Strategic Corporate
tax planning

Strategic Corporate
tax planning

JOHN E. KARAYAN

CHARLES W. SWENSON

JOSEPH W. NEFF

John Wiley & Sons, Inc.

For general information on our other products and services, or technical support, please contact our Customer Care Department within the United States at 800-762-2974, outside the United States at 317-572-3993 or fax 317-572-4002.

Wiley also publishes its books in a variety of electronic formats. Some content that appears in print may not be available in electronic books.

Library of Congress Cataloging-in-Publication Data:

Karayan, John E.
    Strategic corporate tax planning / John E. Karayan, Charles W. Swenson, Joseph W. Neff.
        p. cm.
Includes index.
    ISBN 0-471-22075-2 (alk. paper)
    1. Corporations—Taxation—Law and legislation—United States. 2. Tax planning—United States. I. Swenson, Charles W. II. Neff, Joseph W. III. Title.
    KF6455 .K37 2002
    658.15'3—dc21
                                                                2002005430

Printed in the United States of America

10 9 8 7 6 5 4 3 2 1

about the authors

Formerly Director of Taxes for a New York Stock Exchange-listed high tech multinational, which was then one of the world's largest software concerns, **John E. Karayan, J.D. Ph.D.**, is a tax attorney with a "Big 8" CPA firm background. He retired from professional practice to become a full time university professor, but he has remained active outside of academia as a consultant to entrepreneurs and as an expert witness in complex litigation. Among other things, for the past 15 years Professor Karayan has served on the Board of Directors of the world's foremost manufacturer of anti-terrorist vehicle access barricades. He has published articles in journals ranging from *The Tax Advisor* to the *Marquette Sports Law Review*, and has spoken before professional groups such as the World Trade Institute, California Continuing Education of the Bar, California Society of CPA's, and the Beverly Hills Bar Association. He also was president of the American Accounting Association's 34th Annual Western Regional Conference on Electronic Commerce.

Charles Swenson, Ph.D., is professor of taxation—and the Elaine & Kenneth Leventhal Research Fellow—at the Leventhal School of Accounting of the University of Southern California, where he teaches (among other courses) graduate classes on strategic tax planning. A CPA admitted in California, his professional experience includes service as a tax consultant at one of the world's leading professional advising firms, PricewaterhouseCoopers. Professor Swenson has also been a visiting scholar at the University of California at Los Angeles' Anderson School of Management and a visiting professor at the California Institute of Technology. Winner of several American Taxation Association Outstanding Tax Manuscript Awards, Professor Swenson has published extensively in leading journals such as *The Accounting Review, Advances in Taxation*, the *Journal of Accounting and Public Policy*, the *Journal of the American Taxation Association*, and the *National Tax Journal*.

Joseph W. Neff, J.D., is a partner in the Los Angeles office of PricewaterhouseCoopers. Mr. Neff's expertise and experience in tax planning for entrepreneurs and managers is summed up by his current position in the firm: the U.S. National Partner in Charge of Middle Market Tax Practice. Throughout his illustrious career, he has focused on helping managers integrate tax planning concepts into strategic decision making.

contents

acknowledgments

Like business ventures, management books are often profoundly influenced by many people. Those that did so for this book range from colleagues to staff, professors to students, and partners to clients. They all should be thanked (but not blamed!) for their contributions, but there are too many to do so explicitly. There is room only for a special few to be acknowledged: Sheck Cho and Jennifer Gaines, our talented and patient editors, along with Dr. Glenn Freed, Dianthia Simon, Mike Swenson, Harry Dickinson, Mike Bond, Peter Drucker, and Anne Karayan (my talented and patient bride of 30 years).

introduction

This book shows managers the principles of tax management and how to apply them to every day situations to enhance shareholder value. (The book also shows professional advisors how to become more effective consultants, and investors how to better analyze financial statements.)

Taxes are important to know, but hard to learn. The devil is in the details. But managers and investors do not need to know the details. They just need to be aware of the fundamental principles of taxation and how to apply them when making decisions.

Even this is no simple task. We have tried to do this in two steps. First, over 75 years of experience have been distilled into an innovative framework that organizes tax principles and their applications. This framework helps nontax specialists see tax savings opportunities and also helps managers to apply tax principles to make better decisions.

To make it easier to use, this analytic framework is called SAVANT. (A savant is an exceptionally knowledgeable person.) This is an acronym for how tax planning fits into business decisions: through Strategy, Anticipation, Value-Adding, Negotiating, and Transforming.

Second, after explaining and illustrating how SAVANT works, we show how managers can apply this framework to typical business transactions. These applications are illustrated with numerous examples drawn from real life in the marketplace. To make them more usable, the transactions are organized around a venture's typical life cycle.

The *value-adding* and *financial reporting* effects of tax management are emphasized throughout the book. Each chapter provides a general discussion appropriate to managers. Greater detail is presented in sections called Tax Management in Action and Technical Inserts.

APPLYING SAVANT TO MAXIMIZE SHAREHOLDER VALUE

SAVANT is used throughout this book to show nontax specialists how to critically analyze situations to generate tax-savings opportunities. SAVANT works as follows: To add maximum value to each transaction, decision makers need to stay focused on the firm's strategic plan, anticipating tax impacts across time for all parties affected by the transaction. Managers *add value* by considering these impacts when *negotiating* the most advantageous arrangement, thereby *transforming* the tax treatment of items to the most favorable status. Expert managers (and consultants) use these concepts, derived from economic policy and tax law, to maximize shareholder value.

WHY MANAGERS NEED TO KNOW THE PRINCIPLES OF TAX PLANNING

Reducing taxes is beneficial, but why should managers learn the basics of tax planning? It may seem obvious at first glance, especially to the owner-manager or corporate entrepreneur. But this is an important question, which can be answered differently at different times, in different organizations, and for operations in different countries.

Managers need to learn about taxes because optimizing a venture's total tax burden is important to its success, and managers are the main decision makers in an organization. Knowing the fundamentals of taxation and how to apply them allows managers to make better decisions and thus be more effective in their jobs. Managers who are able to identify tax issues can also make more effective use of tax consultants, because these managers can recognize a problem when it arises and advise consultants of the trade-offs involved.

Taxes impact success because operational decisions are generally based on the risk-adjusted net present value of expected *after-tax* cash flows. In addition, federal and local income taxes, payroll (e.g., Social Security), sales (e.g., value-added, goods and services, or gross receipts), and property taxes often add up to one of the largest expense items of an organization. Furthermore, tax payments typically have a high legal priority claim on an organization's cash flow. That is, not only can taxes be a big expense, but they also must be paid, and paid quickly.

Furthermore, multinational businesses that are publicly traded in U.S. capital markets can be especially sensitive to tax expense. This is because earnings (which usually have a major impact on stock prices) must be reported on an after-tax basis. Indeed, not only must earnings be reduced by taxes paid in the current year, but earnings must also be reduced by any expected *future* income taxes generated by such earnings. Because senior managers' compensation is often tied to earnings via stock prices (e.g., through stock options), key decision makers in multinational organizations often have a high personal stake in optimizing taxes.

SAVANT BALANCES THE BENEFITS WITH THE COSTS OF TAX PLANNING

All in all, there are many factors that combine to motivate managers of organizations to seek to reduce taxes, provided the cost of doing so is not too high. This is because tax planning requires making changes, and doing so is not cost free, nor are the rewards certain. First, the details of taxation are hideously complex. Second, the cost of complying with tax rules (e.g., preparing tax returns and providing details requested by tax auditors) can be significant. Not only can it be costly to figure out how much to pay but also who to pay and when to pay.

Such costs can be particularly high for cross-border activities, which can involve a multitude of different tax jurisdictions imposing different taxes. In addition, similar taxes are often imposed by different jurisdictions using similar but different basic definitions. This raises the specter of multiple taxation (e.g., the same income effectively being taxed at rates exceeding 100%), although governments typically try to avoid this situation through tax treaties and special adjustments, such as the U.S. foreign tax credit.

Finally, although income and payroll taxes may be the province of headquarters staff, and thus savings may not directly affect a divisional manager's annual performance bonus, other taxes almost always do. This is because these taxes are normally charged to strategic business units and thus reduce their individual bottom lines.

Not every idea that saves taxes is a good one. The SAVANT framework helps managers make better decisions because it balances the benefits of tax planning with the costs of doing so.

GOALS OF TAX PLANNING

Most people think that minimizing taxes should be the goal of tax planning. This is short-sighted, because taxes are only one factor, albeit a major one, in the mix of costs and other factors that generate the amounts most often taxed: profits and wealth. Put simply, one can avoid many taxes by neither earning a living nor owning property, but most people do not aspire to a life of poverty, however tax free it is. Furthermore, strategies that reduce taxes are rarely cost free. If nothing else, when focusing on saving taxes, managers are not focusing on increasing sales, improving product quality, or producing goods and services more efficiently. The SAVANT framework recognizes this by striving toward *optimizing* taxes, rather than *minimizing* them. The goal is to balance the benefits against the risks and costs.

Tax strategies are also risky: Changing operations to save taxes (e.g., by operating through multiple corporations) often results in an increase in long-term administrative costs and generates uncertain returns because tax laws can change (and, as the past 15 years have demonstrated in the United States, change can occur dramatically, rapidly, and unpredictably), and tax rules themselves are all too often obscure at best.

In cross-border transactions, the interactions of multiple taxes imposed by different jurisdictions also must be appreciated. Also, tax-savings strategies can be intrusive. Why is it, for example, that profitable businesses in the Los Angeles area, a relatively high-tax location, do not all move to Las Vegas, a very-low tax location? One reason is that it is costly to move. Another is that nontax factors dominate the decision: Many business owners simply want to live in southern California rather than southern Nevada. Yet another reason is that skilled labor, qualified subcontractors, and competitive suppliers are plentiful in southern California, as are (perhaps more importantly) customers.

GENERIC TAX-PLANNING STRATEGIES

Thus, even though total elimination of taxes is not a goal, people and organizations often invest significant amounts of time and resources in implementing tax-reducing strategies. The ultimate goal is to reduce taxes while not excessively intruding on the organization's overall operations. SAVANT explicitly recognizes this.

SAVANT also illustrates that tax strategies are usually based on taking advantage of either the time value of money (e.g., paying taxes later) or differences in tax rates (i.e., tax-rate arbitrage). As already noted, tax arbitrage is typically behind artificial transfer pricing schemes, that is, using accounting entries to shift profits to jurisdictions that impose the lowest net taxes (i.e., the lowest tax costs relative to the benefits received by operating in a particular jurisdiction—e.g., free medical care for all people, including a firm's employees.)

Tax savings strategies usually fall into one of four types: (1) creation, (2) conversion, (3) shifting, and (4) splitting. *Creation* involves plans that take advantage of tax subsidies, such as moving an operation to a jurisdiction that imposes lower taxes. For example, during the past 25 years many engineering and entertainment firms have fled the city of Los Angeles, which imposes a gross receipts tax, and moved to the relatively tax-free city of Pasadena, which is located just a few miles away.

Conversion entails changing operations so that more tax-favored categories of income or assets are produced. For example, advertising in order to sell inventory results in ordinary income, which is usually taxed immediately and at the highest rates. However, equally successful *image* advertising generates an increase in a firm's goodwill, which is not taxed until the goodwill is sold, if at all, and then would likely be taxed at lower capital gains rates.

Shifting involves techniques that move amounts being taxed (also called the tax base) to more favorable tax-accounting periods. A good example is accelerated depreciation, which allows more of an asset's cost to be a tax-deductible expense in early years, thus deferring the payment of taxes until later. Another example is an individual retirement account (IRA).

Splitting techniques entail spreading the tax base among two or more taxpayers to take advantage of differing tax rates. For example, the top U.S. income tax rate on individuals is nearly 40%, but the standard tax rate on the first $50,000 of corporate income is only 15%. Incorporating a sole proprietorship generating $200,000 in profits, and paying a $150,000 salary (provided it is reasonable) to the proprietors, is a splitting strategy that saves $12,500 (i.e., 25% of $50,000 split off and moved into the corporate tax return) of income taxes each year.

Taxes can also be avoided through fraud, which is fairly widespread throughout the world outside of the United States, but relatively small for noncriminal activities within the United States. Those favoring fraud as a strategy generally need not read books like this.

TAXATION: A GLOBAL PERSPECTIVE

For many reasons, people and organizations are increasingly operating in multiple locations and competing in global markets. All of these locations and markets have tax consequences that can be managed through proper planning. For example, a California firm may have two manufacturing facilities—one in Ohio, the other in Singapore. The former sells in all 50 states, the latter in Southeast Asia. Federal income taxes will be due on net taxable income from U.S. operations; Singapore, and perhaps other Asian countries to which sales are made, will assess foreign income taxes. Property taxes will be due in Singapore, California, and Ohio; use taxes will be due in many of the 50 states.

How can such a complex tax setting be managed? Not easily. But if every important transaction is guided by critical analysis triggered by the SAVANT framework in conjunction with a periodic environmental scanning, then organization-wide, global tax management will occur.

WHY DO YOU NEED THIS BOOK?

In sum, taxes can affect the results of a wide variety of decisions, ranging from those made for organizations in which people toil to very personal decisions such as marriage. Sometimes tax considerations are paramount. More often they are important but not dominant. Rather than always trying to minimize taxes, a wise decision maker seeks to optimize tax impacts by balancing expected tax burdens against the costs of reducing them plus the many nontax factors that often are more important in making the best decisions.

Because tax rules are often complex, unclear, and uncertain, even the finest tax experts do not know all of the rules. Instead of trying to help readers learn all of the rules, this book helps managers acquire a critical mass of tax knowledge. Then, using the SAVANT framework, managers can trigger consideration of key tax issues and find and use tax rules to make better decisions in their business, public, and private lives.

Strategic Corporate
tax planning

Understanding Strategic Tax Planning: A Framework

A Framework
for Understanding Taxes

The claim that information would define the future reminded
me of the famous party scene in the 1967 movie The Graduate.
A businessman buttonholes Benjamin, the college graduate played
by Dustin Hoffman, and offers him a single word of unsolicited
career advice: "plastics." I wondered whether, if the scene had
been written a few decades later, the businessman's advice would
have been: "One word, Benjamin: 'information.'"

—Bill Gates, The Road Ahead

How much are people and organizations touched by taxes? Think about
what people do every day. Buy a cup of coffee, and some sort of sales or
value-adding tax is almost certainly included in the amount paid. Make a
telephone call, and an excise tax is likely incurred. Earn income, and a significant portion of the compensation must usually be withheld for payroll
taxes. Make money trading stocks over the Web, and a percentage of the
profits will likely be dedicated to annual income taxes.

One conclusion that can be drawn from this thought experiment is
that taxes seem to be everywhere, embedded in every transaction. This conclusion can be supported by the following set of simple experiments on the
World Wide Web. First, get on a Web browser (e.g., Netscape or Explorer)
and run an Internet search on the word "taxes." Consider the sheer number
of hits generated by this simple task. Run the search again on the Web site
of a national newspaper (such as *www.nytimes.com* or *www.economist.
com*). How many articles discuss taxes? Finally, explore one of the gateway
Web sites in taxation (e.g., *www.taxsites.com* or *www.taxworld.org*). As
you may already know, a gateway is a Web site that consists primarily of
links to other Web sites. Gateways are particularly handy for keeping
track of the constant changes in Web addresses and for finding new sites.
Be sure to look at the Web site for the U.S. Internal Revenue Service (IRS),

3

www.irs.gov, which was one of the first major sites for a governmental agency and is one of the most heavily used. Browse the various publications available there. How many are there? Other very interesting sites to explore are the U.S. Federal income tax calculator, *www.nettax.com,* and the free tax return preparation site, *www.hdvest.com.* It also may be worth your time and effort to view the history of taxation found at *www.uic.edu/depts/ lib/collections/govdocs/tax/taxhistory.html,* and the "Hot Topics in Taxation" page of the University of Michigan's Office of Tax Policy Research at *http://209.69.116.53.*

One reason that taxes seem to be everywhere may be that they are a price paid for government. Not the total price: To some extent (and in many ways, both directly and indirectly), governments support themselves by charging users for specific services provided. For example, some local governments charge a monthly fee to owners of residences that are hooked up to municipal sewer systems. However, throughout the world governments are primarily financed through taxation. Taxes are charges not directly related to goods or services provided, which are imposed on people and organizations located within a government's legal reach. In many locations in the industrialized world, a multitude of governments and their subdivisions—ranging from cities to nations, school districts to metropolitan rapid transit districts—levy a myriad of taxes on a wide variety of activities, such as income taxes on business profits, property taxes on wealth, value-adding taxes on purchases, and payroll taxes on compensation.

Some taxes are periodic. For example, payroll taxes on employees are usually withheld from each paycheck, and income taxes are typically based on one year's earnings. Other taxes are generated if and only if certain transactions occur. For example, sales taxes are usually triggered by the retail sales of goods, and inheritance taxes may arise when title to property is passed to a person's heirs.

The primary purpose of most taxes is to raise revenue to finance governments. But because taxes impose costs on transactions, taxes affect people's behavior, and thus can (and are) used by governments to try to shape society. Indeed, the primary purpose of some taxes—such as excise taxes on the sale of machine guns, tobacco, and pollutants—is to further social engineering goals.

Taxes seem to be everywhere, and triggered by a bewildering array of activities, but how is strategic tax planning important to people who do not devote their lives to tax consulting?

HOW ARE TAXES IMPORTANT IN DECISION MAKING?

Sometimes taxation, and thus tax planning, is one of the most important factors in decision making. Consider the following scenario. Your best friend, who lives in New York City, e-mails you with the news that she has just inherited a large amount of cash. She asks for your help in investing it in U.S. mutual funds, which primarily hold bonds. Look in a financial newspaper or Web site that shows the current earnings of various bond funds. Pick five at random, and calculate their average yield. Now do the same for five that have the words "tax exempt" or "municipal" in their names. (For the uninitiated, this means that these funds invest primarily in bonds issued by U.S. states and local government agencies. Interest paid on such securities is almost always exempt from U.S. federal income tax, and is often exempt from state income taxes as well.) What is the difference in the average yields of the first set of mutual funds and the tax-exempt set? Could a significant part of this difference be accounted for by tax effects?

Tax planning can affect decision making in even the most commonplace of settings. Consider the case of a typical U.S. homeowner whose annual property tax payment must be paid before January of the following year, and it is now December. Almost all people who pay U.S. federal income tax calculate the tax based on their net income—that is, their taxable revenues less their tax-deductible expenses—in each calendar year. Assume that the property tax is a deductible expense, and that the homeowner is in the 28% tax bracket. This means that every dollar of additional income results in $.28 in additional tax. Similarly, every dollar of tax-deductible expense saves $.28 in taxes. If homeowners pay the property tax in December, they will get a tax deduction on their tax returns for the current year. The tax benefit is delayed a year, however, if they wait until January to pay. That is, simply paying this deductible expense a few days earlier generates tax savings a year earlier. This simple bit of planning results in tax benefits through timing, an important component of strategic tax planning discussed in detail throughout this book.

Taxes can even affect the most nonfinancial of decisions. Consider the case of two people who want to get married. Should they be thinking about taxes? Suppose that each will earn about $30,000 of taxable income for the current year. If they stay single, each would owe a little over $5,100 of U.S. income tax for the year. Unmarried, about $10,200 of tax would be generated on their total income of $60,000. However, if they are married at the end of the year, their total tax bill would exceed $11,300. That is, the decision to get married would cost them over $1,000 in U.S. federal income taxes that year. (Note: federal tax liability can be quickly calculated in a variety of ways. One way is to use the tax tables provided by the IRS. These can be found on its Web site at *www.irs.gov* by clicking on "Forms and Publications," selecting "Forms and Instructions," and reviewing "Instructions 1040 [Tax Tables]. Another way is to purchase tax-preparation software or use Web-based programs such as those found at *www.hdvest.com* or *www.nettax.com*.)

Reducing marriage penalties like this has been a perennial target of tax legislation during the past few years. Under the Tax Relief Reconciliation

Act of 2001, for example, there are two changes in this area. First, on joint returns—that is, where married couples elect to file one tax return that combines their incomes—the standard deduction (discussed later in this chapter) is being changed. Currently, it is about 85% of that for two single filers. It is being increased to double that of single filers. This is being phased in over a four-year period starting in 2005 and ending in 2008. The current numbers are:

Standard Deduction

Filing Status	Married Filing Jointly	Single	Head of Household	Married Filing Separately
2001	$7,600	$4,550	$6,650	$3,800
2002	$7,850	$4,700	$6,900	$3,925

Two years are shown here so the gradual, across-the-board increases due to inflation indexing can be seen. *Indexing* applies to a variety of, but not all, fixed dollar amounts in U.S. tax law, such as the standard deduction, as well as that rate brackets.]

The second change is that the amount being taxed at the 15% rate for joint filers is being expanded. This is so that the upper limit of amount taxed at 15%—the so-called 15% bracket—will become twice that for single taxpayers, rather than the current 85%. The current rates are:

Tax Year 2002

Married Filing Jointly		Unmarried	
Taxable Income	Rate	Taxable Income	Rate
First $12,000	10%	Not over $6,000	10% of the taxable income
Over $12,000 but not over $46,700	$1,200 plus 15% of the excess over $12,000	Over $6,000 but not over $27,950	$600 plus 15% of the excess over $6,000
Over $46,700 but not over $112,850	$6,405 plus 27% of the excess over $46,700	Over $27,950 but not over $67,700	$3,892.50 plus 27% of the excess over $27,950
Over $112,850 but not over $171,950	$24,265.50 plus 30% of the excess over $112,850	Over $67,700 but not over $141,250	$14,625 plus 30% of the excess over $67,700
Over $171,950 but not over $307.050	$41,995.50 plus 35% of the excess over $171,950	Over $141,250 but not over $307,050	$36,690 plus 35% of the excess over $141,250
Over $307,050	$89,280.50 plus 38.6% of the excess over $307,050	Over $307,050	$94,720 plus 38.6% of the excess over $307,050

This change will be phased in from 2006 to 2008. Note that highlights of recent tax changes can be found at the various gateway tax sites already listed, as well as in IRS publications such as Publication 553.

Tax planning often represents a significant part of doing business. In some cases, taxes are one of the most important aspects in structuring a transaction. Consider Tax Management in Action 1.1.

This case study illustrates just how important taxes can be in a business transaction. DuPont was able to capture part of Seagram's tax savings by negotiating a lower price for the stock it bought back, and Seagram was able to transform what would have been a taxable transaction (had the DuPont stock been sold on the open market) into a largely tax-free transaction by using the tax law. Moreover, the transaction was motivated by both firms' strategic plans: Seagram, for example, wanted to acquire MCA for strategic business reasons. The decision to sell the stock was motivated by the strategic decision to purchase MCA; only the form—a stock redemption by Dupont of its own shares—was motivated by tax savings. This example shows how good tax planning can *add* significant value to a transaction. Although transactions typically do not have such dramatic tax

---

TAX MANAGEMENT IN ACTION 1.1

DuPont and Seagram

As part of its strategy on moving into the entertainment industry, Seagram's managment decided to purchase MCA from Matsushita. There were many ways to finance this acquisition. Seagram chose to do so primarily by selling 156 million of the 164 million shares it held in DuPont back to DuPont. One of the main reasons to do this was that, by having Dupont redeem the shares, the transaction could be treated for U.S. income tax purposes as a primarily tax-free dividend to Seagram rather than as a taxable sale. Being able to report the nearly $9 billion sale as a dividend saved Seagram at least $1.5 billion in taxes.

The tax savings helped finance Seagram's purchase of MCA, but Seagram was not the only winner. DuPont's reward for its role in the deal was the acquisition of a large block of its outstanding shares at a discount from market price of at least $740 million.

For more information, see Merle Erickson and Shiing-Wu Wang, "Exploiting and Sharing Tax Benefits: Evaluating Seagram's Financing/Tax Planning Decision in its Acquisition of MCA," *Journal of the American Taxation Association,* 21, No. 2 (Fall 1999): 35–54.

effects, the example illustrates how a transaction can have an important tax component.

Taxes are only one of the many factors that people and organizations consider when making decisions. In some cases, taxes are a dominant factor; in others, tax considerations play a minor part. Good decision makers generally seek to manage taxes on every transaction. One way to measure how well a firm is managing its taxes is to look at its effective income tax rate. A firm's effective tax rate is the sum of taxes paid by the firm, divided by its (before-tax) net income. Often, firms' effective tax rates exceed 40%. This is not surprising for multinational firms operating in the United States, because they usually are subject to 35% rate on U.S. income plus an assortment of international, state, and local taxes.

As shown in Tax Management in Action 1.2, even large firms can have widely varying effective tax rates. In the sample shown, however, all have rates well below 40%, which shows that these firms are managing their taxes.

These companies were able to reduce their tax burdens to rates below the benchmark 40% primarily by placing operations so that large proportions of taxable income were derived from locations with tax rates lower than the 35% rate typical for operations in the United States. To put some perspective on this, take a closer look at Johnson & Johnson. By bringing its effective tax rate down to 23%, it saved $270 million in taxes. These tax savings were due to a large proportion of its taxable income being derived from Puerto Rico, which allowed the company to enjoy the U.S. possessions' tax credit. Locating operations in low-tax locations uses the strategic

---

TAX MANAGEMENT IN ACTION 1.2

Effective Tax Rates

Firm	World-Wide Effective Tax Rate
General Motors	36%
Microsoft	33%
Johnson & Johnson	23%
McDonnell-Douglas	35%
Disney	35%
IBM	38%
General Electric	24%
Citicorp	26%

Source: Financial Statements in Individual Firms' Form 10K Reports (1993–1995)

tax planning mechanism of *transforming,* which is discussed throughout this book (and in detail in Chapters 7 and 8).

TYPES OF TAXES

As already suggested, government regulation can be an important factor in economic decision making. This book is intended to help people learn how to better factor the impact of regulation into decision making by studying the effect of one prominent kind of regulation: taxation. Throughout the world, various levels of government impose an array of taxes in order to raise revenue or shape the behavior of people and organizations. This is illustrated by the following overview of taxes in one of the world's most important economies, the United States. The United States was also chosen because although it has one of the most complex systems of taxation, it also has one of the most explicit and documented tax systems in the world. For these reasons, most of the examples in this book are drawn from the United States, and its most important tax, the national income tax.

U.S. Federal Taxes

The U.S. government raises the vast majority of its revenues through taxes. (Statistics showing amounts and trends by type of tax can be found on the Web at sites like *www.taxworld.org, www.taxsites.com,* and the IRS site, *www.irs.gov.*) The major types are corporate and personal income taxes, payroll taxes, estate and gift taxes, excise taxes (e.g., on tobacco, alcohol, and air travel), and import duties. Because collections of excise taxes and duties are fairly small and straightforward, they are not elaborated upon further in this book. (For a discussion of the relative importance of different types of taxes—both in the United States and the rest of the world—explore the Web sites reached by clicking on "policy-reform" in sites like *www.taxsites.com* and the University of Michigan's Office of Tax Policy Research at *http://209.69.116.53.*) For similar reasons, the discussion on U.S. taxes will begin with estate and gift taxes.

Estate and Gift Taxes

Gift taxes are imposed when one person gives property to another with non-business motives like affection and appreciation. Estate taxes are imposed on a person's last gift: the transfer of property to heirs at one's death. In this sense, these two complementary taxes are really one unified tax on gifts people give either while they are alive or when they die. (There is another related tax, too: the generation skipping transfer tax. Because it is extraordinarily complex and rarely triggered, it is not discussed further in this book.) Both of these taxes are imposed on the transferor of property, not on the recipients, and are based on the fair market value of the property transferred. In addition, both use the same tax rates. (For more information on this and other topics, check Web sites mentioned previously, like *www.taxsites.com,* or go to the IRS Web site and see IRS Publication 950, *Introduction to Estate and Gift Taxes.* For example, see what you get when you go to the IRS Web site, click on "Forms and Publications," click on "Search for a Form or Publications," and input the term "gift tax" into the search engine.)

The intent of these taxes on gratuitous transfers of property is not so much to raise revenue as to try to prevent excessive concentrations of hereditary wealth. In doing so, these taxes help provide additional vertical equity in the tax system beyond that provided by the income tax. That is, estate and gift taxes attempt to impose additional taxes on wealthier individuals. Both taxes are steeply progressive, which means that tax rates increase as the tax amount increases. The top rate is 55%. Note that there are no U.S. taxes on the recipients of bona fide gifts or inheritances (although some states in the United States impose such taxes). In addition, recipients do not pay income taxes on gifts or inheritances, nor are income taxes imposed on givers when appreciated property is transferred.

The gift tax is imposed on individuals who transfer property in a bona fide gift. A *bona fide gift* has a donative intent, with no strings attached to the recipient. That is, it is not a disguised sale or form of compensation. There are numerous exceptions to the tax, making its payment fairly rare. The most important exemptions are for transfers of property between spouses (both during marriage and upon divorce) and most donations to public institutions such as charities, universities, and churches (which also are exempt from income tax). In addition, small gifts are not taxed. For example, there is an annual exclusion amount of $10,000 per year per donor per donee. If the donor is married, the gift can be treated as if it came from both spouses, in which case the annual exclusion doubles to $20,000. The annual exclusion is a simple tax-planning method that can be used to avoid taxes when large gifts are given in installments. (See Example 1.1.)

EXAMPLE 1.1

Mr. and Mrs. Smith wish to give their son $100,000. They also want to give $30,000 to their church and $500 to their neighbor's son. However, they would like the neighbor's son to periodically mow their lawn, in return for the $500. What are the gift tax consequences? The donation to the church is not subject to tax. Neither is the $500 to the neighbor's son, because it is not a bona fide gift but taxable compensation to him. The use of the annual exclusion reduces to $80,000 the amount subject to tax on the gift to the son. Note that if the Smiths instead give their son $20,000 per year for five years, gift taxes are avoided altogether.

Like the income tax, gift taxes are calculated and paid annually. Unlike the income tax, the gift tax is a lifetime tax, which is figured by including in the amount subject to gift tax for a year—the gift tax *base*—both the taxable gifts made during the year and all taxable gifts made in prior years (but only those since 1976, when the current unified system was enacted). However, prior gifts are not double-taxed. This is because a credit for the tax on prior gifts is allowed against the current year's tax. That is, every dollar of taxes on gifts made in prior years offsets a dollar of taxes calculated for the current year. Because of the progressive rate structure, which results in increasingly higher rates in each successive year until the top bracket is reached.

Another credit—the unified credit—assures that most people never actually have to pay gift taxes. This credit effectively exempts the first $1 million worth of property (over and above the annual exclusion) given away by any one taxpayer. Under the Tax Relief Reconciliation Act of 2001, U.S. estate and gift taxes are being phased out over a 10-year period. This is being done partly by reducing tax rates and partly by raising the unified credit. The timetable is:

Year	Maximum Tax Rate	Unified Credit
2002	50%	$1,000,000
2003	49%	$1,000,000
2004	48%	$1,500,000
2005	47%	$1,500,000
2006	46%	$2,000,000
2007	45%	$2,000,000
2008	45%	$2,000,000
2009	45%	$3,500,000
2010	0	0
2011	55%	$1,000,000

Due to the vagaries of the U.S. legislative process, these changes could not be extended beyond 2010. Thus, although the taxes disappear in 2010, they will reappear in 2011 unless the changes are extended sometime before then. The changes were enacted in an atmosphere of large budget surpluses projected over many years. Budget deficits are now projected, suggesting that federal taxes may be raised, directly or indirectly, in the near future.

Because of the unified credit, the Smiths of Example 1-1 would not actually have to pay any gift taxes on the $80,000 amount, unless they had made over $1,920,000 ($1,000,000 for Mr. Smith plus $1,000,000 for Mrs. Smith, less the $80,000 taxable gift) of prior taxable gifts. (Such gifts would be included in the Smiths' gift tax base.) Unlike the $10,000 exclusion, which is renewed every year, the unified credit is a lifetime amount. Although the credit can be used in pieces over a period of years, the total credit is not renewed every year. In other words, the Smiths would not avoid gift taxes if they gave away $2 million every year.

The estate tax is imposed on the net taxable estate of someone who dies. This is the fair market value of the decedent's assets at the time of death, plus the sum of prior taxable gifts, reduced by the decedent's liabilities and by certain deductions. The most important deduction is for property left to a surviving spouse. Because of this, the estate tax is effectively a tax on the joint life of a married couple. Deductions also are allowed for contributions to be made out of the estate to qualified public institutions (i.e., the tax-exempt organizations already mentioned), and certain funeral, administrative, and miscellaneous expenses. The combined estate and gift tax is a lifetime tax. Although prior taxable gifts are included in the amount subject to the estate tax (i.e., the estate tax base), gift taxes previously paid are creditable. That is, every dollar of prior gift tax offsets a dollar of estate tax. Because of the progressive estate tax structure, the effect is to tax property passed at death—effectively the last gift people can make—at the highest possible estate tax bracket.

To reduce double taxation—once by the Federal government, and a second time by state governments—there is a credit for state estate or inheritance taxes paid. More important, the unified credit assures that most people never pay an estate or gift tax. As noted, this credit currently exempts the first $1 million given away over and above the $10,000 per year annual gift tax exclusion throughout one's life. The balance of the unified credit not used up during one's lifetime can be used to offset estate taxes. Thus, because most people in the United States have net estates of less than $1 million, few people are concerned about the tax. In addition, as with the gift tax, one of the easiest ways to avoid the tax is by giving one's estate to a tax-deductible beneficiary, such as a charity or a surviving spouse. (See Example 1.2.)

EXAMPLE 1.2

Mr. Jones dies in 2002, leaving behind a wife and a son. The total fair market value of assets in his estate is $10 million, and there are $2 million in liabilities. He has made no prior taxable gifts. According to Jones' will, $5 million will go to his wife, with the remainder going to his son. His taxable estate is $10 million − $2 million − $5 million − $1 million = $2 million.

Income Taxes on Individuals

In the United States, individuals pay a national personal income tax on taxable income received during the year. (More details are available on the Web, e.g., IRS Publication 17, *Your Federal Income Tax,* available at *www.irs.gov.*) As discussed later, most states and some cities also impose a personal income tax modeled after the national system (albeit at lower tax rates). Taxable income is computed as

Gross Income – Deductions for Adjusted Gross Income (AGI) =
AGI – Deductions from AGI = Taxable Income

Gross income includes any realized income that is not subject to an exclusion. For individuals, this typically includes salaries and wages (including year-end bonuses), dividends, interest, rents, royalties, distributions from retirement accounts, and gains (net of losses) on the sales of assets. Adjusted gross income (AGI) is calculated by subtracting the "above the line" deductions (because they are reported on the front of the tax return form). "For" AGI deductions generally are limited to those relating to sole proprietorships, rent and royalty income, and losses on sales of property.

There are two classes of deductions "from" AGI. Both of these are subject to a phase-out for higher income taxpayers, the details of which are not important here but can be found at sites like *www.taxsites.com.* The first class comprises personal and dependency exemptions. The taxpayer receives a tax deduction for self, spouse (if married), and for each dependent. For the year 2002, the amount of the exemption is $3,000 per person. Basically, a dependent is a low-income person being supported by the taxpayer. Whether someone qualifies depends on a five-pronged test, which is surprisingly complex. (As already suggested, those interested in learning more can find a wealth of detail on the Web, such as IRS Publication 501, *Exemptions, Standard Deductions, and Filing Information.*) For a typical taxpayer, the taxpayer's minor children are the dependents. Thus, a married couple with two dependent children would have a $12,000 exemption for the year 2002.

The second category of deductions from AGI is the greater of the standard deduction, or the sum of the taxpayer's itemized deductions. Itemized deductions fall into six classes:

1. Medical and dental
2. Home mortgage interest
3. Charitable contributions
4. Casualty and theft losses
5. State/local/foreign income, and property taxes
6. Miscellaneous

The last category includes items like union dues and employee business expenses, but only if, in total, they exceed 2% of AGI.

The standard deduction is a set amount that varies by the taxpayer's filing status. The numbers for 2001 and 2002 are listed in the first section of this chapter, "How Are Taxes Important in Decision Making?" Filing status, which is limited by a host of detailed rules, comprises the categories single person, married filing jointly, married filing separately, or head of household (typically, a single parent). Filing status is important because it also determines the level of tax rates. Married filing jointly has the lowest, followed by head of household and single.

Tax rates on individuals currently range from 10% to 39%. As previously noted, the United State's income tax is progressive, with higher levels of taxable income being taxed at higher rates. An exception is for net long-term capital gains, which is one of the most complex areas of U.S. taxation. Indeed, one of the longest sentences in the U.S. tax statutes deals with a certain definition relating to long-term capital gains. Consisting of over 500 words, it is 26 United States Code (U.S.C.) Section 341(e)(1). It, along with all of the other U.S. tax statutes (which are typically referred to as the Internal Revenue Code) can be found through various Web sites, including *http://uscode.house.gov/usc.htm.*

Under the Tax Relief Reconciliation Act of 2001, United States income tax rates are scheduled to be reduced in phases over the period 2002–06. The timetable is:

Calendar Year	15% rate	27% rate	30% rate	35% rate	38.6% rate
2002–2003	Partial 10%	27%	30%	35%	38.6%
2004–2005	No change	26%	29%	34%	37.6%
2006 and later	No change	25%	28%	33%	35%

The dramatically unexpected switch from projected U.S. budget surpluses to deficits suggest that phased income tax reductions may be a target for budget-balancing legislation in the near future.

Profits from sales of property other than inventory are generally classified as capital gains. Gains are considered long term if the asset sold has been held for at least 12 months. Capital gains and losses are netted every year, and the maximum tax rate on most kinds of net long-term capital gains is 20%. An exception to this exception is that if the taxpayer's normal tax rate is at the lowest tax bracket, 15%, the maximum rate on that taxpayer's net long-term capital gains is 10%. Certain longer-term gains can be taxed at a maximum of 18% (8% for taxpayers in the lowest tax bracket.) Another exception is for unrecaptured Section 1250 gain, which is generated when certain real estate that has been depreciated is sold at a profit. This gain is subject to a maximum rate of 25%. A final exception is for gains on collectables—such as art, stamps, and coins—which are taxed at a maximum 28% rate. The treatment of capital gains is discussed further throughout this book, in particular, Chapter 10 and the "Transforming" sections of Chapters 2, 3, and 4, which deal with issues such as the choice of the optimal legal form for operating business, executive compensation, and shutting down a business operation. (See Examples 1.3 through 1.6.)

EXAMPLE 1.3

A taxpayer has the following transactions for the year: long-term capital gain of $1,000, long-term capital loss of $200, short-term capital loss of $300, and short-term capital gain of $400. Assume the long-term gains have been held more than 12 months and that the taxpayer's ordinary income tax rate is 36%.
The netting process yields:

	Short Term	Long Term
	<$300>	$1,000
	400	<200>
NET	$100	$ 800

The $100 short-term gain is taxed at 36%; the net long-term gain of $800 is taxed at 20%.

EXAMPLE 1.4

Assume the same facts as Example 1.3, except that the taxpayer's ordinary income tax rate is 15%. Then, the $800 net gain is taxed at 10%.

EXAMPLE 1.5

Assume the same facts as in Example 1.4, except that the net short-term amount is a loss of $100. In this case, the long-term and short-term amounts are also netted, resulting in net long-term gain of $700, which is taxed at 20%.

EXAMPLE 1.6

Assume the same facts as Example 1.5, except that there is a net long-term loss of $800. Here, the long- and short-term amounts are netted together, resulting in a net long-term loss of $ 700, which is fully deductible (because it does not exceed $3,000).

Capital losses are not tax favored. Individuals can only deduct $3,000 per year of net capital losses; any excess is carried forward to be used in future years either to offset capital gains or for a deduction of $3,000 per year. Interestingly, although business fixed assets held more than a year generate long-term capital gain, net losses are ordinary, not capital, and thus do not run afoul of the $3,000 limitation.

Income Taxes on Business Entities

There are a variety of legal forms through which businesses can operate in the United States. As discussed in greater detail in Chapter 3, these include sole proprietorships, partnerships, corporations, and limited liability companies (LLCs). There are tax and nontax benefits and disadvantages to each one of these entities. For income tax purposes, however, business entities in the United States fall into two general classes: regular corporations and flow-through entities. Regular corporations are called C corporations because the basic tax rules governing them are found in subchapter C, Chapter 1, subtitle A of the Internal Revenue Code. This contrasts with corporations that qualify for and maintain a special tax election under Subchapter S, to be taxed as a flow-through entity. These are called S corporations.)

C corporations are taxed on their income, and their shareholders are taxed again when income is distributed to them. Flow-through entities generally are not taxed at the entity level. Instead, the income of a flow-through entity is taxed directly to its owners. This is the case for both income distributed to owners and that which is not. However, when such previously taxed undistributed income is passed out to owners, there is not a second tax. Flow-through entities include partnerships, limited liability companies, and S corporations, and are discussed in more detail in Chapter 3.

The most important general tax rules that apply across business entities are the following:

- *Methods of accounting.* Entities must choose an accounting method that clearly reflects income. The generally acceptable methods are cash, accrual, and hybrid (cash for some items, accruals for others). The cash method has the advantage of giving more control to the taxpayer over the timing of income and deductions. The cash method can be used by noncorporate entities (except for those that maintain inventories) and corporations that have gross receipts of $5 million or less or that perform personal services as their primary source of income. In other cases, the accrual method must be used. Even if not required, the accrual method can be elected, although quite often it is not advantageous to do so.

- **Year-ends.** Flow-through entities (partnerships, LLCs, and S Corporations) usually must choose the same year-end as the majority of the entity's owners. In most cases this implies a calendar year, because almost all individuals elect to be calendar-year, cash-basis taxpayers. Corporations can choose either a calendar or a fiscal year-end. Year-ends (and accounting methods) are elected when taxpayers file their first tax returns; changes normally require the permission of tax authorities, such as the IRS.

- **Depreciation.** For financial accounting purposes, the costs of acquiring plant, property, and equipment are typically written off over the property's estimated useful life using straight-line depreciation. Because managers usually want to report the highest income they can, if they can elect to delay accruals, for example, by using straight-line instead of accelerated depreciation, they will do so. For tax purposes, *personalty* must be depreciated using fixed useful lives based on asset classes. (Personalty are assets that are not realty; *realty* consists of real estate and assets permanently affixed to real estate.) Although the straight-line method can be used, managers typically elect to use accelerated methods. The accelerated methods fall under the modified accelerated cost recovery system (MACRS). Most personalty fits into the 3-, 5-, 7-, or 10-year useful life category. Cars, trucks, and some equipment are depreciated over five years, and most equipment over seven years. The MACRS tables for these four asset categories are shown in Exhibit 1.1.

Note that a half year's depreciation is allowed in both the first and the last year of the asset's life. Special rules apply in certain circumstances, such as where the majority of a firm's assets for a year are acquired in its last half (or quarter) of the year, or where assets are sold before the end of their full recovery period. (See Example 1.7.)

EXAMPLE 1.7

Assume a business acquires and places into service a light-duty truck in January for $20,000. Because it is a five-year asset, the depreciation for the year is $20,000(.20) = $4000. Depreciation for the next year would be $20,000(.32) = $6,400.

EXHIBIT 1.1   Percent Depreciation, by Year, for Personalty

Recovery Year is:	Recovery Period is:			
	3-Year	5-Year	7-Year	10-Year
1	33.33	20.00	14.29	10.00
2	44.45	32.00	24.49	18.00
3	14.81	19.20	17.49	14.40
4	7.41	11.52	12.49	11.52
5		11.52	8.93	9.22
6		5.76	8.92	7.37
7			8.93	6.55
8			4.46	6.55
9				6.56
10				3.28

Like many countries, the United States allows very rapid depreciation in certain circumstances. For example, profitable small businesses can elect to expense up to $24,000 ($25,000 after 2002) per year of most capital expenditures for personalty. Another example is the 30% additional first year bonus depreciation, which applies to most new personalty and qualified leasehold improvements, that was added by the Job Creation and Worker Assistance Act of 2002.

Realty (other than land) is depreciated straight-line. (Amounts can be found in IRS tables.) A 27.5-year period is used for residential rental realty, and 39 years is used for other realty, unless the firm elects to use the longer lives under the alternative depreciation system (ADS). (Thus, annual depreciation can often be calculated simply by dividing a building's cost by either 27.5 or 39.) For the year of acquisition, and the year of disposition, only part of a year's depreciation is allowed. This amount is based on the number of months of the year the asset is held, with a half-month's depreciation being allowed for the first and last month held. (See Example 1.8.)

EXAMPLE 1.8

Assume a business acquires a warehouse in January for $1 million. Depreciation for that year would be $1,000,000/39 = $25,641. This would also be the depreciation in all subsequent years until the year of disposition.

Income Taxation of Corporations

Although the majority by number of businesses operating in the United States are sole proprietorships, the majority of value-adding businesses are C corporations. (Throughout this book, the term *corporation* will refer to C corporations, unless indicated otherwise.) This is primarily because publicly traded companies cannot elect "S" status. There are two main advantages to operating in the corporate form. First, the owners (shareholders) can lose their investment in case of bankruptcy or lawsuit. (An exception is officers and directors, who may have some personal liability for their own actions.) Second, large amounts of capital can be raised through the capital markets (e.g., public offerings of a corporation's own common stock). The major tax impact of choosing the corporate form is that a C corporation's net income is subject to corporate income tax and, in addition, a second tax on distributions to shareholders, resulting in a double tax.

Note that this double tax occurs only when a corporation has taxable income and pays a dividend to a taxable shareholder. No double tax arises for corporations that show no profits (like many family-owned firms) or pay no dividends (like many growth stocks such as Microsoft). Nor is there a double tax when dividends of profitable corporations are paid to tax-exempt shareholders, such as qualified pension plans, mutual funds, and charities.

Corporations pay an annual tax on their taxable income, which consists of taxable revenues less deductible expenses. The tax rates in Exhibit 1.2 apply.

These U.S. corporate income tax rates are from Internal Revenue Code Section 11, which, along with the rest of the code, can be found through a variety of Web sites, (e.g., *www.taxsites.com*). The rates are progressive. For example, a corporation with $200,000 of taxable income would pay tax of

EXHIBIT 1.2   U.S. Income Tax Rates for Regular Corporations

Over	But not over	Tax is	Of the amount over
$ 0	$ 50,000	15%	$ 0
50,000	75,000	$ 7,500 + 25%	50,000
75,000	100,000	13,750 + 34%	75,000
100,000	335,000	22,250 + 39%	100,000
335,000	10,000,000	113,900 + 34%	335,000
10,000,000	15,000,000	3,400,000 + 35%	10,000,000
15,000,000	18,333,333	5,150,000 + 38%	15,000,000
18,333,333	—	35%	0

$(15\% \times \$50,000) + (25\% \times \$25,000) + (34\% \times \$25,000) + (100,000 \times 39\%)$
$= \$61,250$. Once a corporation has taxable income beyond $325,000, all of its income is effectively taxed at a flat 34% rate. For taxable incomes beyond $18,333,333, the tax rate is a flat 35% on all taxable income.

Taxable income is income from the firm's financial statements, with some adjustments. These are discussed in detail in Chapter 12, but the major adjustments are for subsidiaries operating outside the United States, net operating losses (NOLs), dividend income, and depreciation on machinery and equipment.

The following rules are most commonly applicable to corporations. The tax rules are compared to the typical financial accounting treatment.

- *International Operations.* Under financial accounting, net income from international operations is typically included in the firm's consolidated income statement. For tax purposes, the tax treatment is identical for noncorporate overseas operations. That is, such overseas income is included in the consolidated firm's taxable income. However, if such income is generated by an affiliated overseas corporation, the income is not taxed until it is repatriated, typically as a dividend or a royalty. (See Examples 1.9 and 1.10.)

EXAMPLE 1.9

A major corporation has an unincorporated branch located in London. For the last year, the London branch had $1 million in net income. It sent $400,000 of cash back to its U.S. parent during that year. The U.S. parent will pay U.S. taxes on $1 million.

EXAMPLE 1.10

Assume the same facts as in Example 1.9, except that the London business is a corporation. Here, there is U.S. tax only on the $400,000 dividend. The remaining $600,000 of profits will not be taxed until the money is repatriated.

- *Net Operating Losses.* For financial-reporting purposes, net losses cannot be carried forward (or backward) from prior (or future) years. However, for tax purposes, such losses are allowed as a deduction to reduce the current year's taxable income. NOLs generated can be carried back five years and forward 20 years. There are special rules that apply to consolidated entities, as discussed in Chapter 14. (See Examples 1.11 and 1.12.)

EXAMPLE 1.11

A corporation has a net loss of $1 million during 2002. Its taxable income for 1997 and 1998 were $100,000 and $2 million, respectively. The firm paid $20,000 in taxes in 1997, and was in the 35% bracket in 1998. First, it carries back $100,000 of the NOL to 1997, and receives a refund of the $20,000 taxes paid. Next, it carries back $800,000 to 1998, and receives a refund of (.35)($800,000) = $280,000 of the 1998 taxes paid.

EXAMPLE 1.12

Assume the same facts as in Example 1.11, except that in 1998 the firm had taxable income of $500,000. Here, the firm gets a $20,000 tax refund from 1997. But the refund related to the 1998 taxes is limited to (.35)($500,000) = $175,000. The remaining $400,000 of the NOL will be carried forward to 1999.

■ *Contributions to Charitable Organizations.* For financial-reporting purposes, contributions given to charitable organizations are an expense. The same is true for tax purposes, except that the total expense deducted in any one year cannot exceed 10% of taxable income (before the dividends received, NOL, and charitable contributions deductions). Contributions in excess of the limit are carried forward five years. Additional limits apply to contributions made to organizations other than qualifying public organizations (e.g., most recognizable charities, universities, and churches). (See Example 1.13.)

EXAMPLE 1.13

A corporation has the following operations for the year:

Sales revenue	$ 5,000,000
Cost of goods sold	<4,500,000>
Gross profit	500,000
Charitable contributions	<100,000>
Other operating expenses	<300,000>
Net income	100,000

Assuming all the items of income and expense shown are the same for financial and tax purposes, the limit for charitable contributions is (10%)($500,000 − $300,000) = $20,000. Therefore, taxable income is:

$500,000 – $300,000 – $20,000 = $180,000. The excess $80,000 of charitable contributions is carried forward to the succeeding five years.

- *Capital Losses.* For financial purposes, losses on sales of assets are expensed as they are incurred. For tax purposes, losses on sales or other dispositions of capital assets can be deducted only to the extent of current year capital gains. If losses exceed gains, the excess losses are carried back three years, and forward five years. (See Example 1.14.)

EXAMPLE 1.14

A corporation has two capital transactions for the year: a capital gain of $1 million and a capital loss of $1.5 million. The two are netted together, to give a net capital loss of $500,000. The loss must be carried back three years, and if still unused, forward five years.

- *Goodwill.* For financial reporting in most countries, acquired goodwill is not amortized. In the United States, it is tested annually to see if a portion must be expensed to reflect any impairment in its value. For U.S. tax purposes, goodwill is amortized straight-line over 15 years. (See Example 1.15.)

EXAMPLE 1.15

A corporation buys another corporation for $50 million, when the fair market value of the acquired corporation's assets is $45 million. The excess $5 million is considered goodwill. Each year, $5 million / 15 = $333,333 amortization expense is deducted on the acquiring firm's tax return.

- *Warranty and Bad Debts Expense.* For financial purposes, both are accrued using estimation methods derived from experience. For tax purposes, warranties (bad debts) can be deducted only as they actually come due (go bad). (See Example 1.16.)

EXAMPLE 1.16

A corporation makes $10 million in credit sales during the year. Based on historical experience, 10% of the receivables will never be collected. During the year, customers actually default on $300,000 of receivables. Even though the bad debt expense for financial accounting purposes is $1 million, the deduction for bad debts is only $300,000 for tax purposes.

- *Officers' Life Insurance.* Premiums paid by the corporation on a life insurance policy, of which the firm is the beneficiary, are expensed for financial-reporting purposes. They are not deductible for tax purposes. Interest on any money borrowed to buy the insurance is not deductible for tax purposes, but it is an expense for financial accounting.
- *Inventories.* For financial-accounting purposes, firms can use a number of inventory-accounting methods. These include the FIFO (first in, first out method), several LIFO (last in, first out) methods, specific identification, and weighted average. Similarly, for tax purposes firms can use any method that clearly reflects income. One restriction is that if the firm elects LIFO for financial-reporting purposes, it must do so for tax purposes as well. For this reason, managers typically use the same method for both books and taxes.
- *Dividend Income.* For financial-reporting purposes, intercompany dividends are eliminated from net income in consolidated financial statements. Under U.S. generally accepted accounting principles (GAAP), the financial results of subsidiaries are combined with that of their parent into one consolidated statement. However, to avoid duplication, all intercompany transactions—like sales or dividends—are subtracted out (eliminated.) This is done for all subsidiaries of which the parent corporation owns at least 50%.

  For tax purposes, dividends are also eliminated if they are from a subsidiary included in a parent corporation's consolidated tax return. (To be included, the subsidiary must be domestic and at least 80% owned by the parent.) Otherwise, the method used to avoid double taxation is the dividends-received deduction. The deduction applies only to dividends paid out of a corporation from its U.S. source income. If the recipient corporation owns between 20 and 80% of the payor, the deduction is 80% of dividends. If less than 20% is owned, the deduction is 70%. Thus, for the latter two ownership percentages there will be a book-tax difference. (See Examples 1.17 and 1.18.)

EXAMPLE 1.17

A corporation has the following from operations during the year:

Sales revenue	$10,000,000
Cost of goods sold	<8,000,000>
Gross profit	2,000,000
Dividend income	1,000,000
Operating expenses	<1,000,000>
Net income	$ 2,000,000

If the dividends are from companies of which the firm owns only a small percentage, then the dividends-received deduction is (70%) ($1,000,000) = $700,000. Thus, taxable income is $2,000,000 – $700,000 = $1,300,000.

EXAMPLE 1.18

Assume the same facts as in Example 1.17, except that the dividends are from a subsidiary that is 100% owned by the parent. Taxable income thus is $2 million – $1 million = $1 million.

There are a number of other special tax rules that cause such book-tax differences. They will be discussed later in this book, particularly in Chapter 12.

Other Country Taxes

Most jurisdictions apply whatever taxes they impose on all transactions taking place in their territory. Thus, for example, the United States taxes foreigners on income from sources located within the United States (such as rents from U.S. real estate) and from businesses operating in (i.e., effectively connected with) the United States. Similarly, U.S. citizens or residents may be taxed by other countries on income from sources within those countries. International tax issues are discussed throughout this book, particularly in Chapter 8.

Gateway Web sites, such as *www.taxsites.com* and *www.taxworld.org,* provide excellent pathways to authoritative information on taxes worldwide. Some of the more user-friendly sites that can be found this way are those of the Big Four international professional advising (accounting) firms listed in Tax Management in Action 2.2. For example, current news on value-adding taxes throughout the world is streamed on PricewaterhouseCoopers' Global VAT OnLine Web page at *http://www.globalvatonline.pwcglobal.com/*

Similar to the United States, the taxes of most jurisdictions fall into three categories: transactions taxes, wealth taxes, and income taxes. The two most prevalent transaction taxes worldwide are value-adding taxes (VATs) and import duties. Import (and sometimes export) duties are taxes that are imposed on the flow of goods across most international borders. Notable exceptions are flows among members of free trade zones, such as the United States, Canada, and Mexico (NAFTA) and the European Union. Value-adding taxes exist in only a few countries outside the European Union (e.g., Canada's Goods and Services Tax) and not in the United States. Countries that do impose a VAT tend to be larger, wealthier, and more industrialized than those that do not.

VAT is imposed on buyers at each stage of a product's value-adding chain, based on the value-adding at that point. For example, suppose a country has a 10% VAT. If a manufacturer sells its product for $100 to a retailer, and the cost to manufacture it is $80, the VAT is 10% of ($100 − 80) = $2. The manufacturer collects the $2 from the retailer and remits it to the government. If the retailer adds $1 of packaging costs and resells it to a consumer for $110, the consumer pays the retailer a VAT of 10% of ($110 − 100 − 1) = $1(rounded), which the retailer remits to the government. Note that some purchases (such as medicine or a new home) may be exempt from the tax, and some sales (such as those to other countries) are zero rated. This means that the seller enjoys a tax credit for the VAT it paid when acquiring the materials for the goods and services it exports, providing companies in some countries a large incentive to export.

Wealth taxes are imposed by most jurisdictions, typically in the form of property taxes. They are primarily levied on real estate and are usually based on the property's market value. Income taxes are usually the most significant foreign taxes paid by U.S. companies. These taxes are usually levied on in-country income only, with definitions of taxable incomes varying widely. Tax rates vary widely as well. Independent of taxable income definitions and tax rates, tax treaties between a number of countries and the United States reduce the real tax burden to a much lower rate. Additionally, to make sure that both the United States and the foreign country do not tax the same income, the United States allows a U.S. company to reduce its taxes by its foreign income taxes paid. Chapter 8 contains a more detailed discussion of taxation throughout the world, and the features of U.S. tax law that mitigate the specter of multiple taxation of income generated by cross-border activities.

State and Local Taxes

A survey by PricewaterhouseCoopers LLP found that corporate tax managers spent 44% of their time on state and local taxes. State and local taxes also fall into the categories of transaction, wealth, and income taxes. Sales and use taxes are paid by retail consumers of goods. They are remitted to businesses, which in turn remit these transaction taxes to local governments. The primary wealth tax is a property tax, assessed to owners of both realty and personalty. Forty-four of the states impose a corporate income tax. To partly alleviate double taxation, state corporate income taxes are deducted (expensed) on the federal corporate return (i.e., they reduce the U.S. tax bill). State and local taxes are discussed in more detail in Chapter 7.

BASIC PRINCIPLES OF TAXATION

People making decisions face a bewildering array of taxes, imposed by a variety of governments, that can have significant impacts on the results of decisions made. Complicating the process is the uncertain nature of tax rules. Unlike the laws of nature, tax rules are social constructs resulting from political processes. They often result from the complex interaction of a host of official and unofficial actions taken (or not taken) by different governmental representatives at different times. U.S. Federal income tax, for example, is governed by hundreds of pages of the Internal Revenue Code, annual changes to which are explained in thousands of pages of congressional committee reports. These, in turn, are interpreted in tens of thousands of pages of IRS regulations, rulings, and publications, not to mention judicial opinions. These opinions summarize the thought processes of judges deciding cases that arise from controversies between taxpayers and the IRS that have not been resolved through administrative appeals within the IRS but instead are litigated in various U.S. courts.

It is fair to say that no one knows all of the tax rules that apply to many decisions. Nor will one person know all of the tax rules that may affect the result of many decisions, because results can take place in the future, and tax rules can change. However, like many fields of intellectual endeavor, more important than an encyclopedic knowledge of all of the rules is having a critical mass of knowledge that allows decision makers to ask the right questions. (The focus of this book is on helping managers learn how to do this.) Although at the surface, the specific tax rules relevant to a decision may be unclear, uncertain, and changeable, there is a deep structure to taxation worldwide. Knowing the structure helps in posing the right questions to the right sources—be they tax experts or tax information Web sites—and understanding the answers found. The following section outlines the deep structure of taxation and tax planning.

Goals of an Ideal Taxing System

The basic objective of taxation is to raise revenues to finance governments. Governments also attempt to achieve other objectives in designing and implementing tax systems. These objectives are frequently complicated by the dynamics of political, economic, and social forces. Since the writings of 18th-century economist Adam Smith, people designing tax systems have often considered the criteria he identified: *equality, certainty, convenience,* and *economy.*

Equality means that taxpayers should bear a fair level of tax relative to their economic positions (e.g., income, for income taxes). Equality can be defined in terms of horizontal and vertical equity. Horizontal equity means that two similarly situated taxpayers are taxed the same. Vertical equity means that when taxpayers are in different economic positions, the taxpayer with the greatest ability to pay, pays the most in taxes. For the most part, federal, state, and foreign income taxes attempt to adhere to horizontal equity, both in the taxation of individuals and corporations. Vertical equity is prevalent in individual income taxes, but less so in business taxes. (See Examples, 1.19, 1.20, and 1.21.)

EXAMPLE 1.19

Bill's income for the year consists solely of $15,000 in dividends. Ted's income consists solely of $15,000 in interest income. Both pay a tax rate of 15%, or $2,250 in taxes; there is horizontal equity.

EXAMPLE 1.20

X Corporation has net income from the sales of widgets of $15,000. Y Corporation has net income of $15,000 from the performance of services. Both pay a tax of $2,250; there is horizontal equity.

EXAMPLE 1.21

Refer back to Example 1.19. Assume, in addition to the $15,000 of income, Bill has an additional $45,000 of dividend income, giving him a total of $60,000 in income. If he is still taxed a 15% rate, there is no vertical equity; if he is taxed a higher rate (say, 25%) there may be vertical equity, since Bill pays proportionately more taxes than Ted.

Most income taxes are progressive. That is, higher tax rates apply when there are higher levels of the amount being taxed. For income taxes, this amount—called the *tax base*—is taxable income. However, consumption-related taxes (such as VAT) are rarely progressive (and are often considered regressive) because there is typically only one tax rate. For example, consider sales and use taxes. These are usually paid to states and localities by consumers of tangible goods. Because poor people spend much more of their incomes on consumption than do rich people, they pay proportionately more of their incomes on sales and use taxes.

Certainty means that a taxpayer knows when, how, and how much tax is paid. People in the United States generally know that the balance of their income taxes for a year is due on the following April 15, and that taxes will be withheld from their paychecks. Similarly, corporations know that their income and payroll taxes are due quarterly.

Convenience means that the taxes should be levied at the time it is most likely to be convenient for the taxpayer to make the payment. This generally occurs as they receive income because this is when they are most likely to have the ability to pay. Another aspect of convenience is method of collection. Income taxes in the United States are privately determined by individuals and businesses, and are self-assessed. In contrast, import, property, sales, use, and other taxes are calculated and assessed either by governments or (for sales, use, and value-adding taxes) by vendors.

Economy means that a tax should have minimum compliance and administrative costs. That is, it should require a minimum of time and effort for the taxpayer to calculate and pay the tax. Administrative costs are expenses incurred by the government to collect the tax. Compliance and administrative costs are highest for income taxes, because of their complexity.

Tax Rates and Structures

Taxes are computed by multiplying the tax rate by the tax base, that is, tax rate × tax base = tax. The tax base is the amount that is subject to tax. For income taxes, the tax base is taxable income, defined roughly as income less allowable expenses. For property taxes, the tax base is some measure of the value of the property. Consumption taxes, such as VAT and sales tax, are most often based on the sales price of the merchandise sold. For payroll taxes, a common tax base is compensation.

Tax Rates For most taxes there are three types of tax rates: *marginal, average,* and *effective* rates. The marginal rate is the tax rate that will be paid on the next dollar of tax base (i.e., the rate on the next dollar of income for income taxes, or the rate of tax that will be saved on the next dollar of deduction). (See Example 1.22.)

EXAMPLE 1.22

At the end of the year, XYZ Corporation has taxable income of $50,000. Its tax rate is 15%, so it pays a tax of $7500. Suppose it sells some inventory on the last day of the year for a net gain of $20,000. The gain would put the corporation in the 25% bracket. Thus, the marginal rate on this income is 25%.

The average rate is computed as the total tax divided by the total tax base. The average tax rate in Example 1.22 is ($7,500 + $5,000) / $70,000 = 17.9%. The effective tax rate is total taxes divided by economic income. (Because it includes amounts not resulting from actual transactions—like the rent saved by owning a home—economic income is typically estimated.) For corporations, the effective tax rate generally uses financial-accounting income as the denominator. Suppose the corporation in Example 1.22 has financial accounting earnings of $100,000. Its effective tax rate is ($7500 + $5000)/$100,000 = 12.5%.

How is the effective rate important? The further the firm's effective rate is below the statutory rate, the better a job it is doing in managing its taxes.

Tax Rate Structures   Tax rate structures can be thought of as being *proportional, progressive,* or *regressive.* With a proportional (or flat) tax rate, the average rate remains the same as the tax base increases. Other than the income tax, most taxes are proportional. For example, suppose a county charges a 1% property tax on the assessed (fair market) value of property owned. Whether the corporation owns $100,000 or $100 million worth of property, the rate is still 1% (i.e., it is proportional.)

With a progressive tax rate structure, the average rate increases as the tax base increases. Most income tax systems are progressive. Examples are the U.S. Federal individual and corporate income tax, most state individual income taxes, and many foreign corporate and individual income taxes. Using Example 1.22, there again is a progressive structure. The first $50,000 of taxable income is taxed at 15%; thereafter, the rate is 25%.

A regressive structure is one where the average rate decreases when the base increases. Many people consider sales tax regressive. This is because if the total sales tax paid by a taxpayer is divided by income, the average rate decreases by income. (See Example 1.23.)

EXAMPLE 1.23

Tom earns $100,000 per year. He spends $20,000 of this on clothing and other consumer goods, which are subject to a 7% sales tax. Jerry earns $50,000 and spends the same amount on the same items. Thus, both pay $1,400 in sales taxes. Jerry's rate is $1,400/$50,000 or 2.8%; Tom's is $1,400/$100,000 or 1.4%. Thus, this tax is regressive by income.

SOURCES OF TAX LAWS

People who want to learn tax rules consult two basic types of sources. These are primary sources and secondary sources. Appendix A provides more information on how to do tax research. Primary sources are the official governmental pronouncements on the subject. For U.S. income taxation, for example, primary sources include statutes enacted by Congress (such as those embodied in the Internal Revenue Code), regulations and rulings issued by the IRS, and judicial opinions in court cases dealing with tax matters. Primary sources should be consulted (either directly or through a tax specialist) when making important decisions. Although more precise and authoritative than secondary sources of tax law, primary sources can be extremely difficult to understand.

Secondary sources of tax rules are easier to understand and most useful when learning about something for the first time. These are summarized versions of the official tax rules. Secondary sources include the numerous commentaries on tax issues found in newspapers, such as the Wednesday front page tax column of *The Wall Street Journal*. Also included are the multitude of articles found in professional tax journals and treatises published by eminent tax professors, tax practitioners, and their associations, such as the American Bar Association for lawyers and CPA societies for accountants.

As with U.S. federal tax rules, there are legislative, judicial, and administrative primary sources of tax law for most jurisdictions such as states like New York and countries like Singapore. The nature and scope of these varies with the structure of the laws and government. Secondary sources are available, too, for most jurisdictions, but tend to be less useful, and less available, than those for the U.S. government.

To find secondary sources, go to *www.taxsites.com* and click on "Help-Tips-Articles." The Big Four accounting firms and the large international law firms also publish a great deal of excellent tax and tax-related literature both in print and in electronic form through their Web sites. These sources are particularly useful when learning about the basics of taxation in a foreign country. In addition, there are extensive commercial publications devoted to indexing and explaining tax rules worldwide. These, too, are available both in print and electronically. (For example, go to *www.taxsites.com* and click on "Tax Software.")

Secondary sources like these tend to be arranged in two basic ways. The first, called "tax services," are organized like encyclopedias. They are arranged topically. Tax concepts are presented in editorial style and cross-referenced to primary sources through footnotes, much like a very big textbook. For example, for U.S. income tax rules, a tax service might have a 50-page discussion on the various aspects of taxing capital gains. This would be indexed with footnotes citing primary sources like Internal Revenue Code sections, Treasury Regulations, IRS Rulings, or opinions of the U.S. Supreme Court, circuit courts of appeals, or trial courts.

The second approach, called "annotated reporters," is more like a dictionary than an encyclopedia. Annotated reporters are organized around official pronouncements. In the United States, they usually are organized around Internal Revenue Code sections in numerical order. First, the text of a section is presented, along with a brief history of its legislative changes over the years. Following this would be the text of all of the official regulations duly issued by the IRS, under this code section. Each regulation is followed by short—most often only one sentence—summaries of relevant IRS rulings and judicial opinions. Brief editorial commentary appears throughout. In this way, annotated reporters provide a road map to the primary sources of law.

Legislative Sources

Unlike most accounting rules, those for taxation usually result from an explicitly political process. Tax rules result from a complex interaction of a variety of official and unofficial actions taken (or not taken) at different times. For U.S. taxes, for example, officials of all three branches of the Federal government, the legislative (Congress), executive (president), and the judicial (courts), are involved. There are five basic official actions during the progress of federal tax legislation in Congress that generate primary sources of law. The U.S. Constitution requires that federal income tax legislation originate in the House of Representatives. Technically, only a representative may commence the federal tax legislative process, doing so by depositing a bill in the Speaker's hopper. Under current rules, the bill is forwarded to the House Ways and Means Committee (unless the House Rules Committee decides otherwise, an extremely rare event). When this committee receives a bill, it (in actuality, the committee's chairperson) determines whether to proceed. Texts of bills can be found in a variety of places, such as the *Congressional Record.*

If a bill is viable, the Ways and Means Committee schedules public hearings. Traditionally a delegate from the secretary of the treasury's office is the first person to testify, although usually the testimony is merely a recital of a written statement. Following common practice, this is referred to as the secretary of the treasury's testimony even though it is almost always delegated to an assistant such as an undersecretary. The testimony largely consists of reading a carefully prepared paper—it is the text of this paper (which can be edited after the fact) that is printed in the *Congressional Record*—not a transcript of the words actually spoken. This statement is available immediately on news services, such as the *Dow Jones News Wire;* electronic databases, such as *Dialog;* and tax information services, such as BNA's *Daily Tax Reports.*

Because of the presidential veto power, U.S. tax professionals generally view the secretary of the treasury's testimony as the first key indicator of the viability and ultimate provisions of the legislation. So do the capital markets. This is not surprising, because for most U.S. tax legislation since World War II, the secretary's testimony has largely indicated the eventual provisions actually enacted.

After the public hearings close, the Ways and Means staff (almost always in concert with the staffs of the Joint Committee on Income Taxation and the IRS chief counsel's legislative division) rewrite the bill to reflect the committee's desires. The most important reason for this is that (unless the House Rules Committee overrides long-standing practice) no tax legislation reaches the House floor unless passed (by a majority vote) out of Ways and Means (and no amendments can be made on the House floor). The language of the Ways and Means' bill is considered by many tax professionals to be the most telling indicator of eventual federal tax legislation. It is so important that Ways and Means publishes a report (akin to a college textbook, replete with examples and rationales) when it passes a bill. Because the committee votes and issues the report concurrently, the release of the report is a key informational event, and reading the report is a top priority among senior tax professionals in the United States.

The U.S. Constitution also provides that to become law a bill identical to that passed by the House also must be passed by the Senate. Senate bills follow the same pattern as in the House. Senate rules give the Senate Finance Committee jurisdiction. It holds hearings with the secretary of the treasury testifying first. This testimony usually merely regurgitates the House testimony. Like the House committee, the Senate tax-writing committee issues a report when it passes the bill to the Senate floor.

There are two main differences between the processes in the Senate and the House. First, the Senate allows floor amendments after passage out of committee. Senators proposing amendments can document their rationale by inserting a statement into the *Congressional Record*. Such a statement would serve the same function as a committee report as an official source for legislative intent. Floor amendments are rare. More important, the Senate is largely a reactive body—it amends the House Bill—rather than a proactive body—it usually does not create new provisions. Thus, although senior tax professionals pounce on the Senate Finance Committee's report, few surprises are found in most legislation.

Two more steps are involved, however. Unless the House and Senate bills are identical—and they rarely, if ever, are—the bills are sent to a conference committee. Half of its members are representatives and the other half senators; no hearings are held, but a report is issued. A compromise bill then goes back to both houses whereupon, if passed by both, it goes to the president for signature (as with the 1993 Act) or to be vetoed (as with the 1992 Act). Few surprises are expected, or actually occur here. But, as with the 1992 Act, the last-minute logrolling that characterizes conference committees as a whole creates a potential for surprises.

After a bill is passed by both houses of Congress, it is sent to the president, who can either sign the legislation or veto it. (The president cannot veto just part of a bill; there is no line-item veto on tax legislation.) If the president vetoes a bill, it can still become law if upon resubmission to Congress two-thirds of the senators and two-thirds of the representatives vote for the legislation. Neither action results in a report or other official documentation of great use in determining tax rules. Similarly, no official reports interpreting the legislation are issued by the president. Bills that are enacted are published *verbatim* in *Statutes at Large*. There is one last report, however.

Congress has a standing committee that oversees tax policy but is not directly involved in individual bills. Significant new tax legislation is often the subject of many articles and conferences by tax professionals. After about six months of this scrutiny, the staff of the Congress's Joint Committee on Income Taxation may issue a report answering some of the questions raised. This committee is not involved in passing particular legislation, but is a standing committee devoted to long-range considerations. The report is called the *Blue Book*, and is widely consulted by tax practitioners seeking to understand new tax laws. The *Blue Book* summarizes the wisdom of the staff, and reflects the flurry of commentary by tax professionals in conferences and journals that results after new legislation is enacted. One of the most useful features of this report is the numerous examples it usually contains.

For convenience, most U.S. statutes are organized into codes, with legislation usually consisting of amendments to the relevant code. Almost all legislative law changes are inserted into the relevant code, which presents federal law in a highly structured, organized, and stylized manner. For example, most tax legislation is embodied in Title 26 of the United States Code. Codes organize rules topically, with those dealing with similar issues bundled together. Codes have a very logical structure. The basic unit is the code section. Code sections are divided into pieces—subsections, paragraphs, subparagraphs, clauses, and subclauses—and grouped into larger bodies—subchapters, chapters, subparts, parts, subtitles, and titles.

Administrative and Judicial Sources

The administrative agency in charge of enforcing tax rules often issues a variety of rules to guide taxpayers. In the United States, this agency is the IRS. It issues primary sources of law in its weekly publication, the *Internal Revenue Bulletin,* ranging from simple announcements and notices to more detailed rulings (which present rules in a story format) and highly stylized regulations (which present rules much like code sections, except that there are usually more examples given). Tax regulations themselves are codified in the U.S. Code of Federal Regulations, and are referenced by the primary Internal Revenue Code section to which they relate.

A branch of the Department of the Treasury, the IRS shapes tax laws in two basic ways. First, it enforces the laws by choosing the tax returns to audit and the parts of these returns to challenge. More important, however, is that the IRS issues guidance on what the tax rules are. This is done through a variety of publications and official pronouncements. Current publications and pronouncements can readily be found on the IRS Web site. The most authoritative of these are Treasury Regulations, which are official interpretations of specific Internal Revenue Code sections. Indeed, regulations often read much like code sections, except that sometimes there are examples illustrating what the text means. Occasionally, regulations are written in question-and-answer format.

The IRS also issues a variety of rulings, the most common of which are Revenue Rulings. Unlike regulations and code sections, rulings present the IRS's official analysis of cases. First, a fact pattern is presented. Then, an issue is spotted. Next, the issue is analyzed. Finally, a conclusion is stated and supported by citations to primary sources. Rulings are vignettes, much like parables, which the IRS uses to guide taxpayers by showing how it believes the tax rules apply to a standard fact pattern. The IRS also issues other rulings, such as Private Letter Rulings, where it provides the same kind of analysis at a taxpayer's request, for a specific proposed transaction.

As already noted, the IRS also enforces U.S. tax rules by scientifically selecting a few—on average less than 1% annually—tax returns every year to analyze in a tax audit. Disputes arising from audits can be settled during the audit or after the audit through an appeal to a special branch of the IRS devoted to this function. Disputes not resolved in this way can be—although due to cost they rarely are—submitted to the Judicial branch of government, that is, the federal court system.

Judicial sources of law comprise the opinions written by judges dealing with tax disputes that are not settled administratively. Cases start in one of the three trial courts. Taxpayers usually select U.S. tax court, but sometimes choose their local district courts or the U.S. Court of Federal Claims located in Washington, DC. There is an art to forum shopping, that is, choosing the best court in which to try a case, based on factors such as cost, whether a jury trial is available, and the different precedents that govern a particular court. Trial courts are where factual issues are determined. In deciding the case, however, the court also must determine what the applicable rules of law are and how to apply them to the facts of each case. A written judicial opinion typically results. These present the facts, cite the relevant laws, and explain the decision, and can be found via commercial tax services or via the Web (again, it is easiest to find them by starting with a gateway Web site).

If the outcome here is unsatisfactory, the next step is the U.S. Court of Appeals. Appeals courts can reverse trial courts, but only where the rules of law were not properly applied. A very small percentage of cases decided by trial courts are further litigated in U.S. Courts of Appeal. These courts analyze the rules of law applied by trial courts for errors, but do not redetermine what the facts are. Finally, the taxpayer can attempt to go to the U.S. Supreme Court, although tax cases are rarely heard by the high Court. Less than a handful are decided every year by the Supreme Court, the opinions of which become the law of the land. With some exceptions, each of these courts issues its decisions in the form of written opinions, which form precedents that bind future court decisions on similar issues.

IMPORTANT PRINCIPLES AND CONCEPTS IN TAX LAW

This multifaceted system of tax rules may seem bewildering at first. However, most tax systems have developed around fundamental concepts that do not change much and thus provide a deep structure to tax rules. For example, a number of principles and concepts guide how tax laws are structured in the United States. While they cannot be used to provide guidance on all tax rules, they generally explain why many tax laws are structured the way they are throughout the world.

Ability-to-Pay Principle

Under the ability-to-pay principle, the tax is based on what a taxpayer can afford to pay. One concept that results from this is that taxpayers are generally taxed on their *net* incomes. (See Example 1.24.)

EXAMPLE 1.24

X and Y corporations each have sales revenues of $500,000. Expenses for the two corporations are $100,000 and $300,000, respectively. Corporation X will pay more taxes, because it has greater net income and cash flows, and thus can afford to pay more.

This concept does not apply to every tax in every jurisdiction. Nor do the rest of the concepts presented in this section. Furthermore, those that do most often are understood rather than explicit. That is, they are unofficially applied administratively rather than mandated by primary sources of law. These concepts are more likely to have developed in more industrialized societies where tax laws have become more complex, the foremost example being the United States. Nevertheless, by suggesting what the tax rules ought to be, these concepts can help people understand current rules and anticipate what the rules will most likely be in the future.

Entity Principle

Under the entity principle, an entity (such as a corporation) and its owners (for a corporation, its shareholders) are separate legal entities. As such, the operations, record keeping, and taxable incomes of the entity and its owners (or affiliates) are separate. (See Example 1.25.)

EXAMPLE 1.25

An entrepreneur forms a corporation that develops and sells the entrepreneur's software products. During the year, the corporation has $200,000 in revenue and $50,000 in expenses. The entrepreneur also has a salary of $100,000. The corporation will file a corporate tax return showing $50,000 in taxable income, and the entrepreneur will file an individual tax return showing $100,000 of income.

Closely related to the entity concept is the arm's length doctrine. *Doctrines* are principles that, while often not officially appearing in the tax laws, carry the weight of law. In the United States, for example, doctrines are developed through a series of court cases. An *arm's length transaction* is one in which all the parties in the transaction have bargained in good faith and for their individual benefit, not for the benefit of the transaction group. Transactions that are not made at arm's length will not be given their intended tax effect. (See Example 1.26.)

EXAMPLE 1.26

Assume that in Example 1.25 the corporation pays its entire $250,000 in net income to the entrepreneur as a salary for being president of the corporation. Suppose that a reasonable salary for a president of a small software company is $100,000. The effect of the salary is to reduce the corporation's taxable income to zero, so that it does not have to pay any taxes. While salaries in such closely held corporations are deductible in general, in this case the arm's length test is not met. As a result, only $100,000 (i.e., the reasonable portion) of the salary will be deductible by the corporation. The remaining $150,000 will be considered a dividend.

In determining whether the arm's length rule is likely to be violated with regard to expenses and losses, tax authorities look to see if the transaction is between related taxpayers. Related taxpayers generally include individuals related by blood and marriage, and business entities owned more than 50% by a single entity or individual. (See Example 1.27.)

EXAMPLE 1.27

Assume that an entrepreneur sells an asset to his corporation, and that the sale results in a loss. The entrepreneur owns 49% of the corporation's stock; the other 51% is owned by a group of unrelated investors. Since the loss is not between related taxpayers, it may be considered arm's length.

In applying the ownership test, *constructive ownership* is considered. That is, indirect ownership and chained ownership are considered. (See Example 1.28.)

EXAMPLE 1.28

Assume the same facts as Example 1.27, except that the other 51% of the stock is owned by Z Corporation, which is owned 100% by the entrepreneur. By the rules of attribution and constructive ownership, the entrepreneur is considered to own 100% of the stock: by direct ownership in the first corporation, plus the stock owned by the Z Corporation. Thus, the transaction is not arm's length, and none of the loss would be deductible.

Pay-As-You-Go Concept

Related to the ability-to-pay concept is the pay-as-you-go concept. Taxpayers must pay part of their estimated annual tax liability throughout the year, or else they will be assessed penalties and interest. For individuals, the most common example is income tax withholding. In the United States, for example, employers withhold estimated income taxes and payroll taxes from each employee's paycheck, and then remit the withholding to the government. These taxes, and the requirements for withholding, can be imposed by local governments (such as cities) as well as higher levels (such as state and national governments), but are more common of the higher levels.

In many countries, the withholding *is* the tax; in the United States, it is only a prepayment, which is reflected as a credit against further liability when the relevant tax return for the period is filed. If the taxpayer also has nonwage income (that is, income not subject to withholding), the taxpayer must remit one-fourth of the estimated annual tax due on this nonwage income every three months. This estimated tax requirement generally applies only to expected taxes over a minimum level, such as $1,000 for annual U.S. personal income tax. (See Example 1.29.)

EXAMPLE 1.29

Referring to Example 1.26, how should the entrepreneur pay U.S. income taxes on personal income from the corporation? The $100,000 salary portion must have taxes withheld by the employer (the entrepreneur's own corporation). In addition, the entrepreneur is supposed to pay taxes on the $150,000 dividend every three months prior to actually receiving the dividends at the end of the year. If these estimated taxes are not paid in advance, the taxpayer will be subject to penalties and interest.

Under the same pay-as-you-go principle, corporations in the United States (which typically do not have taxes withheld) must remit one-fourth of their estimated annual tax every three months by making estimated tax payments. (See Example 1.30.)

EXAMPLE 1.30

Suppose a corporation expects to owe $200,000 in taxes at the end of the year: $160,000 in U.S. federal income taxes, and $40,000 in state income taxes. It is required to prepay $40,000 and $10,000 to the federal and state governments, respectively, every three months, or else be subject to penalties and interest.

All-Inclusive Income Principle

This principle basically means that if some simple tests are met, then receipt of some economic benefit will be taxed as *recognized* income, unless there is a tax law specifically exempting it from taxation. The tests are as follows (each test must be met if an item is considered to be income):

- Does it seem like income?
- Is there a transaction with another entity?
- Is there an increase in wealth?

The first is a commonsense test meant to eliminate things that cannot be income. For example, making an expenditure cannot generate income. The second test is the *realization* principle from accounting; that is, for income to be recognized, there must be a measurable transaction with another entity. Therefore, accretion in wealth cannot generate income. (See Example 1.31.)

EXAMPLE 1.31

A corporation owns two assets that have gone up in value. It owns common stock in another corporation, which it originally purchased for $100,000 and is now worth $500,000. It also owns raw land worth $1 million, which it originally purchased for $200,000. It sells the stock for its fair market value, but not the land. Income is recognized only on the stock; there has been no realization on the land.

The increase-in-wealth test means that unless there is a change in net wealth, no income will be recognized. This eliminates a number of transactions from taxation. (See Example 1.32.)

EXAMPLE 1.32

A corporation borrows $5 million from a bank, issues $1 million in common stock, and floats a bond issue for which it receives $10 million. Although each of these transactions involves cash inflows and transactions with other entities, there is no change in net wealth. This because for each of the three cash inflows, there is an offsetting increase in liabilities (or equity) payable.

Closely related to the income-realization concept are the concepts of *recovery of capital, claim of right,* and *constructive receipt.* Under recovery of capital, a taxpayer does not usually recognize income on the sale of an asset until the taxpayer's capital is first recovered. Under claim of right, income is recognized once the taxpayer has a legal right to the income. Under constructive receipt, income is recognized when it is available for the taxpayer's use, even if the taxpayer does not collect the income. Note that constructive receipt applies only to cash-basis taxpayers; accrual-basis taxpayers recognize income (if it is realized) regardless of whether it is received. (See Example 1.33.)

EXAMPLE 1.33

A corporation sells inventory for $100,000; its cost to manufacture is $10,000. The sale is for cash. It also receives $100,000 from a customer by mistake; it will eventually have to pay the money back. Finally, it makes another cash sale of inventory for $10,000, with a cost of goods sold of $2,000. The sale was at year-end. The corporation did not pick up the check from the client until the beginning of the next year, even though the money was available to it before year-end.

Under recovery of capital, on the first inventory sale, the corporation is first allowed to recover its $10,000 inventory cost; only the remaining $90,000 is subject to tax. On the second item, there is no income because there is no legal claim of right to the funds; they will legally have to be returned. Finally, the disposition of the last item (constructive receipt) depends on the corporation's method of accounting. If it is an accrual-basis taxpayer, when it receives the cash is irrelevant; income is recognized at the time of the sale. If it is a cash-method taxpayer, constructive receipt occurs this year, since the funds are available.

Note that the concept of recovery of capital also implies that if the taxpayer does not dispose of the asset, the taxpayer can recover the tax basis over time through depreciation. The extant depreciation used, for federal income tax purposes, is the modified cost recovery system (MACRS), discussed later in the chapter. With only minor exceptions, a capital expenditure cannot be expensed but instead must be depreciated over time.

Legislative Grace

Closely related to the income concepts already described is the concept of *legislative grace*. Here, income that would normally be taxed under the preceding rules is either exempt from tax or subject to a lower tax rate due to special rules. In the United States, for example, these can be provisions in the law, such as the Internal Revenue Code enacted by Congress or its equivalent at the state level. For all taxpayers, one example is the federal exclusion of interest income from state and local obligations. For corporations, federal income tax law has a number of exclusions, the most noteworthy being

- Exclusion from U.S. taxation of the income of subsidiaries located overseas until the funds are repatriated (this applies for most, but not all, subsidiaries)
- Exclusion of up to 100% of dividend income received from another corporation

For individuals, there are numerous exclusions related to employment (some fringe benefits, insurance, retirement fund contributions), illness or death (workers' compensation benefits or life insurance proceeds), family transfers (receipt of gifts and inheritances), and education (scholarships, fellowships, and some employee tuition-assistance plans). Perhaps the most significant is the preferential tax rates given to long-term capital gains. The standard U.S. tax rate is 20% on long-term capital gains, a rate substantially below the maximum federal rate of 39%. This rate can be even lower: For individuals who are in the 15% bracket for ordinary income, a 10% rate applies to long-term capital gains. In many countries, gains from the sale of long-held assets are exempt from taxation.

An important aspect of the preferential capital gain tax rate as related to strategic tax planning is the owner's or manager's sale of ownership of the entity. (See Example 1.34.)

EXAMPLE 1.34

An entrepreneur sells the stock in his company to a larger firm. He sells the company for $10 million. His tax basis in the stock, or what he put into the company (in return for stock), is $1 million. After subtracting his basis (concept of recovery of capital), his capital gain is $9 million. The maximum tax rate on the gain is 20%.

The legislative grace concept applies to deductions as well (deductions are expenses that can be used to reduce taxable income). In the United States, no deduction is allowed under federal and most state income tax laws unless it is specifically authorized by the law. For businesses and sole proprietors, the usual types of expenses are generally allowed for tax purposes. This is also true for certain types of expenses related to individuals' investment incomes.

However, other deductions for individuals exist purely by legislative grace. For example, as already noted there is a fixed standard deduction. If greater, however, individuals are allowed itemized deductions (bounded by elaborate ceilings and floors) for medical expenses, charitable contributions, state taxes paid, home mortgage interest expense, casualty and theft losses, and certain miscellaneous types of expenses.

Business Purpose Concept

Business purpose is closely related to legislative grace as it relates to deductions. Here, business expenses are deductible only if they have a business purpose, that is, the expenditure is made for some business or economic purpose, and not for tax-avoidance purposes. The test is applied to a bona fide trade or business, or to expenses for the production of income. The former is a sole proprietorship, corporation, or other business entity. The latter generally includes investment-type income of individual investors. This rule is typically enforced only when the business deduction also gives some economic benefit to the owner; thus, the owner is trying to get something of value in after-tax dollars, when the item is not otherwise deductible. The rule is typically enforced only in closely-held businesses. (See Example 1.35.)

EXAMPLE 1.35

An entrepreneur owns 100% of the stock of her corporation. She has the corporation buy an aircraft to facilitate any out-of-town business trips she might make. The entrepreneur, who also happens to enjoy flying as a hobby, rarely makes out-of-town business trips. Since the plane will not really help the business, and there is a tax-avoidance motive (the plane would generate tax-depreciation deductions), there is no business purpose to the aircraft. Accordingly, any expenses related to the aircraft, including depreciation, are nondeductible.

Accounting Methods

As already noted, some general rules apply when a taxpaying entity wants to choose among cash, accrual, or hybrid (part cash, part accrual) methods of accounting. For individuals, the election is made on their first tax return. Virtually every individual elects the cash method. For businesses, two rules apply. The first is that when inventory is a substantial income-producing factor, inventory (including related sales and cost of goods sold) must be accounted for by the accrual method. Note that this rule still permits the taxpayer to use the cash method for other items of income and expense. The second rule relates to entity type. If the business is a corporation and it has gross receipts in excess of $5 million, it must use the accrual method for all transactions. Aside from the inventory and the entity-type rules, a business is free to choose any method of accounting.

Tax-Benefit Rule

Under the *tax-benefit* rule, if a taxpayer receives a refund of an item for which it previously took a tax deduction (and received a tax benefit), the refund becomes taxable income in the year of receipt. (See Example 1.36.)

EXAMPLE 1.36

A U.S. corporation pays a consulting firm $100,000 for consulting services in one year. Because this is a normal business expense, the corporation takes a tax deduction for $100,000. Early the next year, the consulting firm realizes it has made a billing mistake and refunds $20,000 of the fees. The $20,000 is taxable income to the corporation in second year because it received a tax benefit in the prior year.

Note that the rule applies only to items for which the firm has received a tax benefit. Accordingly, if the firm was in an NOL status in the prior year, or the amount paid was nondeductible (say, a bribe to a lawmaker), the refund would not be taxable income the next year.

Substance over Form

Under the doctrine of *substance over form,* even when the form of a transaction complies with a favorable tax treatment, if the substance of the transaction is the intent to avoid taxes, the form will be ignored, and the transaction recast to reflect its real intent. (See Example 1.37.)

EXAMPLE 1.37

An entrepreneur is the sole stockholder of his corporation. The corporation never pays dividends to the entrepreneur, and instead, each year it pays out 100% of the corporation's net income as a salary to the entrepreneur (who also serves as company's chief executive officer). The doctrine of substance over form empowers tax authorities to tax at least part of the salary as if it were a dividend.

In jurisdictions where substance over form applies, it has quite often been developed in a series of court decisions rather than by explicit legislative action. Examples are cases such as *Gregory v. Helvering* in the United States, *Furniss v. Dawson* in the United Kingdom, and *Regina v. Mitchell* in Canada.

Recovery of Capital and Calculation of Gains and Losses

A fundamental concept, related to the doctrine of recovery of capital, is the idea of *gains and losses*. That is, only the net gain or loss from the sale of property is taxable (or deductible) for income tax purposes in virtually every jurisdiction. Gain or loss is computed as

Amount realized (the value of what is received) –
Adjusted basis of property given = Gain or loss

The adjusted basis of the property given is computed as

Original basis + Capital improvements –
Accumulated depreciation – Other recoveries of investments
(such as write-offs for casualty losses) = Adjusted basis

The original basis usually is the original purchase price. Capital improvements are additions that have an economic life beyond one year. Accumulated depreciation applies only in the case of an asset used in business. (See Example 1.38.)

EXAMPLE 1.38

A corporation buys a factory building for $2 million in 1991. It sold the building for $3 million in the current year. At the time of sale, the building had $600,000 of accumulated depreciation. In 1998, the corporation spent $400,00 on a new roof. The gain is

Amount Realized:		$3,000,000
Adjusted Basis:		
Original basis	$2,000,000	
Add: capital improvements	400,000	
Less: Accumulated Depreciation	<600,000>	
		<1,800,000>
Net Gain		$1,200,000

As already noted, in the United States gains and losses can be capital or ordinary. Capital gains and losses result from the sale of capital assets, which are defined as *any asset other than the following:* inventory, receivables, long-term business fixed asset, and self-constructed assets. All other assets are ordinary and create ordinary gains and losses. As a practical matter, corporations pay the same tax rate (their normal rate) on ordinary and capital gains. However, losses are treated differently for corporations. Ordinary losses are deductible without limit, while net capital losses are not deductible and must be carried back three years, and if still unused, forward five years. (See Example 1.39.)

EXAMPLE 1.39

A corporation sells a machine for $10,000. It had previously bought the machine for $20,000. At the time of sale, it had $6,000 of accumulated depreciation. This results in:

Amount Realized:		$10,000
Less: Adjusted Basis:		
Original basis	20,000	
Less: accumulated depreciation	<6,000>	
		14,000
Ordinary loss		<$ 4,000>

If the corporation is in the 35% bracket, the tax benefit is $(.35)(\$4,000) =$ $1,400. How would the answer change if instead there was a $4,000 gain? Because it is ordinary, the gain would be taxed at the 35% tax rate for a total tax effect of $\$4,000(.35) = \$1,400$ of tax. (See Example 1.40.)

EXAMPLE 1.40

A corporation sells the stock of a subsidiary for $20 million. It originally bought the stock of the subsidiary for $5 million. The difference is a $15 million capital gain, which is taxed at the 35% rate. What if there was a $15 million loss on the sale of the stock? Then, unless the corporation had other capital gains against which to offset the loss, the loss would be carried back three years to offset any possible capital gains in that year.

Multiple gains and losses must be separated into capital versus ordinary. Next, ordinary gains and losses are netted with each other. Separately, capital gains and losses are also netted with each other. Within the capital category, they must be segregated into short term versus long term. As a practical matter, this long- and short-term distinction does not matter for corporations, since the tax effect is identical. As explained later in the chapter, the distinction does matter for individual taxpayers, since there is a preferential tax rate for long-term capital gains, that is, gains on assets that have been owned by the taxpayer for more than one year. (See Examples 1.41 and 1.42.)

EXAMPLE 1.41

A corporation has the following transactions during the year: a long-term capital gain of $100, a short-term capital loss of $1000, a short-term capital gain of $200, an ordinary loss of $300, and an ordinary gain of $500. The netting process is as follows:

	Ordinary	Capital	
		Short Term	Long Term
	<$200>	<$1,000>	$100
	500	200	—
Net	$300	<$ 800>	$100

The net ordinary income of $300 will be taxed at the 35% rate. The net capital loss of $700 cannot be deducted in the current year, and instead will be carried back three years.

EXAMPLE 1.42

Assume the same facts as Example 1.41, except that the taxpayer is an individual. The ordinary income would be taxed at the taxpayer's top rate. The net capital loss would be deductible at the taxpayer's ordinary rate (individuals can deduct up to $3,000 per year). What if there was a $700 net gain instead? If the gain was attributable to long-term assets, then the preferential long-term capital gains tax rate (see later discussion) would apply. If the net gain was primarily from short-term assets, then it would be taxed at ordinary income tax rates.

SAVANT FRAMEWORK

Just as there is a deep structure to taxation—that is, a set of principles that fundamentally shape tax rules—there is a deep structure to tax planning. In other words, the multitude of seemingly disparate techniques for reducing the tax burden generated by various transactions can be classified into groups of tax strategies. This is done in the SAVANT framework, which is explained in Chapter 2.

The idea of an analytic framework that classifies tax planning techniques is based on the answer to a fundamental question: Why tax plan in the first place? It may seem obvious at first glance, but this is an important question, which is answered differently at different times, for different organizations and in different countries. This is because tax planning requires changing operations, and doing so is not cost free, and the rewards are uncertain. However, optimizing a firm's total tax burden can be important to its success. Examples 1.43 to 1.51 illustrate the cost-benefit trade-offs of corporate tax planning.

EXAMPLE 1.43

A software company has excess cash and is considering acquiring a firm. Two targets appear attractive. One is a restaurant business holding company, which has historically earned a 15% return on investment and also has $100 million of tax benefits, which could be used by an acquiring firm. The other is a computer software firm with equal returns, but no tax advantages. Although the discounted cash flows appear higher for the first target, becoming a worldwide dominant software producer is not part of its *strategic plan*. Because management has little expertise in restaurants, returns may actually decline after the acquisition, making the software firm, despite the lack of tax advantage, a better choice.

EXAMPLE 1.44

Marketing management of a breakfast cereal company has presented an idea for a new product that, in their estimation, has a 50% chance of success. If it succeeds, it will generate $10 million of posttax profits annually, increased to $15 million by a $5 million tax credit for research and development. The investment in the new product would be $100 million, and the firm's minimum rate of return is 15%. The new product should be rejected because the *adjusted* (for probability) *value-added* is 10%: ($10 million) plus $5 million tax credit, or $10 million, divided by the $100 million investment.

EXAMPLE 1.45

A bank holding company is considering selling off one of its unprofitable subsidiaries. By selling the subsidiary, conglomerate earnings per share would increase from $4 to $5 per share. However, the subsidiary generates annual free cash flows of $1 million (partly as a result of tax-loss benefits) on a $1 million investment. The after-tax *value-added* is significant, so the subsidiary should be kept.

EXAMPLE 1.46

A pharmaceutical company would like to build an assembly plant in the People's Republic of China (PRC), partly because the current tax rate is 5%. However, managers of other Southeast Asian subsidiaries are convinced that, if anything, the tax rate will increase because of political pressures. Management should *anticipate* that the rate will increase and adjust the expected rate of return accordingly.

EXAMPLE 1.47

A small entertainment firm wants to hire a talented manager away from a larger firm. The manager is currently being paid $10 million annually in salary, which is $2 million more than the small firm can afford. The small firm offers $5 million in cash and $5 million in stock options. Because the options are tax-favored, the manager may find the options very attractive. The small firm has used tax benefits to *negotiate*.

EXAMPLE 1.48

An investment bank has approached a firm about recapitalization. The firm currently has $1 million and $2 million in class A and B common stock, respectively, outstanding. The investment bank has advised that by converting the class A to $1 million worth of bonds, the firm could save $200,000 annually because interest paid on the bonds is tax deductible but dividends paid are not deductible. Before accepting the deal, management must determine what transaction costs are involved, for example, how much the investment bank will charge for its services so that it can determine whether the transaction will result in *value-added*.

EXAMPLE 1.49

Toward the end of the year, engineers from the production department of a manufacturer would like to replace old machinery with new machinery. Tax rates are scheduled to increase in the next year. Thus, tax deductions for future depreciation will have more cash value. Accordingly, management *anticipates* the changing tax rates and structures the transaction to acquire the machinery early in the next year.

EXAMPLE 1.50

A construction company is considering a contract to build a warehouse. Construction would take one year and cost $1 million, with expenses payable currently and $1.2 million to be received on completion of the project. Because of tax-accounting rules, both costs and revenues are not recognized until the second year. Management needs to consider, in determining the project's *value-added*, the time value of the cash flows from this project, with cash flows net of taxes having more impact in year one than in year two, and having a greater impact on value-adding.

EXAMPLE 1.51

A management consulting firm owns a building in eventual need of a new roof. Instead of reroofing, the firm repairs a part each year. Repairs are tax deductible, whereas a new roof must be capitalized; the firm has transformed a non-deductible cost into a deductible one.

CHAPTER 2

Using the SAVANT Framework to Guide Tax Planning

*[T]he fundamentals of federal taxation have a very long shelf
life . . . . Although we watch frequent additions, corrections, and
amendments, they are rather like hanging meat on the skeleton
of the brontosaurus; underneath, the structure remains the same.*

—Professor Richard B. Stephens,
Fundamentals of Federal Income Taxation

To increase firm value, managers engage in transactions. Of course, firm value can increase for other reasons. For example, the value of the firm's assets simply can appreciate due to market factors beyond the control of managers. However, transactions must have occurred when firms acquire such assets, and it takes transactions to convert such assets into cash flow. Managers do things like buy, sell, rent, lease, and recapitalize. If managers structure transactions such that each is value-maximizing, then by year-end the sum of such transactions will have maximized firm value. However, note that each transaction has an uninvited third party: the government. In strategic tax management, when a firm chooses transactions, it keeps tax management in mind. This transactions approach—the SAVANT framework—is shown in Exhibit 2.1.

The firm looks to engage in transactions that maximize end-of-period value. It can chose from a constellation of entities or transactions, and the choice then is put through the lens of the firm's *strategic* objectives. If the transaction (including tax effects) is consistent with the firm's strategic objectives, it may accept the transaction. Otherwise, even if the transaction is highly tax-advantaged, the firm should consider rejecting the transaction.

EXHIBIT 2.1   SAVANT Framework: A Transactions Approach to Tax Management

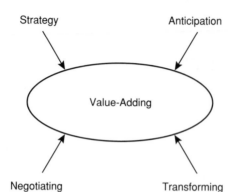

Similarly, the tax aspects of the transaction can be managed in a strategic manner.

Next, the firm *anticipates* its future tax status and chooses the timing— this year or a future year—of the transaction. Because the effects of trans- actions often span more than one year, the firm projects tax effects into the future, using current and expected future tax rates and rules, and factors in management's expectations as to the future tax status of the firm. As discussed more fully in the section entitled "Anticipation," if there is tax advantage to adjusting the timing of a transaction, the firm should do so provided that the nontax economics still make sense.

Taxes are also *negotiated* between the firm and the other entity. As dis- cussed more fully later in the section entitled "Negotiating," the firm seeks to shift more of the tax burden away from itself (and potentially, onto the other entity) by negotiating the terms of the transaction. The firm attempts to minimize tax costs by *transforming* transactions being considered into ones with more favorable tax treatment. For example, managers can work to restructure transactions that might generate nondeductible costs into ones where costs are deductible ones, or work to transform what would have been ordinary income into capital gain income.

What is left, after taxes, is *value-added* to the firm. Like taxes, value- added often inures to the firm over time. Because it is a fundamental prin- ciple that cash inflows are more valuable now than later, tax management takes into account the time value of a transaction as well. The time value of a transaction, after taxes and transaction costs, is what increases firm value in the future. One aspect of a transaction that affects value-added com- prises transaction costs, such as sales commissions or attorney fees. As dis- cussed in the section entitled "Value-Adding," transaction costs reduce the net value of the transaction to the firm. If the transaction costs exceed the net value, the transaction should be rejected.

As explained previously, SAVANT is an acronym for strategy, anticipation, value-adding, negotiating, and transforming. For a transaction to be properly tax managed (and thus best increase firm value), managers should consider all of these aspects.

STRATEGY

A key ingredient of any successful company is a sound and successfully implemented strategy. Tax management should work to enhance the firm's strategy and should not cause the firm to engage in tax-minimizing transactions that deter it from its strategic plan. As an extreme example, a firm could earn zero profits and pay no taxes, but this would be inconsistent with sound strategy. In a business setting, strategy can be thought of as the overall plan for deploying resources to establish a favorable position. The resulting strategy, resulting from the firm's objective appraisal, is often referred to as SWOT: matching internal *Strengths* and *Weaknesses* to external *Opportunities* and *Threats*.

A strategic management imperative results from this analysis. Startegy provides a vision of where the firm wants to go, typically represented by a mission statement. For example, a mission statement might be "to be the global leader in widget manufacture." A more specific business-level strategy is a way to gain an advantage over competitors by attracting customers to the firm and away from competitors. Such strategies typically boil down to doing things better, cheaper, or faster than the competition.

The firm's business-level strategy is typically detailed in operations-level, corporate-level, and international-level strategies. At the *operations* level, the firm's strategy involves gaining advantage over competitors to create value for its customers through its products or services. The operations focus has resulted in many firms reengineering the process by which they execute their business-level strategy. In its competitive analysis, the firm needs to understand whether it has a tax advantage or disadvantage in relation to its rivals. *Corporate* strategy focuses on diversification of the business. Ideally, diversification strategies improve the structural position or process execution of existing units, or, in a new business unit, stresses competitive advantage and consumer value. *International* strategy focuses on taking advantage of corporate and business strengths in global markets. It requires an understanding of local countries and relies on working with foreign governments. As part of the firm's business strategy, it needs to deal with the threats shown in Exhibit 2.2.

How does effective tax management interact with strategy? First, a firm should not alter the form of a transaction in order to manage taxes, if the

EXHIBIT 2.2   General Sources of Strategic Threats to Firms

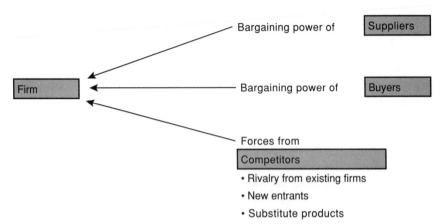

change is inconsistent with its strategy. For example, if a firm wants to acquire another business that is unrelated to its core competency, to obtain tax benefits (e.g., NOL carryovers), it should not do so unless it is clear that the pretax economics make sense.

Second, a firm's competitive strategy may be shaped, in part, by its tax status. Put simply, if a firm is structured so that it has a more favorable tax status than that of its competitors, this can give the firm an overall cost advantage over its competitors. Effective tax management is an important tool in obtaining this kind of competitive edge. (See Example 2.1.)

EXAMPLE 2.1

Suppose the U.S. government announces a 20% income tax deduction for purchasing new equipment. Both a firm and its biggest competitor are thinking about acquiring new equipment. The firm is in the 35% tax bracket; the competitor will be in an NOL situation for several years (i.e., it is in the 0% tax bracket). If new equipment costs $1 million, the firm's after-tax cost is less than this because it enjoys the tax deductions related to purchasing the equipment. The benefit of the new deduction, for example, is 20% of the $1 million cost times the 35% tax rate, or $70,000. Even ignoring other deductions (like depreciation), the firm's after-tax cost of the equipment is only $930,000, whereas the competitor's after-tax cost is $1 million. The firm can use this cost advantage to either buy more equipment, cut prices (and undercut the competitor), or invest in new projects.

The same sort of tax-related competitive advantage can be applied to new entrants and substitute products. It also can be used in developing new products, as discussed in Example 2.2.

EXAMPLE 2.2

Often, firms budget their overall advertising and R&D (research and development) expenses either as fixed amounts or by pegging them as percentages of sales. Taking a competitive analysis into account may be more effective, however. Suppose a firm expects to be in a net operating loss (NOL) situation for the few years and its major competitor is in the 35% bracket. Both are contemplating major product research. For such research, each dollar spent would generate $.20 of tax benefits through two tax savings rules.

The first is a tax credit for R&D and the second is rapid depreciation of R&D equipment. For the competitor, such benefits would yield an after-tax cost of $.80 per dollar spent. If both firms have a $20 million R&D budget, the competitor can spend $25 million of cash and still be on budget. This is because the tax credit will generate $5 million of tax savings ($25 million × 20%) to pay for the extra spending. If R&D is in a race to be the first to develop a patentable product, the firm might be better off staying out of the R&D game (and investing the $20 million elsewhere) until it goes into a positive tax bracket in a few years.

However, where net profits (as opposed to just expenditures) are concerned, the net advantage goes to the NOL firm (see Example 2.3).

EXAMPLE 2.3

Assume two competitor firms have $20 pretax unit contribution margins. Each sells a product for $40 and has fixed costs consisting solely of depreciation of $100,000. Firm A has an NOL carryforward, and firm B is in the 34% tax bracket. Assuming there is a 25% write-off for the depreciable equipment, the strategic advantage goes to the NOL carryforward firm, because it achieves break-even sales at a much lower volume, as follows:

FIRM A: $100,000/$20 = 5,000 units

FIRM B: ($100,000)(1 − .34)(1 − .25)/$20(1 − .34) = 6,964 units

ANTICIPATION

Firms operate in a dynamic environment in which they must attempt to anticipate the actions of their competitors, markets, and governments. Tax-managment firms adjust the timing of transactions in anticipation of *expected* tax changes. (Note that while tax law changes are debated before being enacted, many are applied retroactively.) Firms adjust the timing of their transactions when they are *certain* of their future tax status, or when there is a known change in tax rules. For example, they might know that they have an NOL this year, which will be used next year.

Anticipation and Certain Tax Changes

Suppose it is known that tax rates will rise substantially next January. If it is now December, the rate change can be anticipated. Assuming it is not otherwise harmful, simply delaying December expenses until January means they will have more "bang for the buck" that month by being deducted at a higher tax rate. Examples of such tax management by timing abound. In December 1986, U.S. corporations delayed billions of dollars in taxable income because of the decrease in the federal tax rate scheduled to begin in January 1987. Similarly, in anticipation of a rate increase on individuals, Disney CEO Michael Eisner exercised several million dollars in stock options in late 1986 to accelerate income into a lower-tax-rate-year.

At the corporate level, timing usually focuses on shifting income into lower-tax-rate years, and deductions into higher-rate years. Examples 2.4 and 2.5 illustrate this concept.

EXAMPLE 2.4

What if a company is considering replacing its computer system? The new system would cost $500,000 and would generate first-year depreciation deductions of $70,000. Suppose the firm is currently in the 35% tax bracket, but next year it expects to go into the 0% tax bracket (say, due to various tax credits and losses). If the firm waits until next year, it will receive no tax benefits. However, if it adjusts the timing of the transaction to buy the equipment during the current year, it will get a tax benefit of 35%($70,000) = $24,500.

EXAMPLE 2.5

A corporation is considering selling some unimproved land to generate cash flows. The land would generate a $1 million taxable gain. This year, the corporation is in the 35% bracket, but next year it will be in the 0% bracket. The corporation should adjust the timing of the sale so that it occurs next year. This will save the company (35%)($1million) = $350,000 in taxes.

Effects of Net Operating Losses

As noted in Chapter 1, for U.S. income tax purposes corporate NOLs carry back five years and forward 20. If the firm generates an NOL in the current year, and the loss can be carried back and used in its entirety in the previous years, the NOL should have only minor influence on how the firm adjusts the timing of its current income and deductions. To see this, assume a large firm has an NOL that can be carried back and used in its entirety. Therefore, both its current taxable income and its tax rate are exactly zero. If it is contemplating whether to accelerate $500,000 of income into the current year versus waiting until next year when it is in the 35% bracket, there is no tax difference: The current year's income would be effectively taxed at the standard 35% rate either way.

If the $500,000 were instead an expense, timing would make a slight difference. The expenditure could not be deducted until the next year, so the firm would lose the present value of a one year deferral. As discussed in detail later in this Chapter in the section entitled "Value-Adding, Cash Flows, and Time Value," because one can earn interest on cash received earlier, the value of being paid later is less than the value of being paid sooner. Present value is a mathematical technique that can be used to quantify the benefit of being paid earlier.

However, timing can be very important if the NOL is not used up in offsetting prior years' income but is expected instead to carry forward for a number of years. Here, the discounted value (i.e., the difference between present value and future value) can be significant. Referring to the $500,000 of income in Example 2.4, assume that the NOL will not be used for 10 years and that the firm's cost of capital is 10%, the present value of the tax is only about 40% of what the tax would be without the NOL carryforward. The point is: The presence of an NOL carryforward, particularly one that is large enough to remain unused for a number of years, has an impact on *strategic tax planning*.

Anticipation and Uncertain Tax Changes

The tax-managed firm can anticipate tax changes before they become official. For example, Ronald Reagan campaigned to be U.S. president in 1980 promising rapid write-offs for plant and equipment as part of sweeping tax reform. In anticipation of the Reagan election and subsequent tax act, a number of firms delayed acquisitions of equipment from late 1980 to 1981.

Employing this anticipation strategy entails assigning a probability to the likelihood of tax legislation being enacted. For example, suppose the firm assigns a 50% probability that tax rates will rise to 37% next year from the current 35% rate. The *anticipated* tax rate increase would be 1%, calculated as 50% (37% − 35%). If it can accelerate $1 million of income from next year to this year, the firm's expected tax savings would be $10,000, calculated as 1% of $1 million. (Keep in mind, however, that the expected tax benefits of implementing this strategy would be reduced by any related *transaction* costs.)

In recent years, there have been other U.S. tax law changes that have caused anticipation effects like this. These changes include several extensions of the 20% tax credit for R&D and the exemption of electronic commerce sales from states' sales and use taxes. For the former, each year the credits have been renewed by Congress for a short period. Therefore, an R&D firm must predict whether the credit will be extended and plan how this will affect what it will spend for R&D this year versus next year. (See Examples 2.6 and 2.7.)

EXAMPLE 2.6

Suppose Intel Corporation has a budget of $1 billion per year for R&D. The firm's lobbyists estimate that there is a 30% probability that the 20% R&D credit will not be extended for the next year. If the firm's two-year R&D budget is $2 billion, then the expected tax benefit is $340 million, calculated as $(.2)(\$1 \text{ billion}) + (.2)(1 - .3)(\$1\text{billion})$. If the firm accelerates next year's R&D into this year, however, the tax benefits will be $(.2)(\$2 \text{ billion}) = \$400,000$. Of course, the firm needs to consider whether the acceleration makes good business sense.

EXAMPLE 2.7

Suppose Land's End Corporation is trying to assess the tax costs of mail-order sales into various states. The company is trying to decide whether to establish a Web site with servers in various states to capture some of these sales. A number of states have attempted to subject such sales to sales taxes. However, the U.S. Congress has enacted a moratorium that prohibits states from assessing such taxes this year. Management believes that there is a 50% chance that the law will be extended into the next year. Therefore, the company may want to postpone Internet sales until next year, when the anticipated tax would be less.

Anticipation and Price Effects

Competitors can also react to expected tax changes. At a minimum, a wide-spread reaction has supply-and-demand effects in some markets, causing a price change. Tax cuts cause prices to rise, and tax increases cause prices to fall. (In this way, changes in market prices can mute the effects of tax policy.) This price effect has become known as "implicit taxes."

Firms should attempt to anticipate price effects resulting from tax changes. The magnitude of price effects depends on a number of conditions. These include the elasticities of supply and demand and whether additional suppliers can enter the market (this can occur to some degree in the long run). In practice, such elasticities may not be known, although marketing departments of large firms often have data on price sensitivities to their own products. The point here is that some sort of a price response is likely to occur no matter what types of goods, services, or investments receive the tax break.

A well-known example of the price effects of tax breaks is the case of municipal bonds. As noted in Chapter 1, because the interest income from them is tax free, the demand for municipal bonds is pushed up. Because they are typically sold in even-dollar increments (e.g., $1,000 per bond), the price effect does not *directly* occur. Instead, the effect occurs *indirectly*. The stated interest rates are lower than those for comparable taxable bonds. This can easily be seen by comparing the yields of taxable bonds listed in *The Wall Street Journal* to the yields of state and local bonds listed in its Daily Bond Buyer section.

If there is a tax increase on some goods, services, or investments, the opposite effect occurs: Prices drop. What do these price effects mean to managers? The astute manager should attempt to *anticipate* such price movements. There is a well-known principle in economics that the incidence of a tax (or a tax benefit) falls only in part on the entity *directly* affected by the tax. This effect is shown in Exhibit 2.3, which depicts the hypothetical price effects resulting from a new tax on computers.

Looking at Exhibit 2.3, imagine that demand drops due to an import tax on computers. Market prices drop, too, so part of the tax increase is passed on to computer suppliers via lower prices. (Suppliers can antici-pate tax law changes as well. However, for a supply curve to shift, existing suppliers must leave or additional suppliers must enter the marketplace, which typically occurs over a much longer time period than that for demand curve shifts.)

As shown in Exhibit 2.3, the tax decreases quantity demanded because the after-tax price of computers has increased. This demand decrease pushes the market price down to P from P'. Thus, part of the tax is effectively passed onto suppliers through a lower sales price. Alternatively, suppose a

EXHIBIT 2.3　　Price Effects of an Import Tax on Computers

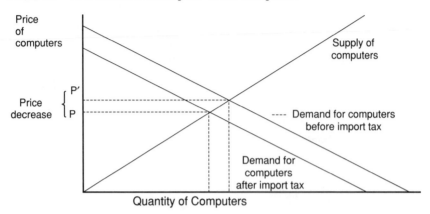

Quantity of Computers

tax break (say, very rapid depreciation) is given for the purchase of computers. What will happen in the marketplace? Because more computers will be demanded, prices will go up, and part of the tax credit will be bid away to suppliers in the form of higher prices. The manager must anticipate such price changes in deciding whether to buy or sell something that is subject to a change in tax rules. (See Example 2.8.)

EXAMPLE 2.8

Suppose a manager knows that on January 1 of next year, a 10% tax credit will be given for the purchase of a new computer system. The manager expects to spend $100,000 on a networked system of PCs to replace an existing system. Assume an additional $8,000 must be spent in programmer time to get the system up and running. The manager hopes the tax savings on the new system of $10,000 (10% × $100,000) will pay for the $8,000 programming costs. However, if the market price, (from increased demand) jumps to around $103,000, then even with the tax break, the anticipated net benefit will be negative: ((10% × $103,000) − $3,000 additional cost) − $8,000 = <$700>.

　　The more familiar managers are with the market, the more accurately they can anticipate and navigate through the price effects. If there is a huge supply market (e.g., PCs), it will take some time before demand pushes the price up. A sharp manager would make a purchase very early on. However, if there is only one supplier (say, Cray Supercomputers), price hikes might occur almost immediately as stockouts occur and marginal costs rise. Thus, unless the manager can effectively negotiate (see later discussion), much of the tax benefit will be lost when dealing in a private market.

VALUE-ADDING

Effective tax management is no different from any other aspect of management insofar as any transaction should at some point be expected to add value. Ultimately, most measures of value-adding are derived from the firm's financial statements. Related to accounting earnings are the firm's cash flows. If the net present value of cash flows from a transaction are positive, then, over time, this will translate into positive financial earnings. Both typically enhance shareholder value and increase management compensation (e.g., where bonuses are based on accounting earnings or stock options are being granted).

Using Cash Flows to Measure Value-Adding

The relationships of cash flows to accounting are illustrated in Example 2.9.

EXAMPLE 2.9

Suppose a firm buys some unimproved land, in 2002, as an investment, for $1 million. At the end of 2003, it sells the land for $2.5 million. The firm's net income before the land transaction, and before management bonuses, for 2002 and 2003 is $10 million and $11 million, respectively. There are 1 million shares of common outstanding. Management receives a bonus of 5% of pretax income. The firm is in the 35% bracket. The value-adding effects from the land transactions are

Items	Cash Flow	Year—2002 Financial Earnings	Cash Flow	Year—2003 Financial Earnings
Purchase price	<$1,000,000>	—	—	—
Selling price	—	—	$2,500,000	—
Gain on sale	—	—	—	$1,500,000
Tax on gain on sale:				
(.35)($2.5m – 1m)	—	—	<525,000>	<525,000>
Management bonus:				
(.05)($1.5m)(1 – .35)*	—	—	<48,750>	<48,750>
Net cash flows	<$1,000,000>	—	$1,926,250	
Net change in financial earnings		—		$ 926,250
Change in earnings per share:				
Above 1 million shares		—		93¢

*Because the management bonus is tax deductible, its after tax cost is 1 – tax rate.

In Example 2.9, the cash-flow analysis yields the same measure of value-adding as does financial accounting income: a $926,250 increase. The cash flows and reported earnings are different just in terms of *when* they are reported. Shareholder value increases by a $0.90 per share earnings per share (EPS); management wealth increases by $75,000 (before they pay their own taxes). Note that cash flows will rarely exactly equal the sum of financial earnings changes over time; however, they will approximate it. The point of this is the following: If managers maximize after-tax cash flows on each transaction, this will also maximize shareholder value, as measured by financial income. Therefore, *discounted cash flow* (DCF) analysis is *critical* in measuring whether a tax management method will increase firm value.

The formulas for present value and discounting, along with on-line calculators, can be found on the Internet. Most are at academic Web sites, such as:

- *http://sks99.com/fm/ch5.htm,* which also outlines the mathematics of finance in general, and its NPV calculator *http://www.sks99.com/fm/presAnn/defPA.htm*
- *http://www.econ.ucdavis.edu/classes/134/lec4.htm*
- *http://www.uni.edu/isakson/CHAP05/,* which provides a concise overview of NPV
- *http://wehner.tamu.edu/finc.www/finc630-lee/glossary05.htm* (formulas and a glossary)
- *http://www.sks99.com/fm/presAnn/defPA.htm*

There are commercial Web sites, too, such as:

- *http://www.cedarspring.com/Components/Finance/TVM/pv.html*
- *http://www.people.memphis.edu/~emkamau/money.html* (calculator)

Value-Adding, Cash Flows, and Time Value

A tenet of business is that a dollar of income now is worth more than a dollar later. Holding tax rates and bases constant, tax management implies deferring income and accelerating deductions. More formally, it is the net present value (NPV) of expected taxes which managers should work to minimize. This implies that not only cash flows, but also discounted cash flows, should be used in determining whether a transaction increases after-tax firm value. (See Example 2.10.)

EXAMPLE 2.10

A firm can make one of two investments. Both have three-year horizons, and both have identical pretax cash flows of $100 per year. The taxes for the first investment are $60 in total, that is, $20 in each of the three years. The taxes for the second investment are also $60, but the tax is all due in the third year. If the firm has a 10% cost of capital, then the present value of taxes under the first investment is: $20(.9091) + $20(.8264) + $20(.7513) = $49.74. (The present value factor for year one is $1/(1 + r)^n = 1/(1.10)^1 =$ .9091. That for year two is $1/(1.10)^2 = .8264$. For more information, see the Web sites listed at the end of the previous section, "Using Cash Flows to Measure Value-Adding.") For the second investment, the tax is $60(.7513) = $45.08 Thus, simply through the time value of deferring the tax, the second investment has a higher value-adding to the company.

Two common gain-deferral techniques used when planning for U.S. income taxes are worth mentioning now. The first is the like-kind exchange. (Governed by IRC Section 1031 it also is called a 1031 exchange.) If a company sells assets (e.g., plant, equipment, or land) for a profit, it must pay taxes on the gain, even if it uses the proceeds from the sale to buy new assets to replace those sold. However, if the requirements of Section 1031 are met, a company that trades in the old for the new is allowed to postpone the tax on the old asset until the new asset is sold. The basic requirement for this favorable tax treatment is that like-kind property must be exchanged: realty for realty, or personalty for personalty. If the firm receives anything other than like-kind property in the exchange (called "boot," from the practice of throwing in other property "to boot" to equalize value in a trade), it is taxed immediately if there is an overall gain on the transaction. (See Example 2.11.)

EXAMPLE 2.11

Suppose a firm has a piece of land worth $5 million, which originally cost $2 million. It wishes to sell the land to generate cash to buy a new plant for $5 million. However, it will have not have enough after-tax cash to do this: $5 million sales price, less taxes on the gain of .34($5 − 2 million) or $1.02 million, equals $3.98 million after-tax proceeds from a sale. On the other hand, if the firm exchanges the land for the plant, there is no tax on the land gain until the plant is sold. If the firm plans to sell the plant in 10 years, assuming an 8% discount rate, the present value of the tax on the gain is .4632($3 million) .34% = .$56 million. By using a 1031 exchange, the manager has saved the firm over half a million dollars.

Of course, the seller of the plant must be willing to take the land in exchange, instead of just receiving cash. The manager should be willing to give the other party up to half a million dollars in addition to the land to get the deal, (that is, negotiate the tax benefits.) However, the manager could find a third firm who might be a willing party to make the exchange, that is, acquire the plant for cash and trade it for the land. Such multiple-party exchanges are not uncommon, and there are well-organized markets for doing so.

Another important tax deferral mechanism is the IRC Section 1033 involuntary conversion, which is important if a gain results when insurance proceeds are received because a firm had a property (realty or personalty) that was destroyed, seized, or stolen. A gain can result if the proceeds exceed the firm's remaining investment in the property. This can happen even if the firm uses the proceeds to replace the lost property. If the requirements of Section 1033 are met, however, taxes on the gain are deferred until the replacement property is disposed of. (See Example 2.12.)

EXAMPLE 2.12

Suppose the firm's factory, located in a foreign country, is seized by the foreign government as part of an antiforeign change in government policy. The factory cost $10 million, and insurance covered the fair market value (mostly due to the value of the underlying land) of $15 million. If the firm uses the $15 million to buy or build a new plant, and the new plant is held 10 years, the present value of the tax is .4632 × .34 × ($15 − 10 million) = $1.48 million. If the firm uses the $15 million for some other type of investment, there is an immediate tax of .34($15 − 10 million) = $1.7 million. By using 1033, the manager saves the firm over $200,000.

Managers do not *plan* to use Section 1033 per se: They do not burn down a plant in order to defer taxes. However, if an involuntary conversion should naturally arise, Section 1033 is a valuable deferral technique.

Other tax deferral methods, discussed in later chapters, include

- Foreign subsidiaries (Chapter 8)
- Installment sales (Chapter 10)
- Recapitalizations (Chapter 13)
- Management stock options (Chapter 6)
- Employee stock option plans (ESOPs) (Chapter 10)

Using Other Measures of Value-Adding

The previous discussion is not meant to imply that discounted cash flow (DCF) is the only method of value increase. On a year-by-year basis, investors and creditors monitor the firm's financial performance. Because

TAX MANAGEMENT IN ACTION 2.1

Economic Value-Added

EVA is a way of measuring an operation's profitability taking into account an important factor that conventional financial measures often overlook. That factor is the operation's cost of the use of capital. All Boise Cascade operations use capital in the form of such things as inventories, equipment, computers, real estate, receivables, timberland, or timber deposits. When a business generates a positive EVA, the operation creates real economic value for the company's shareholders.

Beginning January 1, 1995, EVA became the key financial measure for Boise Cascade. Comparing EVA with other measures, it stands out as a single financial measure that takes into consideration all the essential components of PROTC, ROE, and operating profit. EVA is an effective measure of increases or decreases in shareholder value, and it is becoming a barometer the investment community uses to evaluate how well Boise Cascade and other companies are performing.

Source: Boise Cascade 1996 Annual Report.

DCF information (especially on individual projects) is rarely communicated directly to outsiders, they must usually rely on measures of performance that can be constructed from publicly available financial statement data. Managers thus need to know how transactions affect such measures. Popular annual financial statement measures are earnings per share (EPS), return on equity (ROE)—net income divided by shareholder's equity—and economic value-added (EVA). As an example of EVA, consider Tax Management in Action 2.1, which accompanied Boise Cascade's 1996 *Annual Report.*

EVA has become increasingly popular. It is computed as after-tax operating profit minus the firm's weighted-average cost of capital. Accordingly, even if a transaction minimizes taxes, it may be poor tax management if it decreases EVA.

EVA can be decreased by lower after-tax operating profits, using more capital, or using more expensive capital. Suppose a firm acquires a new plant, which increases annual pretax operating profits by $1 million. Because of the tax benefits of accelerated depreciation, assume there is no tax on the increased earnings. To finance the plant, the firm issues $1 million in bonds that pay 8%. Prior to the transaction, the firm had $100 million in after-tax operating profits, and capital consisting of $200 million in common stock having a cost of 14%. EVA before and after the acquisition is

After-tax Operating Profit   − Cost of Capital = EVA

Before the plant: $100 million − $28 million*   = $72 million

After the plant: $101 million − $28.8 million** = $72.8 million

  * 14% × $200 million
  ** 28 million + (1 million × 8%) = 28.8 million

Thus, from an EVA standpoint the project should be accepted, since it increases annual EVA by $800,000. However, before a definite decision on the new plant can be made, there should be an NPV analysis to consider multiperiod effects (such as tax depreciation becoming smaller in later years).

It is important to note that exclusive use of EVA (or ROE) is not recommended for evaluating long-term projects. For example, suppose the new plant from the preceding example had $1 million in losses in its first two years, but $1.5 million in positive income in subsequent years. Suppose that, when added together, the new plant had a positive NPV. If managers are overly concerned with shareholder response, they might reject the project because, in the short run, EVA (as well as ROE and EPS) is negative.

Maximizing Value-Adding and Potential Conflicts

Maintaining (or improving) value-adding is implicitly a contract between the manager and the firm's shareholders. Closely related are explicit contracts based on financial accounting information. The company may have debt covenants tied to certain financial ratios, and a transaction, while saving taxes, might be detrimental in this regard. For example, suppose a transaction saves $100 million in taxes. However, it is financed with debt that, when added to the firm's existing debt, causes the debt-to-equity ratio to exceed the maximum specified in debt covenants. If it costs the firm over $100 million to renegotiate the debt, the transaction should be rejected. Other contracts based on financial accounting could be with managers (e.g., bonuses), customers, or suppliers.

To see this, refer to Example 2.9. Suppose that you are the CFO of the corporation and are trying to decide whether to invest in the raw land. Recall that the $1 million investment would generate negative cash flows in year 1, and would not have a positive EPS (or other financial statement) impact until year 2. If the firm's middle managers, who receive bonuses based on EPS, can invest $1 million in another project that has a positive EPS impact this year, it may be difficult to persuade them to make the land investment, even if the land investment would have a higher after-tax NPV.

So how should one measure a tax-related transaction's value-added to shareholders? Use NPV, but also consider any important financial statement measures and financial statement-derived contracts.

On Taxes, Value-Adding, and Book-Tax Differences

Another important issue on value-adding and taxes relates to the *timing* and *amount* of tax expense on the firm's financial statements. If a firm never expects to pay a tax on some income, then for financial-reporting purposes, it will not show a tax expense. Such *permanent differences* are the best of all worlds: Neither the firm's cash flow nor its financial earnings are reduced. Although a number of such examples of permanent differences under U.S. accounting rules (GAAP, or generally accepted accounting principles) are mentioned throughout this book, a very important one is income from an overseas subsidiary. Under U.S. tax law, the income of a foreign subsidiary generally does not generate U.S. taxes until the income is repatriated. Under U.S. GAAP, however, the subsidiary's income is included in the parent corporation's consolidated financial statements. This results in accounting earnings that are not reduced by a provision for U.S. income taxes. In many cases the benefit of this permanent difference is 35%—the normal U.S. corporate income tax rate—of these earnings.

More common than such permanent differences are temporary differences. These occur when the only difference in actual taxes paid and the related tax expense on the financial statements is the period in which they occur. That is, there are only timing differences. These result from differences in allowable methods in financial versus tax accounting. One important example is depreciation. Under most countries' GAAP, financial reporting generally uses straight-line depreciation. Some countries, however, allow accelerated depreciation methods for tax purposes. As noted in Chapter 1, one such method—the modified accelerated cost recovery system (MACRS)—is used for U.S. income tax purposes.

As an example, let the following occur in a year:

	Book	Tax
Annual depreciation	1,000,000	2,000,000
Times statuatory tax rate	× 35%	× 35%
Tax effect	350,000	700,000

In future years, book depreciation will be higher than that for tax purposes. That is, the timing difference will reverse. What is the implication for tax management? Because timing differences are numerous and difficult to schedule, managers do not generally worry about them. Instead, the cash flow effects of actual taxes should be considered. However, permanent differences are preferred because they can have an immediate and predictable effect on earnings.

Adjusting Value-Adding for Risk

Both business risks and the risks of tax law changes should be taken into account for effective tax management. A full discussion of risk management is beyond the scope of this text. However, three well-known risk-management techniques are diversification, insurance, and receiving a risk premium. All three can be effectively obtained by using the tax law.

A risk premium is the discount in purchase price that a manager would have to be offered to accept a risky project. (See Example 2.13.)

EXAMPLE 2.13

Suppose a manager is offered two investments, both of which cost $100. Investment A pays $110 with certainty; investment B pays $110 on average, with a 50% chance of paying either $0 or $220. If the manager is risk averse (most people are), she will select project A. Only if the purchase price of B is lowered (i.e., a risk premium is offered by the seller) will project B be selected.

The risk premium aspect is important for two reasons. First, many tax-favored investments have a special tax status because a government is trying to encourage investment in relatively risky investments. Examples include R&D, low-income housing, and inner city investments. Before rushing into one of these investments, a manager should adjust the expected return for a risk premium. Second, the tax benefit may be the equivalent of a risk premium. For example, the U.S. government gives a 20% tax credit for incremental R&D expenses. This effectively amounts to a 20% price cut compared to an investment with an equivalent (but less risky) return (a bond, for example).

The deductibility of losses, combined with taxation of income (gains), results in the income tax system acting as a variance-reducing mechanism for risky investments. That is, the dispersion of anticipated gains and losses is decreased for a risky investment, as shown in Exhibit 2.4. The upper curve shows the range of possible returns without income taxes. The lower curve shows the same returns after the imposition of a tax (the arrow shows the movement from the upper to the lower curve). Thus, assuming the manager is risk-averse (managers will trade off reduced gains for reduced losses), income taxes are good for risky investments.

EXHIBIT 2.4 Risk Reduction with Income Taxes

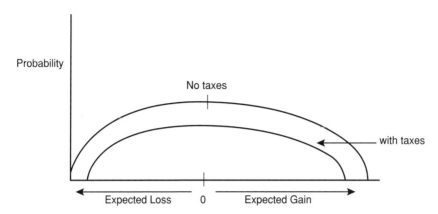

Another way of thinking of this is that the U.S. income tax law effectively provides insurance by allowing loss deductions. Losses on the sale of investments due to theft or casualty are tax deductible. In effect, the government pays the firm for part of the loss. However, such loss deductions are frequently limited in some way. The expected return on a risky investment, therefore, may not be as high as the manager anticipates. These loss-limitation rules are discussed throughout this book, in particular Chapters 3 and 4.

Risk from possible tax law changes must be managed as well. This concept is directly related to anticipation of tax law change. (See Example 2.14.)

EXAMPLE 2.14

Suppose the manager anticipates that there is a 50% probability that tax rates will decrease by 10%. The variance of expected returns will thus be reduced by 5% (10% times 50%) for both gain and loss.

Value-Adding and Transaction Costs

Tax management requires that the tax savings *exceed* the related execution costs in any transaction. Transaction costs might include brokers' fees or legal and accounting costs. Some examples of transactions costs are

- Stock broker fees on the sale of stock
- Attorney, accountant, and investment banker charges on mergers, acquisitions, and recapitalizations

- Lobbying costs to obtain favorable tax structures prior to locating a new plant
- Temporary loss of funds when paying an expense in December instead of January

NEGOTIATING

Effective tax planning involves negotiating tax benefits, both with tax authorities and other entities involved with the firm in a taxable transaction. Negotiation with a nongovernmental party to a transaction is a function of the relative tax status of the parties. That is, the benefits or costs can be shifted between the parties by negotiating the purchase price. (See Example 2.15.)

EXAMPLE 2.15

Suppose a firm is selling an office building with a market value of $2 million, of which tax benefits (through depreciation) are worth $300,000. If the selling entity is in a nontaxpaying situation (e.g., a nonprofit organization that is exempt from U.S. income tax), the tax benefits are worth nothing, so the firm should be willing to sell for less than $2 million. A taxable purchaser should be willing to pay up to $2 million.

The ability of firms to pass on the burden of a tax is known in economics as *tax shifting*. The firm may be able to shift taxes to any number of entities with which it deals, as shown in Exhibit 2.5.

Governments can be negotiated with at all levels. Tax jurisdictions may give special tax breaks to new businesses to locate in their jurisdictions. The

EXHIBIT 2.5   Opportunities for Shifting Taxes to Other Parties

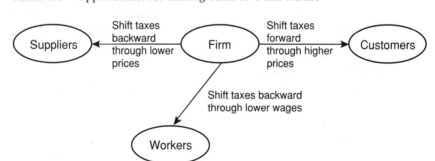

amount of the tax break is a matter of negotiation between the government and the managers of the firm. The local government often finds it profitable to forego property and income tax in order to create more jobs. Managers can negotiate with the U.S. government at two levels. First, they can lobby Congress. (This is discussed in detail in Chapter 12.) Second, managers can work with the Internal Revenue Service to get an advanced ruling on a particular transaction. The latter is particularly useful in a merger. Managers should bear in mind that some forms of negotiation—lobbying and IRS rulings—require large outlays of time and money, which may explain why they are typically used only for significant transactions and by large firms.

At all government levels, one last negotiation level exists: the audit level. If the firm's tax return is audited, agents and their supervisors often negotiate the settlement of taxes owed. This is specifically allowed in the United States. Its *offers in compromise* system allows the IRS to accept a lower amount if a taxpayer does not have the ability to pay the entire additional tax resulting from an audit.

TRANSFORMING

Tax management also includes transforming certain types of income into gains, certain types of expenses into losses, and certain types of taxable income into nontaxable income. Regarding the latter, losses on sales of capital assets (raw land, financial instruments) are deductible only to the extent that the firm has capital gains. Thus, the firm would like to transform capital losses to ordinary losses.

In general, tax management seeks the following transformations:

Taxable income (or gain)	⇨	Tax-exempt income (or gain)
Ordinary income	⇨	Capital gain income
Nondeductible loss (or expense)	⇨	Deductible loss (or expense)
Capital loss	⇨	Ordinary loss

One significant example of gain transformation is the sale of stock. If the corporation sells appreciated assets and then distributes the proceeds to shareholders, the corporation pays taxes on the gain, and the shareholders have ordinary income on the dividend. Instead, if the corporation liquidates, the appreciation is taxed to the corporation, but the subsequent distribution to the shareholders likely is taxed to them as capital gains. If the shareholder is an individual (as opposed to a corporate parent), the maximum tax rate on the gain is 20%. This transformation method can save the shareholder a significant amount of taxes.

Similar transformations can occur through mergers, acquisitions, and divestitures. Of course, capital gains tax benefits have some limitations (this is discussed throughout the book, particularly in Chapters 3, 13, and 14), and there may be significant transactions costs associated with mergers and acquisitions, as well as liquidations. (See Example 2.16.)

EXAMPLE 2.16

The sole shareholder of a small corporation's stock wants to sell the business. The proposed sales price would be $1 million, which is the fair market value of the corporation's assets. The shareholder's tax basis in the stock is $300,000, and the corporation's basis in assets is $200,000. If the corporation sells the assets, then distributes the cash to the shareholder in liquidation, the corporation must pay tax (typically at the standard 35% rate) on the sale, and the shareholder must pay tax (typically at the standard capital gains rate of 20%) on the net proceeds that are given by the corporation to the shareholder.

This would result in $636,000 of after-tax cash flow to the shreholder, as follows:

Sales price of assets	$1,000,000 (1)
Less basis of assets	<200,000>
Gain to corporation	800,000
Corporate tax at 35%	280,000 (2)
Cash given to shareholder: (1) – (2) =	720,000
Less shareholder tax on liquidation:	
0.2($720,000 – 300,000) =	<84,000>
Net cash flow to shareholder	$ 636,000

If instead the shareholder sells the stock, the net cash flow is

Sales price of stock	$1,000,000
Less tax on gain:	
0.2(1,000,000 – 300,000) =	<140,000>
Net cash flow to shareholder	$ 860,000

Selling the stock transforms ordinary income into capital gain. By doing so, the shareholder increases his cash flow by $860,000 – 636,000 = $224,000.

An example of converting a nondeductible loss to a deductible one is profit-taking sales of securities at the end of a year in which previously there were significant sales at a loss. A corporation can only offset capital losses with capital gains. Although net capital losses can be carried back three years and carried forward five years, incurring a capital loss allows a corporation to generate nontaxed revenues immediately by recognizing matching capital gains.

Similarly, a classic example of converting a nondeductible expense to a deductible one can be found in identifying and properly documenting the business purpose for what appear to be nondeductible personal expenses, such as meals, travel, and entertainment. Taking a friend to lunch is not deductible; having a substantial business discussion with a potential client (who also is a friend) can be.

Converting a capital loss into an ordinary loss is not easy, but there are opportunities to do so. One can be found in structuring investments in risky businesses through the use of Section 1244 stock. As discussed in Chapter 4, purchases of capital stock directly from a corporation with no more than $1,000,000 in paid-in capital can result up to $50,000 a year of losses on the sale of that stock being treated as ordinary rather than capital.

Another significant conversion method relates to depreciable plant and equipment. During their use, the firm can take a depreciation expense that is deductible essentially without limit. Later, (as discussed in the section, "Value-Adding, Cash Flows, and Time Value") the gain on a subsequent sale can be postponed with a Section 1031 like-kind exchange.

PUTTING IT ALL TOGETHER: SAVANT CONCEPTS ILLUSTRATED

As CFO of a computer manufacturing company, it has come to your attention that a computer chip manufacturer is for sale for $10 million. It is privately held by the five engineers who started the company. The value of the net underlying assets is $9 million, with $1 million of value attributable to its highly successful R&D department. The reason the company came to your attention is because each year it throws off about $1 million in tax benefits through rapid tax depreciation of equipment and tax credits for its R&D. The tax benefits are very attractive, but you ask the following questions to determine whether the acquisition makes sense from a strategic tax-management perspective.

Does the acquisition fit with the firm's strategic plan? On further inquiry, you determine that the company's chips could be used in the manufacture of your company's computers. Moreover, some management personnel in your company have had experience working for chip manufacturers. Most important, the vertical integration fits with your firm's mission to be a dominant (in terms of quality) computer manufacturer. The acquisition could assure quality by having control over chip manufacture. In that sense, it would give you a strategic advantage over your competitor.

What is the anticipated effect of the sale? Your major competitor has a net tax loss, so it may not make a play for the chip manufacturer, or it may make a lower bid. You anticipate that the tax benefits will continue, with R&D tax credits actually increasing due to a more liberal tax policy that will go into effect next year. Because of the anticipated change in R&D rules, and an expected increase in the tax rate, the timing should be early next year.

Will there be an increase in value-added? The acquisition would be financed with 8% debt; after tax-deductible interest expense, the cost of this capital is 8% × (1 − 34%) × $10 million, or $528,000. After-tax operating profit for the acquisition is $800,000 per year. Thus, value-added is $800,000 − 528,000 = $272,000; this is also the net increase in financial-accounting earnings and the annual cash flow. What transaction costs would be involved? You ascertain that $400,000 of legal, accounting, and loan fee costs would be incurred. Half of them are tax deductible, so the after-tax cost is $400,000 − (.34)(1/2)($400,000) = $332,000. You note that this is $60,000 in excess of the first year value-added. However, assuming you hold the company for 10 years, there is still a positive net present value of −$60,000(year 1) + $4,625,360(sum of years 2 through 10), or $4,565,360. The latter figure uses an 8% cost of capital, for 10 years of annuity, with a resulting factor of 6.7101 less .9259(year 1 factor), or 5.7842 × $800,000 per year. Should there be an adjustment for risk? You assign a necessary 10% risk premium, because chip manufacturing is subject to intense competition. There is no risk that tax authorities will challenge any of the tax benefit.

Can the tax benefits be negotiated? Yes. They are worth $1 million to you each year, but worth nothing to the chip manufacturer or to your rival.

Can any income (gain) or deduction (loss) be transformed? If the acquisition turns out to be bad, it can be sold or part of it spun off to a separate business in a transaction qualifying for capital gain treatment. Alternatively, regarding negotiation, you can give the target company's shareholders stock in your firm in exchange for their stock, which would qualify as a tax-deferred transaction for them. This might result in a lower purchase price.

Therefore, based on SAVANT analysis, you decide to acquire the chip manufacturing company.

Tax Management

Effective tax management means employing the SAVANT principles to every important transaction. It also means periodically scanning the environment to see what has changed that would require new tax-management strategies. Both the transaction-oriented and the time-oriented approaches are discussed in the following section.

Involvement in Transactions

All too often, important business transactions are structured without considering taxes. Subsequently, tax specialists are brought in to clean up the mess, that is, to see how taxes can be saved (if at all) given the already agreed-upon form of the transaction. Instead, managers should consider taxes simultaneously with all other costs. The power to tax a firm's income effectively makes U.S., foreign, state, and local governments partners in the firm. Managers should strive to minimize such partners shares of the firm's value-added.

Scanning the Changing Tax Environment

If the world around the firm never changed, tax management of each transaction would be enough. However, the environment does change, and a manager's due diligence is to scan the environment to see what changes affect the firm, and how the firm should react. While such non-tax environmental changes are in the purview of other business-school texts, there are two key aspects related to tax management. First, such scanning might necessitate a transaction that requires tax management. For example, suppose a competitor drops its price below that of the firm. The firm might respond by lowering prices. To maintain profit margins, the firm might try acquiring components from another firm that had previously been manufactured internally. If the latter approach is taken, there may be tax costs. Such a manufacturing downsizing could produce: (1) extra income taxes, as equipment is sold, (2) possible sales or import taxes, depending on where the new vendor is located, or (3) possible increases in unemployment taxes due to worker layoffs. These tax effects raise the cost of replacing components currently made in-house with those made by other companies, possibly making the outsourcing strategy result in lower profits.

A second type of scanning is for tax-law or tax-rate changes. Taxes constantly evolve through deliberate government policy and through administrative and judicial modifications and interpretation. With Internet availability, important changes can be monitored constantly. It is important to note that a tax change does not beg a reaction: the tax *tail* should never wave the economic *dog*. As an extreme example, suppose the government of Malaysia announces a no-tax policy on foreign investment. If the firm's strategic plan is to become a leader in the Latin American market, it may make little business sense to move the firm's plants to Malaysia. However, an increase in Latin American country taxes invites a *review* of whether plants should be repatriated to the United States.

Here is a sampling of tax changes that have occurred in recent years:

- The U.S. tax rate on capital gains was reduced to 20% (and, in certain cases, to 10%) from 28%.
- The U.K. corporate tax rates were reduced by 1%.
- The U.S. Congress exempted Internet transactions from new taxes by states such as California.
- Tariffs and duties between NAFTA countries, and between EU countries, were reduced.
- U.S. check-the-box rules were passed allowing a business entity to pick whether it will be a taxable corporation or a tax-free flow-through entity.

There are many ways for managers to stay current on tax-law changes throughout the world. At a very general level, *The Wall Street Journal* frequently publishes brief summaries of U.S. tax-law changes, as does the *Financial Times* for EU changes. Some more commonly used research tools available both in hard copy and electronically include Westlaw, LEXIS/NEXIS, CCH, and RIA. As discussed in Chapter 1, a low-cost alternative may be the World Wide Web. Tax Management in Action 2.2 provides samples of some tax Web sites.

TAX MANAGEMENT IN ACTION 2.2

World Wide Web

Tax Information Sites—Scanning The Changing Tax Environment

IRS Related Web Sites
  www.irs.ustreas.gov/
  www.irs.ustreas.gov/cover.html
  www.irs.ustreas.gov/prod/bus_info/index.html
  www.irs.ustreas.gov/prod/ind_info/index.html
  www.tns.lcs.mit.edu/uscode/

Big Four Accounting Firms Web Sites
  www.pricewaterhousecoopers.com/
  www.deloitte.com/
  www.ey.com/
  www.kpmg.com/

Other Web Sites
  www.aicpa.org
  www.taxsites.com

Forming the Enterprise

Choosing a Legal Entity: Risk Management, Raising Capital, and Tax Management

One of the earliest decisions an entreprenuer must make concerns the organizational form of the venture. The choice has important implications for a variety of factors, including taxes, liability, succession, and the ability to attract financing and employees.

—Janet Smith and Richard Smith,
Entreprenuerial Finance

A venture can be operated through a variety of legal forms. In the United States, these include entities such as sole proprietorships, partnerships, limited liability companies, and corporations. Does entity choice make a difference? Consider Tax Management in Action 3.1.

TAX MANAGEMENT IN ACTION 3.1

Limited Liability Companies

The widespread adoption of limited liability company (LLC) statutes in the United States has been a much-heralded development. As of 1999, all states passed such statutes. Because the LLC provides investors with limited liability, pass-through taxation, and far more organizational flexibility than a limited partnership or an S corporation, the LLC is destined to become the business organizational form of the future.

TAX MANAGEMENT IN ACTION 3.1 (CONTINUED)

In 1988, the IRS finally determined that LLC income would be classified as a partnership rather than a corporation, and subject to one level of income tax. According to one estimate, the number of LLCs since 1988 has grown dramatically to approximately 50,000. Two examples of the rapid growth are Utah: 0 to 3,119 LLCs from July 1991 to 1994 and Tennessee: 0 to 7,000 LLCs from 1994 to 1997.

Another sign of the popularity of LLCs was confirmed by Dun & Bradstreet, which conducted a study of 4 million businesses formed between 1990 and 1996. The number of corporate-type entities (including LLCs) grew, while the number of partnerships and proprietorships went down. The number of corporations grew by 5.3% over the period, while the other two formations declined by more than 2.5% each among businesses with 50 or fewer employees.

Much of the impetus for the growth in LLCs versus corporations is the tax advantage of this flow-through entity. However, in strategic tax management, minimizing tax is but one objective in the firm's strategic plan. Even if a firm (or a client) is not an entrepreneur, an *understanding* of the tax treatments of noncorporate entities is critical. As discussed in Chapters 8 and 13, many corporate restructurings and international ventures use noncorporate entities. Thus, a basic understanding of flow-through tax treatments is necessary.

One other important background concept should also be mentioned: the U.S. check-the-box regulations. Under these rules, management can simply check a box on a noncorporate entity's tax return to pick whether it is to be treated as a tax-free flow-through entity or as a taxable corporation. Whether the entrepreneur—or manager of a newly formed subsidiary business—should choose flow-through or corporate treatment is the subject of much of this chapter.

For the entrepreneur, taxes and entity choice are intertwined (see Exhibit 3.1 for the role of taxes).

The entity choice for tax purposes should be based on a strategic planning process that considers a host of nontax strategic goals as well (as discussed in Chapter 2). For tax purposes, the basic entity choices are double-taxed entities (C corporations) and flow-through entities

EXHIBIT 3.1   Interaction of Taxes and Choice of Entity

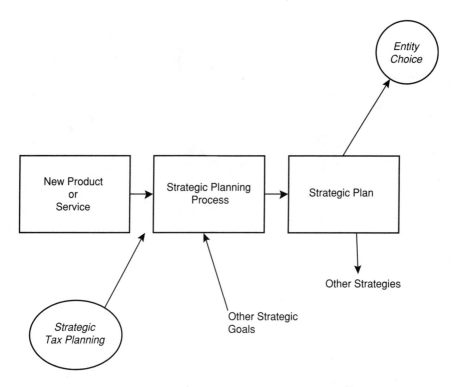

(partnerships, S corporations, and LLCs). Each of these has unique tax attributes, and one cannot unequivocally say that any entity is better than the other.

Depending on the entrepreneur's strategic plan, nontax attributes that differ across entities are

- Risk management
- Managerial control
- Raising capital
- Pretax return

Tax Management in Action 3.2 presents the key tax and nontax attributes.

TAX MANAGEMENT IN ACTION 3.2

Tax Management Attributes of Entity Choice at Early Stage of Life Cycle

	Partnership	S Corporation	Regular C Corporation	LLC
Liability	Unlimited for general partners	Limited to amounts invested and loaned	Limited to amounts invested and loaned	Limited to amounts invested and loaned
Tax rates	Income taxed to owners at marginal tax rates	Income taxed to owners at marginal tax rates	Income taxed at applicable corporate rates	Income taxed to owners at marginal tax rates
Double taxation	No	No, (but, built-in gains and passive income taxes possible)	Yes	No
Pass-though of profits and losses	Yes	Yes	No	Yes
Limitation on entity losses deductible by owners*	Net investments plus net income plus share of debt	Net investments plus net income plus loans to corporation	None deductible	Net investments plus net income plus share of debt
Subject to passive activity loss rules*	Yes	Yes	Generally not	Yes
Limitation on number of owners	No	Yes; 35 for tax years beginning prior to 1/1/97; 75 for tax years thereafter	No	No
Limitation on type of entity which is an Owner	No	Yes, must be individual, certain trusts, or certain tax-exempt entities (new).	No	No

Tiered structure	Yes	No (prior to 1/1/97 tax years); yes for qualified S subsidiaries (applicable post-1996)	Yes	Yes
Special allocations	Possible, if substantial economic effect	No	No	Possible, if substantial economic effect
Fiscal year	May end up to 3 months earlier than the year-end of principal partners	May end up to 3 months earlier than the year-end of principal stockholders	New corporations: any fiscal year; existing corporations: fiscal year with automatic change permitted in certain circumstances	May end up to 3 months earlier than the year-end of principal members
Tax-free fringe benefits	Limited	Limited	All permitted by law	Limited
Public offering	Yes, but some difficulty	No	Yes	Very difficult
Tax-free merger with corporations	No, but possible tax-free incorporation available	Yes, IRC Section 368 provisions apply	Yes, IRC Section 368 provisions apply	No, but possible tax-free incorporation available
Accumulated earnings tax*	No	No	Yes	No
Personal holding company tax*	No	No	Yes	No

*Discussed in Technical Inserts.

STRATEGY

This section discusses strategy in terms of capital raising and management control.

Capital Raising

Exhibit 3.2 indicates capital-raising/return-tax aspects common across entity types. In the short run, the entrepreneur may have limited capital needs, relying on one's own savings and bank loans. As needs expand, however, external financing becomes necessary, either through debt or equity ownership.

Debt and equity each have advantages for entrepreneurs. For U.S. income tax purposes, funds received from outsiders are neither taxable to entrepreneurs nor their operations. As the capital is repaid, however, the return portion is taxable to the capital provider—interest income to

EXHIBIT 3.2   Tax Cycle for External Financing

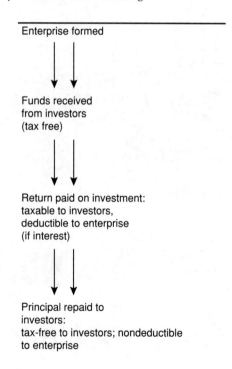

the debt holder or dividend income to the equity provider. Return of the actual principal (as is return of principal in any situation) is tax free. (See Example 3.1.)

EXAMPLE 3.1

An entrepreneur operating in the United States receives $1 million each from two venture capitalists also operating in the United States Venture capitalist 1 receives a bond, due in five years, which pays 10% interest. Venture capitalist 2 receives common stock. During each of the first five years, the corporation has $500,000 of pretax operating profit. The corporation first pays $100,000 of interest. Because the corporation can deduct the interest, the after-tax cost is $(1 - .34) \times \$100,000 = \$66,000$. If venture capitalist 1 is paid a 10% dividend, because the dividend is not tax-deductible to the corporation, its after-tax cost is the same as its pretax cost: $100,000. If and when the stock is redeemed (by design, or through liquidation), the $1 million return of capital to venture capitalist 2 is nondeductible. When the bond is redeemed in five years, the $1 million paid to venture capitalist 1 is not deductible by the corporation.

From the firm's side, interest payments are tax deductible, whereas dividend payments are not. In that sense, debt borrowing is cheaper for the entrepreneur. However, cash flow is more restricted: Debt holders must be paid interest on a regular schedule, whereas shareholders are paid dividends at the discretion of management. An exception is preferred stock, which must be made in regular interest-type (but nondeductible) payments. Furthermore, if a company is liquidated, holders of preferred stock have priority over common-stock holders. This preference is extended to bondholders in many countries, such as the United States, but not in all (notably France, Japan, and Germany).

For a flow-through entity, payments of profits to owners are nondeductible unless they represent interest. This is because the entity itself is not subject to tax. (See Example 3.2.)

EXAMPLE 3.2

Assume in Example 3.1 that the venture was formed as an LLC, venture capitalist 1 received debt, and venture capitalist 2 received an LLC ownership share. Any payment to venture capitalist 2 is not deductible by the LLC. Interest paid to venture capitalist 1 is tax deductible, however.

In terms of costs, the after-tax costs of debt versus equity are functions of market rates of return, tax brackets of the entrepreneur and capital providers, and differences in cash-flow restrictions.

In the initial stages of an enterprise, capitalization will come from private placements. That is, funds will come from venture capitalists, banks, or wealthy investors known to investment bankers. Any of these investor types are compatible with the major entity types (e.g., corporations, partnerships, or limited liability companies). However, if the strategic plan requires a significant capital infusion, a C corporation may be the best choice. Here, there is no limit on the number of owners, and a public offering can be made more easily. Although there are no statutory limits on the maximum number of owners of partnerships and LLCs, public offerings for these entities are difficult. In the United States, limited partnerships are really the only pass-through entities that can be listed and traded on public exchanges. Also, venture capitalists often prefer C corporations.

Tax Aspects of Forming the Entity

When an enterprise is formed, the general U.S. rule is that this event is tax deferred, both to the entity and its owners. When forming a *corporation*, part of the transactions costs are directly related to capital structure. When first formed, the owners receive corporate stock, and any gain on contributed assets may be tax deferred. To the extent the owners receive debt (such as a corporate bond), any built-in gain on property contributed is immediately taxed. The tax problem only arises if noncash property is put into the corporation, and if that property's fair market value is higher than its adjusted tax basis. The latter occurs if the property has gone up in value, or if rapid tax depreciation has driven down the tax adjusted basis.

To be eligible for Section 351 tax deferral, the following must be met:

- The owner transfers property (tangible or intangible) to the corporation.
- In return, receives shares in the corporation.
- Immediately after the transfer, the shareholder who transferred the property in owns at least 80% of the value and voting power of the corporation's shares.

Note that a group of taxpayers can qualify for deferral, as long as they meet the 80% test as a group in addition to each meeting the other two tests.

EXHIBIT 3.3   Tax-Free Formation of a Corporation

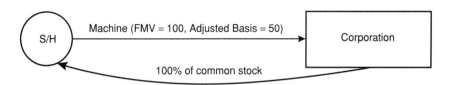

If a shareholder receives something other than stock (such as a bond), it is called *boot*. The gain taxed to the shareholder is the lesser of

- Boot received
- Realized (total) gain on assets transferred to the corporation

Exhibit 3.3 shows an example of this. The realized gain is $100 – 50 = $50. However, because the requirements of Section 351 have been met, the realized gain is eligible for deferral. Since no boot is received, the gain is not taxed. Instead, under the rules of IRC Section 358, the machine has a lower basis to the corporation, so if the corporation eventually sells it for $100, the $50 gain is taxed then. Thus, Section 351 is a *time value/timing* tax-management technique.

What if the shareholder instead received bonds? Then the entire $50 is currently taxed to the owner. However, the machine's tax basis is stepped up to $100, so there will be no built-in gain when it is sold.

What if $100 of cash, instead of a machine, is transferred? Then, there is no gain (and thus no tax) even if the shareholder receives bonds.

If, instead, the owners form a *flow-through entity* (any type of partnership, an S corporation, or an LLC), then the results are similar to the corporate setting. The transaction is not taxable to the entity. It is only taxable to the transferor (owner) if the transaction is a disguised sale of properties, or the flow-through entity interest is received in exchange for services rendered to the entity by the partner (plus some other limited exceptions). Gain inherent in the property transferred is deferred. This is accomplished by reducing the owner's adjusted basis in his or her investment in the flow-through entity.

Entity Metamorphosis

Of course, the entrepreneur is not precluded from changing tax/legal form as capital requirements change. Two common forms of entity metamorphoses are shown in Exhibit 3.4. (See also Example 3.3.)

EXHIBIT 3.4   Changes in Legal Form over Time

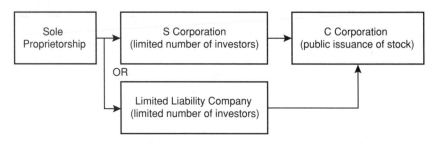

EXAMPLE 3.3

Assume the LLC in Example 3.2 needs an additional $100 million in capitalization. Because this amount requires a public offering, the corporation must first convert to a C corporation. Since the LLC cannot have a public offering, the venture capitalists must either liquidate their LLC ownership shares or convert them into stock. As will be seen in later chapters, transitioning between different entity types, if proper tax management is used, is often tax free. The major problem is that it is very difficult to transition from a successful C corporation to another form without tax costs.

Management Control

Unless operating as a sole proprietor, the entrepreneur who admits other owners may also be admitting fellow decision makers. For corporations (both C and S), such diffusion can be limited by allowing only the entrepreneur (or perhaps a few others) to be actual officers in the company. Investors or shareholders, except in cases of mismanagement, usually do not exercise great power through voting, although it is not uncommon for venture capitalists to want a monitoring role by being on the governing board of the company (e.g., the board of directors). Similar control can be obtained through limited partnerships wherein the entrepreneur can retain operating control by appointment as sole general partner.

Limited partners have less control and are normally silent partners. LLCs are more complicated. Depending on state law, the entrepreneur has varying degrees of control because some investors may be managing associates. General partnerships result in a loss of control: Every owner, as a general partner, can exert managerial influence. (See Example 3.4.)

EXAMPLE 3.4

Refer to Example 3.3. Suppose the venture capitalists had nonvoting LLC interests. Even if they opposed admitting additional shareholders, the entrepreneur may still (as a voting member) force conversion to a C corporation (depending on relevant corporate law). However, had the venture been a general partnership, the venture capitalists would have the right to vote against incorporation.

ANTICIPATION AND TIMING ISSUES

Generally speaking, the advantage of timing is best for C corporations in the United States. Although a corporation's control (unless it has gross receipts of less than $5 million) of the timing of income and expenses with third parties is somewhat constrained because of the required use of accrual accounting, it can control the timing of income to its shareholders. Using dividends as an example, the corporation can chose to pay dividends when a shareholder is in the lowest tax bracket. For salary, the corporation can make bonus payments in a year in which the corporate-shareholder tax differential is greatest. In addition, tax-free perquisites can be paid instead of salary when both the corporation and shareholder are in the highest brackets. (See Example 3.5.)

EXAMPLE 3.5

Assume that a newly formed corporation has a single shareholder, who is also the firm's president. The corporation's taxable income, before any payments to the shareholder, is <$100,000> (i.e., an NOL). Next year, even with the NOL carried forward as a deduction, assume the corporation will have $200,000 in taxable income. Assume also that the shareholder has $100,000 of taxable income (independent of the corporation) in both this and next year, and that she is in the 31% tax bracket in both years. In this case, it makes sense for the corporation to pay a larger salary to the president next year.

For flow-through entities such as S corporations in the United States, the timing of *third-party* income and deduction transactions is more controlled because the cash method of accounting can be used (except for firms carrying inventories). For example, if the LLC provides services to clients in December, it can postpone payment (and thus taxes) until the next year by agreement. Similarly, year-end expenses can be paid in December instead of

January to accelerate the tax deduction. However, these year-end techniques only account for *some* timing control. For the bulk of year-end operations, there is no timing control, because taxable income flows through immediately to the entity owners.

One enormous tax timing advantage of flow-through entities is with respect to NOLs. Such entity-level losses immediately flow through to the owners as a tax benefit; however, C corporations' NOLs must be carried forward and deducted by the C corporation in subsequent years. Because startup enterprises typically have losses, the time value of deducting the losses immediately often swings the decision to start out as a flow-through entity, followed by conversion to a C corporation when the business turns profitable. (See Example 3.6.)

EXAMPLE 3.6

Suppose in Example 3.5 the business is an S corporation. Here, the first year tax loss of $100,000 flows through to the owner, and is deducted on his return. Assume the owner is in the 36% bracket. This gives him a tax savings of $100,000 \times (.36) = $36,000$. Here, the payment of salary is unnecessary for tax purposes and may increase total taxes by triggering extra Social Security taxes.

Anticipation Policy Changes

Strategic tax planning anticipates actions by competitors in markets in which the enterprise interacts, along with actions by governments. As discussed previously, the entities differ on this attribute. For C corporations, there seems to be no clear favorable or unfavorable tax policy trend by U.S., foreign, or state governments. Although recent U.S. tax legislation was favorable to S corporations, little action is planned for the future. Instead, most tax policy in the near term will probably be directed at LLCs, because they are replacing S corporations and limited partnerships. (How markets and competitors react to the entrepreneur's entity choice depends on the nature of the business and the industry it is in, which is beyond the scope of this book.)

VALUE-ADDING

For most businesses, there are constant returns to scale. For example, if the normal return is 10%, a $1 million investment yields $100,000 in pretax profits, and a $100 million investment would yield $10 million. Thus, the more capital a firm can raise, the more total pretax profit (value-adding) it can make for its owners. Also, some industries simply require a large amount of startup capital (e.g., airlines, where each aircraft costs millions of dollars). For such cases, a C corporation is the ultimate entity of choice: Public stock offerings are virtually the only way to such large amounts of capital. However, there are market limitations on how much capital an enterprise can initially raise. Also, the larger the capital stake sought, the higher the cost. Smaller ventures find it almost always cheaper and can raise adequate capital by forming small corporations, partnerships, or LLCs with a limited number of investors.

Adjusting Value-Adding for Risk

The entrepreneur faces both short- and long-term risk. In the short run, cash flows can vary and losses may occur, especially in the early years of an enterprise. Long-run risks involve the potential for more serious losses, such as lawsuits or bankruptcy. Short-run losses can actually be aided by a tax system to the extent that they are deductible: The taxes saved by the deduction reduce the real cost of the loss.

In some jurisdictions, losses are not fully deductible, but are partially deductible or deductible only against future profits. In the United States, losses are generally deductible, but the timing and amount may vary. For a startup C corporation, a net loss for the year must be carried forward to the next tax year as a deduction. If the corporation has a tax loss again the next year, the loss from both years carries forward again, and so on, until there is positive taxable income or 20 years elapses (at which point the loss expires). For established C corporations, losses can be carried back five years and carried forward 20 years. However, if the entity is a flow-through, the loss passes through to the owners and is deducted on their tax returns. Thus, the difference between the two basic entity types for short-run tax losses is simply a matter of timing. (See Example 3.7.)

EXAMPLE 3.7

A startup business in the United States has a $100,000 NOL in its first year, and $50,000 taxable income in each succeeding year. Its owner has $200,000 of her own taxable income, and she is in the 36% tax bracket. If organized as a flow-through entity, the first-year loss is deducted by the owner on her individual tax return, giving her a tax benefit of $36,000. However, years 2 and 3 are taxed to the owner at 36%, with a resultant tax cost of $36,000. If, instead, the organization is a C corporation, the NOL offsets taxable income in years 2 and 3, and saves corporate taxes.

A much bigger difference exists for long-run risk. If the entrepreneur operates without a separate legal entity (i.e., as a sole proprietor) creditors may go straight to her personal assets in the case of bankruptcy or lawsuit. If there is a general partnership, or if the entrepreneur is a general partner in a limited partnership, the same personal liability occurs.

A partial offset for a bankruptcy loss is the tax-deductibility resulting from the worthlessness of the investment (stock, LLC certificate, or partnership interest). However, in the United States such capital losses are deductible only by individuals up to $3,000 per year (in excess of the entrepreneur's capital gains for the year). Investors that are corporations can offset capital losses only against capital gains. As with many U.S. rules, there are exceptions. One here is that if an election is made to treat a qualifying company as a small business corporation, up to $50,000 ($100,000 on a joint tax return) of ordinary loss can be deducted by individuals if the common stock of the company becomes worthless or the shares are sold. This special rule will be discussed in Chapter 4.

Transaction Costs and Value-Adding

Attorney, accountant, broker, and syndicator fees can vary substantially across new entity types. Typically the cheapest entity to form is a sole proprietorship, for which most jurisdictions require little legal documentation. The next cheapest is the general partnership, for which usually only an operating agreement must be kept. Limited partnerships must file articles of partnership, and corporations must file articles of incorporation with the government in the country where they are located. The attorney fees for drafting these depend on the number of owners and the number and complexity of legal arrangements that the entrepreneur desires. LLCs also must file documents with the government, which are more expensive to draft. If outside financing is sought (see Chapter 4 for more details), the transactions costs are typically higher for equity than debt, and increase proportionately with the number of investors and amount of the financing.

NEGOTIATING

As noted earlier, there is variation across tax entities in terms of negotiating the sharing of tax benefits. C corporations in the United States provide some flexibility when the corporation is closely held, especially when the owners are also employees of the corporation. Accordingly, there can be a shifting of tax from the entity to the employee-owner through salary and perquisites. Shifting can also be accomplished by paying interest to equity owners who also provide debt financing, along with rent or royalties to those who provide tangible or intangible property for the corporation's use.

TAX MANAGEMENT IN ACTION 3.3

Tax Consequences of C Corporation–Shareholder (Manager) Transactions

Tax Consequence to _____

Type of payment from corporation to shareholder

Manager	Shareholder (manager)	C Corporation
Dividend	Taxable	Not deductible
Salary	Taxable	Deductible
Perquisites (e.g., company medical or pension plan)	Depending on type, not taxable	Deductible

---

The tax consequences to the corporation and employee/shareholder from such transactions are shown in Tax Management in Action 3.3.

While dividends are ineffectual, salary payments are useful for splitting the tax liability between the corporation and the owner. To see this, suppose a U.S. corporation has $200,000 of taxable income, before paying its sole shareholder/president a salary. If the corporation is in the 34% bracket and the owner is in the 31% bracket, paying salary results in a tax savings of 3% (i.e., 34% to 31%). Similarly, a manager in a large, publicly traded corporation can negotiate part of this tax spread in the form of a higher salary.

There are limits on this tax-saving technique. Only a reasonable level of compensation is deductible, and it is subject to payroll taxes. Perquisites, for a C corporation, are the ultimate tax shelter insofar as they reduce corporate taxes while (depending on the type of perquisite) often being tax free to the managers/shareholders. Similar to salary, managers can negotiate for part of this tax savings in a large corporation. (See Example 3.8.)

EXAMPLE 3.8

The sole shareholder of a corporation is also its president. He calculates that each year the corporation generates $200,000 in free cash flow (i.e., this is the amount he can pay himself in salary plus perquisites). Assume that his personal cash flow needs are only $180,000 and that there are no other employees (i.e., that he can pay all perquisites to himself). To optimize taxes, he can have the corporation pay $20,000 in medical and dental insurance for him. This would be deductible by the corporation and tax-free to him.

TAX MANAGEMENT IN ACTION 3.4

Other Entity Choices

In addition to the entity choices shown previously, other entity types may be selected. Here is a brief overview:

- *Limited Liability Partnership (LLP)*. Now recognized by over half of the states in the United States, an LLP is essentially a general partnership with one important exception. In the case of legal actions, only the partner(s) performing the service can be sued for their personal (nonpartnership) assets. The other partners are thus protected. Many CPA firms (notably Arthur Andersen) have chosen this form of entity, since most states do not allow licensed professionals to practice as LLCs or as limited partnerships. The tax treatment is the same as a partnership.
- *Personal (Service) Corporations* or *Professional Corporations (PCs)*. Many service professionals practice in this form. While not affording the liability protection (of personal assets) that a regular corporation does, the PC offers more protection (depending on state) than does a sole proprietorship or general partnership. PCs can elect either C or S corporate status for U.S. tax purposes.
- *State and Other Country Tax Treatments of Various Entities*. These vary by state and by country, but are similar to that of the United States for the most part.

As discussed previously, S corporations offer fewer chances for negotiating tax benefits. As the corporation generates income, it passes-through to the shareholders and is taxed immediately. The method of passthrough is mechanical (based on ownership percentage), and it is difficult to shift taxes among the owners. However, although income also passes through to the owners in partnerships and LLCs, there is the possibility of *allocating* income in tax-minimizing proportions. The owners can negotiate how this *special allocation* will occur. (See Tax Management in Action 3.4.) Special allocations are further discussed in the Technical Insert at the end of the chapter.

TRANSFORMING

In the United States, C corporations can transform ordinary income into capital gain income by liquidating all or part of shareholders' interests. The strategy is straightforward: Avoid paying dividends for a period of time (to avoid shareholder tax), then have the shareholder sell all or a substantial portion of her shares. The difference between what the shareholder receives and the cost (tax basis) of her shares is taxed at capital gain rates. Assuming the shareholder is in the top tax bracket, she will have saved 19.6% (i.e., the ordinary rate, 39.6%, minus the capital gain rate, 20%) times the amount of the gain through transforming. (See Example 3.9.)

EXAMPLE 3.9

A U.S. resident who is the sole shareholder of a corporation sells his stock for $500,000. His tax basis in the stock is $200,000, and he has held the stock for three years. The gain of $300,000 (calculated as $500,000 − $200,000) is taxed at 20%. This gives the shareholder a net cash flow of $440,000 (calculated as $500,000 − (.2 × $300,000). Were the $500,000 paid to him in dividends, the after-tax cash flow would have been $302,000 (calculated as $500,000 − .396 ($500,000)).

Indeed, the transforming benefits are so attractive that the United States has enacted some corporate penalty taxes to keep entrepreneurs from never paying a dividend and converting all corporate earnings into capital gains. These are discussed in the Technical Insert at the end of this chapter.

A less pronounced conversion occurs with flow-through entities upon liquidation of some or all ownership rights. Any appreciation in value of the enterprise—due to goodwill or appreciation in value of the underlying net assets—manifests itself in a higher liquidation (sale) price to the enterprise (outside buyer), which is taxed at capital gain rates. Unlike a corporation, however, the annual earnings of a flow-through entity cannot be converted from ordinary to capital gain taxation. (See Example 3.10.)

EXAMPLE 3.10

Assume the same facts as in Example 3.9, but instead of selling the stock to an outsider, the entrepreneur decides to liquidate the corporation. The corporation can sell its assets first, and then distribute the cash to the entrepreneur, or the corporation can distribute the assets to the entrepreneur for the entrepreneur to sell. The tax consequences are identical, as follows. Assume that the corporation is in the 35% bracket, and that its assets consist of $100,000 in cash plus equipment with a fair market value of $400,000 (and a tax basis of $250,000).

If corporation sells assets first:

Sales price	$400,000	(1)
Less basis in assets sold	<250,000>	
Gain on sale	$150,000	
Tax to corporation on sale		
(.35) ($150,000)	$ 52,500	(2)

Distribution to shareholder of assets remaining after tax is paid

((1) – (2)) + $100,000 cash =	$447,500
Tax to shareholder on distribution	
(.2)($447,500 – $200,000) =	<49,500>
Net cash flow to shareholder	$398,000

If corporation distributes assets, then the entrepreneur sells assets:

Distribution of assets	
($400,000 + $100,000) =	$500,000
Less corporation's basis in assets	
($250,000 + $100,000) =	<350,000>
Gain to corporation on distribution	$150,000
Tax to corporation on distribution	
(.35)($150,000) =	$ 52,500
Distribution to shareholder	
($500,000 – $52,500) =	$447,500
Less tax to shareholder	
(.2)($447,500 – $200,000) =	<49,500>
Net cash flow to shareholder	$398,000

Thus, while part of the gain is transformed, it is far less than in the case of sale of the stock to an outsider.

In the United States, two special rules also apply just to corporations. These apply both to C and S corporations. One is for *qualified small business* stock, known more precisely as Section 1244 stock. If a C or S corporation so elects, its stock owned by individuals qualifies under this provision. If Section 1244 stock becomes worthless (e.g., the corporation goes bankrupt), up to $100,000 of loss ($50,000 if a joint individual tax return is not filed) can be deducted as an ordinary loss. This is far superior to the normal classification for such losses: The $3,000 per year limit on net capital losses usually applies to corporate stock. Note that this limit applies to worthlessness on partnership and LLC investments.

A second conversion advantage for corporations is lowered tax rates on gains from sale of stock of start-up enterprises. Both of these provisions will be discussed in Chapter 4.

PUTTING IT ALL TOGETHER: APPLYING SAVANT TO ENTITY CHOICE

Suppose you and an associate start a business that produces business software. Under your guidance, programmers have developed the prototypes, which you have beta-tested in small businesses. You have each invested $10,000, which has been used primarily to pay the programmers. You have no formal legal agreements between you and your friend. You have a $150,000-per-year job in another company, and about $500,000 of net worth. Your friend is a graduate student earning $10,000 per year and has $5,000 in savings. You eventually will require about $200,000 to rewrite the software so that it can be used by larger businesses. You are considering doing business through a separate entity, with the stipulation that you and your friend will remain equal owners. Use the strategic tax planning framework to suggest an entity choice.

Strategy

Capital raising, management, and control: You and your friend would like to retain control, so a goal could be to have any new investors brought in to be treated as lenders or passive capital investors. Lenders can be in any entity type, although if an unsecured loan is procured from venture capitalists, they would probably want some potential control. Banks probably would require a loan secured by your personal assets. The tax advantage of debt is deductibility of interest payments.

For capital raising, $200,000 is not large enough to require a public offering, so use of a C corporation is not mandated. Instead, private placements could work, either through sale of S corporation stock, LLC certificates, or limited partnership interests. A limited partnership is a bad idea from a liability perspective, because both you and your friend would most likely be the managing general partners. This would subject your personal assets to creditor's risk. Thus, either an S corporation or an LLC is indicated.

Anticipation

As noted previously, no major changes are expected in any entity type, although with LLCs becoming more prevalent, the legal costs of forming them could become cheaper.

Timing issues The expectation of NOLs early on favors the use of flow-throughs. When positive taxable income is generated later on, the owners can covert it to a C corporation, if desired.

Value-Adding

The double tax on C corporations, at first blush, makes it seem less attractive than the flow-through entities. More taxes paid at the entity level mean less to be reinvested in the business. Although some of the double tax can be mitigated through salary payments, the flow-through entities dominate as the best choice under these conditions.

Adjusting value-adding for risk As noted above, risk management points to either an LLC or an S corporation. The entity would not have to pay a risk premium to investors, either, because only their initial investment would be subject to risk.

Adjusting value-adding for transactions costs An attorney would be needed, who would charge about the following for drafting and filing: corporation: $1,000, S corporation or limited partnership: $2,000, and LLC: $3,000. If any new equity owners are admitted, about $250 per new person would likely be charged.

Negotiating

Because of the nature of the business, you anticipate tax NOLs for the first few years. By forming an LLC, you have the flexibility of allocating these losses among owners through *special allocations,* an option unavailable to S corporations.

Transforming

All entities can be liquidated at capital gain rates. In case the business fails, an S corporation is favored because of the possible use of Section 1244 stock.

Conclusion

After weighing all the factors, you decide to form the business as an LLC.

SPECIALIZED LEGAL FORMS

Although the vast bulk of business transactions in the United States are conducted in the legal form of a corporation, the other forms discussed throughout this chapter—such as partnerships and limited liability companies—are not uncommon. Nor is the technique of using multiple entites, such as a parent corporation with many subsidiaries, or combinations of entities, such as a partnership of corporations. There are specialized legal forms, however, which are not used regularly or are used in certain industries. A good example is the Real Estate Investment Trust, which is explained in Tax Management in Action 3.5.

TAX MANAGEMENT IN ACTION 3.5

Special Entity: Real Estate Investment Trusts

A special, nontaxed, flow-through entity, real estate investment trust (REIT), has become increasingly popular in the United States. Its use is restricted to investments in real estate. A REIT essentially is a corporation that, if it meets certain requirements, is tax free. The requirements include: (1) it has less than 100 shareholders, (2) 95% or more of its income comes from real estate, and (3) it distributes at least 95% of its income each year.

For the income test, its income must not be from the sale of real estate (e.g., a real estate developer or construction company). A number of holding companies are REITs, using the REIT to hold investments in office buildings, shopping malls, and apartment buildings, from which the REIT collects rental income. A number of hotel chains have also used this entity.

Recently, a number of large corporations have begun using REITs to shelter their income from real estate. In response, the IRS is has attempted to place some restrictions on this entity. In particular, the IRS issued a ruling on what is known as "step-down preferred stock." This also is called "conduit entities issuing fast-pay preferred stock." These securities (sold in the private market for institutions

TAX MANAGEMENT IN ACTION 3.5 (CONTINUED)

under the SEC's relaxed Rule 144a), pay a lofty interest rate of 13% to 14% in the first 10 years, and then drop to 1%. Bear Stearns was thought to be among the most aggressive marketer of these securities, which included investors such as Union Carbide and Disney.

Under the practice, preferred stock issues were sold to tax-exempt investors such as pension plans. In the transactions, the buyer and the seller would jointly create a real estate investment trust, each contributing $100 million. Through the REIT, the buyer would get inflated dividends, which, because of the buyer's tax status, would be tax free. After paying the oversized dividends for 10 years, the seller would buy out the buyer's share of the investment for a nominal amount, liquidate the REIT, and distribute the remaining $200 million in assets to the seller.

Under U.S. tax law, such a liquidation is generally thought to be tax free. But what was really happening, the IRS declared, was that the seller was selling preferred stock and not paying taxes on $100 million of income.

As noted in the Introduction, explanations that delve into more esoteric tax issues have been isolated into Technical Inserts throughout this book, so that they can be scanned quickly and found later if the issues arise. The following Technical Insert 3.1 is a prime example, highlighting, as it does, some of the most dense areas of taxation made complex in order to deal with highly sophisticated and perfectly legal tax management techniques.

TECHNICAL INSERT 3.1   LIMITATIONS ON ENTITY TAX PLANNING

General Limits

For partnerships and LLCs, each owner's deductions in any one year are limited to the owners' net investment (or capital account in the entity) plus the owner's share of the entity's debt. In other words, loss is limited to the owner's tax basis. For example:

TECHNICAL INSERT 3.1 (CONTINUED)

Balance Sheet
A-B Partnership

Assets		Liabilities & Equity	
Cash	$100	Liabilities	$175
Plant &		Capital accounts:	
Equipment:	200	A	75
	$300	B	50
			$300

If *A* is a 60% owner, then her basis is her capital account of $75, plus her share of the debt (calculated as 60% of $175 = $105), or a total basis of $180. If the partnership (or LLC) has a tax loss of $400, *A*'s share is 60% ($400) = $240. However, she can only deduct $180 (her basis) in the current year. The remaining $60 carried over to future years until *A* has sufficient basis to cover the loss.

For an S corporation, the rules are slightly different. Substitute "stock equity" for "capital accounts" in Example 3.11. *A* could only deduct $75 of loss, and the remaining $165 would carry over to future years. Unlike partnerships and LLCs, for an S corporation the liability of $175 can only be included in *A*'s basis if it is owed to *A* (i.e., she loaned the S corporation the money).

Thus, choice of entity relates to anticipation (timing and time-value issues), with partnerships and LLCs having an advantage over S and C corporations.

Passive Activity Loss Limitations

Unless the entity owner is actively involved in management of the enterprise, a loss from a flow-through enterprise is limited to passive activity income (or income from other flow-through entity investments) for the year. Using the previous example, if partner *A* is actively involved in management, then her loss is only subject to the basis limitation of $180. If, however, she is simply a passive investor, and she has no other positive income from any other flow-through entities, she cannot deduct any of the loss: The entire $240 carries forward to subsequent years when the flow-through generates positive taxable income. Any unused losses under the passive activity rules can be utilized to offset gain when the owner liquidates her interest, or liquidates the entity, in a taxable transaction.

TECHNICAL INSERT 3.1 (CONTINUED)

There are a number of definitions for active involvement in management. The simplest, and easiest to document, is if the owner puts in at least 500 hours per year of time directly related to the entity.

Special Allocations

An advantage of partnerships and LLCs over S corporations is the possible use of special allocations. Referring back to the A-B Partnership example, suppose partner *A* is in the 35% tax bracket, and partner *B* is in the 15% bracket. Because a tax loss is worth more to partner *A*, it might be best for the partnership (or LLC) to specially allocate 100% of the loss to her. To accomplish this, the allocation must have "substantial economic effect." This test has two requirements:

1. The loss reduces the partner's (here partner *A*) capital account.
2. Any liquidation proceeds must be based on relative capital accounts (i.e., if partner *A*'s capital account is negative, she must pay the balance back to partner *B*).

These two requirements force partner *A* to accept lower cash flow in a later year for any extra tax benefits in prior years. To see how this works, suppose in the previous example that the partnership is liquidated at the beginning of the next year, with net (after liability payoff) liquidation proceeds of $75. Because *A* has a post-special-allocation capital account of $<325>, the first $25 of proceeds go to *B*. Then, the remaining $50 also go to *B*, in proportion to his capital account. The net result of this is that *A* has lost $45 in liquidation cash proceeds (60% of $75) in order to get an extra $56 (40% × 35% × $400) in tax savings. In general, if substantial economic effect can be delayed until liquidation, the higher the net present value of the special allocation. In this case, for example, if partner *A*'s discount rate is 10% and the liquidation occurs 10 years after the allocation, the present value of the lost cash flow is only $45 × .3855 = $17.34.

In addition to the anticipation (timing and time-value) attributes of special allocations, they have a unique negotiation possibility: Partners (and LLC owners) in different tax brackets can NEGOTIATE the tax benefits between the owners.

Accumulated Earnings Tax, and Personal Holding Company Tax

There are penalty taxes, added onto a C corporation's regular tax bill in the United States, if a corporation is audited and found not have

---

TECHNICAL INSERT 3.1 (CONTINUED)

---

paid enough dividends. In effect, these special taxes force certain closely held corporations to pay dividends. (Although the accumulated earning tax technically applies to all corporations, it is extremely rare for the IRS to attempt to impose it on publicly traded corporations.) Because dividends are not deductible by corporations, but are taxed as ordinary income to the shareholders, the result is usually a significant increase in overall taxes.

The accumulated earnings tax is triggered when corporations have retained earnings of more than $250,000 ($150,000 if a personal service corporation), unless the accumulations can be justified by reasonable business needs. Among the accepted needs are working capital and certain reserves for business contingencies such as expansion, self-insurance, and redemptions of stock to pay death taxes.

The personal holding company tax applies even to reasonable accumulations if the corporation has too much passive income. This tax can be imposed only on closely held corporations, but not if they are financial institutions. *Closely held* means that at any time during the last half year more than 50% of the value of its outstanding shares are owned, directly or indirectly, by no more than five individuals. Passive income is from interest, dividends, some rents, and most royalties; too much means that such personal holding company amounts to no less than 60% of the corporation's adjusted ordinary gross income.

The tax typically applies where an individual incorporates herself, or the assets of an active business are sold but the corporation is not liquidated. Using flow-through entities like limited liability companies avoids this tax.

CHAPTER 4

Financing a New Venture

What is happening differently over the last few years . . . is that individual partnerships can and have been borrowing. If you start with a billion dollars of capital, you can borrow a whole lot of money and make very big footprints. Well, if you do that with a billion dollars, or $5 billion, all you got to do is show up in the morning!

—Robert Slater,
Soros: The Unauthorized Biography

Possibly no issue is so critical to the success of a startup business as the methods it uses for finance. This chapter shows how strategies for financing a business fit into the SAVANT framework. There are two basic forms: internal financing and external financing. The former results when firms retain earnings. This occurs when firms have positive net cash flows but do not distribute them all to the firm's owners. Companies that limit expansion by purchasing new property, plant, and equipment only out of cash flows from operations are using an internal financing strategy. External financing is a strategy whereby cash comes from sources other than the firm's own positive cash flow. These sources come in two fundamental forms.

One is debt financing, which can be either short-term borrowing (such as financing purchases through buying on account) or long-term borrowing (such as raising cash by selling bonds or mortgaging property). Students who pay their tuition and books with a credit card are using short-term debt financing; those who use student loans are using a long-term debt financing strategy.

Equity financing is the other form of external financing. Examples of this include corporations that sell common stock (to either new shareholders or existing ones), and partnerships that sell partnership interests to new investors (or receive new contributions of capital from existing partners).

INTERNAL FINANCING

This method of financing typically is not practical until after the early stage of the enterprise, when there are sufficiently steady streams of net positive cash flows from operations (or the sale of assets) to finance a firm's growth. However, as part of its long-run planning, an organization may plan to transition from external to internal financing eventually.

Strategy

Internal financing's two major advantages are control over cash flows and management. Unlike debt (which by explicit contract requires periodic interest payments) and equity (where owners often expect current cash returns, e.g., dividends), retained earnings are generally not subject to pay-out restrictions. Additionally, using internal financing allows the firm to grow without having to give management power (or a share of future increases in the firm's value) to new providers of capital.

Value-added from internal financing is potentially higher than from external financing because neither the enhanced cash flows nor the increased value of the firm resulting from financing are shared with anyone other than the original owners. The value-added from internal financing is higher than that for debt financing when the increased cash flows from debt-financed expansion are lower than the cash that is diverted to debt service (i.e., the required periodic payments of interest and repayments of principal). Internal financing also can add value over equity financing, particularly when the value of the firm increases due to factors not directly related to the projects being financed (such as when speculation created a hot market for *dot-com* companies going public in the late 1990s). However, because internal resources are typically more limited than external financing—consider how many people can pay for a house, a car, or an MBA without a loan—there are usually limits on how much value can be created by internal financing. (See Example 4.1)

EXAMPLE 4.1

A firm has the following:

	Annual Operations	Planned Plant Expansion: Expenditures/Year
Annual free cash flow	$10 million	
Planned expenditures		$15 million

Here, the firm is short at least $5 million per year through internal financing, so either some external financing must be sought or the expansion cut back. If the company properly manages its taxes, it may be able to increase the free cash flows and reduce external financing.

Anticipated tax law changes affect internal financing choice. For example, if taxes are expected to increase, sufficient earnings must be retained to cover the taxes not paid when transactions occur (such as income taxes). Similarly, anticipated tax decreases promise additional internal financing resources. The timing and time-value aspects of internal financing are advantages in that, because there are no lags to commit to investments when the firm simply needs to write a check, managers can control timing of tax benefits and deductions. (See Example 4.2.)

EXAMPLE 4.2

Suppose, in Example 4.1, the firm borrows $15 million per year from banks. Assume that the plant expansion generates $2 million per year in tax deductions. If the firm is in the 39% bracket this year and will be in the 34% bracket next year, it would prefer not to delay deductions until next year. If the bank doesn't follow through with financing until next year, the tax savings lost would be ($2 million) × (39% − 34%) = $100,000. Note that there is less danger of losing such tax benefits if the firm uses internal financing.

Of course, market conditions affect tax choice. If external financing is expensive (cheap), internal financing will be used more (less). Similarly, the nature of a business affects feasibility. High (low) profit margins require higher (lower) ability to use internal financing. The effects of taxes are shown in Example 4.3.

EXAMPLE 4.3

Suppose there are two otherwise identical firms, both needing $1 million for new equipment. Both are in the 35% income tax bracket, but one generates more cash flows, as follows:

	Company A	Company B
Sales	$10 million	$10 million
Cost of sales	<7 million>	<5 million>
Gross margin	3 million	5 million
Operating expense	<2 million>	<2 million>
Net (taxable) income	$ 1 million	$ 3 million

Here, company *B* can use internal financing, but company *A* cannot. In this scenario, taxes should have no great impact on the choice of financing. To see this, assume that the capital expansion is completely deductible. This would generate a cash flow of $(35\%)(\$1,000,000) = \$350,000$, not enough to finance the expansion. Indeed, unless the tax benefits are 100% of the cost (which they cannot be if internal financing is used) so that there is no net cash outflow, taxes do not make a big difference in internal financing. As discussed next, when debt financing is used, taxes can make a difference.

Negotiation of tax benefits is not really affected by the use of internal financing, but, as also discussed later, it is an important factor in structuring debt financing.

While there are no direct transforming advantages to internal financing, there is a definite advantage in the absence of transaction costs (as discussed in the next section). However, increases in firm value are not usually taxed until there is an exchange transaction, such as a sale of corporate stock. Thus an internal financing strategy that bolsters the value of a firm's equity held by existing owners can be quite tax advantaged.

EXTERNAL FINANCING: DEBT VERSUS EQUITY

Before applying the SAVANT framework, it is useful to compare different types of external financing. Short-term debt comes in many forms. *Short term* usually refers to loans that must be repaid within a year, but the phrase also is applied to maturities of up to five years. Short-term debt also is characterized overall by higher interest rates than long-term debt, but can be interest free. Trade credit, where suppliers allow purchasers to buy on account, often is extended interest free for 30 days. (Similarly, people using credit cards need not typically pay interest if they pay the balance within the grace period of about 30 days.) Long-term debt also takes a variety of forms. For large corporations, it usually consists of bonds (secured by specific assets) and debentures (not secured by specific assets), but there are a host of other arrangements.

Equity financing also comes in many forms. Most common are contributions to capital—usually in cash but sometimes in property—by partners in a partnership or owners of a limited liability company, along with the issuance of capital stock by a corporation. For the latter, usually only common stock is issued. Owners of common stock most often have voting control of the corporation, and they have the benefit (and disadvantage) of having residual ownership. For example, payments to common shareholders are made only after all other external financing claimants are paid; most jurisdictions allow dividends to be paid only out of net earnings and at the discretion of management.

Owners of preferred stock usually have no voting rights, but must be paid a specific dividend, which is computed similarly to interest. Hybrid securities are some combination of the above, most typically in the form of debt that can be converted into equity.

Strategy

In strategic planning, managers search for an optimal capital structure in the long run. The optimal mix of debt and equity for an organization depends on the firm's objective. For a not-for-profit organization, debt might be discouraged in order to assure continuity of programs during economic downturns, which may unexpectedly reduce contributions. Similarly, in a for-profit organization, the optimal debt-to-equity mix sought by management is the one that maximizes owner's equity. This is a function of expected risk and return.

For the most common form of business, the corporation, the goal is to enhance shareholder value. If the firm's shares are publicly traded, current finance theory—such as the capital asset pricing model (CAPM)—indicates that the market price they trade for implicitly takes into account both risk and return.

Value-Adding

A key aspect of debt financing is leverage. This can be an advantage or a disadvantage. Debt allows an equity investment to control more assets, which adds value when increased cash flows from debt-financed expansion exceed the cash that is diverted to debt service. In other words, debt adds value when debt enhances cash flows in excess of the required periodic payments of interest and repayments of principal. When this happens, leveraged returns are higher than nonleveraged ones.

For example, suppose that for every $1 invested in equipment a firm can make $1.15 in profit. If the firm's borrowing cost is 10%, every dollar borrowed nets 5% of pretax profit. If the firm can borrow as much as it wants, this 5%, across a large number of units, translates into large profits and economic value-added (EVA). In contrast, because the amount of financing available internally is almost always more limited than that available if external sources also are sought, the number of units that can be made is more limited, thus limiting total profits.

Risk affecting financing choice includes operating risk and financing risk. Operating risk can result from cycles in the economy. If the economy has a down cycle, or the firm has a down cycle, cash flows can decline, affecting the firm's ability to pay interest and principle. Financial risk comes from interest rate fluctuations. Because of this, debt has more financial risk. Taken altogether, risk is higher for debt.

However, cost is often lower on debt financing. The main reason for this is that interest payments are typically tax deductible. In this way, they act as a tax shield to reduce the entity's overall taxes. However, the higher the relative use of debt, the greater the risk of bankruptcy or costly debt renegotiations. This lowers EVA. The relationship is shown in Exhibit 4.1.

Value-added also decreases at some point because of lenders charging higher interest rates for additional loans, as the firm's risk of default increases. This counteracts the increasing returns from leveraged investments.

Optimal capital structure (i.e., the best mix of debt and equity) varies by industry and over time. As mentioned before, some industries are characterized by lower profit margins, so external financing is preferred. Further, lenders may benchmark against industry norms and provide more loans to firms in certain industries. Also, firms with higher effective tax rates (ETRs) benefit more from debt because of the tax shield. In addition, strategically there is an interaction with competitors' tax status and a firm's optimal capital structure. (See Example 4.4.)

EXAMPLE 4.4

A firm and its major competitor's financial statements can be summarized as follows:

	The Firm	The Competitor
Sales	$100 million	$100 million
Net (taxable) income	10 million	10 million
Assets	10 billion	10 billion
Debt	2 billion	7 billion
Equity – Common stock	7 billion	2 billion
– Retained earnings	1 billion	1 billion

Here, financial analysts and creditors will probably rate the firm higher than its competitors because of a lowered debt load. In turn, higher credit rankings usually result in lower costs of acquiring additional external financing.

If the firm is in a positive income tax bracket, and debt and equity have the same pretax costs, the higher financial ratings also may justify adding more debt to the firm's capital structure than otherwise. To see this, suppose both firms operate in the United States and are subject to its highest basic corporate income tax rate, 35%. Also, let debt and equity investors demand a 10% pretax return. Dividends, which are not tax deductible, thus would cost 10% both pretax and after tax. Debt, being deductible, would cost 10% pretax but only 6.5% after tax (calculated as 10%(100% − 35%) = 6.5%).

Under the firm's current capital structure, the annual total cost of capital is $830 million, calculated as follows: cost of debt = $2 billion (10%)(100% − 35%) = $130 million plus cost of equity = $7 billion (10%)

EXHIBIT 4.1   Optimal Levels of Debt in a Firm's Capital Structure

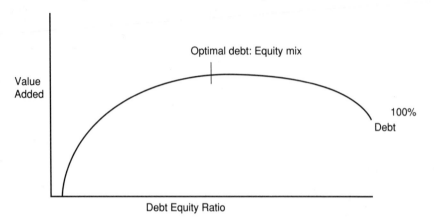

= $700 million. If the firm had the competitor's capital structure, the annual cost of capital would be $655 million—21% less—calculated as follows: $7 billion (10%)(100% − 35%) = $455 million plus $2 billion (10%) = $200 million. Over time, this extra cash flow, reinvested, can give the competitor a significant advantage. This is a trade-off in the long run for having a healthier-appearing financial structure.

In terms of life cycle, firms in the startup stage usually have inadequate internal resources and thus need external financing. Since floatation costs—that is, the transactions costs—of debt typically are half that of equity (around 5% versus 10%), debt may be advantageous. The type of debt used depends on asset structure; if the firm is capital intensive, secured loans or bonds can be used more than debentures.

Adjusting Value-Adding for Risk   As mentioned before, debt has higher risk than equity because of required periodic payments. However, an income tax can act to mitigate some of this risk for investors, and this lowered risk can be passed on to the firm in the form of lower interest rates. For example, under U.S. income tax most interest payments are tax deductible, whereas payments of dividends almost always are not. Similarly, if a firm defaults on debt, the remaining balance becomes a tax-deductible loss to the lender. If the lender is in the business of making loans—as is typical of term loans or short-term financing—the loss is deductible without limit. However, if the lender is not in that business—for example, individuals who invest in bonds—the loss is a capital loss. As discussed previously, such losses are of limited value.

Although equity is riskier, there are possible tax offsets to reduce risk. For U.S. income tax purposes, for example, investors can deduct up to $100,000 ($50,000 if unmarried) of loss during a year on IRC Section 1244 stock as an ordinary (rather than the normal capital) loss. This benefit generally does not apply to publicly traded shares. Instead, Section 1244 applies only to direct investments in certain small U.S. corporations. There are a host of detailed hurdles (e.g., the corporation's stock capitalization at the time of investment cannot exceed $1 million, and the corporation must generate primarily noninvestment-type income).

In addition to softening the impact of losses, income tax rules can cushion profitable investments. For example, in most of the world's tax systems, gains are not taxable until investments are sold or otherwise disposed of. Further, in many systems there is also no tax at all on gains built up during a person's life on property held until death. An exception is the Canadian system, which tends to treat such appreciation as an income-taxable capital gain by the decedent. Canada, however, does not impose estate taxes. In contrast, the U.S. imposes no income tax on the appreciation, but levies an estate tax (albeit only where the decedent gives away more than $1 million) on the value of property held at death.

Another example is that there is no U.S. income tax on 50% of the gain realized by non-corporate shareholders on IRC Section 1202, small business stock. As with Section 1244, Section 1202 contains a host of rules. For example, no more than $10 million of gain can be avoided, and the stock must have been held for at least five years. The stock must have been acquired directly from a C corporation, actively engaged in a U.S. business, with no more than $50 million of gross assets. The remaining 50% of the gain can be postponed by *rolling it over* (reinvesting the sales proceeds) into another company's qualified Section 1202 small business stock, if done within 60 days of the sale of the stock. Although this tax benefit deals with gains, it can be thought of as a risk premium insofar as it increases the expected return on risky stock investments. (See Example 4.5.)

EXAMPLE 4.5

A U.S. venture capitalist contributes $1 million for common stock in a startup Internet company, which meets the rules for Section 1202 "qualified small business stock." Six years later, she sells the stock for $20 million. Of the $19 million gain, 50%, or $9.5 million, is not taxed. Assuming she does not reinvest the proceeds in other qualified small business stock, the tax on the remaining gain is (.20) × ($9.5 million) = $1.9 million.

Note that the benefits of Section 1244, but not those of Section 1202, apply to investments in corporations that elect flow-through S corporation status. Thus, an investor can get tax benefits from flow-through losses and be price-protected in case the business fails. If the business does not fail, once it becomes clear that the business will succeed, it can convert to C status and be eligible for Section 1202 benefits if the stock is sold at a gain. (See Examples 4.6 and 4.7.)

EXAMPLE 4.6

Suppose two individuals start a firm, as follows:

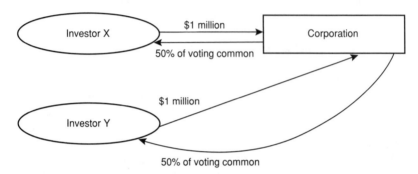

Projected income is as follows:

	Year		
	1	2	3 →n
Taxable income	<$1.2 million>	<$.8 million>	$.8 million

Both investors are in the 38.6% tax bracket and are concerned about bankruptcy, which they see as a real possibility by the end of the first year. Suppose they elect S corporate status, and Section 1244 stock. If the business fails at the end of the first year and the investors do not have other capital gains, then ignoring the time value of money and the benefit of the carry-over of capital losses, the cash flows for *each* investor are

Initial investment	<$1,000,000>
Tax saved from loss pass-through:	
(38.6%)(50%)($1.2 million)	231,600
Tax saved from loss on investment:	
Ordinary: 100,000(38.6%) =	38,600
Capital: $1,000,000 – 100,000	
= 900,000, limited to 3,000 per year	
3,000 × (38.6%) (rounded)	1,200
After-tax loss	<$ 728,600>

At this level of investment, the investors are not really cushioned much by tax benefits.

EXAMPLE 4.7

Assume that in Example 4.6 the business is successful. In year three, the investors may want to revoke S status so that they are not immediately taxed on corporate earnings. (This may not make sense if the firm holds substantial amounts of significantly appreciated inventory.) If they sell the venture for 15 times the earnings, for example, the tax is calculated as follows. The total sales price is 15 × $800,000 = $12 million. The gain realized is the $12 million sales price less the initial investment of $2 million = $10 million. The taxable gain is the $10 million less the 50% Section 1202 exclusion = $5 million. The total tax is $5 million times the standard 20% long term capital gains tax rate = $1 million.

Under this scenario, *each* investor's after-tax return, assuming sale at the end of year three and ignoring the time value of money, averages to over 175% per year, calculated as follows:

Total tax benefits from operations:

Years 1 to 3: (<1,200,000> + <800,000> + 800,000) × 38.6% =	$ 463,200
Total cash flow from sale:	
Cash proceeds (15 × $800,000)	12,000,000
Less tax on gain	<1,000,000>
Total return	$11,463,200
	× 50%
Return to each shareholder	$ 5,731,600

Divided by original $1 million investment = 574%

Over the three-year horizon, this is over a 175% per year return.

Negotiating

In some income tax systems, businesses that suffer operating losses can get immediate tax benefits by carrying those losses back to offset profits. Mature U.S. businesses can carry back to the prior five years and thus generate tax refunds. (The tax benefits of losses are limited in many countries and some states, like California.) However, if the losses exceed these profits, the losses do not generate tax refunds right away. Instead, they are carried forward to offset gains over the next 20 years.

Startups, which usually have nothing but losses, get no immediate benefit from losses under these rules. Losses thus are less important to many new enterprises, for insofar as they simply increase the NOL carry forward, the resulting tax benefits, if any, are delayed. However, if these tax deductions can be transferred to investors, they will effectively reap a higher return on capital.

As noted above, in the United States entities like LLCs and S corporations pass through their losses to their equity owners, and thus investors should be willing to pay more (or accept lower levels of payouts, such as dividends) for startups organized as pass-through entities. (See Example 4.8.)

EXAMPLE 4.8

Refer to Example 4.7 with investor X and investor Y. Suppose that the two investors put in only $100,000 each (to stay within the Section 1244 limit) and plan to issue $800,000 worth of stock to other investors. If investors normally expect a 10% return per year, they expect to get, after tax, ($800,000)(.1)(1 − .396) = $48,320. In this case, however, in year 1 the business lost $1.2 million. Thus the investors receive only a tax write-off (assuming that there is no cash flow from operations and that the shares do not appreciate). The value of the write-off to the new investor group is ($1.2 million)(.396)(.8) = $380,160.

In this way, they actually receive more than their normal rate of return, without receiving any cash flows from operations. Therefore this should be an acceptable investment, at least for year 1. (Tax benefits might not be so great in future years, because deductions for losses can not exceed the total amount invested.) From the firm's perspective, debt at the early stage has no tax benefit, so it should be willing to use debt only if the pretax cost is lower than the after-tax cost of equity financing.

Anticipation

If the firm expects macroeconomic changes that will affect interest rates, or tax law changes affecting interest deductions or tax rates on investors, then it should anticipate how these changes could affect the cost of capital. For example, during 1997 there was ongoing discussion of cutting the capital gains tax rate in the United States. The rate was subsequently cut from 28% to 20% (to 10% for some taxpayers). Had the firm predicted such rate reductions (which actually were enacted in July 1997), it would have been better off issuing stock after July 1997, when the price (driven by tax-induced demand) for stock increased relative to debt. Similarly, if a firm operating in the United States expects the Federal Reserve Bank to hike interest rates, the firm is better off issuing debt now. This is illustrated by the large amount of bonds issued in mid-2002, when the Federal Reserve Bank hinted at a change in its view on the need for lower rates.

EXHIBIT 4.2   Impact of Expected Relative Capital Gains Tax Rate Change on a Firm's Capital Structure

Capital Structure Strategy

Tax rates on firm expected to:	Ratio of capital gains tax rate to ordinary income tax rate on investors, expected to:		
	Decrease	No Change	Increase
Decrease	Issue stock	Issue stock	Depends
Not Change	Depends	Issue debt (stock) If in high (low) bracket	Depends
Increase	Depends	Issue debt	Issue debt

With respect to timing issues, a key issue is how the firm's (and potential investors') tax status is expected to change in the near future. If the firm expects to be in a lower tax bracket (or loss situation), then tax deductions for interest payments are of little use, and the after-tax cost of equity capital may be cheaper than that for debt. The dynamics of timing is represented in Exhibit 4.2.

Three aspects of timing are very important. First, recall that strategic tax management takes into account not just present but *anticipated* situations. Second, also taken into account is the tax status of any party transacted with, since tax benefits/costs become part of the *negotiation*. Third, the *depends* notation used in Exhibit 4.2 means that the decision is a function of the *relative* (firm versus investor) expected tax status.

For example, suppose that the ratio of investors' capital gains to ordinary income tax rates is expected to decrease. For the investor, this favors a common stock investment. However, if the firm is in a high tax bracket and expects to stay there, the firm favors debt. The firm and potential investors thus must negotiate tax benefits in the form of adjusting pretax cash flows. (See Example 4.9.)

EXAMPLE 4.9

Assume current (expected) corporate tax rates of 34% (0 due to an NOL), investor current (expected) ordinary income tax rates of 38.6% (38.6%), and investor current (expected) capital gains rates of 20% (15%). Thus, the ratio of investor capital gains rate to ordinary rate goes from .20/.386 to

.15/.386. This decrease also occurs at the corporate level. The corporation will get a lower tax benefit for interest deductions, which favors issuing stock. Similarly, stock is better for investors because appreciation is expected to be taxed at lower rates in the future.

Such negotiations are made easier when financing is done through private placement rather than through public offerings. In the former, brokers can match clients' and firms' tax status and adjust the pretax yields to align the two parties if necessary.

In each *depends* notation in Exhibit 4.2, the same sort of relative firm/equity owner trade-off may have to be made. Using the previous example, suppose that instead of decreasing, the ratio of personal capital gain to ordinary income tax rates is expected to increase. For example, let the capital gain tax rate be expected to remain at 20%, but have ordinary tax rates be expected to go from 39.6% to 30%. The corporation, still facing decreasing tax rates, would be inclined toward issuing stock. Investors, however, would favor debt. To mediate these competing desires, the firm could issue stock with current, but higher than normal, dividends, so that less investor income would be expected in the form of appreciation. Or debt could be issued at slightly lower interest rates, to make it more acceptable to the firm.

In addition to timing, the time-value aspect of tax benefits is important in the capital structure decision. For investors, timing of payments can be engineered so that they are made in a tax-minimizing way. Dividends can be paid when tax rates decline, or limited dividends can be paid, so that much of the stock's return is in the form of appreciation. Thus, taxes are postponed and thus *transformed* into (lower-taxed) capital gain income. (See Example 4.10.)

EXAMPLE 4.10

Suppose a company earns a $10% return. If a shareholder has $100 worth of stock, this implies that the shareholder should receive $10 in dividends each year. If an investor is in the 38.6% bracket for ordinary income but 20% for capital gains, and has a 10% cost of capital, he is better off instead receiving no dividends for five years and then selling the stock. (The stock can be sold on the open market, or sold back to the company itself. The latter is called a *redemption*.) To illustrate this, assume that the stock can be sold or redeemed for $50. If so, the after-tax present value of these alternatives are

Current dividend: $10(3.7908)(1 − .386) =$ <$23.28>

Sale at end of year 5:

    $50(.6209)(1 − .20)$ $24.84

Advantage to sale/redemption $ 1.56

Effect of Clienteles   As suggested before, the optimal choice for capital structure is highly influenced by the tax status of investors in a firm's debt or equity. This is particularly the case where the investor clientele includes those who do not pay tax at all. This is not uncommon. Some countries do not actually impose significant income taxes on investment earnings; a number do not tax capital gains. Quite a few do not tax dividend income, or allow recipients a tax credit for the corporate income taxes on the profits from which dividends are paid. In many countries, charities are tax exempt; in the United States tax-exempt organizations include pension funds and mutual funds.

In contrast to the situations just presented, tax-free investors may prefer current distributions, such as dividends, to delayed cash flows (e.g., waiting to sell appreciated stock to transform income into capital gains). They also may be indifferent to interest versus dividends. If a firm knows that its clientele will be tax exempt, it can issue debt or equity based on its own needs, disregarding investor tax status. (See Example 4.11.)

EXAMPLE 4.11

A corporation wants to float $100 million of 10-year bonds. The market interest rate is 8% for taxable bonds of similar risk and maturity. By placing the entire issue with a few tax-free pension funds, the corporation may be able to offer the bonds at less than 8%.

Suppose a mature firm in a high tax bracket would prefer to issue bonds. Rather than go to the general bond market, which includes a large percentage of taxable investors, it can arrange a private placement with pension funds that are indifferent to debt versus equity, so long as the pretax returns are equal. Because the lenders are only a few investors, the firm can negotiate interest rates and tax benefits more easily than with a public offering having many investors. Tax Management in Action 4.1 provides data on the volume of such private placements.

TAX MANAGEMENT IN ACTION 4.1

USING PRIVATE PLACEMENTS TO TRANSFER TAX BENEFITS

Investment bankers have increased the number of U.S. private placements under Rule 144a of the SEC. Enacted in 1990, the rule allows firms (acting through investment bankers) to market debt (or debt convertible into equity) without formal procedures. As a result, security sales can be done at much lower cost and almost instantaneously. Most of the investments are sold to institutional investors.

TAX MANAGEMENT IN ACTION 4.1 (CONTINUED)

Some individual examples of private placements (discussed in the article) were as follows. Sakura Capital Funding (Cayman) Ltd., the funding arm of Japan's Sakura Bank Ltd., sold $1 billion of high-grade bonds in a two-part offering through Merrill Lynch & Co. Other big private high-grade offerings this quarter included a $500 million offering for Chrysler Corp.; a $750 million issue for Montell, a Netherlands chemical concern; a $525 million issue for McKesson Corp. and a $700 million issue for Bank of Austria. In the high-yield market, McCaw International Ltd. sold $500 million of bonds via Rule 144a and Innova, a direct satellite company, issued $347 million of securities in the private market.

Source: The Wall Street Journal, April 1, 1997, p. C15.

In many countries, tax timing for interest payments on debt cannot be controlled merely by paying interest at maturity. In the United States, however, interest income must be recognized periodically through amortization of the original issue discount. Accordingly, assuming similar pretax yields, the time value of tax costs is much higher for debt than equity.

From the firm's perspective, the present value of after-tax cash flows of debt versus equity is a function of the firm's tax status and its pretax cost of capital. Thus if a corporation's shareholders are willing to accept nominal dividends in return for stock appreciation, the firm can dramatically increase the present value of stock financing by paying out dividends only after a certain length of time. (See Example 4.12.)

EXAMPLE 4.12

Suppose a corporation has 1 million shares of stock outstanding, on which shareholders expect on average $10 of annual dividends per share. If the shareholders can wait five years and then sell the stock, the tax savings for high-income investors would be $(38.6\% - 20\%) \times \$50 = \$9.30$. If the firm's reinvestment rate of return is 10%, then by reinvesting the cash which would have been paid out in dividends, it can accumulate $\$10(3.79) = \$37.90$ in appreciation per share.

This can be done in most countries. However, as noted in Technical Insert 3.1, the United States has penalty taxes which effectively prevent the use of this strategy by certain closely held corporations.

One last aspect of timing relates to initial public offerings (IPOs). Before a firm goes to the market, it wants to make its financial statements as strong as possible. However, if the firm maximizes financial accounting income prior to the IPO, this may come at the expense of higher taxes. Although tax- and financial-accounting choices are independent, real economic decisions are not. So if the firm accelerates revenues or delays expenditures in order to enhance accounting income, taxes go up. However, the acceleration of taxes by one year may well be exceeded by the present value of cheaper capital over many years, which can be leveraged into higher earnings. (See Example 4.13.)

EXAMPLE 4.13

Suppose a privately owned firm wants to float an IPO next year. Its investment bankers believe that the planned issuance of 5 million shares will be priced at $10 per share, which is based on a price multiple of five times reported net financial earnings. Assume the firm's income statement looks like the following:

	If big expenditure paid this year	If big expenditure delayed until next year
Revenues	$100 million	$100 million
Cost of sales	<55 million>	<55 million>
Gross margin	45 million	45 million
Operating expenses	<40.4 million>	<30.4 million>
Pre tax profit	4.6 million	15.4 million
Taxes at 35%	<1.6 million>	<5.4 million>
Net income	$3.0 million	$ 10 million

If the firm expects its tax bracket to drop to 20% next year, there is loss in tax savings by delaying the expenditure. The loss in savings is the expenditure of $10 million times the drop in tax rate (35% – 20%), or $1.5 million. However, such tax management may be worth it: Net income is $7 million higher, which translates into $7 million × (5) = $35 million more in proceeds from the IPO.

Transactions Cost Effects on Value-Adding   As mentioned previously, debt offerings typically are cheaper than equity (5% versus 10%, depending on circumstances). Because these costs are present at each offering, it makes sense for the firm to try to anticipate future capital needs in order to minimize the number of issuances. This is especially important in jurisdictions like the United States where almost all capital-raising costs are nondeductible.

Transforming

By issuing stock or securities which are convertible to equity, firms can enable either themselves or their investors to transform ordinary income into capital gain, or taxable into nontaxable income. There are a myriad of these hybrid types of securities, many of which are tailored by investment bankers specifically for their large-firm clients. An example appears in the following Tax Management in Action 4.2.

TAX MANAGEMENT IN ACTION 4.2

TIME VALUE AND CAPITAL MARKETS

Large investment banking firms frequently design a number of tax-minimizing financing methods for their clients. In the past, such techniques as straddle sales and "shorting against the box" have been used, before being closed down by tax law changes. One of the newer methods is using debt exchangeable into common stock.

One example of this was the $223 million deal in 1996 by Salomon Brothers. Others have been done by Times Mirror and American Express. Consider Western Southern Life Insurance Company in Cincinnati, which owns shares of Cincinnati Bell. Because the shares had significant appreciation, any sale would have resulted in substantial capital gains tax.

To solve that problem, Salomon Brothers issued a new form of exchangeable notes indirectly backed by the insurance company's Cincinnati Bell shares, then sent on a substantial part of the note proceeds to Western Southern. The deal allowed Western Southern to lock in its profit and free up low-cost cash to invest elsewhere, just as if it had sold the stock, but without incurring any taxes.

Salomon, which originated the exchangeable-note concept in June 1993, called its product a DECS note, for debt exchangeable into common stock. Merrill Lynch and Goldman, Sachs offers similar products under different names, Strypes and ACES, respectively.

To facilitate the Western Southern deal, Salomon Brothers sold the notes to the public and made most of the proceeds available to its client, Western Southern, through a private transaction whose terms mirror the terms of the DECS sold to the public.

When the notes mature, Western Southern can repay its obligation to Salomon with cash or with its Cincinnati Bell stock, either of which Salamon can use to cover what it owes to noteholders. If it pays in cash, no taxes will be owed, because legal ownership of the shares will have remained with Western Southern. In the meantime, it had the use of most of the cash raised from the note sale, free of capital gains taxes.

Some tax agencies, such as the IRS, are attentive to capital structure. Managers need to be careful that debt is not reclassified by them into equity, thereby disallowing interest expense deductions. Some guidelines on avoiding this appear in the Technical Insert section of this chapter. (See Example 4.14.)

EXAMPLE 4.14

A U.S. company's balance sheet shows $100 million of bonds and $1 million of common stock. During the year, the company paid $8 million of interest on the bonds. One year later, on audit, the IRS reclassifies the debt as equity. Interest expense thus is reclassified as non-deductible dividend payments, and the firm owes 35% × ($8 million) = $2.8 million in back taxes, plus interest and penalties.

TECHNICAL INSERT 4.1 DETAILS ON DEBT AND EQUITY

Thin Capitalization

A good example of the reclassification problem is thin capitalization. Because interest is income tax deductible in the United States and dividends are not, there may be a tendency for firms operating there to overleverage. Beyond additional nontax risk, the tax risk is that the IRS, under the auspices of IRC Section 385, may view the firm as *thinly capitalized*. To the extent this occurs, debt will be reclassified as equity, and interest payments as dividends, on an IRS audit. Back taxes and interest also will be owed when interest becomes nondeductible. Although (if issued after October 24, 1992) a corporate issuer's characterization of an initial issue is binding on the taxpayer, it is not binding on the IRS.

Some factors taken into account in classifying debt versus equity are:

- The debtor's failure to repay on time or to seek a postponement
- The economic realities of the transaction
- The business purpose of the transaction
- The names given to the certificates evidencing the debt
- The presence or absence of a fixed maturity date
- The source of payments

TECHNICAL INSERT 4.1 (CONTINUED)

- The right to enforce payment of principal and interest
- Any resulting participation in management
- Whether the debt is subordinate to the corporation's other debt
- Whether the debt is convertible into stock
- The intent of the parties
- Whether there is a high ratio of debt to equity
- Identity of interest between creditor and shareholder
- The corporation's ability to get loans from outside lenders

Although there are no fixed numerical rules, a common sentiment from U.S. practitioners is that debt-to-equity ratios beyond 3:1 may attract IRS scrutiny. However, this certainly depends on industry norms.

Expenses of Raising Capital

Brokerage, legal, and accounting fees directly related to the issuance of new debt or equity are nondeductible *syndication* expenses in jurisdictions that follow the U.S. rules. Such costs are capitalized into the cost of the capital. In particular, stock issuance costs reduce paid-in capital, and debt expenses reduce the debt's principal. New venues usually incur a number of expenses, including organizational, financing, issuance, and operating expenses, most of which are deductible (although some only through amortization over the firm's first five years of operations. Effective tax management includes segregating out syndication expenses and treating them properly. See, generally, IRC Section 248.

Issues Related to Interest Expense

If there is original interest discount (OID) on a bond, in most jurisdictions the firm can deduct interest expense even though not paid, so long as the firm is on the accrual method of accounting. However, in the United States OID is not deductible until paid on junk bonds (where the interest rate is 15% above market), then. Some excellent Web sites devoted to OID, and its calculation, are available through *www. taxsites.com*.

TECHNICAL INSERT 4.2

CORPORATE PENALTY TAXES LIMITING CAPITAL STRUCTURE

Recall from Chapter 3 that a firm's shareholders can postpone their taxes by not paying dividends, then liquidating their interests to *transform* the gain to a 20% capital gain tax rate. Some jurisdictions have special rules designed to limit this. As briefly noted in the Technical Insert 3.1, in the United States, two penalty taxes can be triggered by such a strategy. They are the accumulated earnings tax and the personal holding company (PHC) tax.

Both taxes are assessed only upon IRS audit, and are added to the regular corporate tax bill. The latter tax is assessed only if the corporation is closely held (that is, 50% or more of the value of outstanding stock is held directly or indirectly by five or fewer people in the last half of the year. The former is rarely assessed on publicly traded companies.

Accumulated Earnings Tax

This is a tax on undistributed retained earnings after deducting an allowance. The tax rate is the highest individual income tax rate (e.g., 38.6% in 2002.) The allowance is the greater of $250,000 ($150,000 for service corporations), or "reasonable business needs" of the corporation, less the beginning of year retained earnings.

The phrase "reasonable business needs" is not defined by statute. It has been interpreted expansively by the courts. They include retained earnings for debt retirement, capital acquisitions, acquiring other businesses, working capital, self-insurance for product liability, redemptions to pay death taxes, and investments or loans to suppliers or customer in order to maintain business relationshsips. Most commonly, the tax has been applied where where unreasonable wages, loans, or benefits have been granted to shareholder-employees or related parties, the corporation has made significant investments unrelated to its business, or for reserves providing against unrealistic hazards. As a practical matter, the tax only applies to only mature, highly successful, closely held regular corporations with substantial liquid assets that do not pay dividends.

As an example, consider a manufacturing firm that has beginning and ending retained earnings in 2002 of $500,000 and $600,000, respectively. Assume that it can justify $300,000 for plant expansion but has no other reasons for retaining earnings. If audited, the IRS can assess an additional tax of 38.6% × ($600,000 = 300,000) = $115,800.

TECHNICAL INSERT 4.2 (CONTINUED)

The corporation can avoid the tax by:

- Luck (i.e., it is not audited by the tax authority, or the auditor does not pursue the issue)
- Being able to properly document accumulating the earnings for a reasonable business purpose
- Paying dividends

Personal Holding Company Tax

The personal holding company (PHC) tax applies only to closely held regular corporations that have primarily passive income like interest, dividends, rents, and royalties, and that do not pay dividends. It does not apply to businesses whose primary revenue source is passive type income, such as financial institutions, insurance companies, leasing companies, real estate firms, and software development companies. It is targeted at individuals who try to incorporate their portfolios, their toys (such as yachts), or themselves (such as athletes and entertainers) in order to take advantage of differences in tax rates, or tax bases, between individual and corporate income taxes.

The tax is the highest personal income tax rate (e.g., 38.6% in 2002) of undistributed PHC income. PHC income includes interest, dividends, and capital gains, along with certain royalties and rents, plus personal services income. The latter is not taxed if the person performing the service is not specified in a contract, or if the person specified owns less than 20% of the firm. Rents and royalties are not subject to the tax if they exceed 50% of income (i.e., they are the firm's main business).

For example, assume a firm has $200,000 of income from sales of inventory, and $400,000 of interest income. Because the interest income exceeds 60% of total income, it is subject to a 38.6% tax on $400,000 or $154,400.

The PHC tax applies only if PHC income exceeds 60% of the firm's adjusted ordinary gross income (AOGI) for the year. Typifying the Byzantine complexity of the law in this area, AOGI essentially amounts to gross income decreased by capital gains but increased by gross income deductions for cost recovery (e.g., depreciation or depletion), property taxes, interest, and rents. Unlike the accumulated earnings tax, there is no credit.

Operating the Firm

New Products: Development, Promotion, and Advertising

The need to innovate is mentioned—indeed emphasized—in every book on management. But beyond this the books, as a rule, pay little attention to what management and organization need to be and need to do to stimulate, to direct, and to make effective innovation.... Little thought or space is normally devoted to the entrepreneurial function of creating effectively and purposefully the new and the different.

—Peter Drucker,
Management: Tasks, Responsibilities, Practices

For a business to stay competitive, it must deliver products or services that are perceived to be better, less expensive, or more convenient. Given competitors with the same objectives, this implies a constant evolution in products. This chapter examines the tax aspects of this process using the SAVANT framework.

NEW PRODUCTS AND PRODUCT IMPROVEMENT

The typical product/process development process is shown in Exhibit 5.1.

This process is quite risky, and many products fail. However, the risk is partly borne by many governments through income tax deductions and credits for related costs, such as research and development (R&D) and marketing (see Exhibit 5.2).

Strategy

Although the tax benefits from R&D can be enticing, like other tax incentives they do not justify starting a new product or process that is inconsistent with the firm's mission. For example, an R&D scientist working for

EXHIBIT 5.1   Product/Process Development Process

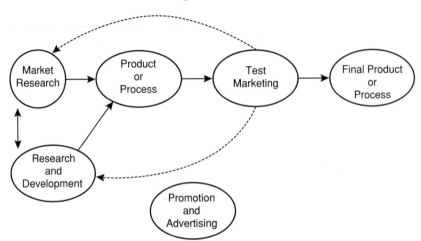

a computer chip manufacturer may stumble upon an idea for an electronic game. If the firm is not in the game business, and gains no strategic advantage by doing so, no amount of R&D tax credits should entice the firm to pursue this product, although the firm may want to *sell* the idea to another firm. Instead, tax benefits should be viewed as a cost- and risk-reduction mechanism for ideas fitting within the firm's strategic plan.

An important part of strategic analysis is the firm's tax status relative to that of its competitors. For example, if the firm is in an NOL carryforward situation, the tax advantages of deductions or credits may be low (or nonexistent). Conversely, if the firm is in the highest income tax bracket, cost and risk sharing is maximized. If competitors are in an NOL carryforward (high bracket) situation, this puts them at a strategic disadvantage

EXHIBIT 5.2   Cost Sharing through Tax Benefits

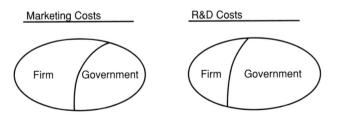

EXHIBIT 5.3 Competitive Advantage Derived from Relative Tax Status

Competitor's Tax Status

		Low Rate	High Rate
Firm's Tax Status	Low Rate	See discussion	Advantage to competitor
	High Rate	Advantage to firm	See discussion

(advantage). (See Exhibit 5.3.) Having the same tax status gives neither a competitive advantage.

For the U.S. income tax, the principle advantages of R&D and marketing expenses are

- A 20% tax credit for incremental (that is, in excess of prior years' average spending) research and experimentation expenditures.
- Current deductibility of R&D expenses not eligible for the credit.
- Expensing or very rapid depreciation of R&D equipment: If it is used only in the R&D project, it is expensed; otherwise, it is subject to rapid depreciation.
- Current deduction of marketing expenses such as marketing research, promotion, and advertising.

Additionally, most states offer R&D credits for corporate income tax purposes, if the research is performed within that state.

Often, firms budget their overall advertising and R&D as either fixed amounts or by pegging them as percents of sales. Taking the competitive analysis just described into account may be more effective, however. (See Example 5.1.)

EXAMPLE 5.1

Suppose the firm is in an NOL carryforward situation for the next couple of years. Its major competitor is in the 35% income tax bracket, however. Both are contemplating basic research toward a series of products. For such

R&D, each dollar spent would generate 20% of tax benefits through the R&D credit and rapid depreciation. For the competitor, such tax benefits yield an after-tax cost of 80%. If both the firm and its competitor have a $20 million R&D budget, the competitor actually can spend $25 million pretax (calculated as $20 million/.80 = $25 million), or $5 million more than the firm. If R&D is in a race to be first to discover a patentable product, the firm *might* be (subject to strategic considerations) better off staying out of the R&D game (and investing the $20 million elsewhere) until it goes into a positive tax bracket in a few years.

Although it may seem counterintuitive, in some cases, the firm may find itself at a competitive disadvantage because of its non-tax-paying status. (See Example 5.2.)

EXAMPLE 5.2

Suppose both the firm and its competitor have budgeted $1 million in pretax dollars for incremental R&D, and the competitor is in a tax-paying situation while the firm is not due to an NOL carryforward status. Because of the 20% tax credit (and tax deduction at the 35% bracket), the competitor can spend $480,000 more pretax (calculated as 20% × $1 million = $200,000 + 35% × (1 million − $200,000) = $280,000).

This competitive disadvantage is not limited to R&D costs. Instead, it is a generic challenge generated by the nature of most tax benefits. Income tax deductions, for example, simply are worth more to higher-tax-bracket taxpayers. Governments are aware of this and can take steps to limit it. The United States, for example, has an alternate minimum income tax, which effectively limits the enjoyment of many income tax benefits by high-income taxpayers. Governments can also phase out deductions for high-bracket taxpayers. In the United States, for example, the standard personal exemption deduction granted to almost all taxpayers is reduced as a percentage of income in excess of a targeted amount, and is reduced to zero for taxpayers with very high income.

Another approach is for policy makers to grant tax benefits through the use of tax credits rather than deductions. This is because the value of a credit does not vary with tax rates. For example, a tax deduction for R&D would generate $35 in tax savings for a 35% bracket taxpayer who spends $100, but only $15 for a 15% taxpayer. However, a 20% R&D credit would grant $20 in tax savings to both. For many reasons, governments also limit credits. The most common way is to make them nonrefundable, that is, a credit can only offset taxes otherwise due. This limits their value to taxpayers who would otherwise expect to pay little or no taxes.

EXHIBIT 5.4 Competitive Advantage from Shifting Tax Benefits

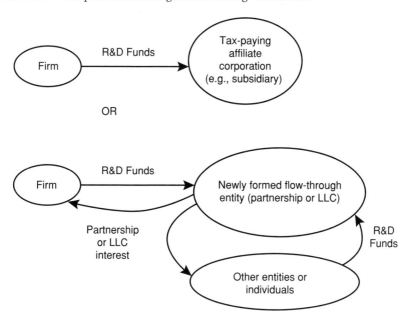

There are techniques, however, that can be used to overcome the possible competitive disadvantage of being a relatively low-tax-paying firm. Underlying them is one basic goal: to shift tax-favored spending (such as R&D) to higher-tax-paying entities in return for negotiated nontax benefits (such as below-market access to technology developed from the R&D spending.) The two basic ways of accomplishing this are shown in Exhibit 5.4.

In some jurisdictions, shifting can be done internally. For example, a firm that expects to be in a loss position could isolate its R&D spending in a 100% owned profitable subsidiary. In most jurisdictions, mechanisms (such as California's unitary tax and the U.S. consolidated return rules) limit the effectiveness of shifting to entities controlled by the firm (or its owners).

Shifting also can be done externally, such as to a newly formed R&D partnership (or LLC) owned at least in part by high-rate taxpayers. To the extent tax benefits can flow through the entity to be used by these other taxpayers, the benefits generate value that the firm can negotiate for. Although there are a host of managerial and legal complications to this approach, it can be successful (at least to some extent) in allowing a low-tax-paying firm to capture tax benefits. For example, in the United States a flow-through entity can allocate almost all of its tax benefits to new investors even though the firm will control the resulting discoveries. (See Examples 5.3 and 5.4.)

EXAMPLE 5.3

Suppose a high-tech firm wants to do $20 million of R&D but is in an NOL situation. There is a 50% probability of developing a product, which will generate $50 million of profit. Thus, the expected return is $(0.5)(\$50,000,000) - \$20$ million $= \$5$ million. A bank loan to finance the project would cost 12%, which would reduce cash flows by $(\$20,000,000)(.02)$ or $2.4 million, for a net cash flow of $2.6 million.

EXAMPLE 5.4

Assume the same facts as in Example 5.3 except that the firm forms an LLC with a nonrival company that needs the tax write-offs. The other firm will provide all the financing in return for 100% of the tax benefits and 75% of expected profits, as follows:

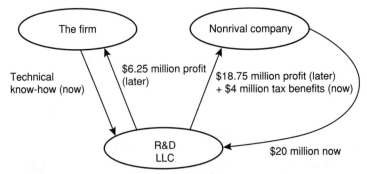

By using this arrangement, the firm's expected cash flow increases by 140%. (This is calculated as $6.25 million – $2.6 million = $3.65 million / $2.6 million.

The scenarios discussed in Examples 5.3 and 5.4 also work with marketing expenses. Thus, if the firm and its competitors' pretax advertising budgets are both $2 million, and the firm (the competitor) is in an NOL carryforward situation (in the 35% bracket), the competitor could outadvertise the firm by $2 million $\times$ (35%) = $700,000, unless some arrangement similar to that just described is made. These arrangements are, of course, subject to transaction cost considerations. Nonetheless, the firm's long-run strategy may suggest having such additional entity choices ready to go in the event that they are needed.

Anticipation

To evaluate potential tax benefits from new product development, actions by competitors and governments should be anticipated. For example, if a competitor is currently in a high tax bracket but may transition into a low one, the competitor may decide to incur tax-deductible, new-product development costs this year but not next year. Just the opposite might occur if the competitor's tax rate is expected to go up.

Tax rate and rule changes should be planned for. But because some changes result from political processes, planning should be flexible. For example, it is not uncommon for government policy makers to establish tax credits to stimulate higher levels of certain types of private sector spending (such as R&D, or hiring low-skilled workers), but have the credits scheduled to expire (sometimes called "sunsetting"). The potential expiration is intended to encourage firms to increase current spending. However, the expiration of many such credits often is deferred—the U.S. R&D credit was renewed several times during the 1990s, sometimes retroactively—which complicates decision making.

Another evolving set of rules in the United States is related to marketing and state taxes. Constitutional interpretations by the U.S. Supreme Court, coupled with odd federal statutes such as Public Law 86-272, limit the ability of a state to tax a firm that has minimal physical contact—called *nexus*—with the state. This does not help a firm that follows a *push* promotion strategy, but can give substantial advantages to a firm that follows a *pull* promotion strategy.

In a *push* strategy, the firm sends employees out to meet customers; with a *pull* strategy, the firm tries to have customers come to it. Thus a push strategy usually requires the physical presence of salespeople and inventory in target locations, which may amount to a table nexus. This is much less likely for a firm following a pull strategy: merely advertising in a state (by TV, radio, email, Web site, or any print medium) does not establish a business link (nexus) to the state as long as the firm has no tangible property or employees in the state. (Note that mailing free samples or coupons and having sample displays in stores are the equivalent of advertising for state tax purposes.)

So, if the firm's sales are generated purely through mail order, telephone, Web sites, or unaffiliated merchandisers, it will not be subject to state income tax, and will not be responsible for collecting sales tax, except where it has a physical presence (such as its headquarters or distribution centers). However, if the firm has property or payroll in a state, nexus (and thus state tax) is established, so the promotion method is irrelevant. (See Example 5.5.)

EXAMPLE 5.5

An office supply company is located in Chicago. It has no offices or salespeople in other states. Instead, it sells to distributors by mail order. Although its products are everywhere, it is subject to state tax only in Illinois.

Another topic requiring anticipation is the taxation of electronic commerce. In the United States, the Internet Tax Freedom Act and its successors exempt Web transactions from new state and local taxes. This law has a built-in sunset provision (which has been extended), so firms should anticipate this possible change and plan accordingly.

Note that although customers are technically responsible for most sales-type taxes, such taxes are not cost free to firms. For example, they must establish an accounting information system for tax collection, file tax returns, remit taxes collected, and submit to tax audits. Furthermore, taxes not remitted by the customer are the firm's responsibility.

As already described, a push marketing strategy involves a physical presence in targeted locations. If this is more than just an occasional traveling salesperson, it may establish nexus and thus liability for state taxes. Under the federal Public Law 86-272, for example, if a firm has an office in a state, or the firm's salespeople perform tasks beyond taking orders, then nexus has occurred. (See Example 5.6.)

EXAMPLE 5.6

Assume the same facts as in Example 5.5, except that the company establishes a sales office in San Francisco. Because it has established nexus, part of the company's profits are subject to California income taxes and it must collect sales taxes on purchases by California residents (even if these sales are handled solely by another division located entirely in the Chicago headquarters).

This business connection problem also occurs internationally. For most countries, simple advertising does not result in taxation. However, if there is a *permanent establishment* (e.g., an office is opened, or sales personnel spend substantial time in the country), the firm may be taxed in the country (either as a branch or as a resident company). As in the state setting, in an international setting a push strategy can result in a tax, even though no services are performed in and no inventory passes through the jurisdiction. Exhibit 5.5 summarizes the state and international tax consequences of a push promotion strategy.

EXHIBIT 5.5   Tax Consequences of Different Promotion Strategies

	Advertising	Salespeople or trade show
State or international tax consequences	None	Tax on at least part of operation

Timing and Time Value Issues   Sales and purchases of new products can be timed in order to increase tax benefits, using the methods discussed previously. Also, the firm can exploit planned changes in tax rules and rates, for example, by planning purchases (sales) to occur in higher (lower) tax years. (See Example 5.7.)

EXAMPLE 5.7

Suppose a U.S. firm wants to buy a machine in December that qualifies for tax depreciation in the 5-year MACRS category. However, the firm is aware that tax rates will go up by 5% next year. If the machine costs $1 million, the tax savings of postponement is $1 million(.05)(20%) = $10,000 by delaying the purchase until January of the next year.

Value-Adding

Like any other investment, product development must pass the value-adding test.

EXAMPLE 5.8

Suppose a manager in a U.S. business can spend $1 million either on new product development (one half of which is for R&D), or for a new machine that will save $200,000 per year in operating costs. For tax purposes, let the machine qualify to be depreciated over five years under the MACRS system. If the new product is successful (based on an estimate of a 50% chance of this), it will generate additional pretax profits of $300,000 annually.

Which investment should be made? Assume existing EVA is 12%, and the firm is in the 35% bracket.

			New Product		
	Year 1	Year 2	Year 3	Year 4	Year 5
Expected pretax income	150,000	150,000	150,000	150,000	150,000
Cash outflows	<1,000,000>	—	—	—	—
Tax credit	100,000	—	—	—	—
Tax on operating income	<52,500>	<52,500>	<52,500>	<52,500>	<52,500>
Net	<802,500>	97,500	97,500	97,500	97,500
Cost of Capital	<120,000>	<120,000>	<120,000>	<120,000>	<120,000>
EVA	<922,500>	<22,500>	<22,500>	<22,500>	<22,500>

The same analysis for the machine is

	New Machine				
	Year 1	Year 2	Year 3	Year 4	Year 5
Cost Reduction	200,000	200,000	200,000	200,000	200,000
Tax increase from cost reduction	<70,000>	<70,000>	<70,000>	<70,000>	<70,000>
Tax shield on MACRS depreciation	70,000[1]	180,250[2]	67,200[3]	40,320[4]	60,480[5]
Cost of machine	<1,000,000>	—	—	—	—
	<800,000>	310,000	197,200	170,320	190,480
Cost of capital	<120,000>	<120,000>	<120,000>	<120,000>	<120,000>
EVA	<920,000>	190,250	77,200	50,320	70,480

[1] $1,000,000 \times 20\% \times 35\% = 70,000$
[2] $1,000,000 \times 32\% \times 35\% = 180,000$
[3] $1,000,000 \times 19\% \times 35\% = 67,200$
[4] $1,000,000 \times 11.52\% \times 35\% = 40,320$
[5] $1,000,000 \times 17.28\% \times 35\% = 60,480$
   [includes half year depreciation from year 6]

These analyses suggest that the new machine is a better investment than the new product, but that despite the tax benefits, neither investment appears worthwhile overall.

As shown by the analysis in Example 5.8, even though an investment may generate superior tax benefits, it is not a sufficient reason to invest in new products if expected EVA declines by approximately $1 million. Of course, this is subject to strategic considerations. If there is a strategic reason for developing a new product (such as to mimic a move by a competitor or improve brand recognition), then negative value-added may not be a good reason for rejecting research on new product development.

Adjusting Value-Adding for Risk   Many aspects of product development are risky in the sense that the manager does not know if it will be a commercial success. However, tax law can act as a risk-sharing partner by absorbing part of the cost. As indicated in Example 5.2, R&D in the United States can shift around 50% of the cost to the federal government through income tax savings. However, other aspects of SAVANT must be considered before a marketing or R&D investment should be made. (See Example 5.9.)

EXAMPLE 5.9

Suppose a U.S. firm contemplates spending $10 million on an R&D project with a 50% probability of yielding profits of $30 million. Let the firm be in the 35% income tax bracket. If the investment fails, there can be two tax benefits. First is the 20% credit of $2 million. Second is the benefit of deducting the rest of the cost (35%)($10 million – $2 million) = $2.8 million. Thus, $4.8 million of cost was shifted to the government. The firm only has $5.2 million/10 million, or 52% of the risk; the government has the other 48%.

But is the investment still worth it from a SAVANT perspective? Some relevant questions to ask are: Is the R&D consistent with the firm's strategy? If the firm usually does not innovate and instead acquires existing products or know-how, mere tax benefits should not induce it to get into the R&D business. What are the competitors doing? If they have an advantage over the firm in doing R&D, the tax benefits alone should not induce it to complete in the R&D area.

As illustrated by Example 5.4, the firm may want to take the investment off its books by shifting R&D to a flow-through entity. This also implies risk sharing through another partner, rather than the government. If the investment is extremely risky, managers are very risk averse, or the firm is in a low tax bracket (e.g., has an NOL carryforward), the tax benefits may be insufficient in and of themselves to adjust for risk.

Value-Adding and Transactions Costs   The costs of starting a new product are currently deductible unless they are capital in nature. Besides buildings, machinery, and equipment (which must be depreciated over time), other capital assets include trademarks, copyrights, and patents. In the United States costs associated with these new-product-related intangibles are amortized over 15 years if they are purchased from another taxpayer. Because intangibles must be written off more slowly than R&D, they are potentially more expensive. Suppose a firm can spend $10 million to either buy an existing patent from another firm or develop the product internally. If bought, the tax savings at a 10% discount rate are ($1 million ÷ 15)(7.61)(.35) = $178,000. If the R&D is done internally and all costs are eligible for the 20% up-front R&D credit, the tax savings are $200,000.

Negotiating

Like other areas of taxation, promotion involves interaction with other parties in which tax benefits can be part of the negotiations. If the firm is in an NOL carryforward setting, it may want to back-load payments in an advertising contract so that more payments are made in years in which the firm is taxable and thus the payments are currently tax deductible. If the firm is taxable and the advertising firm is in an NOL-carryforward situation, the firm can instead front-load payments in return for a lower price on the overall contract. One popular negotiation method involves contracts with celebrities and athletes. Here, the firm can sign a contract with the individual that arranges payments in a manner that reduces taxes. Typically, actual cash payments are back-loaded, but the firm may be able to take tax deductions (on the accrual basis) on an accelerated basis.

By engineering tax benefits, the firm implicitly changes a product's price. By promoting the product's tax advantages, the firm can segment the market. For example, in the United States financial products such as individual retirement accounts (IRAs), 401(k) retirement plans, and municipal bonds all promote their tax-advantaged status. Thus, they target middle- to higher-tax-bracket markets.

Because consumer tax benefits directly affect price, they may become a part of the firm's life cycle based price promotion strategy, as shown in Exhibit 5.6.

In the early adopters stage, consumers may be more affluent individuals or sophisticated firms, for whom price elasticity is unimportant. As the product matures, price becomes an issue (as competitors enter the marketplace), so tax advantages should be promoted. If the product has a business or employee-related use, the firm can promote its tax deductibility. In this stage, smaller business and middle-class individuals may be the principal consumers. (Note that most purchases for nonbusiness use are not tax advantaged.) In the decline/maturation phase, lower-income households may be the principal consumers. For these consumers, tax benefits are not an important promotion tool.

The method of distribution can affect tax-pricing strategy because of sales-type taxes. As noted previously, if the product is sold by mail order to out-of-state customers or foreigners, there is usually no VAT or sales tax. This can be promoted as a pricing advantage over purchases made from local retailers. Similarly, sales made via the Web can be tax exempt. (See Example 5.10.)

EXHIBIT 5.6   Product Life Cycle and Tax Promotion for Certain Products

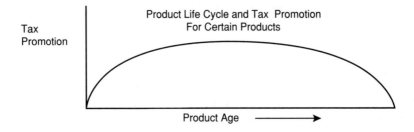

EXAMPLE 5.10

A music company sells CDs for an average price of $13.99 per CD by mail-order sales over the Internet (e.g., Amazon.com). Another music company with retail stores located nationally sells CDs for the same price (e.g., Blockbuster Music). The second company must charge applicable sales taxes to its customers, which puts it potentially at a strategic disadvantage.

The pricing strategy discussed here is more salient in private markets. These are markets where buyers and sellers directly negotiate price. For example, Lockheed might sell aircraft to both TWA and Southwest Airlines. If TWA has an NOL carryforward, the benefits from MACRS depreciation are minimal. So, Lockheed might arrange to make the price lower (higher) to TWA (Southwest) to equilibrate the posttax prices. Other negotiations can occur to transfer benefits between buyer and seller. For example, Lockheed can lease the aircraft to TWA. Here, Lockheed owns the property and can take depreciation on it (while also recognizing lease income), and TWA makes lease payments, which can be lower than loan payments.

EXAMPLE 5.11

Assume a firm sells mainframe computers for $1 million. The equipment has an expected life of five years. Firms can either buy the computers outright or lease them over six years. Ignoring interest, a cash-flow analysis is as follows (assume a 10% cost of capital):

Purchase

Year	Cash flow item	35% bracket	NOL
1	Purchase price: <$1,000,000>	<$1,000,000>	<$1,000,000>
1	Depreciation: $1,000,000(.20)(.9091)*	181,000	—
2	Depreciation: $1,000,000(.32)(.8264)*	264,000	—
3	Depreciation: $1,000,000(.192)(.7513)*	144,000	—
4	Depreciation: $1,000,000(.1152)(.6830)*	79,000	—
5	Depreciation: $1,000,000(.1152)(.6209)	72,000	—
6	Depreciation: $1,000,000(.0570)(.5645)	33,000	—
* Cash flow multiplied by tax bracket		<$227,000>	<$1,000,000>

Lease

1→6	Lease payments: ($1,000,000/6)(4.353)**	<$472,000>	<$ 726,000>

** Cash flow multiplied by 1 − tax bracket

Example 5.11 illustrates that if the buyer is in a tax-paying position, purchasing is better; in an NOL-carryforward situation, the buyer is better off leasing. If the seller knows that the buying firm is in an NOL-carryforward situation, it is more likely, given these facts, to obtain business if it offers a lease. If it knows the buyer is in a tax-paying situation, it should offer a purchase. Providing a similar cash-flow analysis might help persuade the buyer.

Other pricing methods of promotion include coupons (discounts) and rebates. For tax purposes, they simply reduce reported sales revenue when exercised. For financial-accounting purposes, they are recognized (accrued) as expenses when issued, based on an estimate of how many will be exercised.

One other aspect of promotion should be mentioned: free samples. As long as they are small, they are tax free to the recipient and tax deductible to the firm. However, in most jurisdictions the firm must clearly designate (in its records) the items as promotional and not as business gifts. (In the United States, for example, gifts can only be deducted up to $25 per year per recipient.)

Beyond the consumer, taxes can be negotiated with a new product at any point in the value chain, including suppliers (both equipment and materials), workers, and managers, as shown in Exhibit 5.7.

If suppliers have in a high tax status, they can save taxes by selling to the firm on an installment basis. Here, taxes are due as payments are made. (However, recent U.S. law changes have severely restricted this benefit for most retailers.) This has a cash-flow advantage to the firm, also. Alternatively, the firm can agree to such an arrangement subject to other favorable terms, such as a lowered price. If suppliers are in a low bracket (e.g., an NOL-carryforward situation), accelerating purchases to them may result in a lower purchase price. Note that such negotiations depend on market power. For example, a retail giant like Wal-Mart is large enough to obtain such concessions from its suppliers, whereas a smaller purchaser may not be so successful, especially with larger suppliers. (See Example 5.12.)

EXHIBIT 5.7   Negotiating Taxes through Prices: New Products

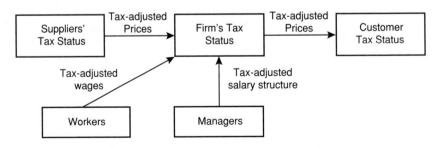

EXAMPLE 5.12

For example, a firm buys $1 million in inventory annually from a relatively small supplier. Purchases are typically made four times a year: March, June, September, and December, in $250,000 installments. Suppose a supplier, currently in the 35% tax bracket, will go into an NOL carryforward status next year. If the firm has a 50% profit margin, making the sale in January (vis-à-vis the normal time of December) would yield:

	Payment made in	
	December this year	January next year
Gross Profit	$250,000(.5) = 125,000	$250,000(.5) = 125,000
Tax	.25(125,000) <32,000>	0
Net cash flow	$ 93,000	$125,000

If the supplier's discount rate is 12%, the month's delay means the January payment is worth 1% less, or $124,000. Still, the advantage of $125,000 − $93,000 = $32,000 is large. This is the amount of tax savings that the supplier should be willing to pass on to the firm in the form of a lower purchase price. Of course, the firm must weigh the costs of having a one-month delay in inventory (e.g., risk of stockouts).

If the firm is in a low tax status, it may prefer to pay employees deferred compensation. Alternatively, if workers are in a relatively high tax brackets, they may prefer tax-advantaged components of their compensation. This could include special pension, medical, and dental plans. (Note that the firm's cash outflows for such items also may be deferred.) The firm may be able to provide less cash compensation in return. Management, in particular, may be amenable to such deferred compensation schemes as stock options, which generate limited (or deferred) tax deductions to the firm, but the firm may need to pay less overall compensation as a result.

Machinery and equipment buyers can be negotiated with by using sales versus leases, installment sales, and componentization of purchase prices. Leases can be used if the buyer is in a low tax bracket. The same is true for installment sales. By providing tax benefits to the buyer, the selling firm may be able to negotiate a higher sales price.

Splitting the purchase price into components also can save taxes. An example of componentization of purchase prices is a computer equipped with software. Bundled, the entire purchase price is depreciated in the United States over five years (MACRS life for a computer). Separated, the software can be written off over much shorter periods. Other examples include structures (such as hotels, pubs, and retirement homes) that contain furniture and fixtures that can be written off over a much shorter life than the building. (See Example 5.13.)

EXAMPLE 5.13

Suppose a U.S. firm sells personal computers for $2,000 each, $500 of which is attributable to software. If a purchasing firm is in the 35% tax bracket, tax benefits of lump sum versus segregated sales prices are as follows (assume a three-year software MACRS life):

Tax Savings on Depreciation*

Year	Aggregate	
1	2000(20.0%)(.35)(.9091) =	127
2	2000(32.0%)(.35)(.8264) =	185
3	2000(19.20%)(.35)(.7513) =	101
4	2000(11.52%)(.35)(.6830) =	55
5	2000(11.52%)(.35)(.6209) =	50
6	2000(5.76%)(.35)(.5645) =	23
		541

Year	Separate	
1	Computer (20.0%)(.35)(.9091)(1500) =	95
	Software (33.33%)(.35)(.9091)(1500) =	53
2	Computer (32.0%)(.35)(.8264)(1500) =	139
	Software (44.45%)(.35)(.8264)(500) =	64
3	Computer (19.20%)(.35)(.7513)(1500) =	76
	Software (14.81%)(.35)(.7513)(500) =	19
4	Computer (11.52%)(.35)(.6830)(1500) =	41
	Software (7.4%)(.35)(.6830)(500) =	9
5	Computer (11.52%)(.35)(.6209)(1500) =	38
6	Computer (5.76%)(.35)(.5645)(1500) =	17
		551

* Assume 10% cost of capital

The difference, $10, is an amount that can be directly part of the negotiated sales price.

In the United States, an important item often overlooked by many firms—at a substantial cost—is sales and use tax. If fixed assets are purchased for resale or to be used in the manufacturing process, suppliers should not charge sales or use tax. However, they often do so. The firm should negotiate directly with the suppliers to make sure this does not occur.

Transforming

There are few opportunities for the firm to convert sales income into tax-favored capital gains. However, if a new product turns out to be unsellable, all costs of unsold inventory, supplies, and equipment can be written off as ordinary losses. (See Example 5.14.)

EXAMPLE 5.14

Suppose a company purchases $1 million of specialized equipment to make a new product. If the product fails, and the machine is unsaleable, the firm can write off the machine that year. In the 35% tax bracket, this is a $350,000 cash inflow, which is much higher than the NPV of writing off the machine over five or seven years.

Firms seeking conversion can try using the *collapsible corporation* technique. Here, instead of selling products individually, a product is developed in an entity and the entity is sold. Classic examples are having a corporation make a film, develop software, or purchase a cellar of newly bottled wine. When the film is finished, the software works, or the wine is sufficiently aged, they are not sold directly. Instead, the common stock of the corporation is sold.

In many jurisdictions, this is treated like any other sale of securities: as tax-advantaged capital gains. In the United Stastes, however, IRC Section 341 was enacted over 50 years ago to reclassify most gains as ordinary income. The rules here are extremely complicated as noted in Chapter 1, Section 3411e)(1) is one of the longest sentences in the code.

As also noted, however, U.S. antiabuse provisions like the collapsible corporation rules provide a road map to sophisticated income tax planning in other jurisdictions (most of which have legal systems abhorring such statutory complexity).

SAVANT AND RESEARCH AND DEVELOPMENT

Because R&D is risky, managers sometimes like to separate it into a separate entity (such as a subsidiary corporation or an LLC). This can get the R&D off the parent company's financial statements, which may also be useful for hiding R&D from competitors. Generally accepted accounting principles (GAAP) in some countries (like the United States), however, limit the ability to shift items (like R&D excuse or debt) off statement.

If an R&D subsidiary corporation is used, the related tax benefits will not be recognized unless either the subsidiary has income or a consolidated (or combined) tax return can be filed with the parent. If one of these two situations is not present, or is too costly to create, the parent instead may want to set up an R&D flow-through entity, like an LLC, so that tax benefits flow through to the parent. Outside investors can also join in the LLC because tax benefits may be sufficient to attract low-cost capital.

In terms of timing and time value, the firm may want to perform R&D in years without NOL carryforwards.

Transactions costs include acquisition of special equipment and hiring of research personnel. These costs may be eligible for the credit plus a deduction. Because tax benefits decrease the real cost, the firm may be able to offer to pay more than market price for R&D (e.g., to attract a top scientist).

One additional time-value strategy relates to R&D equipment. In the United States, it can be depreciated over three years, whereas most equipment is depreciated over five or seven years. (See Example 5.15.)

EXAMPLE 5.15

A biotech company located in the United States buys a mainframe computer for $10 million, which it will use to identify compounds that can treat diseases. The cost of the computer can be depreciated over three years as R&D equipment; if it were used for non-R&D purposes it would be written off over five years. Assuming a 10% cost of capital and a 35% tax bracket, the tax benefits are $(.152)(.35)(\$10\text{ million})(.6209) + (.0576)(.35)(\$10\text{ million})(.5645) = \$250,347 + \$113,803 = \$364,150$ or 4% of the purchase price. (Refer to the bottom half of Example 5.13 for calculations).

TECHNICAL INSERT 6.1   MAXIMIZING THE R & D TAX CREDIT

Rules

A nonrefundable U.S. tax credit is available for incremental research expenses paid or incurred in a trade or business under IRC Section 41(h)(1). Credits that cannot be used due to insufficient taxable income can be carried over. The amount of the research credit that remains unused at the end of the carryforward period is allowed as a deduction under Section 196 in the year following the expiration of that period. Such deduction does not apply to unused amounts claimed under the reduced research credit election of Section 280C(c)(3).

The credit is the sum of (1) 20% of the increase in qualified research expenses for the current tax year over a base amount for that

TECHNICAL INSERT 6.1 (CONTINUED)

year, and (2) 20% of a university's basic research payment. For purposes of item (1), the base amount is computed by multiplying the taxpayer's fixed-base percentage by the taxpayer's average gross receipts for the four preceding tax years. A taxpayer's fixed-base percentage is the ratio that its total qualified research expenditures for 1984 through 1988 bears to its total gross receipts for that period with a maximum ratio of 0.16. Startup companies are currently assigned a fixed-base percentage of 3%.

For purposes of item (2), the amount of basic research payments equals the excess of (a) such basic research payments over (b) the qualified organization base period amount. Basic research payments that do not exceed the qualified organization base period amount are treated as contract research expenses for purposes of the incremental research credit unit item (1), according to IRC Section 41(e)(1)(B).

Finding More Credits

Managers frequently misclassify R&D expenses as something else. For example, specialized computer software that is used in R&D may be misclassified as general and administrative expense. Consultants can potentially save an enormous amount of tax dollars by examining client records to see if reclassification is possible (indeed, all of the Big Four accounting firms perform this service).

CHAPTER 6

Attracting and Motivating Employees and Managers: Company and Employee Tax Planning

There is something sacred about wages.

—Henry Ford, *My Life and Work*

Although direct wages form the vast bulk of employer payments, a multitude of schemes have been used for compensating employees. These plans all have the same basic goal: to improve labor productivity over that derived from simply paying wages. However, they reflect two fundamental approaches to accomplishing this. The first is based on better matching rewards with employee needs. Some of these schemes—such as lifetime employment—are rooted in the classical economist's conception of the diminishing marginal utility of money. Others—such as job enrichment and job sharing—are more specifically based on the perceptions of differences in employees' desires as they become more wealthy or secure, as suggested by management theories like Maslow's Hierarchy of Needs.

The second fundamental approach is to align employee performance more with a firm's strategic goals. Some of these plans, such as piecemeal bonuses for machinists or assembly-line workers, reflect Taylor's conception of the value of rewarding measures of enhanced tangible output. Bonuses for managers, such as those based on Drucker's theory of Management by Objectives, instead increasingly have been targeted at specific, less tangible objectives. These have often been developed during the firm's strategic planning process, sometimes by the managers themselves.

Taxes have also been a key factor in designing nonwage forms of employee compensation. This has particularly been the case when the need to attract and motivate managers is paramount. As with investments, it is not just what one earns that matters, but also what one keeps. It is the expected *after-tax* net present value of an employee's total compensation that matters. Using the SAVANT framework, this chapter explores differential tax treatments of nonwage forms of employee compensation. This is done with an eye toward enhancing worker productivity and the net present value of an employee's compensation at the least after-tax cost to employers.

EXECUTIVE COMPENSATION

Schemes for compensating executives have become quite important in many companies' strategic plans. This may be because executive talent has become increasingly scarce as firms have become more complex, causing firms to compete for talent at the top by offering lucrative compensation packages. The scope of these packages can be seen in annual surveys reported in the business press. For example, in a January 22, 2002, press release, the Economic Research Institute (which among other things publishes the Executive Cash Compensation Index) contrasted cash compensation in 1968 with that of 2001. This was done for both the highest paid executives and the average worker in a sample of about 50 of the most prominent U.S. firms. This survey indicated that the highest paid executive earned an average of nearly $800,000 in 1968 versus under $6,000 for the average worker. In 2001, the executive's compensation rose to an average of $3.5 million. (The highest amount was nearly $17 million for the CEO of General Electric.) This was compared with just a little over $33,000 for workers.

The bulk of top executives' compensation has increasingly been through noncash items, however. For example, the Paywatch section of the Web site of one of the world's leading labor unions—the AFL-CIO—contrasts the average total compensation of the CEOs of major corporations with that of the average worker. On January 20, 2002, it reported that for 2000 these CEOs averaged $20 million in total compensation. Specifically listed were five-year totals of nearly $100 million, $150 million, and $220 million for the CEOs of Bank of America, Conseco, and Sprint, respectively. The average CEO's compensation was over 500 times the total compensation for the average blue-collar worker, and over five times the cash compensation presented in the survey (albeit of a different and smaller group, and in the previous year) discussed in the preceding paragraph.

The results of surveys like these can vary because compensation packages for managers differ widely. They often consist of a mix of factors thought to match both employees' and employers' varying needs. The array of factors can be generalized, however, into six basic components:

1. Annual base wages
2. Year-end bonuses, based on company financial performance measures, such as net income or economic value-adding (EVA)
3. Long-term equity participation, most commonly through stock options
4. Deferred compensation
5. Enhanced retirement and other fringe benefits
6. Employment security arrangements, such as employment contracts and golden parachutes (payments triggered by changes in the firm's ownership)

There are advantages and disadvantages to each component in satisfying employee needs and motivating labor productivity. For example, salary can be adjusted annually. But because it is contracted for ahead of time, it is not ideal as a direct motivator for future performance. Annual bonus payments can fill this role better, particularly if tied to attaining specific strategic objectives for the year. Equity compensation may be more preferable, particularly for senior executives, because the most important objectives may be long term in nature, and because the rewards are congruent with the basic shareholder goals of enhancing the value of the firm's shares.

In addition, components are taxed in different ways. Stock options have a strong incentive effect: If the firm does well, its stock price should increase, as should the value of options to purchase its stock at a fixed price. As discussed in the Stock Options section of this chapter, stock options are also tax advantaged. In the SAVANT framework, this results primarily from anticipation (timing) and transforming characteristics.

NONEXECUTIVE EMPLOYEE COMPENSATION

Before employee compensation packages are discussed, it is important to distinguish the tax treatment of employees from that of nonemployees (contract labor). Periodically, firms will hire temporary help in production (e.g., construction contractors) or administration (e.g., accountants or temporary secretaries). Firms also enter into ongoing agency-type relationship (e.g., sales agents or attorneys on retainer). The trend among large U.S companies in recent years has been toward outsourcing a wide variety of administrative jobs. For tax purposes, these arrangements are considered nonemployee relationships.

One nontax advantage of such relationships is that the firm may not have to pay employee-type benefits to these individuals. In some countries this is required, at least for those working half time. In jurisdictions like the United States, a company does not have to provide medical, dental, or pension benefits, nor are wages automatically subject to union negotiation. Another nontax advantage is flexibility: A firm can easily and more quickly dismiss or hire temporary employees when needed.

Nonemployee compensation typically is deductible just like employee compensation. The only major tax difference, which can be significant, is employment taxes. For U.S. employees, for example, the firm must pay the following:

- FICA (national pension and disability benefits) tax: 6.2% on the first $84,000 of wages for 2002; indexed for inflation in subsequent years
- Medicare (old age medical benefits) tax: 1.45% of all wages
- FUTA (national unemployment benefits) tax: 6.2% on first $7,000 of wages (this amount can partly reduce state unemployment taxes)
- State unemployment taxes: 1–15% (base amount varies by state and rate varies by state and experience)

As noted in Chapter 1, a good gateway Web site to find sites listing tax rates and tables throughout the world is *www.taxsites.com*.

Not only are these direct costs (i.e., value reducing) to the firm, they also entail transactions costs. Record keeping must occur for each employee for each of these taxes and also includes a host of information related to a worker's status as an employee. An example would be amounts withheld from each employee's compensation to be remitted to governments for personal income taxes.

Employment taxes have little impact with respect to executives. For other employees, it can make a cost difference to the employer. This is shown in Example 6.1.

EXAMPLE 6.1

Suppose a company can hire either one upper level manager for $120,000 or two middle managers for $60,000 each. The U.S. employment tax consequences in 2002 would be

		Middle Manager	
	Upper Manager	**Manager One**	**Manager Two**
FICA	7.65%($84,000) = $6,426	7.65%($60,000) = $4,590	7.65%($60,000) = $4,590
FUTA	6.2%($7,000) = 434	434	434
	$6,860	$5,024	$5,024

$10,048

In this simplified example, the employer saves over $3,000 in employment taxes by using one employee instead of two. The savings is about 2.5% of payroll costs. Over a number of employees, this could result in considerable employment tax savings. Note that this example ignores the U.S. Medicare tax, which would be the same in both settings.

Even more employment tax savings might be obtained by having workers classified as self-employed contractors instead of employees. This is hard to accomplish for ongoing jobs, however. Under U.S. law, for example, an employer-employee relationship automatically exists if the firm for whom the services are performed has a right to control and direct the service-performing individuals. This rule is quite expansive. For example, only the right to control, not actual control, is required. The control must extend to the outcome of the work, and to the details and means by which the work is accomplished, however. Factors commonly referred to in testing for employee status are furnishing a place to work, furnishing tools, and right to terminate. These rules apply regardless of whether an individual also is a partner in an organization, an officer or manager, or a substitute for a person normally considered an employee. In most jurisdictions, there is a strong bias against denying mandated employment benefits by trying to reclassify traditional employees as independent contractors.

Attempting to do so also might be a poor tax strategy. Although the firm may pay less in *direct* taxes for independent contractors, it may pay more in *implicit* taxes. To see this, consider a person who has a choice between working in the United States as independent contractor or as an employee. Suppose that, as an employee, the worker would get an annual salary of $60,000. Under U.S. law, one-half of the total Social Security taxes for the worker would be paid by the employer (the employee pays the other half through withholding). Self-employed workers are required to pay both halves of the tax. Were the worker self-employed, wouldn't he require at least the same $60,000 plus the one-half of the Social Security tax he now would have to pay as self-employment tax? Of course, what a firm hiring him as a contractor would actually be willing to pay would depend on negotiation (involving the relative market power of labor versus industry and the like).

Under the definition already given, people in certain professions are almost always considered independent contractors. This includes professionals who offer their services to the public, such as auctioneers, construction contractors, dentists, doctors, freelance professional models, lawyers, public stenographers, and veterinarians. However, such professional status actually works to ensure that payroll taxes are paid by the professional firm. Indeed, firms providing technical personnel (such as engineers, computer programmers, and systems analysts) to clients likely will classify even temporary workers as employees.

EXHIBIT 6.1   Employee Leasing Arrangements

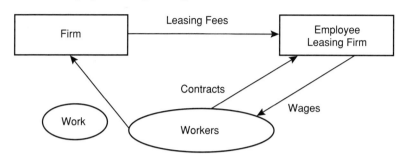

One way to reduce employment and transaction costs related to employment is through employee leasing. Here, a company hires whomever they want, but leases the employees from a company which specializes in doing so. This is depicted in Exhibit 6.1.

Here, the firm pays only (tax-deductible) leasing fees to the leasing firm and is not responsible for employee benefits or payroll taxes. Instead, the leasing firm pays such costs. In many cases, leasing firms provide a lower level of benefits because these firms are smaller, newer, or less unionized. If so, these lowered costs can be passed on to buyers in the form of lower leasing fees. Managers should bear in mind, however, that while leasing may appear to be cost effective, it may not make good business sense. This is because (especially if done to an extreme) there is potentially less control over employee availability, effort, and skill. In addition, firms lose some of the advantages of long-term employee status: innovation, risk taking, and loyalty.

Another way to reduce costs is by controlling the unemployment tax rate. Such rates, set by states in the United States, are highly influenced by experience. That is, rates are higher for employers that have unemployment claims against them or have a history of hiring and then laying off large numbers of employees. Firms can thus reduce costs by reducing the number of employee dismissals. Many states also allow firms to apply to get lower rates. For a new business, unemployment tax rates are generally high. If the firm is a successor—that is, it has bought another firm—it may be able to get a lower rate based on the history of the acquired firm.

In the nonexecutive compensation area, firms can reduce taxes if they take advantage of tax breaks related to hiring new employees. These are usually targeted at high unemployment populations. In the United States, for example, there is a federal welfare-to-work tax credit. Given to the employing firm, it can be seen in Exhibit 6.2.

This law defines qualified employees as a "long-term family assistance recipient" who is certified by a designated local agency. Thus, there is an implicit cost to the tax benefits: The persons being hired may be far less

EXHIBIT 6.2   Example of Tax Benefits from Hiring New Employees

First year for each employee: 35% of the first $10,000 of wages
Second year for each employee: 50% of the first $10,000 of wages

For example, suppose a firm hires 10 qualified employees for $15,000. The firm retains nine of them for at least two years. The credit is:

Year hired: 10($10,000 × 35%) = $35,000
Next year: 9($10,000 × 50%) = $45,000

productive than typical new hires. Also, as is common with creditable expenses, the deduction for wage expense is net of the amount that generates the credit.

Employee Compensation Packages

An important concept in compensation tax planning is that firms are generally indifferent to compensation types. This is because firms get ordinary income tax deductions regardless of the form of the compensation. From the employee's tax perspective, however, there may be differences.

Forms of compensation can be categorized in several ways. Important categories are cash or noncash, and being paid currently or deferred, as shown in Exhibit 6.3.

For the most part, noncash benefits available to all employees are not taxed to the employee (i.e., to be tax free, benefits must be nondiscriminatory between types of employees). The higher the employee's tax rates, the more noncash perquisites are preferred. In addition to exclusion from income taxes, nonwage compensation is often also exempt from payroll taxes (e.g., the Medicare tax in the United States). Of course, each employee has distinct needs, which may or may not include tax minimization. To allow such choices, some companies have so-called cafeteria plans, whereby employees can choose among salary and a variety of benefits.

Compensation packages and tax status interact, as shown in Example 6.2.

EXHIBIT 6.3   Various Components of Compensation

Cash		Non-Cash	
Current	**Deferred**	**Current**	**Deferred**
Salary/Wages	Pension Plan	Medical	Life insurance
	Profit-sharing	Dental	
	Stock option	Meals	
	Bonus	Education	
		Other perquisites	

EXAMPLE 6.2

Suppose a firm offers the following to an employee as part of a cafeteria plan:

Package Component	Annual Value
Salary	$60,000
plus any two of following:	
Stock option—expected capital gain	10,000
Year-end bonus—expected value	10,000
Medical, dental coverage—value	10,000
Group term life insurance—value	10,000

That is, in addition to salary the employee can chose up to $20,000 in other benefits. The tax impacts in the United States are capital gain at 20% (or 10% if the employee's ordinary income tax rate is 15%) on the stock option, bonus taxable when received at ordinary tax rates medical/dental coverage tax free, and group term life insurance (up to $50,000) tax free.

Which would the employee chose? Because the medical-dental and the life insurance are taxfree, they are each equivalent to receiving (if the employee is in the 28% bracket), $10,000/(1 − .28) = $13,888, being taxed on this amount, and using the remaining $10,000 to buy the insurance or medical + dental. Unless the employee can obtain either type of benefit for less than $13,888—doubtful, considering the cost advantages a company has in purchasing such policies at the group level—it is little wonder why companies offer such benefits. (This example ignores the time value of money. In reality, the stock option would be exercised, and the stock sold, in different years, which would require an NPV analysis.)

The choice of stock option versus bonus primarily turns on the employee's tax rate and discount rate. If the employee has a tax rate above 20%, then the stock option is tax favored, because it has a reduced (e.g., 20%) tax rate. The decision also depends on when the option can be exercised and the stock sold. If the employee has a 10% discount rate, what would be the maximum time the employee would be willing to wait to make the option equivalent to a bonus? If the employee's tax rate was 36%, the employee would balance the after-tax result of the bonus with that of the option, as follows (N is the number of years):

$$\$10,000 \times (1 - .36) = \$10,000 \times (1 - .20) \times (1/(1 + .1)^N)$$

$$6400 = 8000 \times (1/(1 + .1)^N)$$

$$.80 = (1/(1 + .1)^N)$$

$$N \cong 1 \text{ year}$$

This suggests that if the employee must wait for over a year to exercise the option, the employee would prefer the bonus. Of course, this is just one example. Often, the value of an option is considerably higher than a bonus. In addition, usually a number of years must pass before possible exercise.

From the employee's perspective, choosing between current and deferred compensation is an application of anticipation (timing). For example, pension plans make income taxable in later tax years (which is often when employees are in lower tax brackets). Choosing noncash over cash compensation is transforming (from taxable to tax free) and, potentially, negotiation. For the latter, the employee can negotiate higher pay by switching to (from) perquisites (salary) in low tax (high tax) years. (See Example 6.3.)

EXAMPLE 6.3

An employee normally in the 28% bracket has $100,000 of cash salary and no tax-free perquisites. If her tax bracket goes up to 36% (for example, due to outside investment income), it may be worthwhile for her to negotiate with her employer to substitute some of her taxable salary for tax-free benefits.

Using the SAVANT framework, the following discusses certain forms of compensation from the firm's perspective.

PERQUISITES

The nature of the firm's industry determines its labor-capital intensity. Because the form of compensation is irrelevant to tax deductibility, the after-tax price that the company pays for labor is really a constant percentage of pretax wage rates. (These, in turn, are a function of the specifics of the firm, nature of the industry, and other non-tax factors.)

To see why the firm is usually indifferent regarding the tax aspects of compensation, refer back to the facts in Example 6.3. The stock option, year-end bonus, medical + dental, and life insurance policies all become $10,000 deductions to the firm. If the firm is in the 35% bracket, each generates $3,500 of tax savings. The only difference in the items is the timing of the deduction for the stock option during which the employee exercises the option. This may happen in a year when the firm is in a different tax bracket.

An additional factor to consider is if the employee lets the options lapse. That is, what if the employee does not exercise them? If they were given to the employee for free, there is no tax consequence. However, if the employee paid for the option, the loss is a deductible capital loss. (As a general note, options on any type of asset are considered capital assets.)

There are transaction costs associated with noncash compensation: Pension plans need trusts and trustees; medical plans need administration. All involve additional paperwork and employees' time.

In deciding on cash versus perquisites, the firm's strategy should be considered. In the long run, is it important that employees be retained? If employee performance of skilled jobs is a crucial success factor (e.g., in airlines or software companies), retaining employees to preserve investment in human capital may be important. Attracting and motivating employees may be important, which implies a need to at least have some benefits plans to supplement cash compensation.

The firm should anticipate some changes in tax rules, too. For example, in since 1983 there has been an increasing trend in the United States for rules that tax fringe benefits. Also, except for defined benefit pension plans (which are discussed later), the direct effects on the firm's financial net income are expenses that, except for minor timing differences, follow the tax expense. That is, for tax purposes, fringe benefits are deducted when paid, while financial accounting rules typically provide for experience-based accruals of fringe benefits (called OPEBs). The accruals, over time, approximate cash-based tax deductions.

PENSION AND PROFIT SHARING PLANS

Pension plans can be defined benefit or defined contribution. The latter fixes the firm's contribution per employee each year. The former requires the firm to make contributions based on actuarial estimates of company-wide expected retirements, life expectancies, and other factors. Because of the transactions costs (for example, hiring actuaries) and value-adding impact (an accrued pension plan funding liability may occur on the firm's balance sheet), defined benefit plans have become increasingly less common.

Under a defined contribution plan, the employer makes annual contributions to a trust account set up for the benefit of the employees. Often this is about 10% of covered employees' gross wages. At the same time, employees typically make their own contributions to the plan. These contributions are normally excluded from each employee's current taxable income. The firm's contributions (typically about 5% of gross wages for eligible employees) are effectively deductible because the contributions from gross wages before income taxes are determined. The transaction is shown in Exhibit 6.4.

The contributions earn a return in the pension trust, which is not taxed. Trusts can be managed by financial institutions (such as banks), but are more often managed by large financial intermediaries, such as Dryfus or Fidelity. In the United States, employees can put in a maximum of 5% of wages plus $11,000 per year; employers, the lesser of (1) 100% of employee's

EXHIBIT 6.4   Contribution Flows in Company-Based Pension Plans

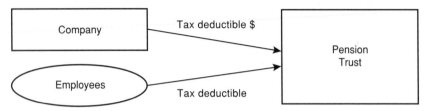

wages (up to $200,000, indexed for inflation), or (2) $40,000 (indexed for inflation) per year, for each employee. (See Example 6.4.)

EXAMPLE 6.4

Under a company's defined contribution pension plan, 5% of wages are paid into the plan by the company, and the employee matches this. If an employee earns $40,000 per year, her employer pays $2,000. The employee's contribution of $2,000 is tax excludible, that is, she pays current income taxes on only $38,000 of wages.

Contributions to pensions are tax deferred, not tax free. Contributions are normally taxed just like wages when withdrawn by employees from pension funds. In exchange for tax-deferred status, there are limitations on the timing of withdrawals. In the United States, for example, there is an extra 10% excise tax on withdrawals made before the employee reaches the age of 59½, unless triggered by certain hardships (such as death, disability, or costs of medical care or higher education).

In addition, while employees can almost always withdraw their own contributions, only that portion of the employer's contributions that have vested can be accessed. Vesting usually does not occur until after three to five years of employment, and even then only with respect to part of the employer's contributions.

The primary benefits to the employee are: (1) tax-free accumulation until withdrawal, and (2) deferral of tax on part of the original wage income. These two occur even if the employee does not vest. After vesting, a third benefit is receiving additional money from the employer. (See Example 6.5.)

EXAMPLE 6.5

Assume an employee receives an annual salary of $60,000. The firm's defined contribution pension plan requires 5% (10%) contributions to the plan by the employee (employer). The plan earns 10% per year. The employee is in the 28% tax bracket. The rate of return, under various years of accumulation, assuming the employee is fully vested after five years, is as follows (where $k = \$1,000$):

Years of Accumulation	PV of Tax Benefit to Employee for Contribution	Accumulation* (vested)	PV of** Tax on Accumulation	Net Benefit to Employee
1	5%(60k)28% = $840	15%(60k) = $9,000($0)	—	TBA
5	5%(60k)28% (3.7908) = $3,190	15%(60k)(5) = 45k(45k)	—	TBA
25 (Retirement)	5%(60k)28% (9.077) = $7,625	15%(60k)(25) = 225k(225k)	<$7,452>	TBA

* Assumes that the employee's and the pension's discount rates are equal at 10%, and thus cash flows need not be adjusted for time value of money.

** Assumes, for one and five year scenarios, that funds are not prematurely withdrawn (and thus no tax and no 10% penalty apply). For the final year, assumes that the entire amount is received as a lump sum, putting the employee into the 36% tax bracket so that the tax is $(.36)(.092)(\$225,000) = \$7,452$.

As shown in this example, the longer an employee can stay in the pension plan, the higher the present value (PV) of wealth accumulation. The effect also is more pronounced the higher the employee's tax bracket is. (See Example 6.6.)

EXAMPLE 6.6

Suppose that an employee can contribute $5,000 per year to a pension fund, or invest it in a money market mutual fund, for 25 years. Assume both the mutual fund and the pension earn 10%. If the employee is in the 28% bracket, the two accumulations are

	Investment in—	
	Money Market	Pension
Annual (after-tax) investment 10% return, 25 years, compounded	$ 5,000 × (1 − .28) 9.077	$ 5,000 × (1 +.28) 9.077
Net accumulation	$32,677	$58,092
Tax at the end of year 25 (pension)(at 28% tax rate)	<0>	<16,266>
Net after tax wealth increase	$32,677	$41,826

From the firm's perspective, the cash-flow effect is the amount of the firm's contribution times 1, minus the firm's marginal tax rate. The nontax cost is the charge to financial-accounting earnings. The pension expense reduces both earnings per share (EPS) and economic value-added (EVA). In addition, any undercontributions (or amounts owed by the firm to the pension at year-end) are shown as liabilities on the firm's balance sheet.

On the plus side, any excess contributions are returnable to the firm. Because a number of employees usually do not stay long enough to vest, the firm effectively keeps some of its prior contributions. These excess funds can be either used to reduce required contributions the next year or reinvested tax free in the pension.

One interesting way in which pension funds are invested is to buy shares of the company's own stock. (See the discussion of employee stock ownership plans—ESOPs—later.) This reduces the number of shares publicly held, potentially motivates employees to work harder, and possibly acts as a deterrent to hostile takeovers. On the latter point, if employees own a large block of the company stock through the firm's pension plan, they are less likely to be receptive to an outsider's bid to buy their shares.

Profit-sharing plans are structured to pay employees a percentage of the firm's earnings each year, and are thought to motivate employees to focus more on the firm's bottom line. Employees can also share in profits by stock ownership. An indirect form of ownership is an employee stock ownership plan (ESOP). This is a trust controlled by the firm and its employees, which holds shares of the company's stock in participant employees' names. Employees can also own stock directly. A good example of this is United Airlines. Among the tax advantages of ESOPs in the United States are that dividend payments to employees are sometimes deductible by the firm, and the original granting of the stock is deductible. (See Example 6.7.)

EXAMPLE 6.7

Under its ESOP, each employee owns 10 shares of the company's common stock. When dividends are paid, these stay in the employee's account. They are not taxed to the employees until the money is withdrawn (for example, upon leaving the company or retirement).

CURRENT AND DEFERRED COMPENSATION

Most large U.S. companies have set up 401(k) plans, whereby the employee sets aside some salary into a retirement-type account. The amounts diverted to the plan are not taxed until withdrawn (e.g., upon termination, retirement, or disability), and earnings on the balance in the plan are also untaxed until withdrawn. Since the annual maximum an employee may contribute is only $11,000, (indexed annually for inflation) these plans are irrelevant to executive compensation.

LIMITS ON DEDUCTIBILITY ON EXECUTIVE COMPENSATION

Executive compensation comes typically in three forms: salary, bonus, and stock options. In the United States, the first two are taxed currently to the executive and are deductible currently to the firm. The deductibility and taxability of options depends on the type of option.

Publicly held corporations are denied deductions for the amount by which certain executives' annual compensation exceeds $1,000,000. This limit applies only to officers listed in the Security and Exchange Commission's (SEC's) Regulation S-K. Those listed are the company's chief executive officer (CEO) and the four other highest paid officers. The limit applies only to compensation that is not performance-based, and thus there is an opportunity for the firm and the executive to negotiate the tax benefit to the employer. Also, stock options can often be excluded from the limit if they meet certain criteria. The most important criterion is that they are performance based. One indication of this is when the original option price is below the stock-trading price at the time of the stock's issuance.

Another limit on executive compensation is the limited deductibility of so-called golden parachute payments. Frequently, executives enter into agreements to protect them from being fired in the event of a takeover by designating a large amount that must be paid if this happens. In the United States any lump sum that exceeds the executive's average base salary over the prior five years is nondeductible by the firm. The executive is also liable for a 20% excise on the excess. Because of these limits, firms often seek some other form of payment that is deductible (such as stock options) in lieu of excess parachute payments. (See Example 6.8.)

EXAMPLE 6.8

An executive's salary has averaged $2,000,000 per year for the last five years. If terminated, he would receive a lump-sum payment of $10,000,000. This would not be tax deductible by the firm if paid.

STOCK OPTIONS

Generally, the option process is as follows:

| Option granted to executive | ⇨ Executive exercises options (receives stock) | ⇨ Executive sells stock |

EXHIBIT 6.5   Tax Aspects of Qualified and Nonqualified Stock Options

	Option Granted	Option Exercized	Stock Sold
ISO			
Taxability to executive	None	None	Capital gain (sales price minus option cost)
Deduction to firm	None	None	None
Nonqualified			
Taxability to executive	If FMV known, FMV minus amount paid. Otherwise, none.	FMV of stock less amount paid	Capital gain (sales price minus previously taxed income)
Deduction to firm	Amount taxable to executive	Amount taxable to executive	None

The profit for the executive comes through sale of the stock. Tax deductibility and taxability have symmetric timing in the United States, depending on whether the option is a qualified stock option—that is, based on an incentive stock option plan (ISO)—or nonqualified. The tax treatment is shown in Exhibit 6.5.

As can be seen, ISOs are more tax beneficial to the executive, with two caveats. First, if substantial enough, the spread between the exercise price and the stock's fair market value (FMV) at the time of exercise is potentially subject to the alternative minimum tax (see Technical Insert 6.1). Second, there are time limits (for example, the stock cannot be transferred by the employee within one year of sale). In practice, for most publicly traded firms reasons such as these time limits result in a prevalence of nonqualified options.

From the corporation's perspective, tax deductibility of the nonqualified option makes it less costly. Of course, the tax status of both the employer and employee must be taken into account: see Exhibit 6.6 and Example 6.9.

EXHIBIT 6.6   Impact of Relative Tax Status on Optimal Form of Stock Option

		Tax Status of Executive	
		High	Low
Tax Status of firm:	High	Negotiated	Use nonqualified
	Low	Use ISO	Negotiate

EXAMPLE 6.9

Assume an executive is in the 38.6% tax bracket, and the firm in the 35% bracket. Assume the following actual and projected information:

Option Grant	Option Exercise	Stock Sale
1/1/98. To buy 10,000 shares at $50 each. Stock currently trading at $45. FMV of option = $1/share.	12/31/2000. Projected Market price = $60 per share.	12/30/2002. Projected sale at $65/share.

If the option is nonqualified, the firm gets a tax deduction for $10,000 = the FMV of the stock options. This is the amount taxable to the executive (a tax of $3,860), and the deduction to the firm (tax savings of $3,500). On exercise, the executive recognizes ($60 − $50 − $1)(10,000 shares) = $90,000 ordinary income, which translates into a $34,740 tax. The corporation gets a deduction for the same amount, which, at its 35% bracket, is a tax savings of $31,500. On exercise, the executive recognizes ($65 − 60) (10,000 shares) = $50,000 of capital gain, which results (at a 20% tax rate) in a tax of $10,000. The corporation gets no deduction. The total tax bill for the executive: $3,860 + $34,740 + $10,000 = $48,600. The total savings for the firm: $3,500 + $31,500 = $35,000.

Note that this example ignores time value. To be precise, one must compare the after-tax NPV for both the executive and the firm.

What if the firm in Example 6.9 had an NOL carryforward, which was expected to keep the firm out of a tax-paying position for a number of years? (This is not unusual for startup firms.) None of the $35,000 tax savings would occur. In this case, from a tax perspective the company is equally well off with an ISO. Also, the executive would be better off from a tax perspective.

How does the use of stock options fit into the SAVANT framework? In large part, the strategic objectives of the firm may be controlling. First and foremost, if the firm is privately held, often the owners do not want ownership given to outsiders such as executives. For publicly owned corporations, if the executive is important to the firm's long-run plans (e.g., Bill Gates of Microsoft), then stock ownership acts as a so-called golden handcuff to provide longer-run incentives. Also, given the huge run up in stock markets throughout the world over the last decade, the potential profit in options can be a source of attracting top managerial talent; however, middle management may be less important to the firm's strategy and less likely to receive options.

In terms of value-adding adjusted for risk, the cost of options to the firm and the executive are both higher. The firm's risk is higher if the executive does little to improve the company, but profits nonetheless due to a run up in the stock market. However, risk should be reduced because in principle the executive will only take actions that are perceived by the stock market to be value-adding. For the executive, there is risk of a downturn in the firm's stock unrelated to the executive's actions. (This risk has proven minimal in practice for a variety of reasons, not the least of which has been the propensity of firms to reset option prices when a downturn in the firm's share price eliminates the value of options previously granted, i.e., the options are *under water*.)

The tax attributes of even nonqualified options act as a risk premium. First, there is anticipation (timing and time value). Executives choose what year (e.g., when their tax brackets are the lowest) to exercise options and pay much of the tax later when the stock is sold. Second, there is transforming: in the United States, options allow what would have been ordinary compensation income (e.g., 36% bracket) to be converted to long-term capital gain (e.g., 20% bracket). With respect to anticipation, executives would want to time selling to years when the capital gain rate was expected to drop. In addition, executives would prefer to receive and exercise in years expected to have lower individual tax rates. (Note that while there are many countries where capital gains are lightly taxed, virtually no states tax capital gains at a lower rate than ordinary compensation income.)

In anticipating changes in tax rates, firms would want to issue options and have them exercised in a year of higher tax rates. (See Example 6.10.)

EXAMPLE 6.10

Refer to Example 6.9, and assume the executive receives nonqualified options. Suppose that at the time of issue the executive's bracket was 39.6%, but was expected to fall to 36% in 2001. In this case, the executive has the timing option of postponing exercise from 2000 to 2001. Assuming the market price in 2001 is also $60, the executive saves (39.6% − 36%)($60 − 50 − 1) (10,000 shares) = $3,240 in taxes. Also, because taxes are deferred for a year, assuming a 10% discount factor, the tax savings is really $3,240/.9091 = $3,564. (The extra $324 illustrates the time value of delaying tax.) In the original example, the $31,500 capital gain tax, which was deferred from 2000 to 2001, had a $31,500(1 − .8264) = $5,468 value associated with the delay of the tax. Finally, in the example, the ability to convert ordinary income into capital gains had transforming value as follows: (39.6% − 20%)($65 − 60 − 1)(10,000 shares) = $7,840 cash flow value to the executive.

One aspect of risk management for the firm relates to transformation. ISOs can be converted to nonqualified options, but the reverse is not true.

Thus one strategy for the firm would be to have its options initially meeting the ISO qualifications. Later, if it turns out to its advantage, the ISOs can always be disqualified (which is not difficult to do).

In terms of the financial reporting aspects of *value-adding*, under U.S. GAAP the firm must disclose in a footnote the value of stock options outstanding and not yet exercised by the executives. (See Example 6.11.)

EXAMPLE 6.11

Refer to Example 6.9. Suppose the firm can reasonably predict that its stock will be worth $65 in 2002, and this is about the time the executive will exercise. The real cost to the firm is ($60 − 50 − 1)(10,000 shares) = $90,000 before taxes. If the firm paid this in salary, the payment would reduce financial statement earnings (and also EPS) by $90,000 immediately.

There is no reduction under the option plan: The firm merely discloses the $90,000 cost off balance sheet (that is, in a footnote). When the option is exercised in 2000, the $90,000 compensation expense reduces earnings, and EPS also is diluted by the 10,000 increase in outstanding shares. The delay in earnings reduction may prove very valuable if the firm is about to issue additional shares or is close to violating debt covenants.

Negotiation is the *sine qua non* of options. Here, executives can negotiate tax aspects directly with compensation committees or boards of directors. (See Examples 6.12 and 6.13.)

EXAMPLE 6.12

Refer to Example 6.9, where the executive receives options for 10,000 shares. Suppose the remainder of the executive's compensation package is a salary of $300,000. Let the executive be in the 38.6% bracket, and be risk neutral (i.e., indifferent between salary that is certain and stock option gain that is speculative). Suppose also that she needs only $100,000 per year in cash flow for living expenses. If not, she should be willing to trade off an additional $200,000 salary for an equivalent value in stock options. The tax savings to the executive could be as high as $200,000(.386 − .20) = $37,200. However, NPV of the five-year delay associated with this is ($200,000 − $37,200) × (five-year factor of .6209) = $101,083 loss in PV.

Thus, in this case the tax delay, even when coupled with conversion, would be insufficient to induce the executive to substitute options for cash.

EXAMPLE 6.13

Assume the facts in Example 6.12, except that the firm has an NOL, which is expected to carry forward (and thus keep it out of a tax-paying situation) for a number of years. Although it would be indifferent from a tax perspective, the nontax benefits are clear: $200,000 cash flow is saved, and the firm's financial statements avoid an earnings charge until 2002. Given the firm's preference, how could it entice the executive to take options? The executive needs $101,083 more in after-tax NPV of options. The firm and executive can negotiate that.

Note that if the firm is in a tax-paying situation, for reasons already discussed it prefers salary to options. In such a case it should negotiate with executives to induce them to accept more salary.

The transactions costs of options involve extra legal fees related to wording the compensation contract. As a final note, stock options have become an increasingly popular form of compensation for celebrities and athletes, as discussed in the Tax Management in Action 6.1.

TAX MANAGEMENT IN ACTION 6.1

Stock Options among Athletes and Entertainers

Star athletes and entertainers have often used their names to endorse products. In recent years, a number of them have received stock options instead of cash compensation from the companies that they endorsed. For example, an April 7, 1997, article in *The Wall Street Journal* reported the following option deals for athletes (sport/company in parentheses):

- Michael Jordan (basketball/various companies)
- Cal Ripken Jr. (baseball/Oakley sunglasses)
- Kent Steffes (volleyball/Foothill 76s)
- Dale Earnhardt (NASCAR driver/Action Performance, Inc)
- Tiger Woods (golf/Official All Star Café—Planet Hollywood)
- Greg Norman (golf/Cobra Clubs)

Some entertainers with option deals are

- Jerry Seinfeld (NBC)
- Bryant Gumbel (CBS)

The lucrative nature of these contracts is exemplified by Greg Norman, who earned $40 million on a $2 million option when Cobra, Inc., went public and was subsequently acquired by American Brands, Inc.

MANAGEMENT BONUS PLANS

A significant portion of executive compensation comes through year-end bonuses. Such bonuses are typically tied to some financial-accounting performance measures. These include net income, operating income, or value-added. While tying performance to reward, bonuses may have two strategic disadvantages vis-à-vis options. First, they encourage short-run payoff projects. Second, they may encourage managers to manipulate accounting information to temporarily increase earnings.

In most jurisdictions, bonuses are taxed as ordinary income. Thus, unlike options there is no tax risk premium to adjust value-added for risk in bonuses. There is a time-value advantage, however. This is because bonuses are taxed when received. There is also a timing advantage. The firm can accrue an immediate tax deduction at year-end on the accrual, albeit in the United States the firm must actually pay the bonus within 2½ months of year-end. (Bonus agreements must be worded carefully to avoid recognition in the current period under the constructive receipt doctrine in jurisdictions that apply the doctrine.)

If the firm or the executives expect a change in tax status, then they can negotiate the timing. Suppose the firm expects a lower tax bracket next year, and the executive's tax bracket is to remain constant. Then the firm should be willing to pay the executive a slightly higher bonus if he is willing to accept the bonus this year. Transaction costs involve legal negotiations relating to the contract. Example 6.14 shows how the negotiating aspect can work.

EXAMPLE 6.14

Suppose a cash-basis firm is currently in the 34% bracket and expects to be in the 35% tax bracket the next year. If an executive's year-end bonus is $1,000,000, it is worth $1,000,000(.35 − .34) = $10,000 more to the firm if it can delay payment until early next year. This would be the maximum amount it would be willing to pay the executive to delay receipt.

A natural tension would arise in the above example if the executive's tax bracket also were due to increase next year. (See Example 6.15.)

EXAMPLE 6.15

Suppose in Example 6.14 that the executive's rate was due to go up to 38.6% from 36%. Then, the minimum the firm would need to offer the executive would be 2.6%($1,000,000)—$26,000 more—to accept the delay.

FINANCIAL STATEMENT/FINANCE VERSUS TAX STRATEGY TRADE-OFFS

For many firms, the form of executive compensation makes a nontax difference. Under U.S. GAAP, for example, such compensation expense reduces earnings. In addition, unexercised stock options are disclosed in footnotes, which the stock market or lenders may perceive as a potential dilution of ownership and EPS. When options are exercised, EPS is reduced by additional outstanding shares. In addition, reduction in earnings can potentially violate contracts (e.g., debt covenants), or reduce bond ratings. Also, if the firm plans an additional stock issue or bond float, the decrease in earnings may cause a reduction in proceeds. Accordingly, the financial accounting impact (in particular, the reduced earnings, net of reduced tax expense) may more than offset the financial accounting gain brought by enhanced executive performance.

How is the tax savings incorporated in financial statements? It is reflected as additional cash on the balance sheet and as reduced income tax expense on the income statement. (See Example 6.16.)

EXAMPLE 6.16

An executive exercises $1 million of nonqualified stock options. The company takes a tax deduction for $1 million. On the firm's financials, income tax (assuming the firm is in the 35% bracket) is reduced by $350,000.

Exhibit 6.7, Consultant's Interview, provides some insight into the relative importance of tax minimization versus financial statement impact for executive compensation planning.

EXHIBIT 6.7   Interview with Leading Compensation C.onsultant

CONSULTANT INTERVIEW

Dennis Ito
Western Regional Director, Personal Financial Services
KPMG Peat Marwick

How important are taxes in structuring Executive Compensation?
Generally, the executive is concerned about the total amount of compensation, when the compensation is received, and whether it will be subject to ordinary or capital gains tax rates. Generally, the employer is concerned about the timing and amount of the income tax deduction and relevant cash requirements, including payroll-withholding requirements.

An employee will generally view the deferral of compensation as a benefit particularly when he or she is otherwise paid a reasonable current salary and bonus and the value of the deferred payment increases by a reasonable rate of return. The value of deferring $1.00 before tax versus, $.55 after tax makes deferred compensation arrangements quite attractive when the creditor risk is manageable against the return paid on the deferred amounts. The securitization of deferred compensation arrangements using Rabbi Trusts is used frequently to mitigate the executive's fear of management changes to deferred compensation arrangements. A deferred arrangement is not necessarily received poorly by the employer as the employer now has a mechanism to *handcuff* the executive for several years.

In addition, the opportunity to obtain capital gain rates via Stock Option programs or restricted stock programs can be a significant motivator. For these executives, taking some equity risk is well worth the possibility of paying the difference between ordinary and capital gain tax rates (i.e., 39.6% versus 20% federal rates). This is particularly apparent with startup companies, but equally applicable within more mature companies poised for growth as well.

The employer will tend to have an affinity to Nonqualified Stock Option programs due to the favorable financial statement treatment and income tax deduction. Employers should also be concerned about the possible application of the *Golden Parachute* rules of IRC Section 280G as well as the $1 million limit on deductions for compensation paid to certain officers of publicly traded corporations under IRC Section 162(m).

At times some of the goals of the executive and the employer have cross-purposes, but usually an appropriate balance can be negotiated between the involved parties.

In startup companies, particularly those with IPOs, is there a fundamental difference in PFP that you do?
Companies contemplating an IPO present tremendous opportunities for the informed executive. All too often we find executives with vast numbers of incentive stock options and nonqualified stock options shaking their heads wondering why they did not exercise sooner. Of course, hindsight is always 20–20, so we should review the decision making process and then determine the reason the executive did not exercise earlier.

We seem to find at least one of the following: (1) They did not want to, read as they did not have the money, to exercise earlier; (2) they did not understand what they have received and how best to utilize the option effectively; (3) by the time it became clear that exercising was appropriate, the tax cost associated with the exercise (either ordinary income from the exercise of NQSOs or alternative minimum tax from the exercise of ISOs) was too expensive; and (4) because of 1, 2, or 3, or all, they decide to wait and do nothing until the time to exercise and sell via a cashless exercise. The rationale being that they have been at no equity risk, and can still take home a nice sum of cash, unfortunately less than they might have received had they made an earlier decision and net of a significant amount of ordinary income tax, but correctly so, without any equity risk.

For those that can afford to accept the equity risk, we encourage executives to negotiate an *early exercise* feature into their ISO and NQSO plans so that the income tax effect of the early exercise can be minimized.

The early exercise and a timely Section 83(b) election allows the informed executive the opportunity to start the capital gain holding period at little, if any, tax cost.

What are some important differences in PFP that you do for closely held versus publicly traded executives?
Generally, we do not see traditional ISO and NQSO programs within the closely held arena due to the lack of liquidity. Instead, alternative equity-based incentive programs or cash programs are more popular. If equity-based, either phantom-stock type programs or restricted stock purchase or bonus programs are popular. A most interesting challenge in building closely held executive compensation programs is incorporating an exit (i.e., liquidation) strategy for the executive. Conversely, if the closely held business owner is attempting to exit, then the challenge is in making the executive compensation program attractive enough to make a management buyout affordable. Due to the different business purposes involved, executive incentive compensation programs for the public company executive compared with the closely held executive are usually quite different in design. Lack of liquidity, valuation methodologies, and buy-sell issues become dominant features of a closely held company's executive compensation program.

How important are issues of negotiation (of tax benefits) and time value of money in your PFP practice?
More and more frequently we are representing the executives' interest in designing and negotiating more executive PFP sensitive programs. Whether the discussion concerns adding an early exercise feature, or making a timely Section 83(b) election, or inserting a *gross-up* feature in conjunction with planning to minimize excise taxes in a change of control situation, or making sure that the performance based programs satisfy the Treasury Regulation requirements, or adding a deferred compensation feature, or whatever, the usual discussion involves the maximization of allowed tax benefits, family wealth transfers techniques, deferral of income, and minimization of taxes.

PUTTING IT ALL TOGETHER:
APPLYING SAVANT TO EXECUTIVE COMPENSATION

You are on the compensation committee of a Fortune 500 company, and you are trying to hire a top executive away from a competitor. You estimate that the executive would bring $5 million per year of additional value-added to the corporation. Your firm has a tax NOL, which is due to expire this year. The company's financial earnings are positive. The executive's current compensation at the competitor firm is $1 million in salary. What sort of contract should be offered?

Strategy

Hiring the executive away from the competitor is a major strategic advantage. To keep her from going back to the competitor, a contract to tie her to the firm is needed; stock options may be the way to accomplish this goal.

Anticipation

You may want to assure her that your stock's value will go up in response to her performance, and that the firm anticipates no debt or equity issuance in the near future.

Timing and time-value issues   Again, because of the expiring NOL, timing of compensation to occur next year is best for the firm.

Value-Adding

The (after-tax expense) financial-accounting charge to earnings should not exceed $5 million per year, regardless of the form taken.

Adjusting for Risk   The fact that she has a pure cash contract at the competitor may indicate some risk aversion. Thus, some portion of the contract may have to be in cash.

Transactions Costs   You estimate it will cost $100,000 in legal and accounting fees to draw up a compensation package.

Negotiating

Because of the expiring NOL this year, you would prefer to defer more compensation until next year. This argues in favor of bonuses or options. However, you may have to pay her more to accept such deferred compensation. Also, the fact that she receives all-cash compensation currently may mean she is in a low bracket. In this case, she would see no tax advantage to stock options.

TECHNICAL INSERT 6.1 INCENTIVE AND NONQUALIFIED STOCK OPTIONS

Incentive Stock Options

The term *incentive stock option* is defined by IRC Section 422(b) as an option granted to an individual, for any reason connected with his

TECHNICAL INSERT 6.1 (CONTINUED)

employment, by the employer corporation (or its parent or subsidiary) to purchase stock of any such corporation, provided the following statutory conditions are satisfied:

- *Shareholder-approved plan.* The option must be granted under a plan specifying the number of shares of stock to be issued and the employees or class of employees to receive the options. The plan must be approved by the shareholders of the corporation within 12 months before or after the plan is adopted (IRC Section 422 (b)(1)).
- *Grant within 10 years of plan.* The option must be granted within 10 years of the date the plan is adopted or the date such plan is approved by the shareholders, whichever is earlier.
- *Ten-year life.* The option must, by its terms, be exercisable only within 10 years of the date it is granted (IRC Section 422(b)(3)).
- *Option price.* The option price must equal or exceed the FMV of the stock at the time the option is granted. IRC Sections 422(b)(4) and (c)(1) provide that this requirement shall be deemed satisfied if there was a good-faith attempt to value the stock accurately.
- *Nontransferability.* The option by its terms must be nontransferable by the employee except by will or the laws of descent, and distribution and must be exercisable during the employee's lifetime by the employee, (IRC Section 422(b)(5)).
- *Stock Ownership Limit.* The employee must not, immediately before the option is granted, own stock representing more than 10% of the voting power or value of all classes of stock of the employer-corporation or its parent or subsidiary (IRC Section 422(b)(6)). This limitation is waived under IRC Section 422(c)(6) if the option price is at least 110% of the FMV of the stock subject to the option and the option by its terms is not exercisable more than five years from the date it is granted.
- *Per-Employee annual Limit of $100,000.* The aggregate FMV of stock, determined when the option is granted, for which ISOs are exercisable for the first time, must be limited by the plan to $100,000 per calendar year, (IRC Section 422(d)). More than $100,000 worth of stock options exercisable in any one year may be granted to an employee, but only the first $100,000 can qualify as ISOs. Options in excess of the statutory ceiling are treated as nonqualified options.

TECHNICAL INSERT 6.1 (CONTINUED)

■ *Designation.* To facilitate granting total options exceeding the $100,000 ceiling while retaining qualified ISO status for options on the first $100,000 of stock, IRC Section 422(b) provides that stock options otherwise meeting the statutory requirements for the ISO treatment set forth in IRC Section 422(b) are not to be treated as such if the terms of the option at the time it is granted specifically provide that the option is not to be treated as an ISO under IRC Section 422.

Nonqualified Stock Options (NQSOs)

Options that are designated as not being ISOs by the grantor, or that do not meet the statutory criteria for ISO treatment, are NQSOs governed by IRC Section 83 (Treasury Regulations (Treas. Regs.) Section 1.83-7(a)). Thus, an option may be an NQSO because the employer prefers it to be or because the option's provisions automatically preclude ISO treatment (e.g., the option price is less than FMV at date of the grant, or the option will be exercisable for a period longer than 10 years).

The critical factor in determining the treatment of NQSOs is whether the option has a readily ascertainable FMV at the time of grant. If so, the grant of the option is subject to taxation (IRC Section 83(e)(3)). If not, IRC Section 83 will apply to the transfer of the stock at the time the option is exercised (IRC Section 83(a) and (b)).

IRC Section 83 is the basic statutory provision prescribing the tax effect of transfers of property in connection with the performance of services. It applies to options only if they have "a readily ascertainable FMV" (IRC Section 83(e)(3)). An option has a readily ascertainable FMV if it is actively traded on an established market. This is a truism of little practical use, because options with the price or duration terms of compensatory stock options are seldom traded. In the absence of an active market, the regulations provide that an option qualifies if its value can be measured "with reasonable accuracy." This is a standard that is satisfied only if (1) the option is transferable and is immediately exercisable in full by the optionee, (2) neither the option nor the underlying property is subject to restrictions or conditions having a significant effect on the option's FMV, other than a lien or other condition to secure payment of the purchase price, and (3) the FMV of the opportunity to benefit from appreciation in the underlying property during the life of the option without risking an capital can be measured with reasonable accuracy (Treas. Regs. Section 1.83-7(b)(2)).

TECHNICAL INSERT 6.1 (CONTINUED)

If an option succeeds in running this gauntlet, the employee is treated by IRC Section 83(a) as though his salary had been increased by the value of the option, requiring this amount to be included in gross income. Having paid his way, the employee thereafter has the status of an ordinary investor who purchased the option for cash at its FMV. This means that exercise of the option is a nontaxable event and that any other disposition of the option—sale, gift, transmission at death, or the like—is governed by the rules applicable to investors, rather than rules of IRC Section 83.

The transfer of an option without a readily ascertainable FMV when granted is not subject to IRC Section 83, but when the option is exercised, the transfer of the underlying property is Section 83. (Treas. Regs. Section 1.83-7(a)). This is in effect the mirror image of the treatment of options with a readily ascertainable FMV. Their transfer to the optionee is subject to IRC Section 83 while the subsequent transfer of the underlying property on exercise of the option is outside the aegis of IRC Section 83.

By rendering IRC Section 83 inapplicable to the compensatory transfer of options without a readily ascertainable FMV, IRC Section 83(e)(3) leaves their tax status to be determined under the *LoBue* case. This means that the grant of the option is not a taxable event. In subjecting the transfer of the property pursuant to the option of IRC Section 83, the regulations reach the same result as is reached under *LoBue* when the option is exercised. The excess of the FMV of the underlying property over the amount paid is includible in the gross income of the person who performed the services. The inclusion in gross income is required in the taxable year of the transfer, or in the first year thereafter when the recipient's rights in the transferred property become transferable or are free of any substantial risk of forfeiture. This is the same rule that applies to other types of restricted property subject to IRC Section 83.

If an unexercised option is sold in an arm's length transaction, the regulations specifically provide that the seller recognizes compensation income (Treas. Regs. Section 1.83-7(a)). No specific rules for other dispositions are provided, and transfers of options are subject to the general rules of IRC Section 83 that cover dispositions of restricted property (by sale, gift, transmission at death, or otherwise) before it becomes transferable or the risk of forfeiture terminates. Other triggering events are compensatory cancellations of restrictions that by

TECHNICAL INSERT 6.1 (CONTINUED)

their terms will never lapse, exchanges of restricted property in non-recognition transactions, and the employer's right to deduct the amount taxable to the person who performed the services (Treas. Regs. Section 1.421-6(d)(3)).

Tax Treatment of ISOs and NQSOs

The following table sets forth the tax effect of ISOs and NQSOs to the employee and the employer at three critical dates: grant, exercise, and sale.

	Income to Executive		Employer Deduction	
	ISO	NQSO	ISO	NQSO
Date of Grant	None	None	None	None
Date of Exericse	None	Ordinary Income	None	Ordinary deduction
Date of Sale	Capital Gain	Capital Gain	None	None

As the table shows, there are two primary advantages if the employee receives an ISO and holds the stock for the requisite time period. These are that income recognition is deferred until the stock is ultimately sold, and the entire appreciation over the option price is capital gain (Temporary (Temp.) Regs. Section 14a.422A-1, Q&A-1).

As noted in the table, the bargain element (FMV of stock at date of exercise less the exercise price) is a positive adjustment for alternative minimum taxable income (AMTI) in the year the option is exercised. (IRC 56(b)(3)).

If the ISO holding period requirements are violated (that is, the executive disposes of the stock before two years from the date of issue or one year from the date of exercise), this "disqualifying disposition" affects both the executive and the corporation. First, gain on the sale of the stock is ordinary income to the holder up to the amount of the bargain element, and any excess gain is capital gain. Second, the corporation is allowed a deduction for the ordinary income recognized.

If the employee receives an NQSO, income is deferred only to the date of exercise, and the bargain element is then taxable as ordinary income. Any further appreciation after exercise is capital gain when

TECHNICAL INSERT 6.1 (CONTINUED)

the stock is subsequently sold. Thus, the bargain element of the NQSO is subject to ordinary income tax at a time when the employee has received no cash from the transaction.

The tax treatment to the employer also differs for ISOs and NQSOs. The employer receives no deduction from the ISO transaction unless the employee disposes of the stock early and triggers ordinary income (IRC Section 421(b)). In contrast, the employer receives a deduction equal to the bargain element at the date of exercise of an NQSO. (IRC Section 83(h)).

CHAPTER 7

Market Penetration: Operating in Different States

The determination of the boundaries of a state's authority
to impose taxes on out-of-state companies has become an
increasingly contentious battlefield....

—Karl Frieden, *Cybertaxation*

In a survey by PricewaterhouseCoopers, corporate tax managers in the United States indicated that they spent 44% of their tax planning time on state and local tax issues. With a myriad of tax incentives and hidden taxes across states, strategic tax management at the state and local level has become increasingly important.

Most firms start out in one geographic area, then expand to other jurisdictions as local demand, costs, and marketing dictates. Indeed, one of the major impacts of the rise of electronic commerce has been the enhanced ability of small firms to reach foreign markets. The World Wide Web is one factor that has led to the end of distance in business transactions. Another one notable feature has been the emergence of the micro-multinational, that is, new organizations with little capital but global reach. Large firms may have physical operations in many states and decide to move into additional ones based on the same dictates. Or, they may do so for strategic presence: If Burger King opens restaurants in a new city, McDonalds may do so soon to avoid loss of competitive advantage.

The tax-management issues that arise when firms operate across jurisdictions are fundamentally the same whether the borders being crossed are between countries or among political subdivisions of the same country. But there are major practical differences, particularly within the United States, in identifying which portions of a tax base are properly associated with which jurisdictions. In the international arena, the methodology focuses on the location of entities. In the local arena, the focus is on the location of a firm's resources. Because the latter is novel to the typical manager, this chapter is devoted to local taxes, particularly on operations across the states within the United States. Tax management of activities crossing national boundaries is presented in Chapter 8.

One aspect of cost analysis is the state and local tax structure. Tax Management in Action 7.1 shows average effective tax rates for each state in the United States. This is computed as total taxes paid by businesses in the state divided by net business income (net value-added) for the state. As can be seen, there is a substantial difference in effective rates, with states in the Northeast and the Pacific coast having the highest rates, and Southeastern states, the lowest. These rates should only be regarded as suggestive of overall state tax policies. They should not be used for individual company decision making, which requires researching specific rates and rules applicable to their company.

TAX MANAGEMENT IN ACTION 7.1

Tax Rates by State

State	Overall Effective	State	Overall Effective
Alabama	12.45	Louisiana	21.46
Arizona	25.7	Maine	19.3
Arkansas	9.96	Massachusetts	16.26
California	15.97	Michigan	39.74
Colorado	14.47	Minnesota	17.74
Connecticut	21.26	Mississippi	16.82
Delaware	32.92	Missouri	14.47
DC & Maryland	14.44	Montana	19.09
Florida	20.92	Nebraska	6.63
Georgia	13.98	Nevada	10.69
Hawaii	7.84	New Hampshire	25.82
Idaho	7.22	New Jersey	23.24
Illinois	21.19	New Mexico	16.86
Indiana	18.76	New York	26.84
Iowa	10.24	North Carolina	12.01
Kansas	14.71	North Dakota	11.14
Kentucky	21.3	Ohio	15.6

TAX MANAGEMENT IN ACTION 7.1 (CONTINUED)

State	Overall Effective	State	Overall Effective
Oklahoma	16.62	Vermont	16.61
Oregon	16.28	Virginia	13.91
Pennsylvania	17.03	Washington	19.87
Rhode Island	18.47	West Virginia	26.89
South Carolina	19.72	Wisconsin	17.5
South Dakota	4.22	Wyoming	42.63
Tennessee	14.62		
Texas	17.65	United States	17.79
Utah	12.63		

Tax Management in Action 7.2 shows the multitude of different types of state and local taxes that U.S. businesses are subject to. Sales and use taxes are excluded (as in Tax Management in Action 7.1) because the aggregate data do not allow a separation of taxes paid by businesses versus individuals.

TAX MANAGEMENT IN ACTION 7.2

Taxes Levied upon Business

Type of Tax	Number of States	% of Total Taxes
Property tax—real	49	41.58%
Property tax—personal	41	11.07%
Property tax	41	6.02%
Alcoholic beverage license	47	0.25%
Amusement license	34	0.19%
Corporation license	48	3.05%
Motor vehicle license	49	7.44%
Public utility license	31	0.30%
Corporate net income tax	45	19.71%
Severance tax	33	4.00%
Document and stock transfer	30	1.89%
Taxes NEC	15	0.16%
Unemployment insurance	49	4.33%
Total		100.00%

GENERAL PRINCIPLES OF STATE AND LOCAL TAXATION

States impose the following major taxes on businesses:

- Income (sometimes known as franchise) taxes
- Property (usually assessed at the county level) taxes
- Payroll (unemployment and disability) taxes
- Other taxes significant in the aggregate: document, capital stock/net worth, real estate transfer

Forty-four states impose an income tax. Most use rules similar to the federal ones, with the following major exceptions: Income from the U.S. government is tax free; interest income from other governments is taxable; and state taxes paid are nondeductible. Depreciation, often the largest deduction other than payroll for firms, is similar to the federal MACRS system, with some variations. Most states do not allow deduction of federal income taxes.

When a firm operates in multiple states, its overall business income is apportioned (and taxed) across states based on the relative sales, payroll, and property in each state. Nonbusiness income, such as net revenues from market investments, is typically taxed where the firm is headquartered rather than apportioned among the states where the firm does business.

Property taxes are imposed on realty (such as land, buildings, and improvements) and certain personal property (such as vehicles, aircraft, and boats). In some states, inventory and equipment are also taxed. Tax rates are typically in the .75 to 2% range, based on assessed value or depreciated cost. Assessed value varies by state and type of property, usually involving fair market value. Fair market value is based on comparable sales prices, replacement costs, or *highest and best use*. Certain types of property are often tax exempt, such as realty owned and used by income-tax-exempt charities.

Payroll taxes are based on unemployment insurance histories of the firm and overall payroll in the state. Other types of state taxes are generally quite low, for which tax management may not be worth the investment of managerial time (i.e., transactions costs may be too high relative to the expected benefits).

PLANNING WITH INCOME TAXES: MANIPULATION OF PLANT, WORKFORCE, AND POINT-OF-SALE LOCATIONS

Corporate income tax rates vary across states, and multistate income is apportioned to individual states based on averaging formulas. Because of this, multistate firms can save taxes by using some straightforward techniques. The method is simple: Cause as much income to be apportioned to the lower tax states. The devil is in the details, because this is done by moving as much of the firm's property, payroll, and sales to lower-taxed states as possible, subject to nontax considerations.

Before illustrating some methods for reducing taxes, the basic principles of state corporate income taxes will be discussed.

State Corporate Income Taxes

The states that impose a corporate income tax require that income of a business be apportioned to the taxing state based on an averaging formula. Usually, it is a three-factor formula: the ratio of sales, payroll, and property within the taxing state to the corporation's total sales, payroll, and property. That is, if a corporation has operations in a state, the income taxable there will be the firm's total income (both within and outside the state) multiplied by the apportionment formula. Most states double-weigh the sales factor in the apportionment formula. Thus, income apportioned to a state is:

$$\text{Total Net Income} \left(\frac{2 \times \text{Sales}}{\text{Total Sales}} + \frac{\text{Payroll}}{\text{Total Payroll}} + \frac{\text{Property}}{\text{Total Property}} \right) \times \frac{1}{4}$$

This is illustrated in Example 7.1

EXAMPLE 7.1

A corporation has taxable sales in state A and state B. Approximately 70% of the firm's overall profit is related to state A. Sales, payroll, and property in state A (state B) are $100 million ($50 million), $40 million ($30 million), and $70 million ($50 million), respectively. Taxable income allocated to state A is: $10 million × (1/4[(2 × $100 million/$150 million) + ($40 million/$70 million) + ($70 million/$120 million)]) = $6.2 million. The remaining $3.8 million of profits is taxed in state B.

Exceptions to the three-factor rule include:

- Iowa and Texas require a single-factor formula.
- Missouri has an election for a single-factor formula.
- Colorado and Hawaii have an election for a two-factor formula.
- Massachusetts has a single-factor formula for manufacturers.
- Illinois now has a single-factor formula.

Some states use different formulas for special industries or allow firms to propose special arrangements to reflect more clearly activities within the state.

States cannot tax firms that have no physical presence—such as employees or inventory—within the state. This is known as the *nexus* requirement. (A very similar concept applies in the multinational arena, and is explicitly dealt with in a *permanent establishment* article of most tax treaties.) Thus a firm that sells products purely through the mail, or via the Internet, to purchasers located in a state cannot be taxed by that state.

Apportioning State Income Taxes: Unitary versus Separate Accounting

In apportioning income, some states use *separate accounting*, in which each legal entity is treated as a separate taxpayer. (This is similar to the approach most countries use when taxing multinational firms.) Other states use the unitary method to combine related entities. This method determines the extent to which a parent corporation's branches and affiliates are included in its apportionable income and the apportionment formula. That is, if an operation is considered to be part of a unitary business, its income (along with its property, payroll, and sales) is included in calculating state tax, even if this operation is a separate legal entity or is not located in the state.

The basic characteristics of a unitary business are that (1) the corporation's operations are dependent upon or contribute to the business conducted by the group, and (2) there is at least 50% common ownership or control between the parent corporation and the other members of the unitary group. (See Example 7.2.)

EXAMPLE 7.2

Assume the facts from Example 7.1, except that the state A and state B operations are run through separate corporations. If states A and B use separate accounting, then $7 million is taxed in state A, and $3 million, in state B. If states A and B are unitary, then the two corporations' operations are combined, and taxable income is apportioned to states A and B as shown in Example 7.1.

The conventional definition of a unitary tax state is one that requires filing of a combined (consolidated) corporate income tax return which indicates that affiliates are considered being part of the unitary business. Two general types of combinations apply: worldwide or water's edge. In a worldwide combination, all affiliates, regardless of the place of incorporation (including the foreign subsidiaries), are included in the apportionable base. *Water's edge* combination requires inclusion only of affiliates that are incorporated in the United States, regardless of where they do business. States rarely require the application of the worldwide method, typically allowing a choice between the two methods. (See Example 7.3.)

EXAMPLE 7.3

Refer back to the facts in Example 7.2, except substitute country B for state B, and assume that state A is a unitary state. If the firm makes a water's edge election, only $7 million of income is taxed in state A. If the firm foregoes the election, part of the $10 million of income is apportioned to state A, so $6.2 million is taxed in state A.

If instead of the unitary method the state uses separate accounting, only the income of the entity conducting business in the state is included on the corporate income tax return. Because of this entity-level restriction, multistate corporations can engineer their tax liabilities by shifting more (less) income to the state if it has a relatively lower (higher) tax rate than that of affiliates located in other states. Intercompany transactions (e.g., transfer pricing), can be used to shift income. (The same rules and tax savings techniques apply generally to multinational taxation.)

However, there is really only one setting where such intercompany transfer pricing schemes work. This setting requires that each of the following three conditions be met: (1) one of the states is a separate accounting state; (2) the transfer is between two corporate entities; and (3) the state's Section 482 rules on transfer pricing allow significant latitude. Most jurisdictions have rules preventing artificial shifting of income or expenses among related parties. That is, only activities priced at *arm's length* are recognized. In the United States this concept is embodied in IRC 482. Similar rules are common in the international arena and can be found in most tax treaties.

For the second condition, note that if either the transferor or transferee is not a corporation (e.g., a branch or flow-through entity), the transferor's and transferee's incomes are "pooled" (as part of the unitary business). This can occur even in separate accounting states. Because over half of the states either require or can enforce combined reporting, transfer pricing is likely to be useful only in certain limited cases. In contrast, taxes in unitary states can be manipulated by altering the location of property, payroll, or sales. Because these are real economic choices, tax minimization may result in decreased pre-tax economic performance, vis-à-vis both a no-tax situation and the separate accounting setting. The next section discusses such incentive effects.

Incentive Effects of Unitary versus Separate Accounting

Because of formula apportionment, one key way for firms to shift taxable income from high-tax states to low-tax states is to shift sales, property, or payroll from high- to low-tax states. However, if firms are already in a profit-maximizing equilibrium, changing such allocations would result in a drop in *pretax* income. Accordingly, it is not immediately obvious, absent a more rigorous analysis, whether firms would find such tax planning profitable.

When the possibility that one of the states uses separate accounting (and the divisions are separate corporations) is included, the analysis becomes even more complex. If the two states have different rates, does it still make sense to move sales, capital, or labor, even though this will have no direct impact on the separate accounting state's tax base? If so, is it still profitable in light of the possible drop in pretax income? To understand this, one should first examine the simplified setting where simply moving sales can reduce taxes. (See Example 7.4.)

EXAMPLE 7.4

Suppose the firm has its manufacturing located in state X, and sells its product in both state X and Y. The tax rates for these states are 10% and 5%, respectively. If the firm sells only by mail order into state Y, it has no nexus and is not liable for any income taxes in that state. That is, all net income is allocated to (and taxed by) state X. By simply filing for a business license in and having sales personnel make regular calls into state Y, the firm can establish nexus there. Accordingly, sales made into the state will be allocated there. Assume the following facts for the firm:

	State X	State Y	Total
Sales	$100	$100	$200
Payroll	$50	$0	$50
Property	$75	$0	$75

Corporate taxable income is $40.

Without nexus in Y, all $40 of income is taxed in X, for a total tax liability of $40 \times 10\% = \$4$. If nexus is established, the amount apportioned to X is as follows:

$$\text{Sales:} \quad \left(\frac{100}{200}\right) \times 2 \quad = 100\%$$

$$\text{Property:} \quad \frac{50}{50} \quad = 100\%$$

$$\text{Payroll:} \quad \frac{75}{75} \quad = 100\%$$

$$\overline{\quad 300\%/4 = 75\% \quad}$$

$40 \times 75\% \times 10\% = \$3$ taxes due in state X.

Allocation to Y is as follows:

$$\text{Sales:} \quad \left(\frac{100}{200}\right) \times 2 \quad = 100\%$$

$$\begin{aligned}
\text{Property:} &\qquad\qquad 0\% \\
\text{Payroll:} &\qquad\quad = \quad 0\% \\
\hline
100\%/4 &= \ 25\%
\end{aligned}$$

Total tax = $3.50. This is a .50/4.00 = 12½% reduction in taxes.

Of course, the firm must counterbalance other aspects of SAVANT before employing this technique. Specifically, are the transactions costs greater than the tax savings? Also, are the annual costs of having sales personnel travel into Y less than the tax savings?

When the firm attempts to manage state taxes by actually moving workers or plants between states, the analysis becomes more complex. Important factors to consider are the transactions costs of moving, and the value-adding with respect to marginal productivity in the new location and its effects on the bottom line.

On Moving Property and Payroll

If all states are unitary, a multistate operation can save taxes by moving physical facilities to a lower-taxed state.

EXAMPLE 7.5

Suppose a firm has operations in state 1 and state 2. Data for the two operations and states are

	State 1	State 2
Property	$2000	$2000
Payroll	$ 500	$ 500
Sales	$1000	$1000
Net (taxable) income	$ 100	$ 100

Assume both states' tax rates are 10%. Applying the formula in state 1, combined income is $200, which results in a tax of

$$10\% \times 200 \times \left(2\left(\frac{1000}{2000}\right) + \left(\frac{500}{1000} + \frac{2000}{4000}\right)\right) \times \frac{1}{4} = 10 \text{ for each of two states}$$

Suppose the tax rate in state 2 goes to 15%. A seemingly simple solution would be to close the state 2 operations and sell directly to state 2 customers without being physically located there. Using this interstate sales technique, because there are only sales (and no property or payroll in state 2), no taxable nexus with the state exists, so state 2 cannot impose a tax. (This is a commonly used strategy, by which the firm either uses mail order or drop shipment through an unrelated state 2 firm.) With the exception of six states, the state 2 sales would still be included in the state 1 apportionment numerator under the so-called throwback rule. Applying this rule, all income would be apportioned to the 10% bracket in state 1.

Despite the apparent simplicity of this sales-shifting solution (see Example 7.5), it is not feasible in a number of cases. First, there may be strategic or cost advantages to a physical presence in state 2. For non-Internet retailers and services, the necessity of a physical presence is clear-cut. Second, there may be cost or marketing advantages to servicing the market with an in-state facility. There may be lower wage rates or shipping costs, for example.

A second solution is to reduce payroll, property, and possibly sales in state 2 and increase them in state 1. This resource reallocation is most easily (and inexpensively) accomplished by expanding (reducing) assets and payroll within state 1 (state 2), as opposed to transfers between states. While shifting allocated income to state 1, this strategy may not be the best overall in the firm. This is because it may interfere with the efficient production structure and the optimal sales plan for the firm.

Acquiring Operations across State Lines

Similarly, when deciding to acquire an operation or subsidiary in a new state, managers and consultants should consider the following:

- Does it establish nexus where none existed before?
- What is the effect on the firm's overall state income taxes because of changes in apportionment?
- What are the pretax economics? What are costs of capital and wages (net of any economic incentives offered), changes in productivity, and effects on value-adding or the bottom line?
- Can incentives be negotiated with local authorities? Can tax benefits or costs be negotiated with the seller? If the seller is in a lower tax bracket, will it be willing to lease instead of selling (note that eight times annual rental values usually are counted as *property* for apportionment). Because moving workers (or hiring new ones) will save the firm income taxes, is it willing to pay them higher wages to entice them to relocate (join the firm)?

- Does the firm anticipate the same tax rates and rules to remain in place? Consultation with state political analysts may enable some forecasting for at least a few years in the future. If the tax climate may get less attractive in the foreseeable future, the net present value of tax savings actually could turn out to be negative.
- Most important, what are the transactions costs of acquiring or moving a subsidiary into a new state? Legal and accounting fees, or actual transportation costs for personnel and equipment, could exceed any tax benefit. (See Example 7.6.)

EXAMPLE 7.6

A retail store, which operates solely in state A, is thinking of opening some stores in nearby state B. This will be done by acquiring the existing stores of a similar business. Both states A and B are unitary, with income tax rates of 10% and 6%, respectively. Annual property taxes in state B average 2% of the value of realty. The company's effective tax rate actually may fall, by apportionment of income from state A to state B. The firm should also negotiate with county officials to (at least temporarily) reduce state B property taxes.

Income Tax Savings through Restructuring

Restructuring can be done by combining entities. This is useful when one entity operates at a loss and the other has a profit. (See Example 7.7.)

EXAMPLE 7.7

Alpha Corp does business in state 1 using $150 million of property, and in state 2, using $250 million of property. It generates a total profit of $400,000. Beta Corp operates only in state 2, having $300 million of property, which results in a $200,000 loss. As separate entities, the tax is (assuming a simple one-factor apportionment rule)

Alpha Corp:
    State 1: $150/400 \times \$400,000 \times 10\% =$ $15,000
    State 2: $250/400 \times \$400,000 \times 4\% =$ 10,000
Beta Corp:
    State 2: $\$300,000/300,000 \times <200,000> =$ 0
Total tax: $25,000

If the corporations are combined:

AlphaBeta Corp:

State 1: 450/700 × $200,000 × 10% =	$12,875
State 2: 250/700 × $200,000 × 4% =	2,857
Total tax:	$15,714
Total tax savings from combining:	$ 9,286

Using Special Purpose Entities When Expanding

If the firm operates in unitary states and plans to expand into separate accounting states, it often can save state income taxes by utilizing special-purpose entities. This is because only the special purpose entity, and not the parent corporation, will establish nexus in the new state. Effectively, the firm transforms taxable into nontaxable income. (See Example 7.8.)

EXAMPLE 7.8

A manufacturer located in a unitary state wants to establish a new plant in a nonunitary state. The new plant will operate as a separate subsidiary and will transfer finished products back to the parent company. The parent forms a new subsidiary in the unitary state, whose sole function is to finish and sell the product from the new plant. Although the entire operation will be taxed by the unitary state, the separate accounting state cannot tax the operations of the parent company, for lack of nexus.

Because many separate accounting states consider intangible property as establishing physical nexus, firms that license patents, copyrights, or other intellectual property rights may wish to use special-purpose intangible entities. (See Example 7.9.)

EXAMPLE 7.9

A coffeehouse, which is incorporated in a unitary state, wishes to open franchises in a nearby separate accounting state. The new operations would be able to use the company's famous trademark name. By forming a subsidiary in the unitary state that holds the trademark, the separate accounting state's taxation will be limited to the special purpose entity. Because the parent company has no nexus, its income will be apportioned to the state.

Note that tax authorities in some states, notably California, have developed doctrines to try to prevent such tax planning.

LOCATION CHOICE:
SOURCING VERSUS PRODUCTION PLATFORMS

When a firm decides to enter a new geographic market, the question of degree of presence arises. If the company provides services or consumer merchandise, it often would make sense to have sales facilities located in the new market, with property and personnel. For example, if Macy's decides it would like to compete against Nordstrom's in an area where it has not previously operated, it may not want simply to advertise mail-order sales. Instead, it might want to invest capital in a store, transfer management personnel, hire some local workforce, and the like.

It must also decide on sourcing. That is, will purchases be made from in-state affiliates, in-state nonaffiliated suppliers, or some combination? By locating affiliated sourcing platforms in the same state, the property factor in the three-factor apportionment formula increases, causing more income to be allocated to that state.

These location choices also have potential property tax considerations. If the firm buys or builds sourcing or production facilities, it will be subject to local property taxes unless a tax abatement can be negotiated. If facilities are rented, part of the lessor's property tax will be passed on to the firm in the form of higher lease payments. Often a net lease is used in which the firm actually pays the lessor's property taxes. As mentioned previously, annual property taxes are typically 1 to 2% of assessed value the latter of which is either estimated current market value or original cost. If cost is used it is reassessed (stepped up to fair market value) upon purchase or completion of new construction.

Property taxes are assessed on almost all realty, most personalty, and, in some states, intangibles. For personal property, tax savings may be obtained by (1) making sure any retired assets are removed from taxing list, and (2) where flexibility exists, classifying assets in the lowest-taxed category. For realty taxes, tax savings can be obtained by establishing the lowest valuation. For any property, one method of valuation is the market method, which uses sales prices of comparable properties. For properties that generate rental income, the discounted cash flows from the property also can be used. This is known as the *income method*. (See Example 7.10.)

EXAMPLE 7.10

Assume a corporation leases a building for $100,000 per year, and its cost of capital is 10%. Comparable properties are valued at $1.5 million. Under the income method, the value is $100,000/10% = $1 million. It would assert a value of $1 million to local tax authorities.

If the firm is unsure about its long-term strategic intent in the new market, leasing may make sense. It avoids property taxes by local governments and keeps any related liabilities (e.g., mortgages) off the balance sheet. Also, in the early stage of operation, it may result in tax losses that would be increased by rapid depreciation. (See Example 7.11.)

EXAMPLE 7.11

A variety store is considering opening a new store in a new city. It is unsure whether it will be successful. Buying a store building would cost $10 million; a year-to-year lease is $2 million annually. Although the second option is more expensive in pretax dollars, it is (1) less risky, (2) keeps the store and its financing off balance sheet, (3) avoids direct property taxes, and (4) has more rapid tax deductions (the building, if owned, would be depreciated over 39 years).

Note that leasing facilities usually does not reduce apportionment of income to the new market. Most states capitalize leases (e.g., multiply the annual lease payments by 8) and make that the property factor for apportionment.

DISTRIBUTION: PLANNING FOR SALES AND USE TAXES

If the firm sells personal (nonrealty) property to end consumers, it must collect applicable sales or use taxes from the customer. If it fails to collect, the firm is responsible for payment of the tax to the appropriate jurisdiction. Whether it is a sales tax or the complementary use tax is determined by what state the consumer is in. (see Exhibit 7.1.)

Although they are intended to complement each other, there may be differences between a state's sales tax and its use tax. For example, the sales tax rate may be slightly higher than that for the use tax. This often occurs because for administrative convenience local taxes may be *piggybacked,* that is, added onto the state rate. Examples include rapid-transit and pollution-control surtaxes.

In the United States, a firm need not collect sales taxes unless it has a substantial physical presence (nexus) in the jurisdiction. (As noted previously, similar rules apply in multinational taxation and are often made

EXHIBIT 7.1   Sales versus Use Taxes: Two Sides of the Same Coin

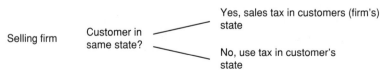

explicit in the permanent establishment provisions of tax treaties.) Substantial presence is triggered by having property or employees in the jurisdiction. It also results from having a sales force based outside the state that, when traveling into the state, performs substantial additional services besides order taking (e.g., bringing in and stocking inventory). (See Example 7.12.)

EXAMPLE 7.12

A Texas firm sells consumer goods in California. Assume that, by virtue of a traveling sales force, it has nexus in California. If it does not have an office in California, it charges its customers the state's 7% use tax. If it opens a California sales office, an 8 to 8.5% (depending on city/county) sales tax will apply to California sales.

One way to avoid these taxes is through mail order or Web sales to customers in another state. As long as the firm has no substantial nexus in the customer's state, the firm is not required to collect sales taxes from the customer or pay sales taxes to the state on the firm's behalf. Because having no tax effectively reduces the total price to the customer, this may give the firm a competitive advantage over in-state firms, which must charge or remit a sales tax. This tax advantage may be undercut by increased shipping costs, however. (In addition, in some states customers my be liable for paying a use tax. This may be limited to nonconsumer items, and, in any event is more honored in the breach.)

In a large organization with many steps in the value chain, it is important to determine in what state sales or use taxes are due. The basic rule is simple: It is the destination state of the final consumer. The state of actual title passage, while determining the location of property for income tax apportionment, is irrelevant for sales and use taxes. (See Example 7.13.)

EXAMPLE 7.13

Suppose a company sends inventory via a *drop shipment* as follows:

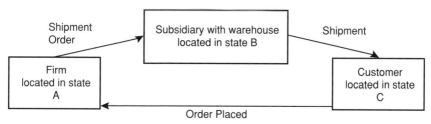

The use tax is due in state C, that is, where the good is used.

Most sales and use taxes apply only to retail sales of tangible personal property. Thus realty, services, and goods that will be resold (or become part of a manufactured product) are all exempt from the tax. If part of the product includes a service, the firm should segregate the service so no sales tax need be charged. Examples include custom-developed computer software and extended warranty contracts.

Taxation of Electronic Commerce

Under current U.S. law, states are prohibited from assessing sales or use tax on purely Internet sales. Although a customer that avoids a sales tax may end up paying its companion use tax, it is still better for the selling firm to avoid such taxes because

- A potentially expensive accounting system, which determines taxes across product type, across a variety of taxes, does not have to be set up. Nor does the firm have to endure the costs and distractions of audits by state taxing agencies.
- Without sales and use taxes, the price of the firm's product is effectively lower. This gives the seller a pricing advantage over sellers having to charge such taxes.
- Sometimes customers do not pay the tax. The seller is then left paying the tax.

Only a small percentage of worldwide sales are made on the Internet, but this is likely to increase substantially. With sellers in one state, Web servers in another, and customers in a third, most jurisdictions do not have a policy on Internet taxation, particularly for value-added or sales/use taxes. How long this will last is uncertain.

The importance of this issue is underlined by the United States having established the Advisory Commission on Electronic Commerce. With 19 members—ranging from the governor of Virginia to representatives from America On Line, Time Warner, Gateway, Charles Schwab, AT&T, and MCI World Com—the group has been struggling to recommend revised nexus rules to Congress. The issues are aptly handled in *The Wall Street Journal* article, "E-Commerce Panels Attempt to Agree on Internet Sales Tax Policy Collapses" (March 22, 2000, p. B2). Indeed, in 2001 Congress extended the three-year moratorium on new state taxes on electronic commerce found in the 1998 Internet Tax Freedom Act.

This ambiguity is currently being utilized by a number of sellers to avoid these taxes, thus giving them a strategic price advantage. (See Example 7.14.)

TAX MANAGEMENT IN ACTION 7.3

Incentives and Location Choice

Many cities, states, counties (and trade blocks, such as the European Union) offer firm-specific incentives to entice business to locate in their area. Many local governments are beginning to demand refunds of previous incentives from companies who reneged on their promises (e.g., by leaving the area or not hiring as many workers as planned). Similarly, some localities are awarding incentives over time, instead of up front.

EXAMPLE 7.14

A California furniture retailer is considering expanding into a national market. If it does so by having a Web site and making sales through the Internet, it will have a 6% (or more) price advantage over local area retailers who must collect sales taxes.

LOBBYING AND TAX ABATEMENTS

Like the European Union and countries such as Israel and Ireland, most states have an active policy of attracting new business. Many, including cities, have well-advertised tax incentives to do so, as discussed in Tax Management in Action 7.3.

Beyond publicized tax incentives, many local jurisdictions provide incentives on a case-by-case basis. These incentives may include:

- Low-cost financing. The city or county may underwrite private activity bonds, which may have a low interest rate due to tax exemption to investors.
- Sale or lease of public property at below-market rates
- Exemption from local (e.g., city) income taxes, license fees, and other charges for a fixed time period
- Reduction or exemption from property taxes for a fixed (tax holiday) period

From the government's perspective, these incentives often pay for themselves by job creation and expansion of the tax base through multiplier effects. (See Example 7.15.)

EXAMPLE 7.15

A company asks a county for a five-year forgiveness of property taxes as a condition of opening a new plant there. The lost property taxes would be $1 million per year. However, after calculating that the ripple-through effect of the plant on increased local sales and income taxes to be $1.5 million per year, the county government officials grant the property tax concession.

From the firm's side, managers negotiate these tax benefits so that value-adding, giving account for the net present value of tax reduction, makes the project profitable.

In terms of strategy, effective tax management does not imply that managers shop around for tax deals. Instead, the economics of deciding whether a new facility should be built and approximate geographic area where to build it (in terms of marketing, overall strategy, and other costs) should identify a set of potential areas. Next, the manager should contact local officials in a number of such areas to get them to compete for the plant by offering tax and other incentives. The local officials can be contacted directly or through state trade and tourism offices. Location choice specialists can do much of the work; the Big 4 accounting firms have such specialists. A perspective by one of the authors, who is a consultant in this area, appears in Exhibit 7.2.

EXHIBIT 7.2   Strategy and State Tax Planning

CONSULTANT INTERVIEW

Joseph Neff
National Partner in Charge, State and Local Tax Practice,
PricewaterhouseCoopers, LLP

How important is state and local tax (SALT) practice to consulting practice, and to clients?
SALT practice is very important; it is one of the fastest growing practice areas. Our SALT consulting services can sometimes be used as an entree to obtain other business, such as the attestation (audit) engagement.

What are some ways that firms can manage taxes?
For all taxes, shifting to lower taxed states is the general idea. In the corporate income/franchise tax area, some methods are

- Shifting location of sales, property, and payroll out of higher, and into lower, tax states
- Setting up separate selling, or expense performing, subsidiaries in certain states
- Establishing (or avoiding) nexus in states which would cause combined-entity taxes to decrease (increase)

In the sales tax area, we do *reverse sales tax audits*. Often businesses have over-paid sales or use taxes, and such a reverse audit can result in sizable tax refunds.

How do timing, anticipation, and negotiation fit into these techniques?
In terms of timing and anticipation, we stay right on top of actual or pending law changes, and advise clients to take these into account before structuring transactions. We have a group in our national office which specializes in location choice; they work (negotiate) with local officials on obtaining possible agreements on local tax matters.

What tensions arise among SALT, financial reporting, and the firm's strategic objectives?
The issue I'll address is not necessarily a conflict, but it is certainly an interaction between financial reporting and SALT. If a proposed SALT method, which saves taxes, can also increase reported financial earnings, it may be a much easier sell to managers whose compensation is tied to financial earnings, such as bonuses or stock options.

TRADE-OFFS WITH LOCAL TAX INCENTIVES: INFRASTRUCTURE, GOVERNMENT COSTS/SUBSIDIES, AND OTHER LOCAL COSTS

Although tax incentives may be quite appealing, nontax factors can easily dominate a location choice decision. Indeed, one reason a local government may offer tax incentives is because some other aspects of the locality would not normally attract investors.

PUTTING IT ALL TOGETHER: SAVANT APPLIED TO MARKET PENETRATION IN OTHER STATES

You are CEO for SALSA!, Inc., which manufactures and sells a bottled salsa that sells primarily in Arizona. Based on a family recipe, it is regarded as high quality and high priced. It sells primarily to grocery stores. It has brand recognition in Arizona, and you are considering expanding to southern California and southern Nevada markets. The first step would be to have the sales force make calls to the super-markets. You are considering whether to open sales offices in San Diego, Los Angeles, and Las Vegas. Income (property) tax rates in California and Nevada are 9% (1%) and 0% (1.5%), respectively.

Strategy

Although you have no formal strategic plan, eventually you would like to become a national leader in high-end salsa. A market analysis reveals that you have no major competitors in either state: All supermarkets sell medium priced, national brands.

Anticipation

You anticipate no major changes in state tax policy in the near future.

Value-Adding

The total costs of additional sales force would be $300,000 annually. Your marketing department estimates that you could sell 200,000 units annually at a gross profit of $3 per jar. Internal financing would be used, that is, there would be no cost of capital per se. Thus, pretax EVA would be $100,000 annually.

Adjusting value-adding for risk   Brand reputation would be at risk if the product failed in the new states. That is, bad publicity might preclude a national sales campaign in the future. Since the pretax profit already is low, you are hoping to obtain some tax benefits to provide a risk premium.

Adjusting value-adding for transactions costs   Some minor business license fees, new automobiles for the sales force, and similar expenses are already included in the $300,000 mentioned above.

Negotiating

Because you are not locating any operations in the state, that might provide significant jobs, there is little hope of obtaining tax concessions from local authorities.

Transforming

There is a major tax advantage of the Nevada operations: Any gross profit from such sales will be subject to a 0% tax rate (that is, it is transformed to tax-free income). You may not want to use this to drop prices because of your prestige pricing strategy, however. So, the tax savings in Nevada may provide enough risk premium alone to greenlight the new market expansion. Based on your overall business judgment and SAVANT analysis, you decide to proceed with the new state campaign.

TECHNICAL INSERT 7.1 OVERVIEW OF SALES AND USE TAXES

In acquisitions, one activity that has taken on increasing importance is the review of potential sales and use tax liabilities. Indeed, for professional advisors, many attestation engagements are awarded because of the tax dollars that can be saved by filing for refunds of overpaid sales and use taxes.

TECHNICAL INSERT 7.1 (CONTINUED)

Specifically, manufacturing or wholesaling clients are exempt from these taxes for any purchased materials that will either be resold or become part of the manufactured product. Thus a manager or consultant involved with an acquisition should examine a sample of purchase invoices and interviews purchasing personnel to determine policies on payment of such taxes. If there is no uniform policy, or personnel are unaware of the exemptions, then a full-fledged *reverse audit* may be in order. Amended sales and use tax returns can be filed with the appropriate states, often resulting in substantial tax refunds. In addition to the cash flow, there is more good news: value-adding. The firm's financial statements can usually be changed to reflect an additional receivable and a reduction in tax expense.

Unfortunately, a reverse audit sometimes brings bad news: sales and use taxes owed. As part of due diligence, managers (and consultants) should also look at the target's sales records. If the firm is selling to ultimate consumers, and the firm has nexus in these states, sales or use tax should be collected from customers. If the firm being acquired has not done this properly, it is usually difficult to go back and ask customers to remit the back taxes, and the firm is left with the responsibility of paying back taxes.

However, if the target has filed sales and use tax returns in the past, the statute of limitations may have run out. In most jurisdictions, there is a three-year limitation period during which the tax authorities must assert claims for additional taxes, provided a tax return prepared in good faith was properly filed. That is, if the unpaid taxes are from more than three years ago, the firm is off the hook, so to speak. However, if the firm has never paid taxes to a particular state, there is no limit: Taxes may be owed back to the beginning of time. Now for the really bad news: The firm must book the back taxes as a liability and as an increase in tax expense. The latter reduces financial-accounting earnings.

This is why it is so important to discover potential liability before the acquisition is completed. If there is a possibility of the target firm owing substantial back taxes, the successor owner, the acquiring firm, would be responsible for them. Once known, however, the client firm can either negotiate for a lower purchase price, or buy the target's assets instead of stock as a means of limiting tax liabilities.

CHAPTER 8

Market Penetration: Company and Employee Tax Planning for Operating in Foreign Countries

Ironically, while companies need to enter and compete in foreign markets, the risks are high. There are many challenges here, including shifting borders, unstable governments, foreign-exchange problems, corruption, and technological pirating. For this reason, one might conclude that companies are doomed whether they stay at home or go abroad. We would argue that companies selling in global industries have no choice but to internationalize.

—Philip Kotler, *Marketing Management*

As a firm grows, a natural consideration is to look toward worldwide markets. Globalization provides a number of tax opportunities that can enhance value of a firm. Effective tax management entails familiarity with the home country (e.g., United States) and foreign tax structures.

SOME BASICS ON U.S. TAXATION OF OVERSEAS OPERATIONS

Unlike almost every other country, a basic principle of U.S. taxation of foreign operations is that a U.S. firm's worldwide income is subject to U.S. taxation. However, the legal form in which a firm operates (e.g., joint venture versus a corporation) makes a difference on the *timing* of the U.S. income tax.

Typically, a U.S. firm begins its overseas operations via direct export. If the firm's products are sold to an unrelated entity overseas (either directly or through an overseas affiliate), the U.S. tax treatment is almost the same as a U.S. sale. If the foreign country assesses a tax on the profit from a firm's transaction, the firm can take a foreign tax credit (discussed later) against U.S. taxes for the foreign income tax paid.

Also, most countries have duties (i.e., import taxes) that are assessed on the value of products imported. The rates vary significantly by country and product. The rules vary also with respect to whether the duty imposed depends on the point of title passage. However, if inventory is sold to a host country importer located in the United States, there are no foreign taxes—duties or income taxes—on the sale.

Once a firm gains experience in international business, it may then establish a physical presence overseas. If the presence is unincorporated, then the U.S. government treats it as a branch. The tax treatment of a branch is essentially the same as for direct export: Net profits are taxed immediately. Because of this, tax management focuses on foreign taxes. Foreign taxes on an unincorporated business are typically the same whether the business is formed as a joint venture (JV), a partnership, an unincorporated branch, or some other legal form.

Finally, a firm can incorporate overseas. For U.S. tax purposes, there is no tax until there is a repatriation of funds to the U.S. parent. This typically occurs via a dividend, interest payment, or a royalty. If the subsidiary is liquidated or its stock sold, any gain is subject to tax. Thus, tax management also involves anticipation (timing) of taxes. Most countries impose some sort of corporate tax as well, although many reduce it by a dividend imputation system. (See Exhibit 8.1 and Examples, 8.1, 8.2, and 8.3.)

EXHIBIT 8.1   Overseas Presence Life Cycle

Common Life Cycle for Expanding across Borders

EXAMPLE 8.1

A U.S. toothpaste manufacturer wants to begin selling in Asia. Based on marketing research, it believes it will have significant markets in countries having large English-speaking populations—Japan, Singapore, Hong Kong, and Thailand. In its first year of operations, it sells directly to foreign wholesalers located in those countries. The foreign wholesalers then resell the toothpaste to foreign retailers. In 2000, the U.S. manufacturer's foreign sales (translated into U.S. dollars) were $10 million. Related cost of goods sold was $4 million. It owes U.S. corporate income taxes on $6 million of income.

EXAMPLE 8.2

In 2001, the U.S. manufacturer sets up manufacturing facilities in the above four countries. The toothpaste is again sold to foreign wholesalers. Sales, less related manufacturing expenses, are $7 million. Of the $7 million in profits, $5 million is sent back to U.S. headquarters in early 2002. The $7 million is subject to U.S. tax for the year 2001. The $5 million distribution in 2002 is tax free.

EXAMPLE 8.3

Assume the same facts as Example 8.2, except that each of the four foreign manufacturing facilities is incorporated in the country where they are located. Only the $5 million is subject to U.S. tax, and is so for the year 2001.

When the firm forms a subsidiary, the required legal form varies by country. Tax Management in Action 8.1 lists some common entity types for some countries.

TAX MANAGEMENT IN ACTION 8.1

Legal Entities to Utilize in the European Union: Corporate-Like Entities

Country of Orgin	Type of Company	Translation
Germany	Aktiengesellschaft (AG)	Corporation
Germany	Gesellshaft mit (GmBH) Beschraenkter Haftung	Cooperative with limited liability
United Kingdom	Public limited company (PLC)	Public limited company
	Limited (LTD)	Corporation
Netherlands	Naamloze Vennootschap (NV)	Limited liability company
Italy	Societa per Azioni (SpA)	Public limited company
Sweden	Aktiebolag (AB)	Joint stock company
France, Latin America	Sociedad Anonima (SA)	Joint stock company

SOME BASICS ON TAXATION BY COUNTRIES OTHER THAN THE UNITED STATES

Basic tax rates and rules for some countries are listed in Tax Management in Action 8.2. A number of countries, such as Britain, France, Germany, and Taiwan—use dividend imputation systems. Under these systems, shareholders (including corporate shareholders) get a deduction or credit for

TAX MANAGEMENT IN ACTION 8.2

Overview of Business Taxes for Select Countries

Country	Tax on Unincorporated Business	Corporate Tax Rate	Tax Rates: Withholding on Dividends	Tax Treatment of Property & Equipment
Australia	36%	36%	10%	P = Straight Line E = Accelerated
Canada	25% + 38%	38%	25%	P = Accelerated E = Accelerated
France	33⅓% + 25% (on undistributed profit)	33.33%	35%	P = Straight Line E = Accelerated
Germany	45%	45%	30%	P = Straight Line E = Accelerated
Ireland	38%	38%	27%	P = Straight Line & Accelerated E = Accelerated
Italy	37%	37%	15%	P, E = Accelerated
Japan	37.50%	37.50%	20%	P, E = Accelerated
Luxembourg	33%	33%	0%	P = Straight Line E = Accelerated
Spain	35%	35%	25%	
Sweden	28%	28%	0%	P = Straight Line E = Accelerated
Switzerland	28.50%	28.50%	35%	P, E = Accelerated
United Kingdom		33%	25%	P = Straight Line E = Accel

dividends (or for the taxes paid on the earnings generating the dividends). However, as is the case with the U.S. system, tax rates are only part of the story: Rules affecting the tax base can have much more impact. In particular, rules related to plant and equipment are quite significant. If the country allows rapid depreciation or tax credits, the firm's tax bill can be reduced significantly. Some general rules in this regard are shown in Tax Management in Action 8.2.

TAX TREATIES

Independent of in-country rules and rates, a number of countries have tax treaties with other countries (notably the United States). Treaties exist to minimize conflicts between countries, to attract foreign investment, to avoid double taxation, and for other policy reasons. As suggested by the Model Tax Convention of the Organization for Economic Cooperation and Development (OECD), most treaties affect firms by reducing withholding rates on dividend, interest, or royalty payments by subsidiaries located in one treaty country to parent companies in the other treaty country (see Tax Management in Action 8.3). Treaties also establish nexus rules. For example, in the U.S., UN, and OECD models, firms resident in one of the treaty partners cannot be taxed by the other unless they have a permanent establishment in the taxing country. Furthermore, *competent authorities* are designated in each country to ensure consistent treatment of transactions. Some treaties also provide specific tax breaks to encourage investment.

TAX MANAGEMENT IN ACTION 8.3

Sample of Treaty-Based Withholding Rates on Payments to U.S. Parent

Australia: 10% on interest and royalties; lower rate on shipping and insurance businesses
Canada: 10% on dividends, interest, and royalties
France: 0% on dividends and interest; 5% on royalities
Germany: 0% on dividends
Ireland: 0% on dividends, interest, and royalties
Italy: 10% or 15% on dividends, interest, and royalties
Japan: 10% on dividends, interest, and royalties
Spain: 10% on dividends, interest, and royalties
Sweden: 0% on dividends, interest, and royalties
Switzerland: 5% on dividends and interest
United Kingdom: 0% on dividends, interest, and royalties

EFFECTIVE TAX MANAGEMENT

Strategy

The firm's decision to do business in foreign countries should be consonant with its strategic plan. If the firm's mission statement is to be "a leading firm in the Midwest," no amount of tax incentives should persuade the firm to set up operations in a foreign country. Likewise, a firm that manufactures and sells in Europe should not locate in Hong Kong (which has low tax rates) without careful consideration of how this location fits in with the firm's strategy.

Once the firm has decided to go international, an important strategic decision is entity choice. That is, what legal form (e.g., a corporation, a partnership, or a limited liability company) should the firm adopt? As mentioned previously, a typical marketing progression is: direct export, joint venture (with a local foreign firm), unincorporated branch, and subsidiary. Generally speaking, for a U.S. firm, this results in a steady decrease in (the present value of) U.S. taxes. Note that by following this normal progression, *tax management* does not necessarily imply *tax minimization*.

Locational choice should also fit into the firm's strategic plan. Labor and material costs may make plant location more desirable in a high-tax area. Alternatively, tax savings resulting from a treaty or other agreement may influence the choice between two countries, both of which would otherwise fit into the firm's strategic plan. (See Example 8.4.)

EXAMPLE 8.4

A U.S. laundry soap manufacturer would like to enter the Southeast Asian market. It wants to locate a manufacturing facility there. One choice is Singapore—good infrastructure, ready access to skilled labor and materials, and other advantages. However, the tax rate there is 30%. The other choice is Shanghai, where there is a 15% tax rate in *enterprise zones*. However, Shanghai's infrastructure is much less developed than that of Singapore. Management estimates that the extra costs due to poor infrastructure more than make up for the extra tax savings. They locate the plant in Singapore.

Once a location and entity choice have been made, tax management of interentity transactions becomes important. Repatriation of funds should not just be tax minimizing (that is, paid only when the parent has a low tax rate or the subsidiary has low retained earnings). The cash flow needs of the overseas operation and the parent should also be considered. Similarly, when transfer prices are set, tax minimization should not be the sole objective. Because pricing results in real economic consequences to both buying and selling parts of the firm, the long-term consequences should be considered. (See Example 8.5.)

EXAMPLE 8.5

Assume that the U.S. manufacturer in Example 8.4 establishes an incorporated subsidiary in Singapore. In its first year of operations, its net income is $10 million. Assume that this is also its taxable income for both U.S. and Singapore purposes. It pays a Singapore tax of 30% × ($10,000,000) = $3,000,000. Because the U.S. tax rate is higher (at 34%), the firm would like to set the transfer price as low as possible. However, this would result in a cash shortfall for the subsidiary, which, at the critical startup phase, is not advisable.

Strategy and Tax Treatment   Treaties commonly provide for tax rates and tax benefits allowed only by the host nations. Typically, these treaty-based rates are well below the general tax rates. Besides setting specific rates and withholding rates, treaties also provide for information-sharing policies between the tax enforcement agencies of the two countries and require that at least one of the countries allow a tax credit to mitigate taxpayers' double taxation. Tax Management in Action 8.4 lists some of the countries with which the United States currently has tax treaties.

TAX MANAGEMENT IN ACTION 8.4

Countries Having Tax Treaties with the United States

Australia	Iceland	Norway
Austria	India	Pakistan
Barbados	Indonesia	Philippines
Belgium	Ireland	Poland
Canada	Israel	Portugal
China	Italy	Romania
Cyprus	Jamaica	Russia
Czech Republic	Japan	Slovakia
Denmark	Kazakstan	Spain
Egypt	Korea (South)	Sweden
Finland	Luxembourg	Switzerland
France	Mexico	Trinidad and Tobago
Germany	Morocco	Thailand
Greece	Netherlands	Turkey
Hungary	New Zealand	United Kingdom

EXHIBIT 8.2   Strategic Impact of Competitors' Relative Tax Rates

A competitor's effective foreign tax rate:	The firm's effective foreign tax rate	
	High	Low
High	No strategic tax advantage to either	Overseas strategic tax advantage to the firm
Low	Overseas strategic tax advantage to the competitor	No strategic tax advantage to either

On Competitive Strategy   A recurrent theme throughout the text is that by effectively managing taxes, a firm's costs decrease, and it can then afford to lower prices and win more market share. While a competitor may attempt to manage taxes, too, a firm can still have the advantage if it has better knowledge of taxes in general, and of its competitors' tax status in particular.

Knowledge of a competitor's tax rates can give one a better prediction of how the competitor will act (or react) internationally. Exhibit 8.2 illustrates the impact of a competitor's versus the firm's effective foreign tax rates:

If a firm has the advantage, it should go into the market (assuming this otherwise makes good business sense), and the competitor should not (absent any non-tax cost advantages over the firm). The opposite holds true if the competitor has the tax advantage. (See Example 8.6.)

EXAMPLE 8.6

Suppose the firm and a competitor are considering manufacturing overseas, in the same country. For both, an overseas subsidiary would send a royalty payment back to the U.S. parent that would be subject to U.S. taxation. Assume that the competitor has enormous foreign tax credit carryforwards, so that it cannot utilize a tax credit for any foreign taxes paid to the proposed new country. This effectively results in a double tax to the competitor, which gives the firm a strategic cost advantage.

How can a firm lower its effective foreign tax rate? One way is to operate in countries with lower tax rates, but only if operating there makes overall business sense. (See Example 8.7.)

EXAMPLE 8.7

Assume the same facts as the previous example. The country being considered is Ireland, because of its 15% tax rate. However, all of the firm's market is in the United States, and shipping costs from Ireland would almost equal the tax savings of operating there. Because any unexpected costs could result in the proposed plant operating at a loss, the plan does not make business sense.

Tax Management in Action 8.5 provides a sample of countries that have significantly lower statutory income tax rates than the United States. Referred to as *tax haven* countries by the U.S. government, some tax problems can be created for a firm that uses these countries to simply funnel income through, instead of conducting legitimate businesses there (that is, where both business activity and customers are located in the country).

Such funneling is called "Subpart F income" (named after the place in the Internal Revenue Code, Subpart F, where the rules are found). Examples have occurred in industries ranging from banking and insurance to shipping and oil and gas. If Subpart F income is generated in a tax haven country by a controlled foreign corporation (CFC)—basically, a wholly owned subsidiary—the United States immediately taxes the foreign subsidiary's income even if no dividends are paid. Thus firms operating in the United States should strongly consider only conducting *real* businesses in these countries in order to obtain full tax benefits.

TAX MANAGEMENT IN ACTION 8.5

A Sample of Low Tax Rate ("Tax Haven") Countries

Antigua and Barbados	Leeward Islands
Aruba	Liberia
Austria	Liechtenstein
Bahamas	Luxembourg
Bahrain	Monaco
Barbados	Netherlands
Belize	Netherlands Antilles
Bermuda	Panama
Cayman Islands	Singapore
Costa Rica	Switzerland
Gibraltar	Turks and Caicos Islands
Hong Kong	Windward Islands

The rules in Subpart F are extraordinarily complex. As noted in previous chapters, this is another of the intricate U.S. antiabuse statutes which codifies principles not yet developed outside the United States and therefore is rarely mirrored in the tax laws of other countries. Ironically, it provides a road map for tax planning for firms operating in those jurisdictions.

Another way to get tax-strategic advantage over a competitor is through use of the foreign tax credit limitation rules. Briefly, if a competitor is in an *excess* foreign tax credit status, and the firm is not, it can generate more foreign income at a lower tax rate. The general rules of the foreign tax credit (FTC) are briefly described in Example 8.8.

EXAMPLE 8.8

Suppose a firm has U.S. and foreign operations as follows:

	U.S. Parent	Foreign Branch
Taxable income from own operations	1000	100
Add: foreign income	100	—
Taxable income	1100	100
Tax (35% United States, 30% foreign)	385	30
Foreign tax credit	<30>	—
Net tax	355	30

As shown, the FTC reduces U.S. tax, so that there is no double tax on foreign income. Effectively, the foreign income is taxed at the U.S. rate of 35%: $30 paid to the foreign government, plus $5 (after the foreign credit) paid to the United States. In this example, there is no excess foreign tax credit, so the full $30 tax credit can be taken.

However, there are at least two situations where the firm cannot use the credit (an excess foreign credit situation). The first is based on the annual limit, computed as

$$\text{FTC limit} = \text{U.S. taxes} \times \left(\frac{\text{Foreign source income}}{\text{Worldwide income}} \right)$$

Using Example 8.8, the limit would be:

$$\$385 \times \left(\frac{100}{1100} \right) = \$35$$

In this example, the firm can use the entire $30 as a credit. What if the foreign tax rate was 50%, causing a $50 tax? Then, only $35 could be used to offset current U.S. taxes. The $15 would be an excess foreign tax credit. This amount could be carried back two years and forward five years to offset U.S. taxes on foreign income in those years. Otherwise, it would not reduce U.S. taxes.

The second way to have an excess FTC is by having excess FTC carryovers from a previous year. In this case, the firm cannot use its current FTC. If it is known that a competitor has an excess FTC, this gives the firm a strategic advantage. This is because effectively the competitor pays a double tax on foreign income. Until this reverses, the firm has a cost advantage to operating overseas.

FTC computations are more complicated than depicted, although this is a good overall example. In actuality, there are *baskets* of foreign income which give separate FTC limits. Also, if the foreign operation is a subsidiary, there is a *deemed paid* credit for foreign taxes paid by the subsidiary.

An additional source of tax-strategic advantage over a competitor is through entity choice. For example, if a U.S. firm operates overseas through a corporation, U.S. tax is deferred until the foreign subsidiary remits funds. If a U.S. competitor has a branch or JV, however, it is U.S.-taxed immediately. Also, if there are startup losses, a firm may want to elect flow-through entity treatment to have the foreign losses reduce current U.S. taxable income. (See Example 8.9.)

EXAMPLE 8.9

A U.S. consumer products firm wants to begin operations in Europe. Its first distribution center is in Germany. Because of low initial sales and labor costs, it expects a loss in its first few years. Accordingly, it forms a GmBH, which is treated as a flow-through entity for U.S. and German tax purposes. The tax loss will flow through to the U.S. parent company as a tax deduction.

In the United States, a specialized entity choice for a corporation is a foreign sales corporation (FSC). If elected, FSC status provides for immediate taxation of a portion of the foreign income but some of the income is effectively tax exempt. Because of various rules, an FSC is typically only used by medium-sized manufacturers with high profit margins that can commit to a long-term foreign presence.

The FSC is discussed in more detail later in the chapter. More important, in January 2002 the World Trade Organization ruled that FSCs are an export subsidy that violates its rules (just as the FSC's predecessor, the domestic international sales corporation, was invalidated under the WTO's predecessor, the General Agreement on Tariffs and Trade. Thus it is almost certain that the FSC rules will change, and likely that a new form similarly redesigned to skirt the export subsidy rules will be enacted if FSCs are eliminated.

Anticipating

When the firm decides to go overseas, it predicts implicitly whether tax rates will change over time. If the firm is offered a tax holiday for a fixed period of time, it must anticipate the amount of tax increase that will occur at the expiration time. Similarly, firms should forecast the extent to which existing general tax rates and treaties will change.

Because treaties are bilateral agreements, firms typically look for signals that changes may occur. For example, the United States publicly announced for many years that it intended to repeal a tax treaty with the Netherlands Antilles. This treaty exempted real estate sales from U.S. tax, and provided only a nominal Netherlands Antilles tax. Accordingly, U.S. firms had a long period to divest themselves of Netherlands Antilles companies before the special tax break was taken away. However, non-treaty changes are harder to predict. For example, Britain's 1997 reduction in corporate rates at a time of budgetary problems came as a surprise. Accordingly, in more politically volatile regimes, anticipation may be more difficult.

In setting transfer prices, the firm must also anticipate the likelihood of a tax audit and subsequent tax adjustment occurring. Because there is some latitude in setting such prices, and the tax authorities know that firms exploit this, audits of transfer prices are common. (See Example 8.10.)

EXAMPLE 8.10

A U.S. electronics firm manufactures most of its components in Asia. Each Asian plant is a wholly owned subsidiary of the U.S. parent corporation. Each subsidiary *sells* its output to the U.S. parent. To minimize audits and provide consistency for the company, it enters into an advanced pricing agreement (APA) with the IRS. Under the agreement, prices will be set at full cost to manufacture, plus a 15% markup (profit for the subsidiaries). Transactions costs are reduced insofar as the number and scope of IRS audits and adjustments are minimized.

Anticipation and Timing   If the firm anticipates a change in foreign tax rates or rules, it may want to adjust the timing of its investments. Timing also affects ongoing transactions. For a separate subsidiary, repatriation of funds (via dividends or royalties) to a U.S. parent should take into account both the parent's U.S. tax rates and its foreign tax credits. Generally, it reduces taxes overall for the firm to make such payments when the U.S. parent is in an NOL carryforward status, or it has excess foreign tax credits that can be used to offset U.S. tax.

Transfer prices, within reason, can be periodically adjusted to reflect changing relative tax rates. If the U.S. parent transits into a lower tax rate, either the transfer price or the quantity of inventory can be adjusted to shift more income into the United States.

Anticipation and Time Value   Regarding organizational form, time value is most salient for corporate subsidiaries. Here, U.S. taxes can be postponed almost infinitely, such that their net present value (NPV) can be nearly zero. Other organizational forms have no such advantage.

Value-Adding

Related to strategy is the fundamental idea that the pretax economics of overseas investment must be sound. Accordingly, foreign tax incentives should influence location choice only at the margin. If a planned operation is profitable solely because of tax benefits, it should be avoided.

Similarly, entity choice is affected by value-adding. On the firm's balance sheet, joint ventures, partnerships, branches, and the like are simply reported as an investment asset, and are not shown in detail.

The impact of foreign business on economic value-added (EVA) and earnings per share (EPS) should be considered. Although investments like this may have a projected positive NPV, this might not dominate the investment decision. Upfront losses, for example, may reduce earnings reported in financial statement, thus affecting share prices (and management bonuses).

Adjusting Value-Adding for Risk   Foreign ventures pose additional risk management problems for the firm. Part of this is mitigated by entity choice. Direct export involves minimal risk; joint ventures and partnerships provide local risk-sharing partners. Branches and subsidiaries put more of the firm's operations at risk.

Tax benefits may act to partly provide a risk premium. With respect to foreign taxes, many developing countries offer tax holidays to prospective firms. However, managers should be cautious. If such tax concessions are necessary to attract business, the country may be lacking in other important infrastructure respects. Alternatively, risk may be higher.

As with domestic operations, U.S. taxes provide something of a risk premium as well. If the operation goes bankrupt or is seized, a tax-deductible loss occurs. However, if it is in a separate legal entity (as opposed to a branch), the loss is considered a capital loss and its deduction is therefore limited. If the international operation incurs NOLs, they flow through to the parent unless the operation is a subsidiary. In this case, the NOLs cannot be used to reduce U.S. taxes. (See Example 8.11.)

EXAMPLE 8.11

A corporation established a manufacturing operating overseas. The operation expects NOLs its first two years of $1 million per year. Assuming the U.S. parent is in the 35% bracket, the operation provides $350,000 per year of tax benefits, if it is not an unincorporated subsidiary.

From a nontax perspective, operating risk can be mitigated by organizational form. Forming a joint venture with a local operation adds the local's knowledge. Forming as a corporate-like entity (see Tax Management in Action 8.1 for entity forms in various countries) also gives the parent firm loss protection against liabilities generated by the foreign venture. This advantage should be weighed against the likelihood that, for tax purposes, the parent's loss may be classified as a capital loss. Recall that a capital loss may take years to deduct for U.S. income tax purposes. In that sense, having a flow-through entity, joint venture, or branch, where losses on individual assets can flow through to the parent, is a better tax-related risk reduction mechanism. (See Example 8.12.)

EXAMPLE 8.12

Assume the GmbH in Example 8.9 projects two-year losses as follows: $6 million (⅓ probability); $3 million (⅓ probability); and $1 million (⅓ probability). The *expected* pretax loss is thus $3 million. This would flow through to the U.S. parent, for an expected after-tax loss of $(1 - .35) \times \$3,000,000 = \$1,950,000$. Thus, the U.S. tax system has absorbed part of the loss. If the entity were instead an AG (a corporation under German law), none of the loss would be currently deductible by the U.S. parent.

Besides operating risk, a major source of international risk is from currency rate fluctuations. A risk occurs, for example, if the dollar devaluates and the firm is holding dollars (or has to pay on a contract not denominated in dollars). A gain can occur if the dollar goes up in value, and the firm holds dollars at year-end or pays on contracts denominated in other currencies. In either case, the gain or loss is ordinary and without limits for U.S. income tax purposes. The tax law thus acts like partial insurance policy on such financial risk. (See Example 8.13.)

EXAMPLE 8.13

A corporation has losses on foreign currency of $1 million. Assuming it is in the 35% tax bracket, it is out of pocket for only $650,000 after the tax deduction.

EXHIBIT 8.3   Forming a New Corporation

Value-Adding and Transactions Costs   Legal and accounting costs are higher for the corporate form, and lowest for direct exports. These costs vary by country and size of operation. In addition to import and export duties, there are other transaction taxes to consider. The most significant in the United States are on entity formation. The first is on formation of a corporation, as shown in Exhibit 8.3.

If the assets transferred have appreciated in value, the appreciation is subject to immediate U.S. income taxation. A simple way to avoid this is to transfer cash, and have the foreign affiliate buy the assets overseas. Alternatively, the subsidiary can obtain overseas financing.

If the overseas operation is instead a newly formed flow-through entity (such as a joint venture), then there is an immediate 35% U.S. excise tax. Again, transfers of cash, or obtaining overseas financing, obviates the problem.

Other Aspects of Value-Adding   As discussed in Exhibit 8.4 international tax planning must be balanced against other value-adding objectives of the company.

EXHIBIT 8.4   Balancing Tax Savings and Strategy in Multinational Ventures

CONSULTANT INTERVIEW

Gregory P. Hickey, Partner
International Tax Practice
PricewaterhouseCoopers LLP

What are some of the tensions that arise between international tax planning, and financial reporting, and other business objectives?

The following conflicts can arise:

- *Foreign tax credit planning.* The tax advisor suggests passing title overseas to generate foreign source income, but operations resists because a change in the way of doing business.
- *State and foreign restructuring to save taxes.* The tax advisor suggests restructuring changes (e.g., new holding company, relocation of warehouse to another country, intercompany charge for services royalties), but operations resists because it causes too much trouble.

- *Purchase price allocations.* The tax advisor wants allocations to short-lived assets to maximize depreciation deductions, but for financial statements (to increase EPS) the desire is to allocate to long-lived assets (building, goodwill, land).
- *Accounting Principles Board Opinion (APBO) 23.* A strategy that earnings of foreign subsidiaries in high tax rate countries are not permanently reinvested can help EPS because the related foreign tax credits reduce tax expense. The problem is that this may force the firm's treasury department to commit to cash repatriation plans that are not advisable, or result in adverse foreign tax consequences when the dividends are paid.
- *Restructuring charges.* This is often a good way to clean up the financials, but it results in some nondeductible charges for tax.
- *Leases.* A finance lease (vs. an operating lease) may be the desired lease for financial statement purposes, but could have adverse alternative minimum tax (AMT) consequences because of the depreciation effect.

Negotiating

Local officials, especially in developing countries, can be frequently negotiated with. This is particularly true with regard to property taxes and other localized fees.

Transfer prices, however, allow for two levels of negotiation. First, if a tax audit occurs, in the U.S. tax auditors are authorized to settle on reasonable prices under the offers in compromise provisions. Although IRS agents are not known for flexibility in this area, some negotiation is possible.

Second, the selling and buying parts of the firm may negotiate the price. This is particularly important if managers are evaluated on accounting profits. Here, tax minimization and performance measures may be at odds. For example, if the overseas selling subsidiary (manufacturer) is in a low tax jurisdiction, tax minimization implies setting the transfer price high. Yet this hurts the profits of the purchasing U.S. firm, which in turn might result in reduced bonuses for the purchaser's managers. Thus, tax and performance objectives may need to be weighed.

Specifics on Negotiation One way to manage international taxes is to negotiate with international authorities for relief. For large corporations, particularly in developing countries, a firm can negotiate local taxes (e.g., those on sales or property) as well as licenses and other fees. Negotiating national taxes, such as the corporate income tax, is much more difficult to do. For national taxes, general low-rate provisions which apply to all firms meeting certain criteria (e.g., creating new jobs) are the typical case. Well-known examples are manufacturers' low rates given in certain areas of Ireland and China.

Another negotiable item is within parts of the firm itself, through transfer pricing. Here, the firm attempts to shift income to the lowest-tax-rate country. To see how this can work, see Example 8.14.

EXAMPLE 8.14

A U.S. parent has an overseas subsidiary, located in a low-labor-cost, low-tax-rate country. The manufacturer ships the product to the U.S. affiliate for resale, as follows:

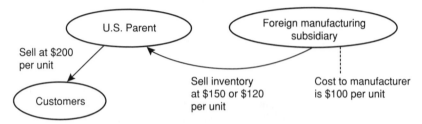

If the U.S. tax rate is higher than the foreign rate, the firm would like to set a high transfer price. Assume the U.S. and foreign tax rates are 35% and 20%, respectively. The analysis setting a low(higher) transfer price is as follows:

	High Transfer Price (Price = 150)		Low Transfer Price (Price = 120)	
	U.S. Parent	**Foreign Sub.**	**U.S. Parent**	**Foreign Sub.**
Selling price	$200	$150	$200	$120
Cost of goods sold	<150>	<100>	<120>	<100>
Income	50	50	80	20
Tax rate	× 35%	× 20%	× 35%	× 20%
Tax	17.5	10	28	4
Total tax	$27.5		$32	

Thus, the firm saves $4.5 per unit on taxes by setting a high transfer price. What if the foreign country has a higher rate? Then, a low transfer price should be set. If the countries' tax rates are reversed, the high transfer price yields a total tax of $22; the low transfer price a tax of $27.5.

The negotiation aspect of transfer pricing relates to the managers in the two parts of the company, and to tax authorities. On the former, if managers of the buying and selling division are evaluated on profits that result from tax-based transfer prices, there is a potential conflict. For the high transfer price case, the selling firm manager has a windfall gain, and the purchaser an undeserved loss. The opposite holds true for low transfer price.

Thus, centralized management should become involved to compensate the losing manager in another manner. In the alternative, a separate transfer pricing scheme for internal reporting purposes should be established. However, such a separate accounting system may be prohibitively costly. (See Example 8.15.)

EXAMPLE 8.15

A U.S. corporation has a subsidiary located in Ireland for tax purposes. The subsidiary sets relatively high transfer prices on goods shipped to the parent. For management-compensation purposes, the Irish subsidiary is treated as a cost center. That is, management is to focus on controlling costs, and bonuses are based on this. Thus, transfer prices do not affect compensation.

Negotiation with tax authorities may be necessitated if there is a tax audit. Note that firms cannot set ridiculously high or low prices: Some general guidelines must be adhered to. Most countries have their own specific rules that tend to be more flexible than in the United States. Currently, the OECD is working on more restrictive standards. There are a number of acceptable pricing methods for U.S. tax purposes, including those based on similar products, on cost to produce, and like metrics. All involve some degree of flexibility.

The inherent flexibility of intrafirm pricing allows room for tax planning, and even a challenge by tax authorities can be potentially negotiated to a lower tax. In some cases it may be worth entering into an advanced pricing agreement (APA) with the national tax authority. Here, the firm locks in a transfer price that cannot be changed (for a period of time) and likewise (generally) cannot be challenged on audit.

Negotiation with Employees   A final area of negotiation is with respect to transferring employees overseas. In some cases, key employees must be transferred overseas against their preferences. In such cases, the firm can help persuade employees to move through incentives. One such incentive is favorable U.S. tax treatment. As noted in Chapter 2, the U.S. taxes its citizens and residents on their worldwide incomes, regardless of where earned. However, an expatriate who meets certain tests can exclude up to $80,000 per year from U.S. taxation. The employee must be a bona fide resident of a foreign country, or be physically outside of the United States for 330 days in any consecutive 365-day period. Note that this does not allow exclusion from taxation by the foreign country, however. (See Example 8.16.)

EXAMPLE 8.16

Suppose a U.S. executive spends a year in the London office of a U.S.-based firm. The executive earns $200,000, and the U.S. (U.K.) tax rates are 35% (30%). The tax consequences are (assume no other income, deductions):

	U.S.	U.K.
Taxable income before exclusion	$200,000	$200,000
Exclusion	<70,000>	n.a.
Taxable income	130,000	200,000
Tax rate	× 35%	× 30%
Tax	$ 45,500	$60,000
Foreign tax credit	<39,000>	—
Net tax	$6,500	$60,000

The credit is limited to foreign taxes paid on nonexcluded income (which in this case is 30% of $130,000). Note that the foreign tax credit (FTC) is computed much the same as the FTC for a foreign corporation. It eliminates double tax by reducing the U.S. tax paid by foreign taxes paid.

Another employee negotiation item is housing costs. If the employer pays for the employee's foreign housing costs, the employee can exclude reasonable amounts for housing in excess of $10,000 of such reimbursements from U.S. taxation. This amount increases each year with federal cost of living indices. Note that under normal U.S. tax rules, any amounts received from employers, including cost reimbursements, may be taxable.

Finally, favorable taxes in the foreign country itself may be part of the negotiation. A number of Middle Eastern countries, for example, impose no income taxes on foreigners (e.g., Kuwait.) This effectively increases the real compensation of an employee from a country that does have these taxes.

Transforming

By utilizing a foreign subsidiary, a U.S. parent effectively transforms taxable income into nontaxable income by deferral. Also, some types of expenses, which are typically nondeductible, can be deducted. Certain payments (e.g., bribes and kickbacks) that are nondeductible if paid to U.S. officials, can be deductible if paid to foreign officials. Another popular way to transform is by using offshore entities, which are often located in island nations in the Caribbean ocean. Tax Management in Action 8.6 discusses one such off-shore venture.

TAX MANAGEMENT IN ACTION 8.6

Using Offshore Ventures

A common tax planning mechanism is for companies to establish so-called offshore businesses. These are most often established in small countries, such as many of the Caribbean Island nations. The advantages are purely tax: low (or no) taxes by the offshore (e.g., Caribbean Island) country, and certain home country tax advantages. These businesses are typically a small office, which processes paperwork for investment income such as lending, sales of realty in another country, or insurance. (Their use for e-commerce is as yet unknown, but is a distinct possibility.)

A recently popular offshore investment was a U.S.–Bermuda partnership. The tax rate is zero in Bermuda. A U.S. company would form a partnership with a financial services company (such as an insurance company) from another country. Many of these ventures were set up by major U.S. investment banking firms.

Such operations are under constant IRS scrutiny. In late January 2002, news reports suggested that Enron paid less than $200 million a year in U.S. income tax on its billions of dollars of revenues primarily through offshore ventures sprinkled throughout the Caribbean. Unusually, the IRS often pursues such cases through the court system rather than negotiate settlements out of court. An article in *The Wall Street Journal* (March 8, 1997, by Randall Smith) reported the result of one such case decided in the U.S. Tax Court. The decision disallowed approximately $100 million in losses claimed by Colgate-Palmolive in a Bermuda partnership arranged by Merrill Lynch & Company.

At a trial in New York on the matter, one Merrill investment banker said other Merrill clients that did similar transactions included Allied Signal Inc., American Homes Products Corp., Borden Inc., Brunswick Corp., Dun & Bradstreet Corp., Paramount Communications Inc. (now part of Viacom Inc.), and Schering-Plough Corp.

The Merrill plan put Colgate into a Bermuda investment partnership with Merrill and a Dutch Bank, Algemene Bank Netherlands (ABN, now a unit of ABN Amro Holding NV). Then a number of switches in the partnership's investments and ownership resulted in a paper profit for the Dutch bank in 1989, followed by a paper loss for Colgate two years later. As a non-U.S. taxpayer, the Dutch bank did not owe U.S. taxes on its gain, but Colgate tried to apply its losses against a $105 million capital gain from the 1988 sale of its Kendall health-care division.

TAX MANAGEMENT IN ACTION 8.6 (CONTINUED)

At the trial, Colgate argued that it aimed to use the partnership as a vehicle to buy back debt and manage its interest rate exposure. However, the court disagreed, and sustained the IRS's disallowance of the losses as *sham transactions.*

Foreign Sales Corporations   Another popular method of transforming is by use of a foreign sales corporation, (FSC). Most large multinational firms prefer regular overseas corporations (CFCs) to FSCs because they establish a more permanent active foreign presence, as in manufacturing. Midsized companies, as well as companies with high profit margins (e.g., above 50%) often use FSCs. In addition, FSCs are used as lessors that receive lease income, a portion of which will be exempt from U.S. taxation.

As already noted, the European Union successfully challenged the legality of domestic international sales corporations (DISCs the forerunner of FSCs) under the General Agreement on Trade and Tariffs (GATT), and was recently successful in challenging FSCs under GATT's successor, the World Trade Organization (WTO). Just as in the case of DISCs, legislation to change FTCs so that they meet WTO standards is pending before the U.S. Congress.

FSCs are not allowed a tax deferral on export income. Instead, a certain percentage (about 15 or 16%, depending on taxpayer status) of export income (exempt foreign trade income) is exempt from U.S. taxation. Pricing methods are provided for determining exempt foreign trade income. FSC tax benefits now available for software companies enable computer software to be treated as export property, even in cases where an agreement provides that the software may be reproduced overseas.

To elect FSC status, a foreign corporation must meet the foreign presence requirement. (An exception to this requirement is provided for small FSCs, where the foreign corporation's export receipts do not exceed $5 million.) The foreign presence requirement includes the following: (1) maintaining a foreign office, (2) operating under foreign management, (3) keeping a permanent set of books in the foreign office, (4) conducting foreign economic processes (e.g., selling activities), and (5) being a foreign corporation. In addition, the corporation must have no more than 25 shareholders during the taxable year and have no preferred stock outstanding at any time during the taxable year.

Most FSCs operate as commission FSCs. Rather than buying the item produced by the parent and then reselling it, they receive a commission for arranged sales. The maximum profit allowed the FSC cannot exceed the greatest of (1) 23% of the combined taxable income (CTI) of the related exporter and the FSC, (2) 1.83% of foreign trade gross receipts (not exceeding 46% of CTI), or 3) taxable income using IRC Section 482 pricing provisions (see Technical Insert for Section 482 provisions). (See Example 8.17.)

EXAMPLE 8.17

An FSC was incorporated in a U.S. possession by D Corp, the U.S. parent. It operates as a commission FSC for D Corp's export sales of its product. Sales results for first the year of operations are as follows:

D's gross sales	$80,000
Cost of goods sold	<44,000>
Gross income from sales	$36,000
Expenses attributed to export sales	<9,500>
Net income from sales before FSC	$26,500
Expenses paid by FSC	<2,000>
CTI	$24,500
FSC profit under CTI method (23%)	$ 5,635
FSC profit under gross receipts method (1.83% of gross sales)	$ 1,464

Because the CTI method results in more profit to the FSC than the gross receipts method, the FSC is allowed to earn a profit of $5,635. The FSC's commission is determined as follows:

Maximum profit allowed	$ 5,635
Expenses incurred by FSC	2,000
FSC commission	$ 7,635

The tax attributable to FSC activity is calculated as follows:

Commission income: $7,635	
$8/23$ of commission income	$ 2,656
Expenses incurred by FSC: $2,000	
$8/23$ of FSC's expenses	<696>
Taxable income	$ 1,960
U.S. tax at 34%	$ 666

The exempt foreign trade income is $3,675 = ($7,635 − $2,000) × 15/23. This is equal to 15% of $24,500.

PUTTING IT ALL TOGETHER: PENETRATING FOREIGN MARKETS FROM A SAVANT PERSPECTIVE

You are advising a CEO of a United States-based soft drink company on opening up bottling and distribution centers overseas. The company's marketing staff has identified central Europe and more developed parts of South America as good markets with favorable infrastructures. Specifically, the two sites are Sao Paulo, Brazil, and Budapest, Hungary. One site must be chosen as a test market. About 20% of the company's key employees would be transferred.

Strategy

The move appears consistent with the firm's strategic plan to internationalize. How will competitors react? Will they also enter this market? And will they operate in nearby countries that offer better tax advantages, thereby reaping a cost/pricing advantage? You find out that the national corporate tax rates for Brazil and Hungary are 25% and 18%, respectively.

Value-adding

The overseas operations will appear on the consolidated financials, thus they will directly affect EPS and EVA. Accordingly, having favorable tax treatment would be important. Use of a flow-through entity would avoid tax locally. However, U.S. tax would be immediate. The opposite would occur if corporate form were elected. Transfer pricing could be the answer if tax-reducing prices could be established.

However, going overseas will clearly be risky. Forming a JV with locals could help. From a tax perspective, incorporating would defer U.S. tax and provide something of a risk premium.

Value-adding is potentially reduced by transactions costs. If assets are transferred over, federal income (corporate) or excise (flow-through) taxes will be assessed. Much of this can be avoided by having the subsidiary purchase assets overseas. However, the IRS will (rightfully) assert that technical know-how, particularly patented soft-drink formulas, are intangible assets subject to the tax. The firm should attempt to minimize the value of intangibles through careful documentation.

Anticipation

Both countries' plans for tax revisions need to be investigated. Also, what is the likelihood of audits from either country's tax authorities? In terms of timing and time value of money, entity choice is critical. A discounted cash-flow analysis should be done on corporate versus flow-through forms.

Negotiating

If transfer prices are used to manage taxes, how will managers' compensation and incentives be affected? When employees are transferred, what individual tax rates will they be forcing in either country? Will U.S. tax law exclusions make the move any more inviting?

Transforming

By postponing taxes through an overseas corporation, the present value of U.S. taxation can become so small that it is effectively converted into nontaxable income. Unless funds are needed domestically, either the Brazilian or the Hungarian subsidiary could accomplish this.

TECHNICAL INSERT 8.1 TRANSFER PRICING

As discussed previously, transfer pricing deals with the sales of goods and services between related parties. By definition, the transactions at issue are not entirely mediated by the invisible hand of the market. Indeed, they often deal with trade secrets and other intangibles for which there are no comparable market transactions. Thus, it is difficult to determine proper prices. This, in turn, provides ample opportunity for shifting net income artificially in order to reduce taxes or achieve goals other than the clear reflection of income among the parties involved.

Not surprisingly, most countries scrutinize related party transactions. The international standard is that they must be priced as unrelated parties would do in an arm's length transaction. This is the standard in the United States, which is set forth in IRC Section 482 and Treas. Reg. Section 1.482.

Under IRC Section 482, the IRS is empowered to reallocate income, deductions, and credits between related taxpayers to more clearly reflect income. This does not give the IRS *carte blanche* power to adjust transfer prices. But it does require that the taxpayer to establish the reasonableness of any transfer-pricing arrangement.

As noted already, the U.S. rules are far more detailed and explicit than those for other countries as a whole. For example, the regulations provide that for the simplest class of transactions—the sale of inventory (and other transfers of personal property)—one of the six following methods must be used:

1. Comparable uncontrolled price (CUP) method
2. Resale price method

TECHNICAL INSERT 8.1 (CONTINUED)

3. Cost-plus method
4. Comparable profits method
5. Profit split method
6. Unspecified methods

These methods are detailed in the regulations. For example, the first method sets the transfer price equal to the price that the company charges to an outside party. However, in many cases (especially for partly completed products), no outside sales of internal goods occur, so this method cannot be used. The resale price method is designed to be used for transfers to the retailing part of the company. Here, the sales price charged by the retailer, less the normal profit markup, is the transfer price.

The cost plus method uses the cost of producing the inventory, and adds a normal profit markup percentage. The unspecified methods are any other reasonable methods. In general, the IRS prefers methods in the order listed previously.

The rules on the pricing of intangibles (such as copyrights, patents, and trade secrets) are even more complex. However, as noted throughout this book, because these rules are explicit and accessible, they provide a road map of what a manager can do to reduce taxes in countries other than the United States.

CHAPTER 9

Operations Management

We're in the business of dramatically reducing the cost
of distributing technology. To do that, we are going to get
closer and closer to our suppliers and customers

—Michael Dell, CEO, Dell Computers

Once a venture starts up, it must decide on how to manage ongoing operations. This chapter discusses two important aspects of operations management that are impacted by taxes. The first is production design and process selection. The second is strategic capacity planning.

PRODUCTION DESIGN AND PROCESS SELECTION

Materials and Inventory

A firm's purchasing decisions involve a number of choices. These include three key strategic decisions. The first deals with sourcing locations. The issue here is to what extent will suppliers be local (e.g., in state), regional (e.g., out of state, but in country), or foreign. The second is the strategic method, that is, whether the firm will seek to cooperate with suppliers. The third is a matter of timing: Will the firm seek to acquire materials and inventory just in time, or will it seek to keep stock on hand?

Generally, strategic method and timing have little differential tax effect. However, sourcing location can have a significant tax effect. This is illustrated in Exhibit 9.1. The issue here is to what extent the firm will try to purchase materials and inventory from suppliers located in the same state as the plant, warehouse or in other location where the firm will be using these items. Income taxes are the primary consideration because no sales or use tax will apply since these purchases will be either used in the manufacturing process or resold. (There could be a sales tax if the items purchased are inconsequential enough to be considered mere supplies. However, because of

EXHIBIT 9.1   Tax Effects from the Location of Operations

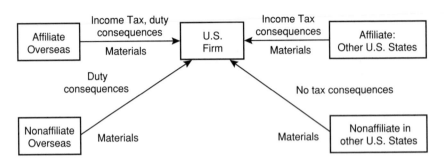

use taxes, the same result would apply regardless of whether the supplier was in state or out of state.) Similarly there should be no property tax impact to the decision in question (i.e., deciding whether to buy from vendors located in the same state as where the items will be used.) This is because most jurisdictions exempt materials and inventory from property taxes.

If materials come from nonaffiliates, there is no income tax consequence, either. However, if an affiliate sells to the firm, there may be a transfer pricing issue. If both states require combined (consolidated) tax returns, then transfer prices are irrelevant. However, if the firm or the seller are in a separate reporting state, tax minimization requires setting the transfer price high (low) if the seller is in a low- (high-) tax-rate state.

For foreign sourcing, duties (both at the foreign and U.S. ports) may apply. There should be no sales tax impact from foreign sourcing because most countries do not impose a sales tax. Nor should the decision on whether to buy from foreign sources turn on value-added taxes (VAT) (as in Sweden) or goods & services taxes (GST) (as in Canada). This is because sales across borders are usually zero rated, and thus no VAT or GST is imposed.

However, purchasing from a vendor located in a VAT jurisdiction could result in lower purchase prices. With zero-rated sales, there is a tax credit to the seller for the VAT that the seller paid when it purchased the goods being resold. (Some claim that this amounts to a government subsidy on exports from countries, like those of the European Union, that impose VAT.)

For income taxes, if the supplier is unaffiliated, there is no tax consequence. If there is an affiliation, however, much the same transfer pricing situation occurs as in the interstate case: The overseas affiliate can set the price high (low) if it is in a country with a lower (higher) tax rate.

Setting transfer prices affects real profits of both affiliates, whether interstate or intercountry. Accordingly, they are subject to negotiation. (See Example 9.1.)

EXAMPLE 9.1

To illustrate the impact of various taxes on materials and inventory, assume the following multistate and multinational firm (in $ millions):

Parent Co. (New York)		Subsidiary Company A (Illinois)	
Sales	$100	$50	sold to parent
Cost of sales	<60>	<30>	from unrelated company
Gross margin	40	$20	
Operating expenses	30	10	
Net income, pre tax	$10	$10	

Unrelated supplier (Turkey)		ubsidiary Company B (India)	
Sales to subsidiary (India)	$5	Sales (to parent)	$10
		Cost of sales	<5>
		Gross margin	$5
Taxes:		Operating expenses	2
Income: United States = 34%		Net income, pretax	$3
New York = 10%			
Illinois = 9%			
India = 25%			

U.S. duties on imports from India: 5%
Note that both New York and Illinois are unitary states

How can the firm manage its taxes with respect to inventory? The first step is to calculate what taxes the firm is actually paying. A good way to do this is first to get a grasp on the intercompany purchases, shown graphically in the following diagram (in millions of dollars):

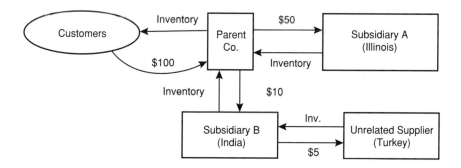

- *State Taxes.* Because both Illinois and New York are unitary, the incomes of the parent and subsidiary A are pooled, and there is no way to really manage state income taxes on transfers between these two. Note, however, that there are no sales or use taxes on such interfirm sales.
- *Foreign Income Taxes.* Subsidiary B pays a 25% Indian tax on income. Thus, manipulating transfer prices changes Indian income tax at 25% and U.S. income tax at 34%. Assuming managers can justify it to tax authorities, tax-minimization implies increasing the price as high as possible. Every dollar of price increase reduces worldwide income taxes by 34% − 25% = 9%.

  However, there is a countervailing effect on import duties. This is because for every dollar of price increase, import duties increase by 5%. Still, there is a net 4% gain on increasing the transfer price. On the India purchases from Turkey, there are likely to be import and income tax consequences. In addition, if profits from India are later repatriated to the United States, they are subject to a U.S. tax (net of a possible foreign tax credit for Indian income taxes paid by the Indian subsidiary).
- *U.S. Income Taxes.* The primary effect of purchasing materials and inventory from outside the United States for use in U.S. locations is the same as that described in the previous paragraph. The impact of a difference in tax rates is affected, however, to the extent the U.S. indirect foreign tax credit applies. These complex rules allow U.S. income taxes to be reduced if and when dividends are paid to a U.S. parent from a non-U.S. subsidiary. The credit is limited to the foreign income taxes traceable to the earnings and profits from which the dividends were derived. In addition, U.S. taxes would not be reduced to the extent the foreign tax rate exceeded the U.S. tax rate.

  Based on this information, a recommendation would be to increase the subsidiary-parent transfer price. Taking the principles of the SAVANT framework into account is critical, however.
- *Anticipation.* Will tax authorities challenge the new price? What is the expected adjustment?
- *Value-Adding.* If (as is likely) the Indian subsidiary will be included in the consolidated financial statements, changing the transfer price will have no direct effect on financial statement earnings. However, the timing difference from the reduced taxes will increase consolidated net income. There are other factors to be considered, too. If the tax authorities challenge the transfer price, what is the expected adjustment? What about transactions costs, such as the expense of changing accounting systems for the new transfer price?
- *Negotiating.* This may be the key stumbling block. Will managers of the U.S. parent be willing to accept a higher price on purchases, which in turn yields lower net income? If their bonuses are based on profit

without taking into account specific tax-minimizing firmwide adjustments, corporate headquarters may have to negotiate with these managers to obtain the price concession.

INVENTORY: METHODS OF ACCOUNTING AND INCLUDABLE AMOUNTS

Whether the firm is a merchandiser (having only finished inventory) or a manufacturer (having raw materials, work is process, and finished goods), the firm can use anticipation by selecting among a variety of timing options for accounting for inventory. In the United States, these include

- Specific identification (impractical unless there are a small number of inventory items)
- FIFO (first in, first out)
- LIFO (last in, first out)
- Weighted average

From an income-tax-minimizing perspective, LIFO tends to be the best choice. During periods of rising prices (the general case over the last 65 years), LIFO results in lower ending inventory, higher costs of goods sold, and lower taxable income (and thus lower taxes). The opposite is true of FIFO.

This tax reduction under LIFO does not come without a price, however. For example, U.S. tax authorities require conformity of financial and tax accounting. If the firm uses LIFO (FIFO) for its financial statements, it must do so for tax as well. This gives rise to the trade-offs in Exhibit 9.2.

Thus, there is direct effect on value-adding through financial earnings. Note that if the firm is in an NOL status, electing FIFO is clearly dominant from a financial-accounting perspective and harmless from a tax perspective. (See Example 9.2.)

EXHIBIT 9.2   Earnings versus Tax Savings Trade-off for Choice of Inventory Accounting Method

Inventory Accounting Choice	Effect on	
	Financial Accounting Income	Taxes
LIFO	↓ Net Income	Taxes ↓
FIFO	↑ Net Income	Taxes ↑

EXAMPLE 9.2

Suppose a firm is on FIFO, and is contemplating a switch to LIFO. Comparable statistics under the two methods are as follows (in $ millions):

	FIFO (now in use)	LIFO (proposed)
Beginning inventory	$ 10	$ 15
Cost of goods sold	100	120
Ending inventory	15	10

If the firm is in the 35% tax bracket, then the $20 million increase in cost of goods sold results in a $7 million tax savings. The trade-off is on the firm's financial earnings. A switch results in a drop in current financial statement earnings of $20 million − 7 million = $13 million. This leads to a concurrent drop in both earnings per share (EPS) and economic value-added (EVA). Using LIFO may be a bad trade-off if (1) debt contracts are tied to earnings, (2) managers receive earnings based on net income measures, or (3) the stock market takes into account the financial earnings drop instead of the cash-flow savings.

If the firm is in a net operating loss (NOL) status for income tax purposes, LIFO has no tax advantage over FIFO until the firm can transition into a tax-paying status. Note that the tax savings from LIFO is often not just a temporary or one time only event. This is because as long as prices rise, LIFO cost of goods sold will always be higher than cost of goods sold under FIFO.

Two important strategic considerations arise in the LIFO-FIFO choice. First, does the firm set its prices to customers based on inventory costs? If so, using LIFO may allow the firm to charge a lower price than its competitors. Second, what method do the firm's competitors use? If its competitors use LIFO, the firm can look better than its competitors in terms of higher earnings on its financial statements. If the firm uses FIFO, the reverse occurs. Note that a competitors' inventory choice, too, may depend on whether the firm has (or expects to have) NOL carryforwards.

Can the firm switch between LIFO and FIFO? Yes, in the United States. However, the LIFO-FIFO switch requires IRS approval. (A switch back and forth is rarely approved). There are also transactions costs involved. These include the cost of changing accounting systems. The IRS also requires a catch-up adjustment on ending inventory, which affects taxable income. If the firm is switching to LIFO (FIFO), the adjustment decreases (increases) taxes. Taxes (or refunds) resulting from such adjustments must be normally spread over three years.

A final LIFO-FIFO consideration is the impact of a so-called LIFO liquidation. This occurs when the firm sells more of its ending inventory than usual. This results in part of beginning inventory being charged to cost of goods sold. If (as is usual with LIFO) the beginning inventory is at a level lower than current replacement cost, cost of goods will artificially decrease, triggering a corresponding increase in net income and taxes. The former may be welcome; the latter is usually not. The point here is that managers need to be aware that these results can occur at any time. (See Example 9.3.)

EXAMPLE 9.3

Because its competitors are using FIFO, a firm decides to switch to LIFO in 2000. The new method will result in lower cost of goods sold and higher financial accounting income. The switch results in an increase of $10 million in taxable income. The firm pays taxes on $3,333,333 of income in each of 2000, 2001, and 2002.

Amounts of Inventoried Costs

For U.S. financial-reporting purposes, a firm's inventory is carried at full absorption cost. That is, inventory costs include direct materials, direct labor, and a share of manufacturing overhead. This is also true for tax, with one important difference: Some general, administrative, and selling expenses are added on. These expenses are added on if they are postacquisition or presale costs incurred, as shown in Exhibit 9.3.

For example, additional inventoried purchasing costs include freight-in, warehousing, and depreciation on the warehouse. Additional presale inventory expenses include similar items, plus packaging and some selling expenses.

EXHIBIT 9.3 Book Tax Differences in Costs Capitalized into Inventory

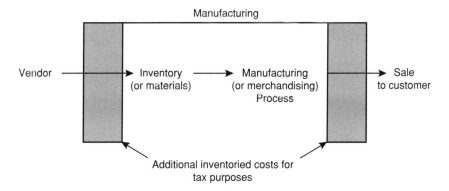

Note that these rules (see Technical Insert 9.1's "Uniform Capitalization Rules") affect only the *timing* of taxes. That is, they merely convert what would be a period cost into a product cost. Switching the firm's accounting methods on its financial statements to match tax rules would increase value-adding by increasing financial earnings, but this must be weighed against the resulting transactions costs. (See Example 9.4.)

EXAMPLE 9.4

Assume the following costs for a merchandising firm:

Cost incurred during the year:	
Freight-in	$ 100,000
Warehouse rental	200,000
Insurance on storage facilities	50,000
Cost of purchases	2,000,000
Shipping to customers	30,000
Packaging costs	200,000
Commissions to sales force	300,000

Assume that there was no beginning inventory, 900,000 units were sold during the year, and 100,000 units were left in ending inventory. Thus $1/10 \times (100,000/1,000,000)$ of the inventoried costs will stay in ending inventory and become part of cost of goods sold next year. The following table illustrates the differing results under tax and financial accounting rules:

	Tax Inventoried Costs	Tax Period Cost	Financial Inventoried Costs	Financial Period Cost
Freight in	$ 100,000	—	$ 100,000	—
Warehouse rental	200,000	—	—	$200,000
Insurance on storage facilities	50,000	—	—	50,000
Cost of purchases	2,000,000	—	2,000,000	—
Shipping to customers	30,000	—	—	30,000
Packaging costs	200,000	—	—	200,000
Commissions to sales force	—	$300,000		300,000
	$2,580,000	$300,000	$2,100,000	$780,000

Because only $9/10$ of inventoried costs will be expensed this period, cost of goods sold will be $.9(\$2,580,000) = \$2,322,000$ for tax purposes and

.9($2,100,000) = $1,890,000 for financial statement purposes. Added to period costs, tax and financial total costs for the year are $2,622,000 and $2,670,000, respectively.

In this case, the firm has an incentive to make financial reporting conform to taxes: it can increase reported earnings (thus, value-added) by $48,000 this year. This is not unusual because tax rules often result in higher taxable income than financial income. Further, transaction costs are reduced because there is no longer a need to have different inventory accounting systems for book and tax purposes.

Inventory Costs and Decision Making

Managers make a number of inventory-related decisions based, at least in part, on what they believe to be the cost of inventory. Such decisions include the number of units to make (break-even analysis), make or buy decisions, and accepting additional orders. Taxes are a component of inventory costs, and thus should be considered in making these decisions. Like nontax costs, whether tax costs are variable or fixed has a significant bearing on decision making.

Exhibit 9.4 summarizes the role of taxes in inventory.

The mixed-cost nature of income taxes results from certain tax-deductible items being fixed (such as depreciation) and other items (such as those relating to sales less cost of goods) being variable. (See Example 9.5.)

EXHIBIT 9.4   Taxes as Fixed or Variable Inventory Costs

	Fixed	Variable
Raw Materials (Manufacturer) or Purchases (Merchandiser)		
Duties		✔
Direct Labor		
Payroll taxes, such Social Security, Disability, or Unemployment		✔ Up to a maximum amount per employee
Overhead		
Property taxes	✔ Within a relevant range	
Income taxes—federal, state, or foreign	✔ and	✔

EXAMPLE 9.5

Consider a merchandising firm that currently buys and resells 1 million units of inventory per year on average, though this amount can fluctuate between 800,000 and 1,200,000. Assume management gathers the following cost data for these sales ranges:

Costs (Taxes only)	Sales in units 800,000	1,000,000	1,200,000
Import duties ($1/unit)	$ 800,000	$1,000,000	$1,200,000
Payroll taxes	300,000	350,000	350,000
Property taxes	1,000,000	1,000,000	1,000,000
Income taxes:			
Federal	3,000,000	4,000,000	5,000,000
Foreign	40,000	50,000	60,000
State & local	300,000	400,000	500,000
	$5,440,000	$6,800,000	$8,110,000

Which costs vary with sales? Import duties and all income taxes. Payroll taxes have a $300,000 fixed component and a variable one that tops out at $50,000. Property taxes are fixed at $1 million. (Note that were the company to double its sales, it would have to expand its facilities. This would increase property taxes. Within the relevant range of production, however, property taxes are fixed in nature.)

What are the costs per unit, which is the amount that should drive decision making? Adding the variable costs at the high and low levels of production results in

Low sales:

$$($800,000 + 300,000 + 3,000,000 + 40,000 + 300,000)/800,000 \text{ units}$$
$$= $4,440,000/ 800,000 \text{ units} = $5.55 \text{ unit.}$$

High sales:

$$($1,200,000 + 350,000 + 5,000,000 + 60,000 + 500,000)/1 \text{ m units}$$
$$= $7,110,000/1m \text{ units} = $7.11/\text{unit.}$$

Accordingly, it is estimated that variable costs increase by $7.11 − 5.55 = $1.56 unit.

As with other items, tax NOL carryforwards offer a competitive advantage. (See Example 9.6.)

EXAMPLE 9.6

Suppose two firms both have variable costs of $20 to produce a unit (excluding taxes). Both have excess capacity, but one firm has an NOL that is not expected to be utilized in the next several years. The other firm is in a tax-paying status. If they both receive an offer to produce and sell at $21, the NOL carryforward firm has an after-tax profit of $1, but the other firm has after tax profit of $(1 - .34)(\$21 - \$20) = \$.66$.

Consider break-even point analysis as another case in point. It is calculated as

$$\frac{\text{Total fixed cost}}{\text{Contribution margin per unit}} = \text{Break-even point in units}$$

EXAMPLE 9.7

Continuing with Example 9.6, assume both firms have $20 pretax unit contribution margins, a sales price of $40, and fixed costs consisting solely of depreciation of $100,000. Firm A has an NOL carryforward, and firm B is the 34% tax bracket. Assuming the cost of depreciable equipment is deductible at 25% per year over four years (that is, there is a 25% write-off), the strategic advantage goes to the taxable firm. The analysis is

Firm A:
    100,000/$20 = 5,000 units is break-even point

Firm B:
$(100,000 \times (.75) \times (1 - .34))/(\$25 \times (1 - .34)) = 3,000$ units is break-even point

Example 9.7 illustrates that taxable firms with large depreciation tax shields can have an advantage over a nontaxed firm that is also capital intensive. Similarly, having a NOL carryforward (or a lower tax rate) can hold a strategic advantage in pricing decisions. Pricing decisions should be made in light of a number of considerations, such as market analysis and competitive analysis. Cost-based pricing plays a part, too. Lower-tax-rate firms have lower costs, and thus can potentially undercut their competitors.

Generally, one can apply standard microeconomic analysis to production/sales decisions like these. Exhibit 9.5 shows total costs (TC) and total revenue (TR) curves for high-tax and low-tax firms, respectively.

The top curves are total revenues, and the lower curves are total costs. The much larger shaded (profit) area of the effectively tax-managed firm can be converted to lower prices, giving the firm a strategic advantage over its competitors.

The firms' total revenue and cost functions are shown as curves because beyond a narrow range of sales/production they are nonlinear (this is confirmed by many studies in industrial economics). Consider a firm that is

EXHIBIT 9.5 General Tax Impacts on Total Costs and Revenues

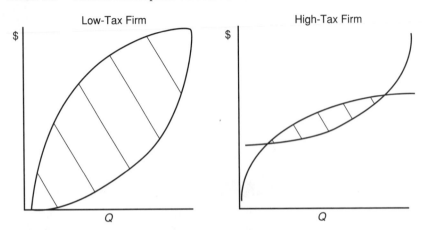

large enough in its industry to be able to affect price and demand. This implies a downward-sloping demand function. For example, suppose total revenues are: $TR = 1,000Q - (.01Q)^2$. At a production level of 1,000 units, total revenue is $90,000.

Similarly, as firms produce up to their capacities, total costs decrease in production with no fixed costs changes. Once capacity is reached, however, additional production necessitates expanded plant size, thus increasing costs. (See Example 9.8.)

EXAMPLE 9.8

Assume that for the firm in Example 9.7 the total costs are as follows: $TC = \$50Q + (.1Q)^2$. At a production level of 1,000 units, total cost is $40,000, and profit is $50,000.

When taxes enter into the equation, the lower-taxed firm has a competitive advantage. (See Example 9.9.)

EXAMPLE 9.9

Assume two competitor firms, both with the same TC and TR functions. The first firm has a 0% tax rate, while the second has a 35% rate. Here, both firms have the same $90,000 of pretax profits. However, the first firm has after-tax profits of $90,000, while the second has $58,500. The first firm could lower prices by $58,500 in an attempt to eliminate its competitor.

How can one know a competitor's tax status, or anticipate the competitors' future tax rates? If the competitor is publicly traded in the United States, the tax footnote required in the firm's annual form 10K filing with the Security and Exchange Commission (SEC) reveals this. If the competitor is privately held, however, this ready source of information is not available, and items like this can only be estimated using competitive intelligence.

STRATEGIC CAPACITY PLANNING: PLANT VERSUS PEOPLE

There are often some choices about human versus mechanized production in service, manufacturing, and merchandising firms. The choice depends in part on productivity and costs. Although machinery could perhaps make them more efficiently, Nike shoes are made largely by hand in China where labor costs are cheap. In contrast, Saturn cars are made mostly in robotized plants, and ATMs have substituted capital for labor in banks throughout the world.

The most fundamental income tax difference between labor and capital is the timing of deductions. Labor expense usually is deducted as it is incurred; capital is almost always deducted over time using depreciation. Prices for both of these factors of production can be reduced by taxes. For example, if governments offer more rapid depreciation expense for tax purposes, then after-tax cost of capital is reduced and may result in the firm's replacing workers with machines. Alternatively, governments can offer tax incentives to hire workers. For example, the U.S. government has a targeted job credit for companies that hire physically challenged individuals, ex-convicts, and others who have difficulty getting jobs.

After-tax factor costs can *increase* as well. Labor cost increases can result from higher payroll taxes. For plant and equipment, lengthening the useful tax lives or making write-offs less accelerated effectively increases the cost of capital. (See Example 9.10.)

EXAMPLE 9.10

Suppose a firm has the following features:

Factor	Annual Tax Deduction	
Factory	$ 1,000,000 cost/39 yrs = $ 25,600	depreciation expense
Equipment (100 machines)	10,000,000 cost/7 yrs = 1,429,000	depreciation expense
Employees (100 workers)	2,000,000	salary expense
Total annual deductions	$3,454,600	

Assuming the firm is in the 35% tax bracket, the annual tax savings from these deductions $1,209,110. Suppose payroll taxes (such as Social Security) taxes decrease by 2%. This reduces the cost of labor by $40,000 before tax annually and by $26,000 after tax. One way to think of this is as an increase in the cost of capital vis-à-vis labor.

A clearer example would be if tax-depreciation rules on equipment changed so that they were depreciable in three years, instead of seven. (See Example 9.11.)

EXAMPLE 9.11

If a new machine is bought for $100,000, the annual tax depreciation cash flow benefit is changed by: $(100,000)/(\frac{7}{3})(.35) = \$81,667$ per year, or 43% across time (ignoring the time value of money).

A change in the relative prices of labor and capital requires managers to review the possibility of a change in input structure. If the tax-price change is expected to be temporary, then the manager should simply adjust the *timing* of inputs; if nontemporary, a permanent adjustment in the mix may be called for. (See Example 9.12.)

EXAMPLE 9.12

Suppose a company makes a manufactured product that requires the inputs of any combination of workers and machines that adds up to four. (Assume at least one machine and one worker is required, however.) Currently, company uses two of each, as follows (assume the firm is in the 35% tax bracket):

Machines: Cost = $100,000 each.

Annual tax depreciation = $20,000 each (approximately). If time value and interest are ignored, and the machine costs are paid off evenly through five years, the annual after tax cost of a machine is $100,000/5 = 20,000$ less tax savings from depreciation: $(100,000/5)(.35) = 7,000$. So, after-tax annual costs = 13,000.

Workers: annual cost of salary and benefits = $20,000/year.

After-tax cost = $(1 - .35)(20,000) = \$13,000$.

Suppose the government gives a 50% tax credit for hiring workers located in economically depressed areas. If the firm can hire equally skilled workers in this category, it may be worthwhile for the firm to replace one of the machines with an additional worker.

However, the firm needs to try to anticipate the permanence of the tax credit. If it is expected to be temporary, then it may not be worthwhile to make such a major production change for a temporary tax savings.

The timing adjustment is often associated with anticipated tax policy changes. Suppose the government allows for rapid depreciation of equipment under a new law this year, which is expected to be repealed at the end of the year. If the firm is considering replacing some plant and equipment in the near future, it may want to accelerate the purchase to this year, to take advantage of the tax benefits. Of course, this plan is contingent on whether the time value of the early acquisition is higher than keeping the old machine, after considering borrowing costs, tax benefits, and increased efficiency (see Capital Budgeting, Chapter 11). (See Example 9.13.)

EXAMPLE 9.13

Suppose a U.S. company is considering replacing its computer system (server, workstations, and the like). The current system is a seven-year MACRS property, which cost $300,000 when purchased five years ago. The firm would like to replace the system next year. However, next year it anticipates that it will generate an NOL which will carry forward for many years. If the system costs $500,000, what should be the timing of the acquisition? Assume the new computer system's effect on productivity and cost is not easily quantified, and the firm is in the 35% bracket.

	Acquire Now	Acquire Next Year
Year 1 Depreciation tax benefit	$500,000 (.1429)(.35) = $25,008	0*
Years 2 → 8 depreciation tax benefits	0	0*

* Tax benefits carried forward until NOL expires;
   NPV may be so small as to be close to zero

Thus, it saves the firm $25,008 in taxes by accelerating the purchase into this year. Note that the tax benefits in years 2 through 8 are identical. Also, one must consider the transaction costs of making the switch (such as the gain on sale or commissions). If they exceed the transactions costs that would be incurred were the sale made next year by more than $25,008, the firm may want to make the purchase next year.

However, if the manager believes the tax policy change to be permanent, then a change in the capital-labor input mix may be called for. For example, suppose an auto manufacturer can make a certain car part with any combination of machine hours (machine intensive) or labor hours (labor intensive). A well-known representation of this from microeconomics is the following equation:

$$\frac{MRP_L}{MRP_K} = \frac{MC_K}{MC_L}$$

Where MRP_L and MRP_K are the marginal revenue products of labor and capital, and MC_K and MC_L are the marginal costs of capital and labor. The equation means that any marginal change in capital structure should follow the rule that additional revenue will be proportional to additional relative cost. (See Examples 9.14 and 9.15.)

EXAMPLE 9.14

Suppose, before a tax-law change, the auto part could be made with any combination of five hours of machine or labor time, machines cost $100,000 and last three years, and that labor costs are $20,000 per year per worker. If the corporate tax rate is 34%, the machine is depreciated straight line, and each worker (machine) can produce 10,000 (20,000) units per year, the analysis would be as follows:

Machine:

Marginal product (three years)	60,000 units
Marginal cost (three years)	
Up front cost (assume no financing)	$100,000
Less time value of tax benefits (at 10%)	
Year 1: ($100,000/3) × .909 × 34% =	<10,300>
Year 2: ($100,000/3) × .826 × 34% =	<9,360>
Year 3: ($100,000/3) × .75) × 34% =	<8,560>
	$71,780

Worker:

Marginal product (three years)	20,000 units
Marginal cost (three years)	
$20,000 × 3 years × (1 − .34)	$39,600

Suppose management does a productivity analysis, and determines that productivity of parts follows the following function:

$$\text{Production of parts} = 5 \; (L^{0.4} \times K^{0.5}).$$

Then if 100 labor hours and 100 machine hours are applied, total parts produced is: $5(100^{0.4} \times 100^{0.5}) = 5(6.31 \times 10) = 315.5$. Using differential calculus, we can find the marginal product of labor and capital is as follows:

$$\frac{\partial Q}{\partial L} = 2L$$

$$\frac{\partial Q}{\partial K} = 2.5K$$

Therefore, the profit-maximizing solution is

$$\frac{2L}{2.5K} = \frac{71,780}{39,600} = 2.27K$$

that is, for any given budget for the year, 2.27 times as many workers should be hired for each machine.

EXAMPLE 9.15

Assume the facts as in Example 9.14, and suppose that tax policy changes so that equipment can be expensed in the year of acquisition. The marginal cost of capital is then $100,000 \times (1 - .34) \times .909 = \$59,094$. The new analysis is then:

$$\frac{2L}{2.5K} = \frac{59,094}{39,600} = 1.49 \text{ worker per machine}$$

Note that the analysis is sensitive to assumptions about the production function, cost of capital (here, it was assumed to be 10%), and marginal (after-tax) costs.

It is important to realize that the analysis in Examples 9.13 and 9.14 is with respect to *marginal* decisions. For a discussion of longer-run input-planning decisions, such as capacity planning, or single versus multisite selection, see Chapter 11, "Capital Budgeting."

PUTTING IT ALL TOGETHER:
OPERATIONS MANAGEMENT FROM A SAVANT PERSPECTIVE

Nutraherb, Inc., is a U.S.-based producer of herbal health food remedies such as natural pain relievers and vitamins. One of its raw materi-

als suppliers is in Thailand, and Nutraherb is considering purchasing the supplier. The firm sells $10 million per year in herbs primarily to Nutraherb, on which a 5% duty is paid. The annual purchase price is $25,000,000. The supplier sells at a 100% markup. Thai corporate income taxes are 30%. For liability purposes, Nutraherb would like to keep the supplier as a corporation. Nutraherb is in the 35% bracket for U.S. income tax purposes and is concerned about managing taxes. Nutraherb's main competitor is also considering making a bid for the company.

Strategy

The acquisition makes strategic sense. It enables Nutraherb to control timing, quantity, and quality of supply. Moreover, it may put the firm's competitor at a strategic disadvantage.

Anticipation

No tax law changes, or changes in either firm's tax status, appear relevant.

Value-Adding

The firm may be able to see significant dollars by the acquisition. Because there is a 100% markup, it could cut the cost of materials by $5 million per year, which, ignoring time value of money and cost of capital, would pay for itself in five years. Because the target would appear in Nutraherb's consolidated financials, there may be significant EPS and EVA benefits as well.

However, taxes complicate the issue. Setting a lower transfer price reduces import duties: A $5 million per year transfer price drop would save the firm $250,000 per year in duties. However, income taxes would increase. A $5 million transfer price drop decreases Thai taxes by $1,500,000 but increases U.S. taxes by $1,750,000. This would result in a net income tax increase of $250,000 per year. Thus, the net tax impact overall would be 0.

Two further tax issues arise: uniform capitalization rules (UCR) and LIFO-FIFO choice. Because the subsidiary is located outside the United States, it will not be subject to UCR. Electing LIFO will increase the transfer price, which acts to increase total taxes. This has little effect on the firm's financials because such intercompany transactions are eliminated upon consolidation.

Regarding transaction costs, making the acquisition will reduce U.S. duties. However, the firm should also consider the cost of legal and accounting fees for the acquisition. That is, if external financing is necessary to raise the purchase price, what additional legal, brokerage, and loan fees will be incurred?

There is some risk that U.S. and Thai tax officials will challenge the transfer price. Thus, the expected return should be risk-adjusted.

Negotiating

If managers of the target and the parent are evaluated based on profitability, setting a very low price will hurt the subsidiary's management. Nutraherb may have to negotiate with these managers to get them to agree on the low price.

Transforming

By deferring payment of dividends over many years, target's earnings essentially will be transformed into nontaxable income.

TECHNICAL INSERT 9.1 INVENTORY TAX ACCOUNTING

Uniform Capitalization Rules (UCR, or UNICAP)

According to the U.S. Treasury Department, the overall purpose of UNICAP is to create a system that is consistent among all taxpayers in determining the cost of inventories and the basis of certain assets. UNICAP increases the amount of costs that are not currently deducted. This results in a temporary book/tax difference, which generally originates unfavorably as inventory levels increase and reverses as inventory levels decrease.

A taxpayer must

- Include in inventory costs the allocable costs of property that is inventory (IRC Section 263A (a)(1)(A))
- Capitalize the allocable costs of any other property (IRC Section 263A(a)(2)(B)). The *allocable costs* are the following:
  - The direct costs of the property (IRC Section 263A(a)(2)(A))
  - The indirect costs, to the extent of the property's share of the costs (IRC Section 263A(a)(2)(B))

Allocable costs include all depreciation deductions with respect to the taxpayer's assets. Interest is an allocable cost, but only where the underlying debt was incurred or continued to finance certain produced property. Taxes are allocable indirect costs (IRC Section 263A(a)(2)(B)).

TECHNICAL INSERT 9.1 (CONTINUED)

Tax Effects of Switching to and from LIFO

LIFO. Under the last-in, first-out (LIFO) method of inventory valuation, the most recently purchased merchandise is treated as sold first (IRC Section 472(b)(1)). LIFO may be used only when inventory is valued at cost (Treas. Reg. Section 1.472-2(b)). If a taxpayer had written down inventory to a lower market value, the difference between that value and cost must be restored to income ratably over a three-year period (starting with the LIFO election year) (IRC Section 472(d)).

LIFO Recapture Tax. When a corporation uses the FIFO method for its last year before electing to become taxed as an S corporation, any built-in gain will be recognized and taxed as the inventory is sold. This is not true for a LIFO-basis corporation, unless it invades the LIFO layer during the following 10-year period.

To preclude deferral of gain recognition under LIFO, the law requires the income recognition of a LIFO recapture amount upon making an election to be taxed as a flow-through entity under Subchapter S. A C corporation using LIFO for its last year before making an S election must include in income the excess of the inventory's value under FIFO over the LIFO value.

Any change in the method of valuing inventory, with the exception of a change to LIFO, requires IRS approval.

CHAPTER 10

Financing Ongoing Operations and Tax Planning

You have to divorce yourself from the stock price and just focus on the business
— Howard Schultz, CEO of Starbucks

Firms need a certain amount of working capital to finance ongoing operations, take advantage of unexpected opportunities, and fulfill longer-run strategic plans. Examples of the first of these include payments to suppliers and scheduled payments to creditors and bondholders. The last includes cash for plant expansion and for acquisition of other firms. Firms manage this by preparing an annual master budget that forecasts operating needs, including any cash needs.

Beyond the cash budget objectives, there are value-adding considerations to cash flows as well. Capital markets may perceive low levels of cash as a sign of a weak or risky firm. High levels may be seen as healthy. They can also be seen as a sign of poor investment management, or of managers misusing funds (that is, an agency problem).

To finance ongoing operations, firms can generate cash flows from a variety of sources. These include

- Operating earnings (i.e., net income from sale of products or services)
- Sale of operating assets (such as plant and equipment)
- Sale of investments (such as stock, bonds, or raw land)
- Short-term borrowing
- Accelerating, factoring, or selling receivables
- Decrease in dividends
- Payment of stock dividends instead of cash dividends

- Stock buybacks (by the firm or management) to reduce dividend payouts
- Employee stock option plans (ESOPs)
- Receipt of dividends from subsidiaries (domestic and foreign)

Each of these methods has tax implications that can be analyzed using the SAVANT framework.

OPERATING EARNINGS

Operating earnings, after payment of federal, foreign, and state or local taxes, add to retained earnings. As discussed previously (at the end of Chapter 5, for example), earnings retained without a legitimate business purpose may be subject to special penalty taxes, such as the U.S. accumulated earnings tax.

SALE OF OPERATING ASSETS

Gains (losses) on the sale of operating assets are taxable (tax deductible). Gain or loss is the difference between an asset's sales price and its adjusted basis. Adjusted basis is original cost, plus improvements, less accumulated depreciation. Gains generally are treated as capital gains. As noted in Chapter 1, capital gains are not taxed in many jurisdictions. In those where they are, capital gains usually are taxed at ordinary income rates unless offset by other capital losses. Losses on the sale of operating assets usually are treated as ordinary losses and are fully deductible.

Note that depreciation previously taken reduces an asset's basis. This generally results in reducing the loss or increasing the gain if the asset is sold. Thus, the tax benefit of depreciation flows from time value. (See Example 10.1.)

EXAMPLE 10.1

Suppose a U.S. firm buys a $1 million machine, which can be depreciated as a five-year MACRS property. (MACRS depreciation rates can be found in IRS Publication 946; those used here are on page 64 at page. As noted previously, tax related publications like this can be found on the Web via gateway sites like *www.taxsites.com*.)

Let the firm sell the machine for $900,000 at the beginning year 3. If the firm's tax rate is 34% and its cost of capital is 10%, the present value (PV) of the cash flows is as follows:

Item	Year	Cash flow	Discount Factor	Discounted Cash Flow
Purchase	0	<$1,000,000>	1	<$1,000,000>
Depreciation	1	1,000,000 × .20 × .34 = 68,000	0.9091	61,819
	2	1,000,000 × .32 × .34 = 108,800	0.8264	89,912
Proceeds on sale	2	900,000	0.8264	743,760
Tax on sale				
Proceeds	2	900,000		
Less adjusted basis*		< 823,200>		
Gain on sale		$ 76,800 × .34 = 26,112	0.8264	<21,579>
Net present value				<$126,088>

*Adjusted basis = cost less accumulated depreciation
= $1,000,000 − 68,000 − 108,800

Here, the PV of the tax benefits from depreciation is $61,819 + $89,912, which total to $151,731. This exceeds the PV of the tax on the gain, which is $21,579.

Had the machine been sold for its original purchase price, the PV of the tax benefits would still exceed the PV of the tax on the gain. This is because the discounted cash inflow on sale would increase by $100,000 × .8264, but the discounted tax outflow would only increase by $100,000 × .34 × .8264.

Selling operating assets simply to generate cash flow may not make business sense. This is because unless the asset is traded in for a new asset, its absence will decrease value-added. Because there is also a financial accounting gain or loss, there is an effect on earnings that may in turn affect management bonuses. Finally, the timing of any gain on the sale can be negotiated with the buyer. That is, if the buyer is willing to accept payment over time, the tax on the gain can be recognized ratably over time.

SALE OF INVESTMENTS

Investments are income tax favored throughout the world. In the United States, they usually are capital assets, generating capital gain or loss on sale. Such gains and losses are netted together for the year. If there is a net gain, it is taxed like any other income for corporate taxpayers but at very reduced rates for most individual taxpayers. Net losses, however, are nondeductible for corporate taxpayers and must be carried over. Upon carryover, such losses can only be used to offset capital gains. The carryover period is three years back and five years forward. (For individuals, up to $3,000 of losses can offset other income, and the excess is carried forward indefinitely.)

Like net operating losses (NOLs), a regular corporation that generates a net capital loss for a year applies the loss in a stylized way. First, the corporation's tax return for the year three years before (e.g., 1999 for a loss in year 2002) is reviewed. If there were net capital gains for the year, the return would be restated and a tax refund calculated by offsetting these gains with the current year's loss. If this loss exceeds the capital gains, the excess is carried forward to the second previous year. This is repeated until the fifth year after the net loss. After the fifth subsequent year, any remaining carryover disappears.

Otherwise, the same tax-management principles of timing and negotiation that apply to operating assets also apply to investments. However, the sale of investments can have a very different impact of on a U.S. firm's financial statements than the sale of operating assets. Under U.S. GAAP, unrealized gains or losses on operating assets are not recognized, and thus their net book value remains at depreciated historical cost. However, unrealized gains and losses on marketable securities are typically recognized under mark-to-market accounting. Thus, their net book value often is much closer to their current market value, and the gain or loss reported in financial statements in the year of sale year minimal. (See Example 10.2.)

EXAMPLE 10.2

Suppose a firm has blue chip stocks purchased in 1999 for $10 million, with the following basis and fair market value:

	Basis	Market Value
As of Dec. 31, 2000	$10,000,000	$50,000,000
As of Dec. 31, 2001	$10,000,000	$75,000,000

If the firm sells the stocks in 2001, there will be a taxable gain of $75 million − $10 million = $65 million. The gain is capital (assuming the firm is not a dealer in securities). Unless there are some unused capital losses to offset against it, the gain will be taxed like ordinary income. If the firm is in the 35% bracket, there will be $22,750,000 of taxes due. If the firm is in an NOL carryforward status, no taxes will be due.

If the firm trades in marketable securities (that is, it had an active business buying and selling securities), and it had elected mark-to-market-accounting, there would be little tax due on the sale. Under this method, the firm would have recognized $50 million − $10 million = $40 million gain in 2000, and paid tax of $14 million. In 2001, only the $25 million of appreciation occurring that year would be taxable. The tax for 2001 would be $8,750,000, so the total tax (not discounted for time value) would be the same as in the previous paragraph, $22,750,000.

SHORT-TERM BORROWING

Cash flows from borrowing are not taxable. However, subsequent Interest payments on the debt normally are tax deductible. Interest payments on short-term debt (such as bank notes) are usually higher than those on long-term debts. Firms may favor such junior debt because it does not typically violate debt covenants on existing long-term financing. Transaction costs include loan fees, which must be capitalized and amortized over the term of the loan. (See Examples 10.3 and 10.4.)

EXAMPLE 10.3

Suppose a firm borrows $1 million on July 1, 2002 to finance its short-term working capital needs. The bank charges 2%, and the loan is due in two years. Interest is at 10%. The tax savings related to the borrowing are as follows (assume a 35% tax rate):

	2002	2003	2004
Interest expense:			$100,000(½ yr)
(10% × $1,000,000) (½ year) =	$50,000	$100,000	= 50,000
Amortization of loan cost:			
(2% × $1,000,000)/24 =			
$2083 per month × ½ year =	12,500	25,000	12,500
Total deductions	$62,500	$125,000	$ 62,500
Tax savings at 35%	$21,900	$ 43,800	$ 21,900

EXAMPLE 10.4

What if the firm in Example 10.3 expects to have a lower tax rate in 2004? (Assume the firm uses the cash method of accounting.) While it may appear to save taxes by prepaying in 2003 the interest due in 2004, the deduction is not allowed until 2004.

The opposite is not true. If the firm expects to be in a higher tax bracket in 2004, it would save taxes by delaying interest payment until 2004. (The deduction for the loan fee amortization is not delayed, however.) Of course, the lender may not agree to the delay, or it may change penalties. The delay also might impair the firm's credit ratings. These must be weighed against the tax savings.

ACCOUNTS RECEIVABLE

Cash can be generated from customer receivables in a number of ways. Offering discounts for early payment (e.g., 2/10 / net 30) may affect the timing of cash flows, but the timing of taxable income recognition is usually unaffected. This is because taxable income is already recognized under the accrual method for most firms.

Selling and factoring of accounts receivable results in recognizing a tax loss, if the firm has already accrued the sales revenue for the entire sale. This is because the buyer (factoring institution) pays less than the actual receivable amount.

The firm, subject to cash-flow needs, may want to engineer the timing of the factoring to coincide with higher-tax-rate years. Suppose a firm can sell $1 million of receivables for $800,000, at the end of 2002. If its 2002 tax rate is 0, (e.g., from an NOL carryover) and its 2003 rate is 35%, it can save $200,000 × 35% = $70,000 by simply postponing the factoring until January 2003. Of course, if the firm's cash needs are so critical that the sale cannot be delayed, tax savings should not induce a postponement.

The impact of bad debts should be mentioned at this point. For financial-accounting purposes, bad debts usually are expensed based on an expectation. For example, the firm may have historically had 5% of credit sales become uncollectible. So, it would accrue a bad debt expense of 5% of each year's sales. However, for U.S. tax purposes, bad debts are written off only as they actually go bad.

The write-off can occur only when the debt becomes worthless, not when the firm gives up attempting to collect. Because this may take years to occur for some loans, the present value of the tax deduction can be diminished. For substantial bad debts (e.g., a bank's loan to a defaulting poor country), a tax management opportunity exists. If the firm is certain of the debt's uncollectibility, it can postpone final, worthlessness-proving efforts until it is in a high tax bracket. Or it can accelerate such efforts into higher-tax-bracket years. Of course, transactions costs should be considered. (See Example 10.5.)

EXAMPLE 10.5

Suppose a customer owes $10 million to a firm, which it will never pay. The firm can pay $50,000 in legal fees to sue and obtain a judgment this year for a fraction of the $10 million. If the firm is currently in the 35% bracket but expects to be in the 25% bracket next year, the net savings of ($10 million)(.35 − .25) = $1,000,000 makes the $50,000 legal expense worth accelerating the worthlessness.

DECREASE IN DIVIDENDS

Firms can increase internal cash flows by decreasing dividend payments to shareholders. All other things being equal, shareholders should not mind a lack of dividends, as long as the firm can invest the money and receive at least as great a return as the shareholder would have received when investing it. This is because the stock's value should increase by the amount of the unpaid dividend plus any return on it.

Shareholders may reap a tax advantage from decreased dividends. Dividends are taxed when received. However, if (as is likely) retaining cash from reduced dividends increases a firm's value, shareholders will recognize income only when stock is sold. This occurs whether the stock is sold to a third party or redeemed by the corporation itself. This creates a timing advantage, because shareholders can chose when to recognize income by selling stock in favorable years (or not at all).

There can be transforming benefits as well. Dividends are taxed as ordinary income, whereas stock sales usually generate capital gains. In many countries, these are not taxed at all; in the United States, shareholders who are individuals are taxed at favorable rates (e.g., 20% versus 40%) if the stock has been held for at least a year.

Because most institutional investors in the U.S. capital markets are exempt from income taxes, these tax advantages do not dominate, and, for other reasons, publicly traded firms have some dividend history. However, it is rare when all earnings are paid out.

When dividends are paid to a nonexempt shareholder, such as an individual investor, there can be a double tax: once to the corporation when it has the earnings, and again to the shareholder when the dividend is distributed. Thus, the dividend preferences of the firm's shareholders depend on their tax-paying status. Recognizing these differences, firms often divide shareholder groups into separate tax clienteles. (See Example 10.6.)

EXAMPLE 10.6

Suppose the firm's shareholders are owned equally by the following groups:

	Individuals	Taxable Financial Institutions	Tax-Free Pension Funds
Tax rate on dividends	36%	35%	0%
Tax rate on capital gains	20%	35%	0%

What are the shareholders' dividend preferences? From a tax perspective, individuals prefer having no dividends. This is because it is better recognize income in the most favorable years, which can be accomplished by timing the sale of their stock. In addition, income recognized from stock sales enjoys favorable capital gain status. Of the other two clienteles, financial institutions prefer dividends (from a tax perspective) because these generate a special dividends received tax deduction. Pension funds are tax exempt, and are thus indifferent between dividends and capital gains from a tax perspective. If the majority of a firm's shareholders are individuals, the firm thus may be able periodically to reduce dividends to finance its operations.

STOCK DIVIDENDS

One option available to the firm is to pay stock dividends. Then, the firm can retain cash, and instead incur only the transaction cost of determining shareholders and printing additional shares. Such stock splits are nontaxable so long as they are prorated. By providing a greater number of shares, existing shareholders can sell smaller portions of their holdings, and per-share purchasing ability is enhanced for both existing and new shareholders. (See Example 10.7.)

EXAMPLE 10.7

Suppose a firm declared a two-for-one stock split for all of its common shareholders. Let the firm's outstanding shares be

	Before Split	After Split
Number of shares	10,000,000	20,000,000
Par value ($millions)	$10,000,000	$10,000,000
Par value per share	$10	$5

Each shareholder ends up with twice as many shares, but there are no tax consequences to the firm or the shareholder. If, however, some shareholders are offered cash for their shares, or some are offered more (less) that the 2:1 split, the entire transaction becomes taxable to all the firm's shareholders.

STOCK BUYBACKS

If the firm redeems its own shares (that is, it purchases treasury stock), it generates a negative cash flow in the short run. However, in years after the buyback, more cash can be retained because fewer dividends need be paid. There is an increase in value-adding if earnings per share increase due to there being fewer shares outstanding. The buyback has no tax consequences to the firm, but the shareholders usually recognize capital gain or loss on the difference between the redemption price and their tax basis in the shares. Buybacks can sometimes result in dividend income to the shareholder, as explained in Technical Insert 10.10. (See Example 10.8.)

EXAMPLE 10.8

Suppose a firm's stock is priced at 2 times earnings, which it feels is quite undervalued. The firm is contemplating buying back 20% of its 1 million shares at $200 per share. The firm typically pays out 50% of its annual earnings in dividends. Actual and forecasted financial statistics are as follows:

	Actual	Forecast by Management				
	2001	2002	2003	2004	2005	2006
Earnings ($m)	$100	$110	$120	$130	$140	$150
No. shares (m)	1	1	1	1	1	1
EPS	$100	$110	$120	$130	$140	$150
Cash dividends	$ 50	$ 55	$ 60	$ 65	$ 70	$ 75
Market price per share	$200	$220	$240	$260	$280	$300

If the firm bought 200,000 shares before dividends were declared in the year 2001, it saved the following:

Purchase price: 200,000 × $200 =	<$40,000,000>
Savings in dividends (NPV):	
Year 2001: 200,000 × 50 × 1.00000 = $10,000,000	
Year 2002: 200,000 × 55 × 0.90909 = $ 9,999,990	
Year 2003: 200,000 × 60 × 0.82645 = $ 9,917,400	
Year 2004: 200,000 × 65 × 0.75132 = $ 9,767,160	
Year 2005: 200,000 × 70 × 0.68301 = $ 9,562,140	
Year 2006: 200,000 × 75 × 0.62092 = $ 9,313,800	
Subtotal savings	$58,560,490
Net gain to firm (NPV)	$18,560,490

Note that in Example 10.8 the discount factor was set at 10% and the dividend-saving horizon was limited to management's forecasting horizon.

In a stock buyback, there are no tax consequences to the firm, and the tax consequences to the shareholder are usually favorable. (See Example 10.9.)

EXAMPLE 10.9

Suppose a shareholder owns one share of the stock in the firm in Example 10.8, which she purchased for $110 several years ago. If she is in the 39.6% bracket, she would project the following if she sold the share in the year 2000 before the dividend was issued:

Sales proceeds	$200	$200
Less tax basis	<110>	
Tax gain	$ 90	
Tax at 20%		<18>
After-tax cash flow		$182

Occasionally, a firm's officers (management and board of directors) may buy stock from other shareholders. If the amount is significant enough to concentrate voting control with them, it is referred to as a *management buyout* (MBO). If all publicly traded shares are purchased, the firm goes private. This occurs often when the founding shareholders decide to buy back their company. The tax consequences to the selling shareholders for an MBO are identical to those of firm buybacks: capital gain or loss. There are no gain or loss consequences to the purchasing shareholders. By taking the firm private, it can avoid transaction costs (such as CPA audits, if lenders do not require audits). The firm also has a strategic advantage over competitors because no publicly available information from Securities and Exchange Commission (SEC) filings need be in circulation.

USING EMPLOYEE STOCK OWNERSHIP PLANS

The U.S. income tax favors employee stock ownership plans (ESOPs). An ESOP is a firm-sponsored plan where shares of the firm are owned (through a fiduciary) by the firm's employees. Dividends paid to the employees via the ESOP are deductible as compensation expense. If the firm borrowed money to buy shares (on the open market) to be put into the ESOP, the interest expense is tax deductible (as long as it does not exceed 25% of the compensation paid to employees).

The after-tax cash flow generated is affected by the tax-deductibility of the dividends. (See Example 10.10.)

EXAMPLE 10.10

Suppose 40% of a U.S. firm's 1 million shares are owned by its ESOP. The rest are owned through the market. If a dividend of $10 per share is declared, and the firm is in the 35% tax bracket, the after-tax cost to the firm is

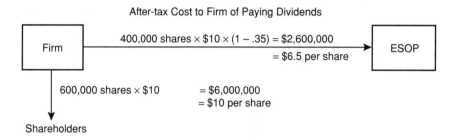

After-tax Cost to Firm of Paying Dividends

Without the ESOP, the after-tax cost of paying dividends equals its pretax cost: $10 × 1 million = $10 million. With the ESOP, the tax savings from deducting dividends to the ESOP reduces the after-tax cost of paying $10 million in dividends to $8,600,000.

The annual tax savings associated with an ESOP does not come without a price. The firm may have to buy the shares on the open market, although newly issued shares can be used. There are also initial and annual legal and accounting fees associated with the ESOP trust. These transactions costs must be weighed against the transforming aspects of the ESOP (converting non-deductible dividends into deductible ones).

RECEIPT OF DIVIDENDS FROM SUBSIDIARIES

As in most jurisdictions, in the United States the payment of a dividend is a tax-neutral transaction to a subsidiary: It cannot take a tax deduction for dividends paid. As shown in Exhibit 10.1, the income tax consequences to a recipient U.S. corporation depend on whether the subsidiary is located overseas and on the degree of ownership.

For overseas subsidiaries, payment of a dividend instantly triggers income that had previously been deferred. However, there is a dividend-received deduction to the extent that the income that generated the dividend was originally from U.S. sources. Because U.S. tax can be almost indefinitely deferred by not paying dividends and then eventually liquidating or selling the corporation so that the resulting build-up in value is treated as a capital gain (that is, transforming), multinationals avoid dividend payments.

EXHIBIT 10.1   Tax Impact of Ownership Percentage

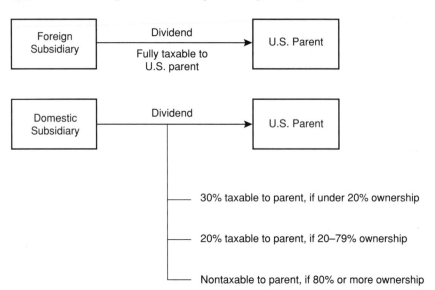

However, as noted in Chapter 9, U.S. income taxes on dividends received from foreign subsidiaries can be reduced by a foreign tax credit. The credit is based on the taxes that were paid on the earnings that generated the dividend. The credit is the lesser of actual foreign taxes paid (or deemed paid) or a set limit. The limit estimates the U.S. tax paid on the underlying income and is calculated as follows:

$$\text{Total U.S. tax} \times \left(\frac{\text{Foreign source income}}{\text{Worldwide income}} \right) = \text{Foreign tax credit limit}$$

Example 10.11 illustrates the impact of the foreign tax credit and its limitation.

EXAMPLE 10.11

Assume Widgetco is a U.S. corporation with a Canadian subsidiary. Their operations are as follows:

	U.S. Parent	Candian Subsidiary
Net (taxable) income	$1,000,000	$200,000
U.S. taxes paid	$ 250,000	
Canadian taxes paid	—	$ 60,000

Let the Canadian subsidiary pays its net earnings of $140,000 ($200,000 − $60,000) to the U.S. parent. Assuming the $140,000 is included in the $1 million of taxable income, the foreign tax credit then is the lesser of:

$$\$60,000, \text{ or}$$

$$\$250,000 \times \left(\frac{140,000 + 60,000}{1,000,000 + 60,000} \right) = \$47,170$$

The difference between the Canadian taxes paid and the FTC limit is $12,830. This is an excess foreign tax credit, which can be utilized in subsequent years.

To improve the timing of tax credits, management may want instead to pay

$$\frac{60,000}{47,170} \times \$140,000 = \$178,079$$

in dividends. This will be U.S. tax free, since it exactly equals the foreign tax credit. Note that there can be complex *grossing* up calculations involved to assure that the Canadian taxes are not both deducted and credited.

The analysis presented in Example 10.11 must be modified if the foreign government assesses a withholding tax on dividends paid to the parent. Many countries impose such taxes in the 15 to 30% range; these count as additional foreign taxes eligible for the credit. These taxes are often reduced on both sides through tax treaties.

For dividends to a U.S. parent from a domestic subsidiary, most of the payment (70 to 100%, depending on ownership percentage) is deducted in determining the taxable dividend. Even more can escape taxation if the timing of the payment is adjusted to correspond with either an NOL carryforward of the parent or low retained earnings of the subsidiary. The latter is important because the amount of the dividend taxable is limited to retained earnings of the paying corporation. Thus, paying a dividend during the NOL carryforward years, or during a subsidiary's low retained earnings year, may completely eliminate any tax on the dividend. (See Examples 10.12 and 10.13.)

EXAMPLE 10.12

Suppose a group is trying to decide when a 70% owned subsidiary should pay a dividend to a parent. The information is as follows:

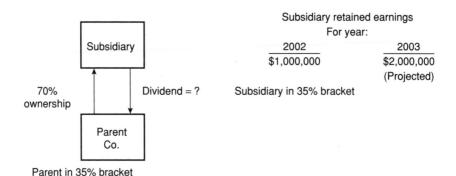

The subsidiary will pay a $2 million dividend*, and the choice is between 2002 and 2003. If the dividend is paid in 2002, it will be taxable to the parent only to the extent of the $1 million of retained earnings. Less the 80% dividends exclusion, the total taxable amount will be $200,000. Paying $2 million in 2003 will be fully taxable. That is, after the 80% dividends received deduction, $400,000 will be taxable.

* It is important to note that a firm can pay so-called partial liquidating dividend (i.e., the dividend exceeds current retained earnings).

EXAMPLE 10.13

Suppose that in Example 10.12 the subsidiary has $1 million of taxable income in 2002, but a $2 million NOL is projected for 2003. Then, it makes sense from a tax perspective to pay the entire dividend in 2003, because it will be completely tax free.

In situations like those presented in Examples 10.12 and 10.13 managers should take into account the cash-flow needs—independent of the tax consequences—of both the parent and the subsidiary, for all years. Furthermore, if the parent owns 80% or more of the subsidiary, timing (at least from a tax perspective) is irrelevant: After the dividend received deduction, none of the subsidiary's dividends would be included in the parent's taxable income.

Dividend payments from a domestic or foreign subsidiary should be consistent with the firm's strategy, and may require negotiation. If the subsidiary needs the working capital more than the parent (for example, to expand its market or to recapitalize) tax advantages of paying a dividend (e.g., during an NOL year) should be only part of the decision. If the firm's subsidiaries are decentralized, there may be required negotiation with the dividend-paying subsidiary's manager, since its operation's cash flow (and related financial ratios) will be impaired. (See Example 10.14.)

EXAMPLE 10.14

Refer to Example 10.13. The parent company still requires a $2 million dividend as working capital needed to cover 2002 operations. If it does not obtain this cash from the subsidiary, it will have to obtain a short-term line of credit from a bank at 10% interest. Assume also that the subsidiary has $2 million in working capital needs. What if it must also borrow at 10%? In this situation, because both companies are in the 35% bracket, the after-tax costs of borrowing are identical at $10\%(1 - .35) = 6.5\%$. Thus, the original solution will not change. So, the subsidiary should remit the entire $2 million dividend in 2002.

Part of the dividend-paying decision is the interaction of financial accounting, value-adding, and management incentives. (See Example 10.15.)

EXAMPLE 10.15

Suppose a parent needs $1 million of working capital for the year. It can either obtain it from its subsidiary or borrow it at 10%. Management receives a year-end bonus of 10% of after-tax income. The subsidiary is in the same situation as its parent, but actually has the $1 million cash, which it can either pay to the parent or retain for its own working capital needs. Assume that $1 million borrowing by either parent or subsidiary would cause a technical default on debt agreements, requiring $500,000 of legal costs to circumvent (or to renegotiate terms). Assume financial statistics for the parent and subsidiary as follows (in millions of dollars):

	With Dividend	
	Parent	Subsidary
Net income, before borrowing, interest, dividends	$10	$5
Dividend income	1(.3) =.3	—
Interest expense	—	10%(1) = <.1
Debt renegotiation costs	—	<.5>
New taxable income	10.3	4.4
Tax at 35%	<3.605>	<1.540>
After-tax net income	6.695	2.86
Management bonus	0.67	0.286

| | Without Dividend | |
	Parent	Subsidary
Net income, before borrowing, interest, dividend	$10	$5
Dividend income	—	—
Interest expense	10% (1)	—
	= <.100>	
Debt renegotiation	<.500>	—
Net taxable income	9.4	$5
Tax at 35%	<3.29>	<1.750>
After-tax net income	6.11	3.25
Management bonus	0.611	0.325

Under the dividend-paying scenarios, consolidated after-tax income is $9,555,000. Under the borrowing scenario, it is $9,360,000. Thus, from a company-wide perspective, paying the dividend is better. However, this strategy does not come without a cost: the subsidiary's management loses 325,000 – 286,000 = $39,000 of bonus. Thus, the firm may have to negotiate with these managers to persuade them to have the dividend paid. Because paying the dividend will benefit the firm $9,555,000 – $9,360,000 = $195,000, it would actually be cheaper for the firm to give the managers the $39,000 outright to persuade them to pay the dividend.

PUTTING IT ALL TOGETHER: FINANCING ONGOING OPERATIONS FROM A SAVANT PERSPECTIVE

A medium-size corporation has a $10 million working capital need for the upcoming year. It can provide $6 million from its own operations, and also must find $4 million from external sources. Management has put together the following options, each of which can generate the $4 million. For simplicity, the firm would like to choose only one of the following:

■ *Sale of marketable securities. The securities have market (book) values of $6,000,000 ($5,000,000). They pay 12% per year, on average.*
■ *Short-term (1 year) bank borrowing at 10%.*
■ *Sale of a warehouse that is not being used to full capacity. Inventory could be easily (and costlessly) held in other warehouses. The warehouse, plus underlying land, could be sold for $7 million. Adjusted tax basis is $5 million.*

- *Choose not to pay dividends,* or instead issue a stock dividend (a 2:1 split was contemplated), since most of the $4 million working capital needed is for dividends.
- *Factoring some uncollected accounts receivable.* There are $50 million in receivables; a factor specialist has offered to buy any of them at 50% of face value.
- *Pay a dividend from one of its 70% owned subsidiaries.* The subsidiary has $10 million in retained earnings.

The corporation has a $10 million NOL carryforward that is expected to offset the current year taxable income, and carry partially over into the next year. Even with the NOL offset, the firm expects to be in the 35% tax bracket next year. Management receives a bonus based on 5% of pretax income. The firm's financial statistics are

Net income before taxes, and effects of any financing choices from preceding list	$1,000,000
TAX: NOL carryforward	<2,500,000>

Analyze each of the proposals from a SAVANT perspective:

- *Sale of marketable securities.* The net proceeds are $6 million, and the taxable gain of $1 million is tax-free due to the NOL. Despite the tax advantage, there is an arbitrage disadvantage: The securities earn 12%, but borrowing costs are 10%. The net financial statement impact is $1 million gain; loss of 12%($6 million) = $720,000 interest income, and net effect is $280,000 net income increase for the current year.
- *Short-term borrowing.* The annual interest cost is $4 million (10%) = $400,000. This also is the reduction in financial earnings, because there is no tax deduction with the NOL.
- *Sale of warehouse.* The gain is $2 million. Even with the tax of $2 million(.35) = $700,000 there is still more than enough to cover the $4 million working capital needs. Net effect on the financials is a gain of $2 million.
- *Stock dividends.* There is no tax effect here as long as the split does not involve cash, or non-pro-rata distributions. No effect on the income statement, either.
- *Factoring accounts receivable.* There is no current tax effect on the tax loss of $4 million(50%) = $2 million. The tax loss simply adds to the NOL and will be used next year. Net effect on the financials: $2 million loss.

- *Dividends from subsidiary.* Even though 30% is subject to tax, the NOL absorbs the income, resulting in no tax. If the subsidiary is accounted for under the equity method of accounting, there is no financial-accounting income effect.

In summary, from a tax and financial accounting income perspective, the win-win choice looks like sale of the warehouse. There are other aspects of SAVANT bearing on the decision.

Strategy

Since the warehouse is unused, this will not harm any strategic production plans.

Anticipation

Much of this has to do with the firm's transition out of NOL status. See above analysis.

Value-Adding

See the preceding analysis. Also, some strategies might be viewed negatively by the firm's shareholders, especially the stock dividend. If so, the firm's stock price would drop, raising its cost of capital. In terms of transactions costs, sales of marketable securities would involve brokerage commissions, and sale of the warehouse, realtor's commissions.

Negotiating

Under the sale of warehouse plan, this is directly not applicable. Under the stock dividend plan, the firm may have to offer something extra to share-holders to get them to accept no dividends. Under any plan reducing financial earnings, management would have to be negotiated with, to persuade them to take reduced bonuses.

Transforming

Because of the firm's current NOL, any gain-generating transaction is tax free. On the other hand, a plan which generates losses does not create a deduction that can be used.

TECHNICAL INSERT 10.1 STOCK TRANSACTIONS IN THE UNITED STATES

Stock Dividends (Stock Splits)

Stock dividends are tax-free, unless one or more of the following conditions holds:

- It is non-pro-rata. *Pro-rata* means that, after the stock dividend, each common stockholder owns the same percent of stock as before the stock dividend.
- A stock dividend is paid to any preferred stockholders.
- Convertible stock is given, and one or more shareholder might turn it into a disproportionate stock holding through exercise of the options.
- Preferred stock dividends are given to common shareholders.
- There is any distribution of convertible preferred stock.

See, generally, IRC Section 305. Most state income tax laws have similar statutes.

Buybacks or Redemptions

If a firm buys back stock, the selling shareholders are presumed to have ordinary dividend income for the entire purchase price, unless at least one of the following conditions are met (in which case the transaction is eligible for capital gains treatment):

- It is *substantially disproportionate*, which means that after the redemption, the shareholder owns less then 80% of what he owned prior to the redemption, and less than 50% of the total stock.
- The shareholder completely terminates his interest (including management), except as a creditor.
- If there is a meaningful reduction in the shareholder's interest, and it is not essentially equivalent to a dividend.
- It is a redemption in partial liquidation of a corporate shareholder. Here, a subsidiary distributes proceeds from sale, or insurance payments resulting from destruction of part of the business. It must be from a genuine contraction of an active trade or business.
- The shareholder's estate redeems shares to pay the decedent's death taxes (federal or state). The shares must be at least 35% of the decedent's assets at death.

TECHNICAL INSERT 10.1 (CONTINUED)

For the first three points, the redeeming shareholder is considered to constructively own shares owned by any relative (spouses, lineal ascendants, or descendants) or any entity also owned by the shareholder. An exception to the constructive ownership rules applies, but only if

- The shareholder promises to acquire no interest in the corporation for the next 10 years
- If such acquisition does occur, the shareholder notifies the IRS immediately

The redemption rules are designed primarily to prevent closely held corporate shareholders from receiving dividends at capital gains rates. Many large companies are closely held. For tax purposes, a closely held corporation is one that is more than 50% owned, directly or indirectly, by five or fewer individuals. To see how this works, assume Ann and Bob each own 50% of the stock of a corporation. Ann redeems 30 of her 50 shares for $300 (her cost basis for the shares is $200). Since she owns less than 50% of the total stock and less than 80% of her prior ownership after the redemption, this qualifies as a substantially disproportionate redemption, and she receives capital gain treatment. To see the dramatic difference between this and dividend treatment, assuming Ann is in the 30% bracket:

Redemption: 28%($300 − $200) = $28 tax
Dividend: 30%($300) = $90 tax

CHAPTER 11

Capital Budgeting

I love the factory. That's what business is all about. Making things. Not this Wall Street stuff, not this consulting stuff, not this lawyer stuff. None of that adds value. You gotta make something.

—Scott McNealy, CEO, Sun Microsystems

In the ongoing operations of a firm, capital acquisition and disposition decisions are common. Effective tax management for such decisions is crucial, because proper planning can significantly reduce their after-tax costs. This is particularly the case for state and local sales, property, and income taxes. Because of their importance in most ventures, capital budgeting decisions is the focus of this chapter and is examined in the following contexts: fixed asset acquisitions, make versus buy decisions, and multiple versus single plant choices.

FIXED ASSET ACQUISITION

Managers are frequently faced with choices on acquisition of additional, and replacement of old, equipment. As with other projects, capital acquisitions should have net cash flows that have a positive net present value. The other principles of SAVANT should be applied too. The principal tax considerations are outlined in this section.

U.S. Federal Income Tax

The depreciation tax shield derived from the modified accelerated cost recovery system (MACRS) provides the primary tax incentive. Other Federal tax incentives include

- The 20% tax credit for incremental research and development (R&D) expenses
- The welfare to work credit

Foreign Income Taxes

Many of these incentives were discussed in Chapter 9.

State and Local Taxes

What tax incentives are offered? For depreciation, most states have adopted Federal accelerated cost recovery rules.

Like the European Union, most U.S. states offer enterprise zone incentives. (An *enterprise zone* is a locale with a very depressed economy.) These include sales tax reductions along with credits for equipment purchases and wages paid. Exhibit 11.1 shows enterprise zone incentives by state.

EXHIBIT 11.1   Enterprise Zone Tax Incentives, By State

State	Income Tax (law cite) and/or Sales/Use Tax Incentives (law cite)	State	Income Tax (law cite) and/or Sales/Use Tax Incentives (law cite)
Alabama	41-23-30	Montana	
Arizona	41-1522 and 41-1525	Nebraska	77-27 and 188
		Nevada	
Arkansas	15-4-1104	New Hampshire	
California	17053.70 and 17053.74	New Jersey	18:7-15.1
		New Mexico	
Colorado	39-30-104	New York	
Connecticut	3 and 12-217v	North Carolina	
Delaware		North Dakota	
Florida	290.007	Ohio	CCH Para. 13-173
Georgia		Oklahoma	690.4
Hawaii	CCH Para. 13-152	Oregon	37
		Pennsylvania	
Idaho		Rhode Island	13-152
Illinois	35 ILCS 5/203	South Carolina	CCH Para. 13-183
Indiana	6-3.1.10-1	South Dakota	
Iowa	15A.9	Tennessee	13-28-106
Kansas		Texas	171.501 and 171.1015
Kentucky			
Louisiana	51:1786	Utah	9-2-401 through 9-2-414
Maine			
Maryland	10-702	Vermont	
Massachusetts		Virginia	13 VAC 5-111 270
Michigan	13-178	Washington	
Minnesota	469.171	West Virginia	1.1
Mississippi		Wisconsin	
Missouri	135.225	Wyoming	

If the firm is multistate, how will additional capital change its apportionment factors? The net effect will be to apportion more income to the state in which the acquisition is made. Thus, if the tax rate in the capital-expansion state is higher than in the other states in which the firm operates, overall taxes may increase despite enterprise zone incentives.

Sales Taxes

In most jurisdictions, capital acquisitions of personalty (such as machinery and equipment) are subject to sales-type taxes, like Germany's value-added tax (VAT) and Canada's goods & services tax (GST). Most of the states in the United States impose a sales tax on retail sales of tangible personal property by in-state vendors. To prevent taxpayers from avoiding sales tax merely by buying out of state (e.g., over the Web), a complementary use tax is imposed on property used in the state that was purchased out of state.

Most states do not impose these taxes for purchases made from the U.S. government. Nor are they imposed on very infrequent *casual* sales, or for personalty that will become part of a product manufactured for resale. Additionally, many states allow credits for personalty purchased in enterprise zones, and some waive sales and use taxes for personalty sold within these zones.

One method for postponing sales or use taxes on equipment is by leasing instead of purchasing it. Note that enterprise zone benefits typically do not apply to leased property. However, significant tax savings can occur by delaying sales or use taxes through the use of a leasing company.

Normally, if a company is planning on purchasing equipment, it should expect to pay sales or use tax. One way to postpone tax is by forming a leasing company, as shown in Exhibit 11.2.

In this setting, the first transaction is not subject to sales or use tax, because it is a purchase for resale. The second transaction is subject to sales or use tax, but over time (i.e., as payments are made). Thus the tax savings flow from the reduced present value of tax costs. This is an example of timing. Of course, one should check with local tax law to see if the above tax treatment is respected. (See Example 11.1.)

EXHIBIT 11.2 Using a Leasing Company to Defer Taxes

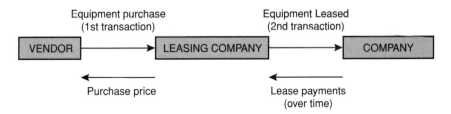

EXAMPLE 11.1

Smithco manufactures communications equipment. In the current year, it budgets for the purchase of $1 million of manufacturing equipment, and $2 million of office equipment. Because the manufacturing defined by most states as a business input, it is exempt from sales tax. For the office equipment, Smithco forms Leaseco, a subsidiary. The subsidiary buys the office equipment, and then leases it to Smithco over five years. Leaseco collects sales taxes from Smithco on the $2 million sales price over five years.

Property taxes

If the capital expansion involves realty, there will be an increase in property taxes. If the expansion (or new site) is significant enough, the firm can negotiate with local officials for tax relief. If the expansion involves a combined purchase of personalty and realty, the firm can try to allocate the purchase price so that all taxes are minimized. This is illustrated in Tax Management In Action 11.1.

TAX MANAGEMENT IN ACTION 11.1

Incentives and Location Choice

In an article appearing in the *The Wall Street Journal* ("Localities Force Firms to Keep Their Promises", October 26, 1996, A2), it was reported that many cities, states, and counties offer firm-specific incentives to entice business to locate in their area. The article reported the results of a KPMG Peat Marwick survey of Fortune 1000 companies. In the survey, 160 of the 203 respondents said they received the following incentives:

Property tax rebates	51%
Income/franchise tax incentives	48%
Job training	11%
Employment or payroll tax credits	9%
Utility rebates	8%
Other	14%

The article also reported on a trend of local governments to demand refunds of previous incentives from companies who reneged on their promises (leaving the area, or not hiring as many workers as planned). And some localities are awarding incentives over time instead of upfront.

ANALYSIS FROM A SAVANT PERSPECTIVE

Strategy

Any equipment acquisition should make business sense independent of the tax consequences. The firm should first consider strategic aspects, for example, will the new equipment result in the firm gaining competitive advantage by producing products cheaper or better, or by delivering them faster?

Consider an express delivery business, where most of the productive assets are delivery trucks. Suppose that the trucks currently are being depreciated over a seven-year life using the double declining balance method per the modified accelerated cost recovery system (MACRS). (MACRS is described in IRS Publication 946. As noted previously, tax related publications like this can be found on the Web via gateway sites like *www.taxsites.com.*)

Now consider the impact if the U.S. government (and the state, by conformity to the federal) changes to the three-year useful life category. Because the tax depreciation is more rapid, the present value of the tax savings generated by depreciation increases, driving down the after-tax cost of a truck.

Should the older trucks (using seven-year MACRS) be replaced with new ones (using three-year MACRS)? More rapid tax depreciation on the replacements may translate into lower cost, which may allow the firm to lower prices to undercut competitors. In addition, from a nontax perspective, the new trucks may allow faster and more reliable delivery.

However, even though tax benefits may be substantial it may not make strategic sense to replace existing trucks. This could be the case if the new trucks would not enable better customer service. It also might be the case if competitors do not purchase new trucks due to capital constraints, or net operating losses (NOLs) that obviate tax benefits.

Anticipation (Timing)

Will the tax laws on depreciation change? If so, this should affect the timing of transactions. This especially is the case for year end acquisitions. If new laws are about to make tax depreciation more rapid, firms should anticipate the change by evaluating whether delaying acquisitions until the beginning of the next tax year makes more sense.

Using the delivery service example, suppose that the five-year MACRS life is expected to go into place in January of the next year. In that case, from a purely tax perspective it makes sense for a tax-paying firm to postpone the acquisitions until the beginning of the next year. However, if the firm is in an NOL carryforward status, it would not make sense to postpone any necessary truck replacements. Indeed, if a competitor is in a tax-paying position, and will delay truck replacements until next year, it would actually give the firm a temporary competitive advantage because the firm would be the *first mover.*

The tax aspects of timing normally do not outweigh nontax business aspects. For example, suppose the delivery service firm estimated it could gain a 10% increase in market share by buying new trucks at the end of this year. Unless the net present value (NPV) of the profit on this increased market share is less than the NPV of accelerating the tax depreciation by one year, the tax changes should not be sufficient to delay truck replacement.

If a manager expects changes in tax rules, then the year in which the assets are acquired should be adjusted. There are potential effects for changes both in tax rates and in depreciation methods. If rates are expected to increase (decrease), acquisitions should be accelerated (delayed). This is because capital budgeting projects should have positive pretax cash flows (due to enhanced revenues or cost savings) that yield a positive taxable income. If tax depreciation is expected to become more (less) favorable, then investment should be delayed.

In evaluating capital projects, after-tax cash flows should be discounted. Accordingly, accelerated tax depreciation methods (MACRS) increase the NPV of projects. (See Example 11.2.)

EXAMPLE 11.2

Using the previous delivery service example, suppose each delivery truck costs $100,000. If the trucks are depreciated under five-year MACRS, and are scheduled to move to three-year MACRS, assuming a 10% cost of capital and 35% federal tax rate, the NPV will be:

Year	5 Year MACRS		3 Year MACRS	
1	$100,000(.20)(.35)(.9091)	= $ 6,364	$100,000(.3333)(.35)(.9091)	= $10,606
2	100,000(.32)(.35)(.8264)	= 9,256	100,000(.4445)(.35)(.8264)	= 12,857
3	100,000(.1920)(.35)(.7503)	= 5,048	100,000(.1481)(.35)(.7513)	= 3,894
4	100,000(.1152)(.35)(.6830)	= 2,754	100,000(.0741)(.35)(.6830)	= 1,771
5	100,000(.1152)(.35)(.6209)	= 2,503		—
6	100,000(.0576)(.35)(.5645)	= 1,138		—
NPV		$27,063		$29,128

If an 8% state tax rate is factored in, the NPV of the three-year (five-year) tax savings will go to $33,290 ($35,782). Thus, although the total depreciation on the truck is $100,000 under either method, the shorter life will increase the NPV of tax savings by approximately 7.5%.

Negotiating

Capital budgeting, more so than any other area except mergers and acquisitions, can involve negotiating tax benefits where (as is typical) a large acquisition is made from one vendor. For example, a firm in a positive tax bracket may be able to purchase a factory from an NOL carryforward firm for a below market price simply because the NOL carryforward firm does not need the tax benefits. However, if the firm has an NOL it may lease from a vendor because the firm does not need the depreciation write-offs. (See Examples 11.3 and 11.4.)

EXAMPLE 11.3

Suppose a firm can buy or lease a new computer system. The system can be leased over six years with annual lease payments of $100,000 or purchased outright for $436,000 (this is the present value equivalent of six payments of $100,000 each). If it were in a tax-paying position, the firm would prefer a purchase. This is because MACRS depreciation is accelerated, giving more than $100,000 of deductions in the early years. But what about the seller? If the seller is in an NOL carryforward position, it might prefer a sale, which triggers all of the income in the year of sale.

EXAMPLE 11.4

Suppose the seller's status is as follows:

- Current year: NOL of $400,000
- Next year, and subsequent five years: 35% Federal bracket

Consider the federal income tax consequences. Suppose the firm's profit on the computer is $400,000. If it sells the machine outright, it pays no taxes and its after-tax cash flow is $400,000. If it leases, it recognizes the following (assuming a 10% discount rate). First, examine the federal tax consequences, assuming a 35% Federal tax rate:

Year	Lease Payment	Tax: 35% of 4/6 (100k)	Net Cash flow	Discount Factor	PV of cash flow
1	$100,000	$23,000	$77,000	0.9091	$70,000
2	100,000	23,000	77,000	0.8264	63,600
3	100,000	23,000	77,000	0.7513	57,900
4	100,000	23,000	77,000	0.6830	52,300
5	100,000	23,000	77,000	0.6209	47,800
6	100,000	23,000	77,000	0.5645	43,500
					$335,100

The difference between purchase and leasing is $436,000 – $335,000 = $101,000. If an 8% state income tax rate is added in, the difference increases to $129,000.

This $129,000 is the tax-induced negotiable amount. That is, the computer seller should be willing to drop its price by up to $129,000 in order to induce the customer to buy rather than to lease the machine.

Value-Adding

A project that has a positive net present value will also increase firm earnings-based performance measures, such as earnings per share (EPS) and economic value-added (EVA). However, there are collateral financial-statement effects to be considered. If debt financed, does the debt increase the chance of violating preexisting bond covenants? In the short run, bonuses may decrease due to increase financial statement depreciation, especially if bonuses are tied to pretax earnings. (See Example 11.5.)

EXAMPLE 11.5

To see this, assume a U.S. firm wants to acquire a new building. The building will cost $10 million, and will be 90% debt financed (with an 8% mortgage). The firm is in the combined (e.g., federal plus state) 40% tax bracket. Assume that the NPV of tax savings for depreciation is $2 million, and that the PV of principle and interest payments is $20 million. If so, the NPV of the building is

Down payment	<$1,000,000>
PV of interest, principle payments	<20,000,000>
PV of tax savings (depreciation, interest)	2,000,000
NPV—cost	<$19,000,000>

Currently, the firm has a year-by-year lease of a building at $2,000,000 per year. Assume the NPV of this is

PV of lease payment	<$30,000,000>
Tax savings: PV of deduction of lease payment	6,000,000
NPV—cost	<$24,000,000>

Based on the data given, buying the new building increases firm value. This is because the NPV of the cash flows is higher, and, at least in the long run, financial-accounting measures (such as EPS and EVA) will also increase.

However, there is a U.S. financial reporting drawback to buying the new building rather than to continuing the lease. In a purchase, the mortgage (as well as the building) appears on the balance sheet. In contrast, an operating lease is off the books. That is, the cost of the use of the building is not included in assets, nor is the obligation to make lease payments included as a liability. Instead, they are merely described in a footnote.

In a purchase, if a mortgage is a significant portion of the firm's liabilities, it may cause the firm to violate existing debt covenants. Or, by affecting other financial ratios, it may affect the firm's equity and debt ratings. These two drawbacks may be finessed by leasing rather than buying. (The actual effect on shareholder value is not clear: loan covenants may include restrictions on leases as well as more tradition debt, and financial analysts may be able to estimate the impact of leasing on ratios.)

In evaluating whether a project has a positive value-added, transactions costs should be considered. Involved are items like information acquisition costs, title transfer fees, document taxes and commissions (if realty), and professional fees (if an entity is acquired). (See Example 11.6.)

EXAMPLE 11.6

Suppose a firm wants to buy an existing factory. The cost would be $10 million. The PV of tax savings would be $5 million (related to depreciation). By replacing the old factory, the PV of production cost savings (after-tax) would be $6 million. The firm's management estimates that, between travel costs and lost productive time, the cost of managers making two trips to thoroughly examine the factory would be $500,000. Realtor's commissions, at 7%, would be $700,000. What is the NPV of the project?

Upfront cost	<$10,000,000>
PV of tax savings	5,000,000
PV of operating cost savings (after-tax)	6,000,000
Transactions costs:	
Investigative time (after-tax)	<500,000>
Realtor's commission (after-tax)	<700,000>
NPV	<$ 200,000>

In this particular example, transactions costs have turned a positive NPV project into a negative one.

If the project involves risk, then such risk should somehow be offset by a higher after-tax cash flow. Generally speaking, the longer-lived the project, the more possible things that could go wrong, so the higher the risk. Because capital budgeting decisions typically involve plant or equipment acquisitions that have multi-year lives, risk becomes an issue. This particularly is the case when comparing investments with differing cash flow variances or useful lives. (See Example 11.7.)

EXAMPLE 11.7

Suppose a firm can invest $1 million in one of two projects: a new computer system or R&D aimed at discovering a specific product. First, examine only federal income tax effects. Assume the firm is in the 35% income tax bracket, and the R&D expenditures are fully eligible for the 20% credit. Projections are as follows:

	Computer System	R & D Best Case*	R & D Worst Case*
Cost	<$1,000,000>	<$1,000,000>	<$1,000,000>
Cost savings (PV)	3,500,000	—	—
Expected revenue (PV)	—	7,000,000	0
Expected net profit (NPV) before tax savings	$2,500,000	6,000,000	<1,000,000>
Tax on profit (PV), or tax savings (PV)	<875,000>	<2,100,000>	350,000
Savings from R&D tax credit (PV)	0	200,000	200,000
Expected net after-tax profit	$1,625,000	$4,100,000	<$ 450,000>

*50% probability of each; firm in 35% tax bracket ignores reduction in R&D deductions caused by taking the 20% credit

Without the tax benefits, the expected value of the R&D project is .5($6,000,000) − .5(1,000,000) = $2,500,000. This is the same as the riskless project, so a manager with any degree of risk aversion would chose to invest in the computer system. After tax, however, the expected value of the riskier R&D project is .5($4,100,000) − .5(450,000) = $1,825,000, which exceeds the $1,625,000 NPV of the less risky project. The riskier project has a greater NPV due to tax benefits. The tax system thus provides a risk premium for the riskier project. That is, it adjusts the (variance on) return.

Next, consider the effects of state income taxes. Assume an 8% tax rate. The expected after-tax profit for either setting is $2,000,000(1 − .08) = $1,840,000. However, if the state does not allow NOL carryforward (or limits them), then state taxes would cause a risk adverse manager to prefer the computer system. What if the state offers an R&D tax credit? (Many do). If the credit is at least as great as the NOL, then state taxes do not distort the decision. In this example, there would be no distortion if the R&D credit were at least $160,000. This implies a $160,000/$1,000,000 = 16% tax credit, which is beyond what states typically offer. Thus, while a state R&D tax credit can make R&D more inviting, it may not be able to compensate for state NOL limitation rules.

PUTTING IT ALL TOGETHER: SAVANT CONCEPTS APPLIED TO CAPITAL BUDGETING

You are the CFO for a major overnight delivery service. You are considering replacing your aging fleet of aircraft (Boeing 747s) with new aircraft (Boeing 767s). You need 20 of these aircraft, which cost $10 million each. You can receive $250,000 each, after tax, on the sale of each old aircraft. Due to increased fuel efficiency and decreased maintenance, you expect to save $2,000,000 per year per aircraft over their 10-year useful lives. Your cost of capital is 8%. Assume a seven-year MACRS useful life, a federal tax bracket of 34%, a state tax bracket of 8% (and that the state conforms to federal MACRS rules), and a state sales tax rate of 7%.

Strategy

If the project has a significant enough positive cash flow, you may be able to drop delivery prices. Also, there is a promotional advantage to having new aircraft: customers may infer your delivery more reliable than that of competition having older aircraft.

Negotiating

Because Boeing is in a high tax bracket, it may prefer to lease the aircraft to you, and recognize income ratably over time. So, a lease-purchase agreement is called for, whereby you (based on your intent to purchase the aircraft) treat it as a capitalized lease purchase. This saves Boeing $5,000,000 in (discounted) taxes, half of which they may willing to pass on to you in the form of lower prices. Also, under a lease, the sales or use taxes that you would have to pay would be made ratably over time.

Value-Adding and Anticipation

Should value-adding be adjusted for risk? If the lease is cancelable by the lessee, it actually is less risky than an outright purchase, assuming the aircraft are reliable and your customer base is unlikely to decrease. Although technically Boeing could cancel the lease, you believe this unlikely to occur. You also expect no changes in tax rates or depreciation rules, so accelerating or otherwise adjusting the timing of acquisition is not required. First, examine the effects of federal taxes. The cash flows by year are expected as shown in Exhibit 11.3.

EXHIBIT 11.3   Expected Cash Flows Form Airplane Leasing Deal

Year	Description	Amount (in $ millions)	Discount Factor (7%)	Discounted Cash Flows (in $ millions)
1–10	Lease payments	<19.75>[A]	7.024	<$138.72>
1–10	Operating cost savings	1.32[B]	7.024	9.27
1–10	Tax depreciation	—	—	155.68[C]
				$ 26.23

A = [20 aircraft × ($10,000,000 − $250,000)] / 10 years = $19,750,000

B = $2,000,000(1 − .34) = $1,320,000

C =	Year	Tax Depreciation in $ millions	Discount Factor	PV of Tax in $ millions
	1	(197.5)(.1429)	0.934	26.36
	2	(197.5)(.2449)	0.873	41.88
	3	(197.5)(.1749)	0.816	28.19
	4	(197.5)(.1249)	0.763	18.82
	5	(197.5)(.0893)	0.713	12.58
	6	(197.5)(.0892)	0.666	11.73
	7	(197.5)(.0893)	0.623	10.99
	8	(197.5)(0446)	0.583	5.13
				155.68

So far, the acquisition's positive NPV suggests positive value-adding. What about the impact of state and local taxes? Again, assume sales (income) tax rates of 7%(8%). For most states, sales or use taxes would be due as lease payments are made: the PV = 7%($138,720,000) = $9,710,000. From an income tax perspective, the operating cost savings will increase the PV of state taxes by 8%($9,270,000) = $740,000. The tax depreciation decreases the PV of state taxes by $35,600,000. So, the net effect of state taxes is to increase the NPV of the project by $25,200,000.

What of the effect on the firm's financials? On the balance sheet, the arrangement can be treated as a capitalized lease, so both assets and long-term liabilities increase by the present value of the lease payments (which is $138,720,000). Upon investigation, you determine that the increase in long-term liabilities does not violate any debt covenants. Further, because there is a net increase in financial accounting income, bonuses for the company's managers will actually increase from the arrangement.

Finally, in terms of timing, if no changes in rates or rules are anticipated, so the transaction should occur when the economics are sensible.

MAKE OR BUY DECISIONS

Manufacturing firms are frequently faced with the decision of making or buying a component integral to the manufacture of their products. An advantage of internal manufacture is complete control over timing and quality of product. However, outsourced components (particularly if manufactured in low cost countries) can be less expensive, especially if there is competition in this market. Whether or not it is less expensive to buy outside depends in part on avoidable overhead costs. *Avoidable* overhead costs are those that would not be incurred if the component is outsourced. (See Example 11.8.)

EXAMPLE 11.8

Suppose that a computer manufacturer has the opportunity to outsource the manufacture of motherboards. Competitive bids, controlling for quality, yield a best price of $280 per board. Internal costs to manufacture are $300, as follows:

Direct labor	$100
Direct materials	100
Overhead:	
Indirect materials	30
Factory utilities,	
Insurance, and taxes (Allocated)	70
	$300

Because the $70 is nonavoidable, the *real* cost to manufacture internally is $230, before transactions costs. Note that if the manufacturing is done in a single state, state income taxes play no role per se; under either manufacture or purchase, costs are deductible.

Tax-related transactions costs may be important if the manufacture or purchase is across tax jurisdictions. If the good is manufactured by the firm in a different state, stopping manufacture may mean that the firm's nexus with the state will disappear. This would eliminate allocation of the firm's income to the state. If this state has a higher (lower) tax rate than the average for the firm's rest of the operations, cessation of manufacture results in a negative (positive) transaction cost.

EXAMPLE 11.9

To see how this might work, assume a California firm was buying a component from its wholly owned subsidiary in Illinois. Financial statistics (in millions of dollars) are as follows:

Annual Financial Data

Illinois Subsidiary		Parent California Manufacturing Company	
Total production costs:	$ 50,000,000	Purchases from sub:	$100,000,000
Total revenues:		Revenues from	
Sales to U.S. parent	$100,000,000	finished products:	$500,000,000
State tax rate	6%	State tax rate	8%

Number of units transferred: 5,000,000

Taxable income	$ 10,000,000	Taxable income	$ 50,000,000
Property	$200,000,000	Property	$300,000,000
Payroll	$ 20,000,000	Payroll	$ 30,000,000

Suppose the parent is considering selling the subsidiary and buying the components from an unrelated supplier. The effect on apportionment of state income taxes needs to be considered. First, one should examine state income taxes assuming the subsidiary is retained:

Apportionment to Illinois:			Apportionment to California:		
Property 200/500	=	.4	Property: 300/500	=	.6
Payroll: 20/50	=	.4	Payroll: 20/50	=	.4
Sales:	=	0	Sales	=	2.0
Average		.2			.8
Times taxable income		× 60,000,000			× 60,000,000
Apportioned TI		12,000,000			48,000,000
Times tax rate		× .06			× .08
State Income tax		$ 720,000			$ 3,840,000

Thus, the total state income tax burden is $4,560,000. If the subsidiary is sold, all taxable income is apportioned to California. To keep the example comparable, assume that the parent company would obtain a purchase price so that its profit from that part of the value chain would be $10,000,000 (that is, the current profit of the subsidiary).

The state income tax would be	
Taxable income	$60,000,000
Multiplied by California tax rate	× .08
State income tax	$ 4,800,000

Example 11.9 shows that by severing its ties with a subsidiary located in a lower-taxed state, the firm's state taxes will increase overall. Thus, for the sale to add value, the nontax cost savings from buying from an outsider must be at least $4,800,000 − $4,560,000 = $240,000 each year.

Note that the reverse would be true were the subsidiary located in a higher-tax-rate jurisdiction. To see this, suppose the rates were reversed (that is, the subsidiary is in an 8% bracket, and the parent is subject to a 6% rate). By keeping the subsidiary, total taxes are $3,600,000: $12,000,000(.08) + $48,000,000(.06). Without the subsidiary, taxes are also $3,600,000: $60,000,000(.06).

Although outsourcing may save costs, there are also strategic considerations. Suppliers can reneg on contracts (that is, adjustment for risk may be necessary) in the long run, and it may be very costly for the firm to restart manufacture. If, however, a cooperative supplier relationship can be established, negotiation of tax costs can occur. For example, if the firm expects to be in a higher tax bracket in the next year, it can request the supplier to postpone sales on deliveries until then in return for a slightly higher sales price. (See Example 11.10.)

EXAMPLE 11.10

Assume the following annual operating data:

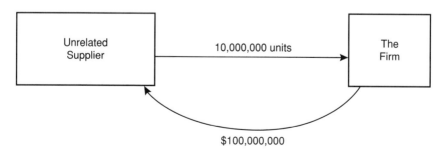

Suppose that sales to the firm constitute 50% of the supplier's sales. Also, suppose that transactions occur evenly throughout the year on a quarterly basis. What if by the final quarter it was realized that the firm will be in an NOL situation next year? If it is in a 35% (8%) Federal (state) tax bracket this year, it may make sense to postpone the last quarter's purchases until the first quarter of next year. The tax savings would be: 35% + 8 % = 43% ($100,000,000/4) = $10,750,000.

This is the maximum amount the firm would be willing to pay the supplier to delay fourth quarter sales. If it has a *captive* supplier, it may be willing to accept much less in the negotiation process. Note that this sale acceleration or delay technique is particularly important for state (and non-U.S.) income tax purposes. This is because many states (and most countries) have NOL carryback/carryforward restrictions, or do not allow NOL deductions at all.

CAPITAL BUDGETING AND PLANT CAPACITY

If the firm needs to expand plant capacity, it may do so by expanding the current plant or by building additional, separate facilities. Because of the interrelationship of federal, international, and state and local taxes in many businesses, it is important to consider all of the taxes in Exhibit 11.4.

EXHIBIT 11.4 Differential Tax Impacts of Expand versus Buy Decisions

	Expand Existing Plant	Build (Buy) Additional Facilities
Property Taxes	Increase	Increase, unless tax holiday obtained
Income taxes		
—Federal	Tax shield from depreciation	Tax shield from depreciation
—State and local	Tax shield from depreciation	If located in new state or "nexus" established; increase (decrease) in taxes if in higher (lower) tax jurisdiction
—Foreign (assumes plant not separately incorporated)	Not applicable	If located in higher (lower) tax country, net foreign & U.S. taxes

This is illustrated in Example 11.11

EXAMPLE 11.11

To see this in action, suppose a firm needs additional plant capacity sufficient to make one million more units per year. In either a plant expansion
or a plant purchase, the following would apply:

Cost of new plant/existing plant expansion	$10,000,000
Increased annual production	1,000,000 units
Increased annual operating profits before	
depreciation expense and taxes	$ 3,000,000
(profits are 30% of sales)	
Increased payroll (costs included in above	
operating profits)	$ 4,000,000

Assume the following tax information. The existing plant in California has:

Annual payroll	$15,000,000
Annual sales	$50,000,000
Book value of plant	$40,000,000
Taxable income	$20,000,000

Assume that California tax rates are 9% on corporate income and 1%
on the value of property. Because the firm sells its manufactured products
to wholesalers, there are no sales taxes. This is the firm's only plant, and it
sells only to California merchandisers.

The proposed new plants could be purchased in Nevada or Mexico.
Relevant tax rates in these jurisdictions would be as follows:

	Nevada	Mexico
Property tax rate	1.50%	1%
Income tax rate	0%	25%

For either location, all manufactured product would be sold to California wholesalers. Under either a new plant or expansion of existing facilities, asset/MACRS categories would be as follows:

Asset Classification	Cost	MACRS Life
Land	$1,000,000	N/A
Building	$6,000,000	39 yrs
Machinery, equipment	$3,000,000	10 yrs

What are the important tax effects under the alternative? For simplicity, assume a 10-year planning horizon and that machinery and equipment are exempt from property taxes.

Expand Existing Plant (in California)

State, local tax consequences:

Annual income tax:	
Operating profits before depreciation	$3,000,000
Property taxes	<70,000>
Depreciation (see federal taxes)	<453,846>*
State taxable income	$2,476,154
Tax at 9%	$ 222,854
Annual property tax: 1% of land & building	$ 70,000

*California, like many states, uses an MACRS—like (or similar) system; see schedule for depreciation the following table

Federal tax consequences:

Operating expenses before depreciation and state & local taxes	$3,000,000
Depreciation:	<453,846>
State, local taxes deduction $70,000 + $222,854 =	<292,854>
Federal taxable income	$2,253,300
Taxes at 35%	$ 788,655
Total taxes, plant expansion: $292,854 + 788,655 =	$1,081,509
Depreciation:	
Building: Straight Line for 39 years ($6,000,000/39) =	153,846
Plant, equipment: Average over a 10 year period ($3,000,000/10) =	300,000
	$ 453,846

What are the important tax effects if a new plant is purchased in Nevada?

Buy New Plant in Nevada

State, local tax consequences:

Income taxes: Nevada	$0
California	63,000
Property taxes: 1.5% of ($1,000,000 + $6,000,000) =	105,000
	$ 168,000

The effect of the Nevada location is to apportion (under California's unitary system of taxation) some California income into Nevada. This would be as follows:

Apportionment to

	California	Nevada	
World-wide income	$20,000,000 + 2,500,000	$22,500,000	
Payroll	15,000,000/19,000,000	4,000,000/19,000,000	0.21
Property	40,000,000/46,000,000	6,000,000/46,000,000	0.13
Sales .2	2.0	All sales into California =	0
Sum	3.66		.34
Average: sum/4	0.92		0.08
Income apportioned into state: average factor ratio times worldwide income	$20,700,000	$1,800,000	
Less income previously taxed in California	<20,000,000>	—	
Increased taxable income	700,000	1,800,000	
Times tax rate	9%	0%	
Increased tax	$ 63,000	0	

Federal tax consequences:

		Nevada	
Operating expenses before depreciation, deduction for state, local taxes		$3,000,000	
Depreciation		<453,846>	
State, local tax deduction		<168,000>	
Federal taxable income		2,378,154	
Taxes at 35%		832,354	
Total taxes—Nevada plant: $832,354 + $168,000 =		$1,000,354	

Thus, purchasing a new plant in Nevada would reduce total taxes to $1,000,354 from $1,081,529, a savings of over $80,000.

What if the plant were in Mexico instead of Nevada?

Buy New Plant—Mexico

Mexican tax consequences:

Income taxes: ($3,000,000 − $453,846 − $70,000) × .25 =	$ 619,038
Property taxes: 1% of ($1,000,000 + $6,000,000) =	70,000
	$ 689,038

Federal tax consequences:

Operating profit before depreciation	$3,000,000
Mexican property taxes	<70,000>
Depreciation	<453,846>
Federal taxable income	$2,476,154
Taxes at 35%	$ 866,654
Less foreign tax credit for Mexican income taxes paid	<619,038>
Net U.S. tax	247,616
Total taxes = 247,616 + 689,038 + 63,000=	$ 999,654

These calculations assume that the plant is not in a separate corporation, so transfer pricing between the related companies cannot be used to optimize income taxes. Also, note that the actual Mexican taxes paid are below the U.S. foreign tax credit (FTC) limit. Thus all of the taxes paid to Mexico can be used to offset U.S. income taxes. Were the Mexican taxes above the FTC limit, the excess could not be used that year. However, such excess FTCs can be carried back two years and forward five years to offset U.S. taxes on foreign income in those years.

Finally, one must consider California tax consequences. Like most states, California allows a resident company to either pay a flat fee (the so-called water's edge election) or include international income in the state tax base without the flat fee (the worldwide method). Assuming the firm elects the latter, additional California taxes are $63,000, just as in the Nevada plant-site selection.

Total tax consequences for Mexico plant:
$689,038 + $247,616 + $63,000 = $999,654

EXHIBIT 11.5   The Impact of Taxes on Projected Cash Flow

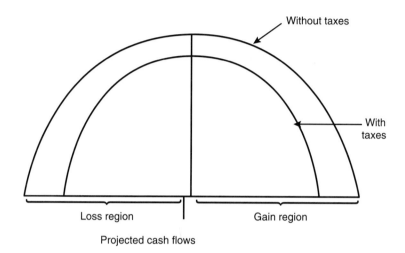

Effect of Income Taxes—Capital Project Cash Flows

This suggests a total tax savings of about $1,000 over a Nevada plant, and $80,000 over expanding the California plant.

After an analysis of the complex interactions of a variety of taxes, the capital budgeting decision based solely on an NPV analysis would be to buy a new plant in Mexico. However, the advantages are not great and may disappear when other business aspects are considered. For example, NPV calculations for a plant in a foreign country should be adjusted for any extra risk involved due to language and cultural differences (as well as other factors).

RISK CONSIDERATIONS

Because capital budgeting involves longer-run horizons, there is inherently more risk that cash flows may vary from projections. (Note that the depreciation tax shield, absent a change in the firm's effective tax rate, is invariant). Because income taxes decrease with decreased revenues, they act as a variance (and hence risk) reduction mechanism. (See Exhibit 11.5.)

Example 11.12 quantities these curves in order to better illustrate this concept:

EXAMPLE 11.12

Consider a firm that invests $10 million in advertising to launch a new product. Management is uncertain about its outcome, but feels there is a bell-shaped curve over a range of possible outcomes, as follows:

Possible profit Ranges—New Product

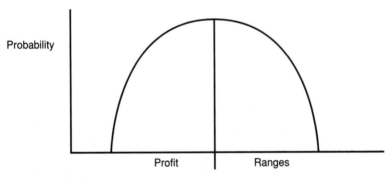

Probability

Profit   Ranges

Worst case	Most likely: Net profit = $1,000,000	Best case
Least likely:		Least likely:
Loss of $10,000,000		Net profit of
advertising plus		$20,000,000
operating costs		

Although management felt that expected profits could fall over a broad range, they prepared some simplified point estimates, first considering only the effects of federal taxes:

	Worst Case: 25% probability	**Most Likely:** 50% probability	**Best Case:** 25% probability
Profit	<$11,000,000>	$1,000,000	$20,000,000
Taxes at 35%	3,850,000	<350,000>	<7,000,000>
Net profit	<$ 7,150,000>	$ 650,000	$13,000,000

Thus, the expected net profit is: .25(<7,150,000>) + .5(650,000) + .25 (13,000,000) = <1,787,500> + 325,000 + 3,250,000 = $1,787,500. What is the effect of federal income taxes? Using a tax rate of 35%, divide the outcomes by (1 − .35) = .65, to get: <$2,750,000> + 500,000 + 5,000,000 = $2,750,000. This pretax result is $962,500 higher than the after-tax outcome. Thus the tax effect is $962,500.

Does that mean that management would find this a more attractive investment if there were no taxes? Most likely, actual tax effects in situations like that illustrated in Example 11.12 would actually make the investment more palatable. This is because of the loss reduction aspect of federal taxes.

For example, in the worst-case scenario, a possible $11 million pretax loss is converted into a $7,200,000 after-tax loss. If the company cannot afford the former loss, or a manager's evaluation (possibly considering her own bonus based on after-tax earnings) hinges on the investment, taxes can actually help in a risky capital budgeting project. However, if the loss creates an NOL at the entity level, the effect of state income taxes can make the loss less palatable. This is because of NOL restrictions in most states. The same applies to many countries.

CHAPTER 12

Financial Statement Analysis and Proactive Tax Planning

As the lens on a business, financial statements, focused with the techniques of financial statement analysis, provide a way of interpreting the business in a way that enables readers to understand the value it generates for shareholders.

—Stephen Penman,
Financial Statement Analysis and Security Valuation

The mature firm's decision making involves an interplay between financial accounting information and taxes. This chapter analyses both internal and external accounting information for such decision making. The discussion of internal use focuses on segmental analysis. External use focuses on tax-related footnotes found in competitors' financial statements.

SEGMENTAL ANALYSIS

Part of a manager's ongoing analysis is to determine whether particular components of a company should be retained or discontinued. In large measure, this decision depends on whether, after factoring out noncontrollable costs, the segment has a profit. One component of cost is taxes. (See Examples 12.1 and 12.2.)

EXAMPLE 12.1

Suppose a firm operates two retail stores with revenues and costs as follows:

	Combined	Head Office (Chicago)	Store A (Las Vegas)	Store B (New York)
Sales	$7,000,000	—	$3,000,000	$4,000,000
Cost of goods sold	<3,000,000>		<2,000,000>	<1,000,000>
Gross margin	$4,000,000	—	$1,000,000	$3,000,000
Other expenses:				
S,G&A	<300,000>	<200,000>	<50,000>	<50,000>
Property taxes	<360,000>	<10,000>	<150,000>	<200,000>
Income taxes:				
Federal	<1,000,000>	—	<500,000>	<500,000>
State	<340,000>	—	<170,000>	<170,000>
Net income	$2,000,000	<$210,000>	$ 130,000	$2,080,000

This initial analysis leads to scrutiny of the Las Vegas store. The profitability on sales, $130,000/$3,000,000 = 4\%$, is well below the firm's target threshold of 15%. Suppose that a closer look at the other expenses reveals the following: Sales, general, and administration expense (S,G,&A) and property taxes were costs incurred by each office or store; taxes, however, were firmwide and simply allocated evenly across these two stores. Nevada has no corporate income tax, so the entire state tax burden is due to New York operations. Reallocating federal and state income taxes, based on how they are controllably incurred, yields:

	Store A (Las Vegas)	Store B (New York)
Gross margin	$1,000,000	$3,000,000
S,G&A	<50,000>	50,000
Property taxes	<150,000>	200,000
State income taxes	0	340,000
Segment profit before federal income taxes	800,000	2,410,000
Federal income taxes^	<250,000>*	750,000
Segment profit	$ 550,000	$1,660,000
As % of sales	55%	55%

*$800,000/(800,000 + 2,410,000) = 25\% \times $1,000,000$ total FIT = $250,000

This controllable cost segmental analysis reveals the Las Vegas store is as profitable as the New York store. (Note that in firms which focus on other metrics, such as economic value-added (EVA), the Las Vegas store might be viable even if its profitability were lower than that of other stores, provided it performed above the firm's target EVA.)

The same sort of analysis can be used for foreign taxes and product line decisions.

EXAMPLE 12.2

Suppose a company sells computer products in California and in Mexico through separate branch offices. It sells two products: computers and printers. The company's financial records show the following:

	Consolidated	Headquarters	California Computers	Printers	Mexico Computers	Printers
Sales	$7,100,000	0	$5,000,000	$1,000,000	$1,000,000	$100,000
Cost of sales	<2,840,000>	0	<2,000,000>	<400,000>	<400,000>	<40,000>
Gross margin	$4,260,000	0	$3,000,000	$ 600,000	$ 600,000	$ 60,000
Other expenses:						
S,G,&A	<1,000,000>	<500,000>	<150,000>	<150,000>	<100,000>	<100,000>
Federal taxes	<900,000>	<900,000>				
California taxes	<300,000>	<300,000>				
Mexican taxes	<90,000>	<90,000>				
	$1,970,000	<$1,790,000>	$2,850,000	$ 450,000	$ 500,000	<$ 40,000>

The company is concerned that printers may not be profitable, particularly in the Mexican market, and perhaps should be dropped. A further analysis shows that while sales, general, & administrative expense has been allocated appropriately, taxes should be allocated as shown in the next table in this Example.

As the posttax segmental data indicate, printers per se are not unprofitable. Instead, only those sold in the Mexican market are unprofitable. Management should consider a number of other factors before deciding to drop this market/product line. These include (1) cross-elasticity (that is, will sales of computers in Mexico fall if printers are unavailable), (2) Strategy (for example, is it important to maintain a strategic presence, despite the losses), and (3) Anticipation and timing (for example, will the losses turn around in a subsequent year).

	Market			
	California		Mexico	
	Computers	Printers	Computers	Printers
Sales	$5,000,000	$1,000,000	$1,000,000	$100,000
Gross margin	3,000,000	600,000	600,000	60,000
S, G, & A	<150,000>	<150,000>	<100,000>	<100,000>
Federal taxes	<685,000>	<105,000>	<120,000>	10,000
California taxes	<255,000>	<45,000>	0	0
Mexican taxes	0	0	<82,000>*	<8,000>
Segment margin	$1,910,000	$ 300,000	$ 298,000	<$ 38,000>
As % of sales	38.20%	30.00%	29.80%	−38.00%

*Assumes Mexican taxes are not creditable against U.S. taxes
If the U.S. foreign tax credit were allowable, margins would improve to 38% & −30%.

OTHER TAX ASPECTS IN SEGMENTAL ANALYSIS

Besides the current impact of a segment on taxable income, some other tax aspects are

- Taxes and fixed assets
- Net operating losses
- State and local income taxes
- Foreign operations

Taxes and fixed assets

When fixed assets are disposed of, gain or loss may occur. This has an impact immediately for U.S. financial-statement purposes and for U.S. tax purposes as well (unless the sales price is paid in installments). The tax shield provided by depreciation on the assets will be lost, too. (See Example 12.3.)

EXAMPLE 12.3

Suppose a firm is considering dropping a product line with the following costs (none of which are allocated):

Sales	$500,000
Cost of sales	<400,000>
Gross margin	100,000
Less S, G, & A	<120,000>
Cash flow from operations	<20,000>
Depreciation	<80,000>
	<$100,000>

The information shows that, pretax, the product has a negative value-added effect on the rest of the firm. However, the *true* cash-flow effects must take into account that depreciation's cash-flow effect is only from the tax shield it provides. Accordingly, the analysis is

Cash flow from operations	<$20,000>
Add tax savings from preceding table (assume 35% federal, 8% state)	8,600
Add depreciation tax shield (assume 35% federal, 8% state)	34,400
After-tax cash flow	$23,000

Assume that if the product line is liquidated, disposition of the assets will result in a tax loss of $10,000. This loss also creates a positive cash flow from the tax effect of .43($10,000) = $4,300. Thus, the cash-flow effects from keeping the product are $23,000 per year; from disposing, a one-time positive cash flow of $4,300. Opposed to this are the financial statement effects, after the provision for income tax expense, as follows:

Keep:	
Pretax loss	<$100,000>
Add: tax savings at 43%	43,000
Financial accounting annual loss	<57,000>
Dispose:	
Financial-accounting loss	<10,000>
Less tax savings	3,400
One-time loss	<$ 6,600>

Because the cash-flow analysis indicates keep, but the financial accounting analysis points to dispose, management should weigh the relative importance of cash flow versus EVA. (Note that other taxes, such as local property taxes, should also be considered.)

Net Operating Losses

If a business segment has an annual tax NOL but the remainder of the firm has positive taxable income, the firm should consider that this NOL tax shield would be lost were the segment dropped. However, if the rest of the firm has an NOL, the segment's NOL may do little good. If the segment has positive taxable income, but the rest of the firm has positive taxable income, the opposite is true. This can be illustrated as

Rest of the firm	Segment Taxable Income	
Taxable income	Positive	NOL
Positive	None	+
NOL	+	None

Note that these effects depend on the extent to which the jurisdictions involved allow deductions for NOLs. Many U.S. states and most countries severely limit (or do not allow) NOL deductions. (See Example 12.4.)

EXAMPLE 12.4

A U.S. computer game manufacturer has annual pretax profits of $20 million. One of its game products loses $2 million each year. If the product is dropped, pretax profits will increase to $22 million. However, the firm will lose (.35)($2,000,000) = $700,000 in annual cash flow (from the loss tax shield) in dropping the game.

State and Local Income Taxes

If the segment operates in the same U.S. state as the rest of the firm, then its effect on the firm is simply the segment's taxable income multiplied by the applicable state income tax rate. However, if the segment operates in a different state, then the relative tax rates of the segment's state, versus the average state tax rate of the rest of the firm, must be considered. Regardless of whether the segment has an NOL or not, part of the rest of the firm's income is apportioned to the segment's state, and out of other states. Thus, the following applies:

Segment State Tax Rate	Effect of Segment on Firm's Income Taxes
Higher than rest of firm	Negative
Lower than rest of firm	Positive

(See Example 12.5.)

EXAMPLE 12.5

Assume the facts as in Example 12.4, except that the firm operates in a state with a 9% income tax. By dropping the game, the firm loses cash flows from the state tax shields of $(.09)(\$2,000,000) = \$180,000$ annually.

Foreign Operations

If the segment operates across foreign borders, its impact on the rest of the firm raises issues similar to the state tax analysis presented previously. Thus, if a segment operates in a country having higher (lower) tax rates than the rest of the firm, then its effect on the firm's overall taxes is negative (positive). For example, suppose a U.S. firm sells in Hong Kong. If it discontinues this segment, its taxes could conceivably go up: the Hong Kong standard tax rate is 15%, versus 35% for the United States.

The analysis above ignores cash-flow effects. If there is a repatriation of funds, either by a current dividend or liquidation, the results can be quite complex and are beyond the scope of this text. However, mechanisms like the U.S. foreign tax credit and tax treaties exist to minimize double taxation. The result is generally that income taxes are imposed at the higher tax rate between the country where income is derived and the country to which it is repatriated.

SAVANT and Segmental Analysis

Beyond the preceding analysis, the firm's segmental decisions should consider the following:

- *Strategy.* Even if there is a negative financial-statement or cash-flow impact of the segment, is there an important strategic presence impact?
- *Anticipation.* Could a current *loser* segment potentially turn around?
- *Value-Adding.* Is there enough risk associated with the segment that its return should be discounted even more? In terms of transaction costs, are there significant legal and accounting fees that follow from a discontinuance? Will severance pay, unemployment claims, and the like be significant?
- *Negotiating.* Can local tax authorities, at the threat of losing the segment moving or going out of business, be negotiated with to reduce taxes?

Any of these considerations may act to countervail the cash-flow or EVA analysis. (See Examples 12.6 and 12.7.)

EXAMPLE 12.6

Assume the same facts as Example 12.4. Assume the firm determines that the following costs will result from discontinuance of the game: severance pay to executives of $2 million and an increase in the firm's unemployment insurance experience rating, which will result in an additional $50,000 per year of unemployment insurance on the rest of the firm. The present value of these cash flows should be factored into the decision.

EXAMPLE 12.7

Assume the same facts as Example 12.4. Suppose the facility that makes the game pays $200,000 per year in property taxes and employs 1,000 people. Management may be able to convince local authorities that it is worthwhile for them to forgive the $200,000 property taxes in order to protect the local jobs.

STRATEGIC ANALYSIS: USING COMPETITOR'S TAX NOTE AND SEGMENTAL DATA

If a competitor is publicly traded in the United States, then it is required to file an annual Form 10K report with the Securities Exchange Commission (SEC). The report is publicly available and is a source of competitive intelligence. Among other things, a Form 10K includes audited financial statements for several years, financial information of the performance of the segments of the firm, and extensive footnotes disclosing a wide variety of pertinent information.

Segmental Data

In its Form 10K, the firm is required to separately report financial information of any segment (either geographic or line of business) that is a substantial portion of the business. Managers thus can acquire competitive intelligence on firms operating in the same markets. Beyond nontax data on competitor profitability, one can infer tax data as well.

Suppose a competitor has United States and Canadian operations. If it is found that the competitor's Canadian operations earn substantially more than those in the United States, it may be difficult to stay competitive. Even without a Form 10K, finding out where the competitors' plants are located is not difficult. However, finding out each plant's profitability is very difficult without a Form 10K. If the competitor has substantial operations in Canada, they will be discussed in the competitor's Form 10K supplementary segmental data.

Note that all substantial non-U.S. operations are reported, and that they are lumped together. Thus, if a significant portion of this competitor's non-U.S. operations are located in countries other than Canada, it may prove difficult to isolate purely Canadian activities.

Note also that Form 10K information can be used—in conjunction with tax note data (discussed next)—to determine the competitor's after-tax profitability. In fact, much of the segmental data analysis performed for one's own company can be done with competitors' data as well.

Tax Footnote Information

If a firm is publicly traded in the United States, its Form 10K also must include a note that reconciles the firm's statutory worldwide income tax rate to its actual effective tax rate. Any differences result from book treatment (of items included in the financial statement) that is different from tax treatment. This analysis must include a separate disclosure of any component of income that accounts for more than 2.5% of this book-tax difference. Such components can include classes of items (e.g., book-tax differences in depreciation), as well as individual significant transactions (e.g., sale of a subsidiary).

One general bit of information contained in the competitor's tax note is whether it is in a tax-paying situation. If it is an NOL carryforward situation, one can infer a number of strategic behaviors that it may be more likely to manifest. This could include, for example, (1) accelerating taxable income through dispositions of assets or operations, (2) avoiding investment in tax-favored assets (e.g., building a plant in Ireland), or (3) purchasing tax disfavored investments (e.g., acquiring a new subsidiary with positive taxable income).

If the competitor operates in international markets, the tax note also will indicate the extent to which its worldwide effective tax rate differs from its U.S. rate. The difference indicates how successful the firm is in managing taxes overall. It also may suggest changes in the competitor's strategy. For example, if the note shows excess foreign tax credits (often, but not always, the result of a U.S. NOL), then the competitor has an incentive to generate additional foreign source income in future years. This can be done by expanding overseas operations, either by new investment or shifting domestic investment abroad. As an alternative, transfer prices can be changed, or dividends repatriated.

Perhaps more important, significant individual transactions that do not appear on other parts of the financial statements may appear in the tax notes. Such disclosures can be for

- Sales of investments
- Sales of subsidiaries
- Extra taxes as result of tax audits
- Tax loss carryforwards
- Tax credit carryforwards
- Other special tax attributes

Example 12.8 shows how significant information can show up in footnotes to financials statements:

EXAMPLE 12.8

An examination of a competitor's tax note reveals that its statutory tax rate decreased to 15% from 35%. This suggests that, unless the competitor moved locations, it was able to obtain some special tax treatment in its existing operations. This may have given the competitor a strategic cost advantage.

Examples 12.9 through 12.12 show information for four companies and illustrate how footnotes to financial statements can be used for competitive intelligence.

EXAMPLE 12.9

Consider the following tax notes for Lucent Technologies. The firm resulted from a spin off from AT&T Bell labs. Since the 1996 report is for its first year of business, competitors in the high-tech communications industry should have found it of interest. An excerpt follows:

Tax Note: Lucent Technologies, Inc. and Subsidiaries

The following table presents the principal reasons for the difference between the effective tax rate and the United States federal statutory income tax rate (in millions of dollars):

	Nine Months Ended September 30, 1996	Year Ended December 31, 1995	Year Ended December 31, 1994
U.S. federal statutory income tax rate	35%	35%	35%
Federal income tax provision (benefit) at statutory rate	$128	<$398>	$274
State and local income taxes, net of federal income tax effect	5	<57>	23
Amortization of intangibles	—	29	12
Foreign earnings and dividends taxed at different rates	15	140	36
Research credits	<18>	<3>	<27>
Other differences—net	13	18	<16>
Provision (benefit) for income taxes	$143	<$271>	$302
Effective income tax rate	39.00%	23.80%	38.50%

The following table presents the U.S. and foreign components of income taxes and the provision for income taxes:

	Nine Months Ended September 30, 1996	Year Ended December 31, 1995	Year Ended December 31, 1994
Income (Loss) Before Income Taxes			
United States	$101	<$1,253>	$ 405
Foreign	266	115	379
Provision (Benefit) for Income Taxes:			
Current:			
Federal	$242	$199	<$119>
State and local	53	42	<40>
Foreign	98	141	123
	393	382	<36>
Deferred:			
Federal	<198>	<523>	267
State and local	<45>	<130>	76
Foreign	<6>	1	<4>
	<249>	<652>	339
Deferred investment tax credits	<1>	<1>	<1>
	$143	<$ 271>	$302

As can be seen, Lucent is in a taxpaying status; its effective tax rate is 39%. We can also see that

■ Its state and local tax is $5 million. This amount suggests that Lucent is doing a good job of managing these taxes, because it is less than 4% of total taxes.
■ There is a $15 million additional foreign tax rate; the firm has likely operated in high-tax jurisdictions outside of the United States.
■ There is a substantial U.S. research and development (R&D) tax credit. The actual amount that Lucent spent on R&D in the year can be estimated from this, knowing that the credit rate is 20%.

The note goes on

	September 30, 1996	December 31, 1995
	35%	35%
Net Current Deferred Income Tax Assets:		
Employee pensions and other benefits	$584	$512
Business restructuring	317	519
Reserves and allowances	589	537
Valuation allowance	<38>	<117>
Other	182	143
Total current deferred income tax assets	1,634	1,598
Current deferred income tax liabilities	<17>	<116>
	$1,617	$1,482
Long-Term Deferred Income Tax Assets:		
Employee pensions and other benefits, net	$1,317	$1,425
Business restructuring	101	267
Net operating loss/credit carryforwards	67	28
Reserves and allowances	69	9
Valuation allowance	<170>	<25>
Other	371	270
	1,755	1,974
Long-Term Deferred Income Tax Liabilities:		
Property, plant and equipment	<518>	<738>
Other	<258>	<364>
	<776>	<1,102>
Net long-term deferred income tax assets	$ 979	$ 872

This information indicates that Lucent had a number of deferred income tax assets. These occur where financial accounting income is lower than taxable income. The specifics show that the firm had an enormous pension plan, and that the firm took a large charge for business restructuring that far exceeded its related tax deduction. Finally, the note goes on to say

> Lucent has not provided for United States federal income taxes or foreign withholding taxes on $4,289 of undistributed earnings of its non-United States subsidiaries as of September 30, 1996, since these earnings are intended to be reinvested indefinitely. It is not practical to determine the amount of applicable taxes that would be incurred if any of such earnings were repatriated.

This is standard wording. It means that for U.S. financial-accounting purposes, the firm did not have U.S. tax expense related to its non-U.S. subsidiaries because there was no plan to repatriate their earnings. Moreover, the note indicates that Lucent's foreign subsidiaries made $1.3 billion of net profits. This gave competitor-information on the extent of foreign operations.

EXAMPLE 12.10

Appliance Recycling Centers of America (ARCA) is the largest U.S. recycler of major household appliances. In its 1996 tax note, the provision for (benefit of) income taxes consisted of the following:

	1996	1995	1994
Current:			
Federal	<$415,000>	<$ 4,000>	$669,000
State	—	—	157,000
Deferred:	650,000	<586,000>	<161,000>

The financial accounting NOL for the year is $415 million. The report then reconciles the firm's statutory and actual (effective) tax rates as follows:

	1996	1995	1994
Income taxes at statutory rate	<$2,462,000>	<$566,000>	$539,000
State taxes, net of federal	<208,000>	<24,000>	126,000
Permanent differences	110,000	—	—
Change in valuation allowance	235,000	—	—
Effect of NOL with no current tax benefit	2,560,000	—	—
	$ 235,000	<$590,000>	$665,000

The information shows that there is a tax loss (for financial-accounting purposes) of $2.4 billion, which started in 1995. The note goes on to describe the actual tax return loss as follows:

At December 28, 1996, the Company had net operating loss carry-forwards of $4,515,000 that expire in 2011.

The information can provide important information about competitors. For example, in Example 12.10, there is no tax incentive for the company to enter into tax-advantaged transactions for a number of years. Moreover, the losses may make the firm a tempting takeover target. (This is discussed in detail in Chapter 14, which deals with mergers and acquisitions).

Throughout this book, cost savings through a variety of tax-savings mechanisms has been pointed out as a source of competitive advantage. As mentioned in Chapter 8 (on international aspects of tax planning), one such mechanism has been the foreign sales corporation (FSC). It provided a reduced U.S. tax rate on non-U.S. income. (As noted in Chapter 8, FSC-like arrangements have twice been successfully challenged under the World Trade Organization and its predessor, General Agreement on Tariffs and Trade (GATT), only to be replaced by a slightly different form.) Whether a firm has elected FSC status can usually be determined only in the tax note. This is illustrated by Example 12.11; a tax footnote showing an FSC for General Electric.

EXAMPLE 12.11

Reconcilation of U.S. Federal Statutory Tax Rate to Actual	1996	1995	1994
Statutory U.S. federal tax rate	35%	35%	35%
Increase (reduction) in rate resulting from Inclusion of after-tax earnings of GECS in before-tax earnings of GE:	—	—	—
Amortization of goodwill	1.1	1.1	1.1
Tax-exempt income	<2.1>	<2.1>	<2.4>
Foreign Sales Corporation	<1.7>	<0.9>	<1.1>
Dividends received, not fully taxable	<0.6>	<0.5>	<0.5>
All other—net	<0.2>	<0.1>	<0.4>
	<3.5>	<2.5>	<3.3>
Actual income tax rate	31.5%	32.5%	31.7%

The note shows that the reduction in taxes due to FSCs is one of the more important of GE's tax management techniques.

Another tax based mechanism for competitive advantage is an employee stock ownership plan. (ESOPs were discussed in Chapter 6. Often the only public source of information about whether a firm is using an ESOP are the tax notes to the firm's financial statements. This is illustrated by Example 12.12.

EXAMPLE 12.12

Northrop Grumman is in an industry with only a few—but nonetheless highly competitive—rivals. Any information by rivals is thus very important. The following is from one of the firm's tax footnotes:

Dollars in Millions:	1996	1995
Income tax expense at statutory rate	$135	$143
Goodwill amortization	16	13
Provision for nondeductible expenses	2	4
Benefits from ESOP dividends	<3>	<3>
Dividend exclusion		
Retroactive effect of statutory rate increase		
	$150	$157

As can be seen, the firm is in a tax-paying status. The note also indicates that the firm has an ESOP. Further details reveal the following:

Dollars in Millions:	1996	1995
Deductible temporary differences		
Retiree benefit plan expense	$602	$421
Provision for estimated expenses	79	25
Income on contracts	49	14
Other	41	35
	771	495
Taxable temporary differences		
Purchased intangibles	<110>	<124>
Excess tax over book depreciation	<64>	<71>
Income benefit plan income		<18>
Administrative and general expenses		
period costed for tax purposes		<2>
	<174>	<215>
	$597	$280

This part of the company's tax footnote shows that

- The firm has a substantial pension plan.
- The firm is making extensive use of accelerated tax depreciation, such as the modified accelerated cost recovery system (MACRS).
- The firm is managing taxes by using the installment method of accounting for long-term contracts.

In some industries, accessing Form 10K information may be impractical when there are numerous firms. In this case, a Lexus-Nexus or Web search, perhaps using select criteria (e.g., "net operating loss"), may be a better approach to finding useful competitive data.

Changing Original Form

Restructuring

I think the results speak for themselves. We had a dramatic restructuring of the balance sheet the first year

— George Fisher, CEO, Kodak
(describing the firm's eighth downsizing since 1983)

Reacting to increasing competition in global markets in the early 1980s, U.S. businesses began a process of restructuring. Restructuring now is ongoing for many firms throughout the world. Its focus is to increase shareholder value. This chapter discusses how, once the firm has committed to restructuring, proper tax management can enhance value-adding.

FINANCIAL RESTRUCTURING

Firms develop a capital structure policy as part of their corporate-level strategy. As with business-level strategy, a firm's financial structure must respond to the evolving needs of the firm and to the changing environment in which it operates. This part of the chapter focuses on firm recapitalizations and their related tax consequences.

Early Retirement of Bonds

When a firm redeems its bonds, under U.S. GAAP and tax-accounting rules it recognizes a gain or loss. The amount is the difference between the price paid (the call) and the bonds' principal amount, less accrued interest. Any accrued interest becomes interest expense. Firms call bonds most often if they are paying an interest rate much higher than the market and the transactions costs do not exceed any interest savings. Another reason is that often the difference generates a financial-accounting gain. This is because in virtually all cases the call price of the bond is higher than its face value.

In the United States, even though there is a book gain the firm can make the call tax free (a type E reorganization) if it reissues bonds to the existing bondholders. To qualify, the principal amount of the debt surrendered cannot be less than that of the debt received. (See Example 13.1.)

EXAMPLE 13.1

Assume the following example:

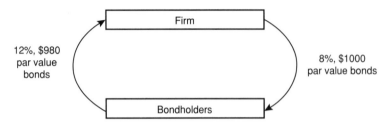

This is a common transaction, where the firm takes advantage of decreased interest rates. Note that here the transaction is tax free to both the bondholders and the firm. What if the firm offers some bondholders either cash or stock? Then the entire transaction becomes taxable.

Converting Bonds

If bonds are converted into common stock, there is no gain or loss to either the corporation or the shareholder if (1) the conversion is prorata (or if the bonds are designed to be convertible prorata), and (2) no boot is given in addition to the stock. (Boot is consideration, other than stock, given by the corporation to the bondholders. An example would be cash. It is called boot because it is added to boot to balance the value of major items being exchanged in a deal.) The result does not change regardless of whether the firm calls or converts the bonds or shareholders decide on their own to convert. (See Example 13.2.)

EXAMPLE 13.2

Assume the following transaction:

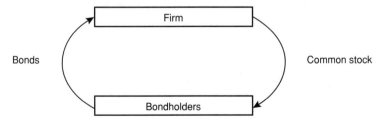

This is a tax-free transaction as long as each bond is tradable for the same amount of common stock and cannot be traded for preferred stock.

Stock Redemptions

If common stock is convertible into another type of common stock or into bonds, in the United States the conversion is tax free to both the corporation and the stockholder as long as the convertibility feature is proportional and no boot is given. (See Example 13.3.)

EXAMPLE 13.3

Either of the following transactions is tax free to both shareholders and the firm, if the distributions are pro rata and do not involve preferred stock:

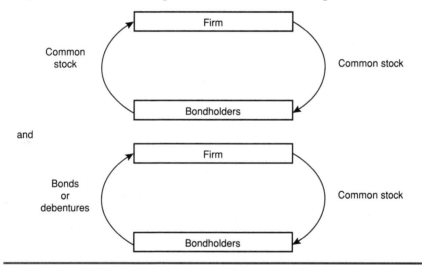

Sometimes the firm simply buys back some outstanding shares for cash. In 1996, for example, such buybacks amounted to $172.6 billion, up from $99.1 billion in 1995 (*Mergers & Acquisitions*, March–April 1997). As noted previously, buybacks have no tax consequence to the firm and are taxed as capital gains to shareholders.

FINANCIAL RESTRUCTURING IN THE SAVANT FRAMEWORK

Strategy

Because interest on bonds is deductible and dividend payments are not— except for employee stock ownership plans (ESOPs)—the firm's current and

EXHIBIT 13.1   Impact of Firm's Tax Status on Optimal Capital Structure

	Taxable	NOL Carryforward
Debt	Tax Advantage	Tax Disadvantage
Equity	Depends	Depends

anticipated tax status affects its after-tax cost of capital. Assuming that pretax dividend payments are equal to interest payment on bonds, the firm's tax status favors capital structure as shown in Exhibit 13.1.

A strategic advantage of convertibility is that if the firm transits in or out of a taxpaying status, it can adjust its capital structure accordingly. Of course, transaction costs should not outweigh the benefits of financial restructuring. Further, the firm should attempt to anticipate its tax status if it is to effect its tax-minimizing strategy.

Value-Adding

In addition to the after-tax cost of capital consideration, tax management should consider the effects on the firm's financial statements. For example, will a change to more debt result in costly debt covenant violations? Because interest expense reduces financial earnings, would such a recapitalization reduce earnings per share (EPS) and have negative effects on market value or managers' bonuses? (See Example 13.4.)

EXAMPLE 13.4

Suppose a firm has decided it wants to replace existing common stock with 8% bonds. The motivation for the decision was two-fold: undervaluation of the firm's common stock, and transition from a period of NOL carryforwards into a taxable status. The transaction would be

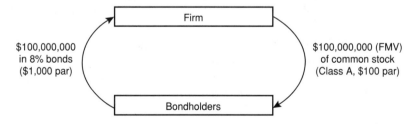

In the United States, dividends usually are not tax deductible but interest expense is. At a 35% tax bracket, the switch to debt would save the firm 35%(8%)($100 million) = $2,800,000 per year in taxes. Assume also the

firm was paying the equivalent of an 8% dividend each year. Assume the following condensed financial statements before the transaction ($ millions):

Income Statement		Balance Sheet	
Net income before taxes*	$50	Assets:	$200
Taxes at 35%	<17.5>	Equity:	
Net income	$32.5	Common	
EPS (Class A common)	$32.5	Class A	$100
(not in $ millions)		Class B	30
		Preferred	30
		Retained earnings	40
			$200

*Includes management bonus of 10% of pretax income

What nontax effect will the recapitalization have? Without considering managements' bonuses, the new financial statements would be

Income Statement		Balance Sheet	
Net income before		Asset:	$200
interest, taxes	$50	Equity:	
Interest	<8>	Common	
Pretax income	42	Class B	30
Taxes at 35%	<14.7>	Preferred	30
Net income	$27.3	Retained earnings	40
		Bonds payable	100
			$200

Note: Assumes earnings paid out to shareholders.

Two negative effects occur. First, management bonuses decline by about 10%($50,000,000 − $42,000,000) = $800,000, unless the firm somehow negotiates with management. Second, the firm's debt equity ratio goes from 0% to 50%. How this is perceived (in terms of riskiness) by debt and equity markets might not be too bad, if the ratio falls within industry standards.

Anticipation

Firms should engineer their debt-equity mix to maximize after-tax value-added. This is most important when tax rates, or a firm's tax status, are likely to change. One way to obtain flexibility in the event of changing tax situations is to issue debt or equity securities that are convertible at the firm's discretion. For example, if convertible stock is issued, it can be converted into bonds if the firm's tax rate goes up. This would allow the firm to convert payments of nondeductible dividends paid on the stock into deductible interest paid on the bonds.

BUSINESS RESTRUCTURING

Process Restructuring

As part of business-level strategy, many firms in the 1990s changed their business processes. Referred to as either core process reengineering (CPR) or total quality management (TQM), process restructuring identifies what products or services the firm is best suited to continue (or start), and redesigns the firm's systems to deliver products or services better, cheaper, or faster than competitors.

The U.S. tax treatment of the costs of process restructuring depends on their nature. If the costs are related to improving the actual manufacturing process, then they are eligible for the 20% research and development (R&D) tax credit. Capital expenditures related to process R&D are eligible for three-year tax write-offs, unless the equipment cannot be put to an alternative use, in which case it is expensed. Other costs are almost always expensed as incurred. (See Example 13.5.)

EXAMPLE 13.5

Suppose a company pays a consulting firm $500,000 for advice on reengineering its manufacturing process. As a result, $300,000 is spent on process R&D, $400,000 is spent on new equipment, and new personnel are added at a cost of $600,000/year in salary. The tax treatment is as follows:

Management consulting fee	Deductible
Process R&D	Tax credit at 20%
New equipment	Depreciate under MACRS
New Salaries	Annual deduction

LEGAL ENTITY RESTRUCTURING

In the late 1990s, there was enormous divestiture activity worldwide in the form of spin-offs, split-offs, and split-ups. (These are different legal forms of basically the same thing: isolating a piece of a large firm and shifting its ownership more directly to shareholders. They are described later in this section, and pictured in Examples 13.2, 13.3, and 13.4.) For example, in 1996 there were 54 major companies spun-off in the United States alone. The values involved numbered in the billions of dollars (*Mergers & Acquisitions*, April–May 1997).

Much of the impetus behind these divestitures is to separate high and low performing lines of business. Under U.S. GAAP, all of a firm's business units—whether isolated into separate corporations or not—are consolidated into one financial statement presented to capital markets. After a divestiture, capital markets are given a separate financial statement for each of the newly separate businesses. Each of these, having their own net incomes and stock, will show separate EPS. If done properly, under U.S. law such transactions qualify as a D reorganization and are tax free to all parties involved. (It is called a D reorganization because it is defined in IRC Section 368(a)(1)(D), which describes the various types of tax free reorganization. Other forms, ranging from A to G reorganizations, also take their names in this way.) Tax-free spin-offs, split-offs, and split-ups are discussed next.

Spin-Offs

Exhibit 13.2 depicts the predominant form for spin-offs.

EXHIBIT 13.2   Tax-Free Spin-Off into a New Subsidiary

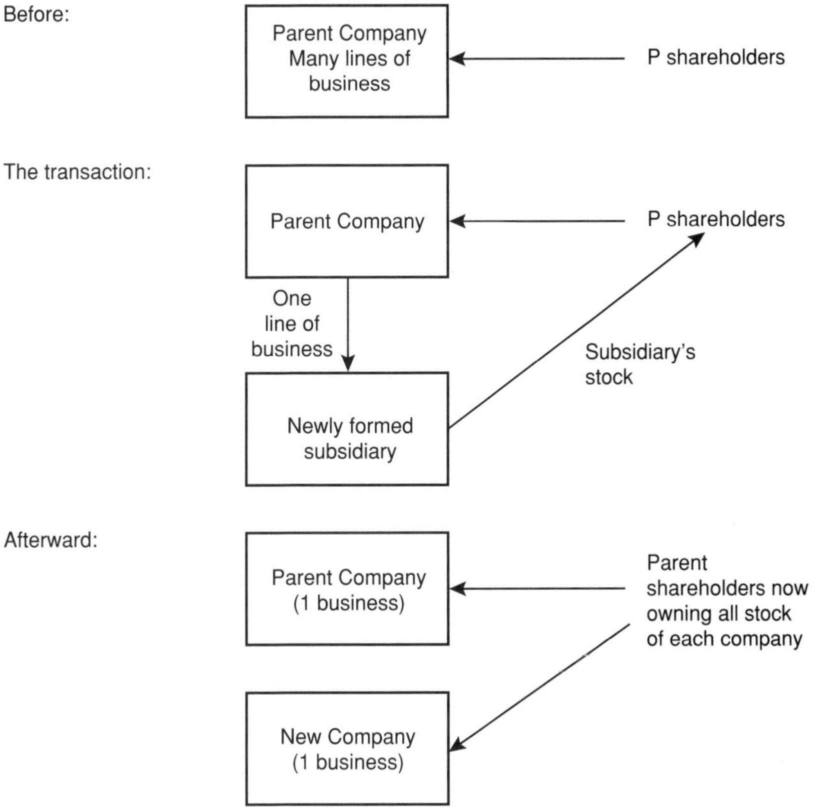

EXHIBIT 13.3 Tax-Free Spin-Off of an Existing Subsidiary

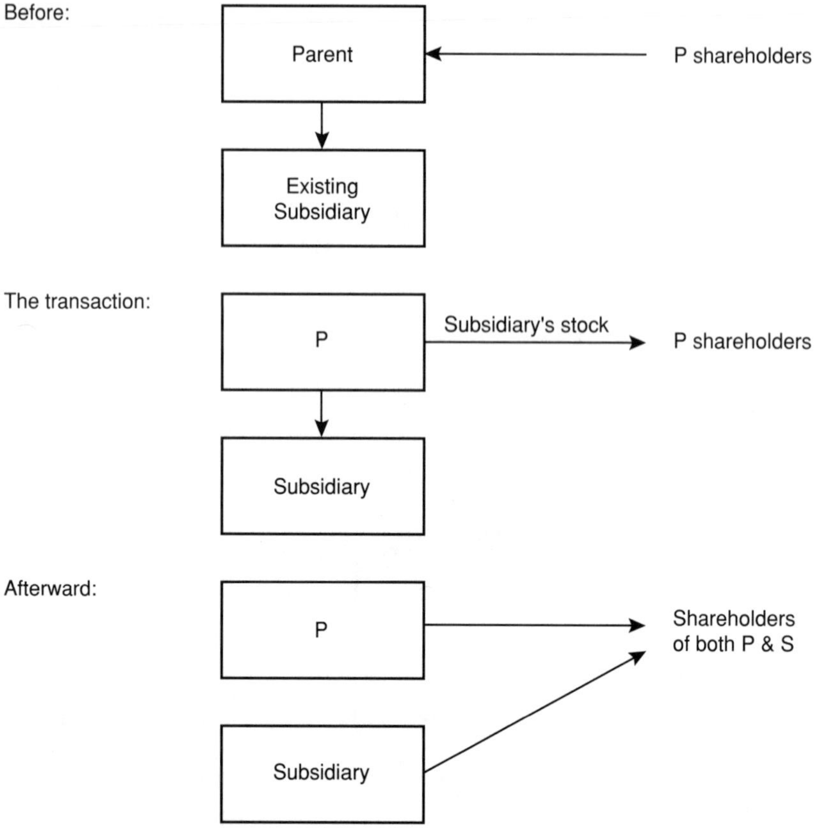

Before:

```
┌─────────────────┐
│     Parent      │ ◄────────────────  P shareholders
└─────────────────┘
         │
         ▼
┌─────────────────┐
│    Existing     │
│   Subsidiary    │
└─────────────────┘
```

The transaction:

```
┌─────────────────┐   Subsidiary's stock
│       P         │ ────────────────────►  P shareholders
└─────────────────┘
         │
         ▼
┌─────────────────┐
│   Subsidiary    │
└─────────────────┘
```

Afterward:

```
┌─────────────────┐
│       P         │ ──────────────►   Shareholders
└─────────────────┘                   of both P & S
┌─────────────────┐           ──────►
│   Subsidiary    │ ──────────
└─────────────────┘
```

Another valid method of spin-offs can be seen in Exhibit 13.3.

In both forms of the spin-off shown in Exhibits 13.2 and 13.3, the subsidiary's stock must be distributed to the parent corporation's shareholders pro rata—that is, in proportion to their percentage ownership in the parent.

Split-Offs

Two variations on spin-offs are split-offs and split-ups. A split-off occurs when a parent corporation isolates one of its businesses in a subsidiary and transfers the shares of the subsidiary to the parent's shareholders. This can be seen in Exhibit 13.4.

EXHIBIT 13.4   Illustration of a Split-Off

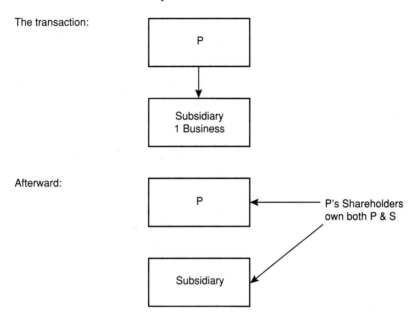

The transaction:

Afterward:

P's Shareholders own both P & S

Split-Ups

In a split-up, a parent corporation divides itself into two (or more) subsidiaries and then distributes their stock to its shareholders. It can be seen in Exhibit 13.5.

If certain conditions are met (see Technical Insert 13.1), the basic U.S. tax treatment is that spin-offs, split-offs, and split-ups are tax free. That is, they do not trigger income taxes for any of the parties involved in the reorganization. Note that tax free means no current taxes, rather than no future taxes. The transaction, like most tax-free reorganizations, actually is tax deferred. This occurs because the tax basis of the assets transferred carries over to the new corporation(s), thus preserving any untaxed gains or losses that had accrued prior to the reorganization. If the tax-free requirements are not met, then a spin-off is taxed as a dividend to the shareholders, a split-off is taxed as a stock redemption the shareholders, and a split-up is taxed as a liquidation.

The shareholders' basis in their stock in the new corporation is determined by reference to their basis in the stock of the original corporation. With a spin-off and a split-off, the basis in the original corporate stock is

EXHIBIT 13.5   Depiction of a Split-Up

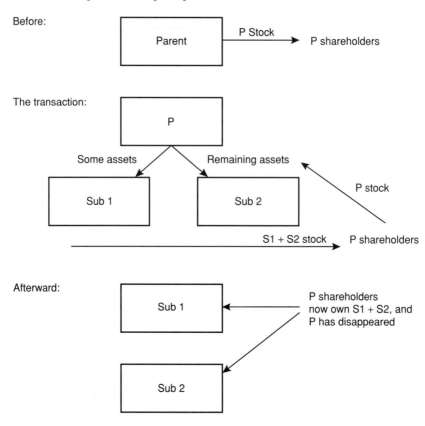

allocated between the original and new stock based on the relative fair market value of each. With a split-up, the basis of the relinquished original stock carries over to the new stock. (See Examples 13.6, 13.7, and 13.8.)

EXAMPLE 13.6

Nancy owns 200 shares of Originalco stock with a total basis of $40,000. Before the spin-off, the 200 shares are worth $100,000. In a spin-off, she receives a distribution of 100 shares of Newco stock valued at $20,000 (this reduces the value of her Originalco stock to $80,000). Nancy surrenders none of her Originalco stock. The basis she had in her Originalco stock is allocated between the Originalco stock and the Newco stock, using the fair market value of each. Thus, $80,000/$100,000 of the

$40,000 is allocated to the Originalco stock. The 200 shares now have a total basis of $32,000.

EXAMPLE 13.7

Assume instead that a split-off occurs. Nancy surrenders 75 shares of Originalco stock for 50 shares of Newco stock. Let the 50 shares of new stock be worth $37,500. After the transaction, her remaining 125 shares of Originalco stock are worth $62,500. Her basis of $40,000 is allocated between the Originalco and Newco stock using the fair market value of each. Thus, $37,500/$100,000 of the $40,000, is allocated to Newco stock.

EXAMPLE 13.8

Lynn and Lew are the sole shareholders of Pubco, a publishing corporation. Pubco was organized six years ago and has been actively engaged in publishing both books and periodicals. Because of antitrust problems, Pubco wishes to divide the business. Two new corporations are formed: Bookco and Periodicalco. All the assets relating to periodicals (books) are transferred to Bookco (Periodicalco). Lynn exchanges all her stock in Pubco for the stock in Bookco. Lew exchanges all his stock in Pubco for stock in Periodicalco. Pubco is liquidated. The transaction qualifies as a split-up. Neither Lynn nor Lew recognizes any gain.

One requirement for a valid tax-free spin-off, split-off, or split-up is that stock representing control of the new corporation must be distributed to the shareholders of the original corporation. In addition, the assets transferred and those retained must represent active businesses that have been owned and conducted by the original corporation for at least five years before the transfer. The distribution also must not be used principally as a device for distributing earnings of either the distributing or the controlled corporation. (See Example 13.9.)

EXAMPLE 13.9

Pacific Corp has been engaged in manufacturing. It also owns investment securities. Pacific transfers the investment securities to a newly formed corporation and distributes the stock of the new corporation to its shareholders. The transaction does not qualify as a tax-free divestiture. This is because holding investment securities does not qualify as a trade or business. The shareholders of Pacific are taxed upon receipt of the stock of the newly formed corporation as if they had received a dividend.

DIVESTITURES IN THE SAVANT FRAMEWORK

When is it more advantageous to sell business outright, versus separating it and keeping it in shareholders' hands?

Strategy

If the business is worth retaining from a strategic perspective, then a divisive reorganization may be called for. For example, in a vertically integrated operation, it may be worthwhile to keep downstream organizations in the conglomerate to assure a level of reliability. However, it may be worth selling the operation outright (and outsourcing) if internal quality and cost are not competitive. Other strategic decisions include

- For legal liability purposes, is it better to have the business in a separate entity, or divested (sold) completely?
- Would a sale give a strategic advantage to a competitor?
- Should current management be retained, or should they be subject to dismissal in the event of a sale?

In terms of value-adding, if one line of business is quite unprofitable, it may be better to sell it than divide it. Another question is whether the firm needs multiple lines of business? Also, two tax items affect the tax provision and financial earnings. First, a sale results in a possible double tax—once at the corporate level (from the sale itself), and again when the proceeds are distributed to shareholders as a (normally taxable) dividend. In a divisive reorganization, shares of the business are put tax-free into shareholders' hands. The shareholders can then decide when to generate income (if at all) by timing the sale of stock. If the shareholders are individuals, they can decide whether to sell at favorable (e.g., 20%) capital gains tax rates, or not.

Transaction costs are typically lower for a divisive reorganization, unless the firm decides to incur legal and accounting fees to obtain a revenue ruling from the IRS. A sale, however, may entail other costs such as appraisals, negotiations, and the like.

The second tax effect deals with anticipation. If a business unit generates a tax loss, then it may be worth waiting until the NOL expires before getting rid of the unit. Alternatively, these tax benefits can be negotiated with a buyer in the event of a sale.

SELLING OFF PARTS OF THE BUSINESS

In recent years, a number of conglomerates worldwide have divided their operations. This has been done by selling off business units or hiving them off into subsidiaries. Much of the incentive to do this has been to separate profitable business units from unprofitable one. Combined, the entities may show low performance. This may hurt share prices, which in turn may hurt the firm's access to capital markets (and talented employees who are motivated by stock options). Separated, however, capital markets can more readily discern which parts of the firm are better performers. Furthermore, some business units may be in industries that are in greater favor with investors (that is, these units have higher earnings multipliers than that of the conglomerate). Isolating these business units in separate legal entities thus may enhance the overall market value of the conglomerate. Alternatively, if part of the business does not fit in with the firm's strategic plan or is very unprofitable, or if the firm needs to sell assets to generate cash, the firm may simply divest itself of certain business units entirely.

SELLING A BUSINESS TO AN OUTSIDE ENTITY

If a business is incorporated, it can be disposed of in two ways: by selling its shares or by selling its assets. If a business is not separately incorporated, then it can only be disposed of by selling its assets. They can be tangible—such as inventories; receivables; or plant, property, and equipment (PP&E)—or intangible, such as franchise rights, goodwill, patents, and covenants not to compete. There are advantages and disadvantages to buying and selling assets rather than shares. Purchasers often strongly prefer buying assets because this will ensure that they will acquire no unexpected or contingent liabilities. For example, if there is a lawsuit pending against a corporation, the purchasing firm will inherit this liability if it purchases the corporation's shares. There is no inherited liability when only assets are purchased, except in very limited circumstances.

Upon sale, the firm recognizes gain or loss on an asset-by-asset basis. Whether the character is capital or ordinary depends on the type and use of the asset sold. (See Examples 13.10 and 13.11.)

EXAMPLE 13.10

For example, suppose the firm has two separate businesses, a chain of resort hotels and a cruise line. It decides to sell the hotel chain for $100 million. Suppose the tax basis (in $ millions) to the seller, and related FMVs, of the major asset categories are as follows:

Major Asset Group	Tax Basis	FMV	Gain or Loss on Sale
Land	$20	$50	$30
Buildings	40	20	<20>
Furniture & fixtures	5	5	0
	$65	$75	$10

Because $100 million was paid for $75,000,000 of tangible assets, the additional $25 million is allocated to the purchase of an intangible (such as goodwill, or the company logo). Because the seller has no tax basis in this asset, the entire $25 million is taxable income. This would be characterized as a favorably taxed capital gain, unless the firm's primary business was creating or trading this kind of intangible. The land sale would be treated similarly. In the United States it would generate a capital gain under IRC Section 1231, which also would characterize the loss on the building as favored ordinary loss.

EXAMPLE 13.11

Suppose instead that the hotel business is operated through a separately incorporated subsidiary, as follows:

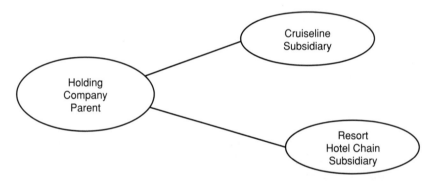

Let the holding company sell the stock of the hotel chain for the same price, $100 million, and its basis in the subsidiary's shares be the same as its basis in the underlying assets in Example 13.10, $65 million. The sale would generate the same $35 million amount of gain, and its character would be a favorably taxed capital gain. This is because the gain was generated by the sale of shares and not by the sale of the underlying assets.

The extent to which selling in corporate or asset form is more advantageous, and other tax-mitigating techniques, will be discussed next in the SAVANT framework.

Strategy

If the firm has already made the decision to sell off one of its businesses, it has presumably already thought through the strategic implications. If the strategy is to reinvest the sales proceeds in operating assets (either in retained businesses or a new business), then there are some ways of structuring the sale to minimize taxes.

Additionally, the firm may try to arrange a like-kind exchange. In the United States, this can be done tax free under IRC Section 1031. What qualifies as like-kind property is quite liberal: any personalty for personalty, and any realty for any realty. At the extreme, the firm might be able to trade all of its assets with other firms, and defer taxes of $25,000,000 \times 35\% = \$8,800,000$.

If the business is separately incorporated, one tax-deferral method is to *trade* subsidiaries with another firm that also wants to get out of its business. (See Example 13.12.)

EXAMPLE 13.12

Suppose the firm wants to get into the restaurant business. If it can find a conglomerate willing to exchange a restaurant business for the hotels, the transaction could be structured tax free as follows:

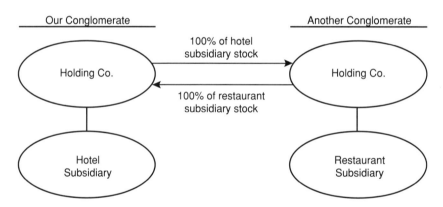

This qualifies as a tax-free B type reorganization, and is discussed more fully in Chapter 14.

Value-Adding

Presumably, EPS or other measures of value-added will improve by disposing of the business. However, if the business is disposed of in a taxable manner, the time value of value-added might be negative in the year of disposal and positive thereafter. In terms of adjusting for risk, if the firm *swaps* subsidiaries, there is a risk of unknown liabilities relating to the acquired corporation. In terms of transaction costs, the search, legal, and accounting fees will be higher for the stock-swap setting, second highest for the 1031 assets exchange, and lowest for the straight asset or stock sales. These costs should be weighed against the tax savings.

Negotiating

If the value of the to-be-sold business assets exceeds the value of the tangible assets, the excess will be allocated to some intangible. Regardless of the designation of the type of intangible, under U.S. tax law the buyer amortizes it over 15 years under IRC Section 197. (As explained in Chapter 1, under most countries' GAAP, goodwill is not amortized. In the United States, acquired goodwill is tested annually to see if it should be written down due to impairment of its value.)

Generally, the allocation of purchase price must be made in proportion to the relative values of the assets involved using arm's length standards. The negotiation aspect lies in determining fair market value. For many assets (especially unique assets), there is some flexibility. The buyer normally wants most of the purchase price allocated to assets with the fastest tax write-offs. In the hotel business example, the purchaser's hierarchy of preferences is as follows: (1) Furniture and fixtures (five- or seven-year tax write-offs); (2) intangibles (15 years); (3) buildings (31.5 years); and (4) land (not depreciable, so no tax write-off). The selling firm may be able to negotiate such tax benefits into a higher purchase price.

TECHNICAL INSERT 13.1 DIVISIVE REORGANIZATIONS

For a tax-free divisive reorganization, the following conditions must be met. These are detailed in IRC Section 355:

- The property distributed must consist solely of stock or securities of a corporation that was controlled by the distributing corporation immediately before the distribution. The parent corporation must own and distribute stock possessing at least 80% of the total combined voting power of all classes of stock entitled to vote and at least 80% of the total number of shares of all other classes of stock.
- The persons who directly or indirectly owned the controlled corporation(s) prior to the distribution must maintain a continuing equity interest in one or more of the corporations following the division. A substantial number of the shareholders who owned the stock of the distributing corporation prior to the division must

TECHNICAL INSERT 13.1 (CONTINUED)

maintain a continuing equity interest in the parent or subsidiary corporations following the division. The distribution of stock and securities does not have to be pro rata. Disproportionate distributions may be used to eliminate the stock ownership of a dissenting shareholder group. In a split-off transaction, some shareholders may exchange all of their parent corporation stock for all of the subsidiary's stock.

- The distributing corporation must distribute either (a) all of the stock and securities in the controlled corporation held by it immediately before the distribution or (b) an amount of stock in the controlled corporation constituting control. The distributing corporation is allowed to retain some stock if it can establish to the satisfaction of the IRS that it was not retained as part of tax-avoidance plan.
- The distribution must have a substantial corporate business purpose. Qualifying distributions include those made to comply with antitrust litigation and those made to separate businesses where the shareholders have major disagreements.
- The distribution must not have been used principally as a device to distribute the earnings and profits (E&P) of the distributing corporation, the controlled corporation, or both. (E&P are the earnings of a corporation that have not yet been subject to tax at the shareholder level. A good approximation of E&P is the corporation's retained earnings.) Whether a transaction has been used as a device to distribute the E&P is a matter of the facts and circumstances in each case. A sale or exchange of stock of the distributing or controlled corporation after the distribution is evidence that the distribution was used as such a device. This especially is the case if the sale was prearranged.
- Immediately after the distribution, the distributing corporation and the controlled corporation each must be engaged in the active conduct of a trade or business that also was actively conducted for at least five years prior to the distribution. The main reason for this requirement is to prevent a corporation from spinning off a newly formed subsidiary whose only assets are unneeded cash and other liquid assets. The shareholders could then sell or liquidate the subsidiary and obtain the liquid assets in an exchange transaction rather than as a dividend.

TECHNICAL INSERT 3.1 (CONTINUED)

Once these six requirements are met, other tax rules come into play. For example, the transferring corporation does not recognize gain or loss on the assets unless (1) the new corporation assumes or acquires liabilities from the transfer or corporation that, in total, exceed the adjusted bases of the assets transferred, or (2) boot property received by the transfer or corporation is retained. Boot property is anything other than stock or debt in the new corporation.

The controlled (newly formed) corporation recognizes no gain or loss on the transaction. Its basis in assets acquired is a carryover of the transferee's basis (plus any gain recognized by the transferor). Furthermore, in determining the new corporation's holding period for the assets, that of old corporation is added (tacked) on.

On the distribution of stock and/or securities to the shareholders, no gain or loss is recognized to the distributing corporation, and no gain is recognized to the shareholder unless boot is received.

CHAPTER 14

Mergers and Acquisitions

But often the CEO asks a strategic planning staff, consultants or investment bankers whether an acquisition or two might make sense. That's like asking your interior decorator whether you need a $50,000 rug. The acquisition problem is often compounded by a biological bias: Many CEOs attain their positions in part because they possess an abundance of animal spirits and ego. If an executive is heavily endowed with these qualities—which, it should be acknowledged, sometimes have their advantages— they won't disappear when he reaches the top. When such a CEO is encouraged by his advisor to make deals, he responds much as would a teenage boy who is encouraged by his father to have a normal sex life. It's not a push he needs.

—Warren Buffett,
Chairman Letter to Berkshire, Hathaway shareholders

A major component of corporate-level strategy is acquisition and diversification. For the last decade, the trend worldwide has been toward same-business acquisitions, as firms focus and capitalize on their core competencies. Tax Management in Action 14.1 shows some summary statistics on U.S. merger and acquisition (M&A) activity by industry.

Whether the acquisition is vertical or horizontal integration, the goal of M&A activity is maximizing shareholder value. Applying the principles of SAVANT can help in this objective. The following are the principle tax considerations for all parties to an M&A transaction. Understanding all parties' motivations can help the manager employ the SAVANT framework to increase firm value.

The following are some principal tax considerations:

■ *Buyer:* whether the buyer will obtain a cost or carryover basis in property acquired (either stock or assets), whether the buyer will inherit the target's tax attributes, and whether such attributes will be subject to limitations

TAX MANAGEMENT IN ACTION 14.1

M&A Activity, by Industry (U.S. during calendar year 1996)

Industry	No. of Acquisitions	Value ($Billions)
Commercial Banks	287	52.3
Telecommunications	86	20.6
Insurance	152	16.6
Food	84	4.5
Health Services	344	20.7
Chemicals	99	10.9
Aerospace & Aircraft	17	4.2
Nondurable goods Wholesaling	118	2.6
Investment and Commodity Firms	128	11.8
Oil & Gas	180	8.1

Source: Mergers & Acquisitions (March–April 1997)

- **Target.** whether the target will recognize gain or loss on the sale of its assets to acquirer, whether the target's tax attributes will be subject to limitations
- **Target shareholders.** whether the shareholders can defer any gain or recognize any loss realized on their target stock

The remainder of the chapter discusses these considerations in detail.

SOME GENERAL TAX RULES

Firms may acquire other firms in two basic ways: taxable and tax free. A more precise description of the latter is tax deferred although income taxes are not immediately triggered by the acquisition, the potential for tax is preserved by having the basis of the assets acquired remain the same. This carryover basis preserves the assets' built-in gain (or loss).

In the United States, tax-free M&As come in three fundamental forms: (1) statutory mergers and consolidations, (2) stock-for-stock swaps, and (3) exchanges of the acquiring company's voting stock for substantially all of the target company's assets. These are known as A, B, and C reorganizations. The letter is shorthand for the subparagraph of the Internal Revenue Code section where these tax-favored reorganizations are defined.

(For example, a statutory merger is defined in IRC section 368 (a)(1)(A).) Because they are somewhat restrictive in form, and because of the transaction costs involved, tax-free methods are less commonly used than taxable M&A transactions.

If the requirements for a tax-free reorganization are met, income taxes are deferred for all of the parties involved: Not only the acquired and the acquiring corporations, but also their shareholders. If these requirements are not met, taxes are a burden primarily on the shareholders of the acquired firm. However, taxable transactions have the advantage of removing the potential for future taxation caused by built-in gains. (These result from the pre-M&A appreciation of the assets involved.) The potential is removed because in a taxable M&A, there is a step-up in income tax basis of the acquired firm's assets. That is, the assets' bases are revalued to fair market value (FMV).

Because taxable acquisitions can take many forms, but tax-free reorganizations can only take a few forms, the latter are discussed next.

TAX-FREE MERGERS AND ACQUISITIONS

General Requirements

Although each of the tax-free reorganization provisions of U.S. tax law has its own requirements, all must meet the following tests (which are based on judicial doctrines).

Business Purpose   Under the business purpose doctrine, the transaction must be motivated by at least one valid business purpose. That is, a transaction will not qualify as tax free if it is undertaken for no other purpose than tax avoidance. However, a transaction motivated principally by tax avoidance—as long as it has at least one significant nontax motivation—will qualify. (See Example 14.1.)

EXAMPLE 14.1

Big Corp. wishes to acquire Little Co. for its significant NOL carryovers. Because Little is in the same line of business, potential synergies make the company worth acquiring, independent of the NOLs. This acquisition meets the business purpose test.

Continuity of Business Enterprise   This doctrine requires that, after the reorganization, the acquirer either uses a significant portion of the targets' assets in its business or continues a significant line of the target's business.

If there is more than one line of business acquired, only one of them has to be continued. (See Example 14.2.)

EXAMPLE 14.2

Assume the same facts as in Example 14.1, except that soon after the acquisition, Big sells off 80% of Little's assets. This fails the *continuity of business enterprise* test, and the transaction is taxable to Little and its shareholders.

Continuity of Shareholder Interest   This doctrines requires that a *material part* of the consideration received by the target's shareholders consist of stock of the acquirer. (See Example 14.3.)

EXAMPLE 14.3

Assume the facts as in Example 14.1 and that Big buys Little's stock directly from its shareholders for cash. The transaction will fail the *continuity of shareholder interest* test, and the sale will be taxable to Little's shareholders.

STATUTORY MERGERS AND CONSOLIDATIONS

These type A tax-free reorganizations must be made in accordance with state statutes that define mergers for basic corporate law purposes. Because state statutes are often difficult to exactly comply with, a type A reorganization is not often used. The compliance issues are (1) shareholders of both corporations must approve the plan, and (2) dissenting shareholders may request appraisals. A further cost is that all liabilities of the target corporation must be assumed, including unknown and contingent liabilities. A statutory consolidation combines two corporations into a new entity, and the old corporations disappear. A statutory merger results in one corporation disappearing as it is merged into another one.

These are depicted in Exhibit 14.1 and Example 14.4.

EXAMPLE 14.4

Big Corp. acquires all the Little Co. properties in exchange for 5,000 shares of Big stock. The Big stock is distributed to Little shareholders in complete

EXHIBIT 14.1   Mergers and Consolidations Pictured as a result of the statutory merger, Little Co. disappears, and its shareholders instead own stock in Big Corp.

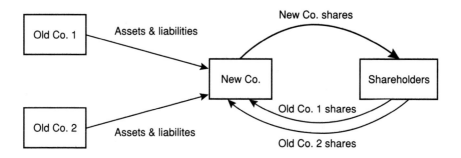

Statutory Consolidation

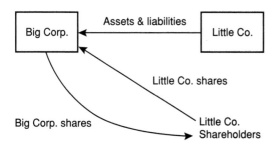

Statutory Merger

liquidation of Little. This transaction qualifies as an A reorganization, assuming that all the other requirements of state law are met. It is a statutory merger.

A variation is a *triangular merger*. This is commonly used if the acquiring corporation is unsure about the target corporation's liabilities. A triangular merger also is used when the acquirer is located in a different state than the target and needs an in state affiliate to meet local laws. The acquiring firm forms a new subsidiary to acquire the target; see Exhibit 14.2.

Another variation is a *reverse triangular merger*. Here, the subsidiary is merged into the target corporation, and the target corporation remains as a

EXHIBIT 14.2 Illustration of a Triangular Merger

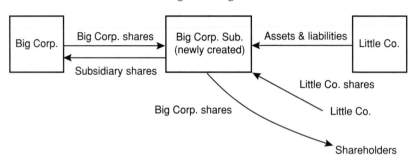

subsidiary of the acquiring company. Among the reasons for this is to preserve the trade name, contracts, or other value inherent in preserving the acquired corporation.

Stock-for-Stock Acquisitions

Type B reorganizations are the simplest type of tax-free reorganization because only shares of stock can be used. In particular, the acquiring corporation can give only its voting stock in exchange for the stock of the acquired corporation.

As shown in Exhibit 14.3, after the transaction, Little is a subsidiary of Big, and the previous shareholders of Little now own part of Big. One difficult aspect of the B reorganization is that no boot can be given. Only the acquirer's voting stock can be given to the targets' shareholders; no cash or other consideration can be thrown in to boot to make the deal work. Also, at least 80% of the voting stock must be surrendered. This means that at

EXHIBIT 14.3 Depiction of Stock for Stock Reorganization

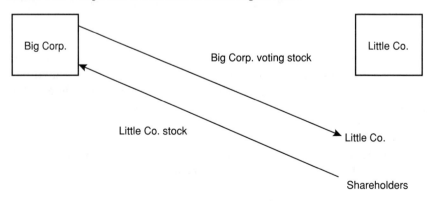

most 20% of the acquired corporation's original stock can remain in minority (dissenting) shareholders' hands. (See Example 14.5.)

EXAMPLE 14.5

Big Corp. gives 5% of its voting stock to Little Co.'s shareholders in exchange for 80% of all classes of Little's stock. The exchange qualifies as a B reorganization; Big becomes Little's parent.

To have a B reorganization, the sole consideration must be voting stock and the acquiring corporation must end up owning at least 80% of all classes of the target corporation's stock. The 80% control requirement must be attained immediately after the reorganization. This does not mean that all 80% must be *acquired* from the restructuring: Stock previously purchased in a separate transaction can be counted in determining the 80% ownership. Further, the stock may be acquired either from the shareholders directly or from the target corporation. (See Examples 14.6 and 14.7.)

EXAMPLE 14.6

Five years ago, Large Corp. purchased 30% of Small Co.'s stock for cash. In the current year, Large acquires another 50% of Small through the issuance of voting stock. Even though some of Small's shares were acquired with cash, the requirements for a B reorganization are met.

EXAMPLE 14.7

Grey Corp. is the parent of Large Corp. Large also owns some stock in Grey. Large exchanges voting stock in Grey for stock in Small. This qualifies as a B reorganization; Small is now Large's subsidiary.

A variation on this is the *triangular B reorganization*. Here, the acquirer forms a new subsidiary, putting its own voting stock into the subsidiary. Next, the subsidiary exchanges the parent stock for stock of the smaller company. That is, the target company's shareholders end up owning stock in the acquiring (parent) corporation.

Asset for Stock Acquisitions

In a C reorganization, the acquiring corporation obtains substantially all of the target corporation's assets in exchange solely for the acquirer's voting stock and a limited amount of other consideration; as is shown in Exhibit 14.4.

EXHIBIT 14.4 Illustration of C Reorganizations

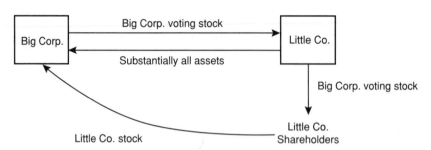

An advantage of a C reorganization is that the acquirer does not have to assume any of the acquired company's liabilities, known or unknown, fixed or contingent. Furthermore, the acquiring company's shareholders do not typically need to approve the transaction. The disadvantages include that many unwanted assets may have to be acquired to meet the *substantially all* test.

Note that to preserve tax-free status, the firm cannot dispose of them for a five-year period after the acquisition. In addition, liabilities which are assumed by the acquirer count as boot. Thus, if too much of the target's liabilities are assumed—for example, if they amount to more than 20% of the purchase price—this would prevent a tax-free acquisition. (See Example 14.8.)

EXAMPLE 14.8

Suppose Big Corp. buys all of Little Co.'s assets for $50 million. If the consideration is completely in Big Corp. stock, the transaction qualifies as a valid C reorganization. If part of the consideration is cash or bonds of Big Corp., the transaction becomes taxable to Little Co.'s shareholders.

Comparison of Tax Attributes

In a tax-free merger or acquisition, gain or loss realized are not recognized—that is, they are not taxed—by the acquiring corporation, its shareholders, or the acquired corporation (unless it does not distribute boot proceeds to its shareholders). However, the shareholders of the acquired corporation are also not taxed, except if they receive boot (which is anything other than voting stock of the acquiring firm, or that of another party to the reorganization). If they do receive boot, they are taxed on their gain realized but only to the extent of the FMV of the boot received.

This is not a problem in B reorganizations, because no boot is allowed. In A and C reorganizations, the amount taxed is the lesser of realized gain or the FMV of boot received. (However, the gain is not limited by the FMV of boot received if the boot given amounts to more than 20% of the purchase price.)

Other tax attributes include carryovers of asset basis and net operating losses (NOLs). In all three types of reorganizations—A, B, and C—the tax bases of the acquired corporations' assets carries over. This means, for example, that depreciation continues as if no ownership change had occurred. Because the original corporation disappears under an A or C reorganization, the NOL carries over the acquirer corporation. This is a definite advantage. However, for a B reorganization the acquired firm is a separate subsidiary, which keeps its preexisting NOLs. As with taxable acquisitions, there are limits to the amount of NOL which can be used by acquiring firms with each of the tax-free reorganizations. These limitations are discussed in a subsequent section.

The following sections discuss the relative advantages and disadvantages of each type of reorganization.

A Reorganizations

- Merger or Consolidation
  - *Advantages.* No requirements that voting stock be used; as much as 50% of consideration can be cash without tax consequences for receipt of stock. (Cash and other property received are taxed, however.)
  - *Disadvantages.* State law must be followed—dissenter's rights and required shareholder meetings may represent problems; all liabilities of target corporation are assumed by acquiring corporation as a matter of law.
- Subsidiary (Triangular) A
  - *Advantages.* Because parent is majority shareholder, problem of securing approval of majority shareholders is removed; subsidiary, rather than parent, assumes the liabilities of the target corporation.
  - *Disadvantages.* For reverse triangular merger, must have 80% control of target corporation, and only voting stock of the parent may be used.

B Reorganizations

- *Advantages.* Stock may be acquired from shareholders; procedures to effect reorganization are not complex.

- *Disadvantages.* Only voting stock of acquiring corporation may be used; must have 80% control of target corporation and may have minority interest in target corporation.

C Reorganizations

- *Advantages.* Less complex as to state law than A reorganization; cash or property can be used as consideration for 20% or less of fair market value of property transferred.
- *Disadvantages.* Substantially all of assets of target corporation must be transferred; liabilities count as other property for 20% rule if any consideration other than stock and liabilities is used; and target corporation must distribute the stock, securities, and other properties it receives in the reorganization to its shareholders.

TAXABLE MERGERS AND ACQUISITIONS

Any M&A transaction that does not meet one of the tax-free reorganization provisions is a taxable transaction. Although the acquiring corporation or its shareholders normally do not recognize gain or loss, the acquired firm's shareholders recognize gain or loss on the difference between the FMV of what they receive on the transaction minus the adjusted basis of any stock given up. As to corporate tax attributes, NOLs stay with the acquired corporation if it is acquired as a subsidiary. If the assets are acquired, and the shell corporation is liquidated, any NOL expires.

An advantage of a taxable acquisition is that the acquired firm's assets are stepped up to their FMVs. This allows for greater depreciation deductions (except where an asset's FMV is less than its preexisting tax basis).

An important choice in a taxable acquisition is whether to purchase the target's assets or its stock. In employing the SAVANT framework, the manager needs to know the tax motives of all parties involved, for each type of transaction. Such tax implications—stated in terms of advantages and disadvantages—are discussed next.

Stock Purchases

The seller's motivations for a stock purchase are favorable when

- The shareholders have a higher basis in their target stock compared to the target's aggregate basis in its assets (resulting in a lower taxable gain on stock sale).

- Capital loss carryovers are available to shareholders to offset gain.
- The seller has tax-exempt status.
- The seller wants to rid itself of target's future obligations, such as contingent liabilities or contractual commitments.

The buyer's motivations are favorable for a stock purchase in order:

- To preserve target's favorable tax attributes
- To avoid a step-down in target's assets if such assets have depreciated in value
- To take advantage of transaction costs when they are lower than in an asset purchase
- To acquire target's contract rights if they otherwise would be difficult to transfer

The buyer's motivations for a stock purchase are unfavorable if

- Target's asset basis cannot be stepped up to fair market value.
- Hidden liabilities and claims against target remain intact.
- Little flexibility exists regarding unwanted assets and liabilities.
- Target's tax accounting methods cannot be changed without IRS approval.

Asset Purchases

The seller's motivations for an asset purchase are favorable if

- The tax on the sale of target's assets is less than the tax on the sale of target's stock (e.g., when target has loss carryforwards to offset the gain).
- Target will have a net loss on the asset sale that can be carried back to prior years to obtain refunds.
- A majority shareholder will not be taxed on the liquidation of target because the corporate shareholder owns 80% or more of target stock.
- The shareholders want to preserve the legal status of target and target's favorable tax attributes.

The seller's motivations for an asset purchase are unfavorable if

- Gains will be taxed twice, first to the seller and later to its shareholders when sales proceeds are distributed as dividends or upon liquidation.

- Target is subject to an unacceptably high tax burden, including state and local income, sales, or property taxes.

The buyer's motivations for an asset purchase are favorable if

- The buyer desires to select (cherry-pick) the specific assets to be purchased or liabilities to be assumed.
- The buyer desires minimal exposure to target's hidden liabilities and claims.
- Buyer desires to adopt a new accounting method for the purchased assets without obtaining IRS approval.

The buyer's motivation for an asset purchase is unfavorable if

- The buyer must step down the basis of acquired assets that have depreciated in value.
- The target cannot readily transfer contractual rights, obligations, agreements, franchises, and licenses to the buyer.
- The buyer incurs significant transaction costs.

The U.S. tax consequences to the target in an asset sale are as follows. The target will recognize gain or loss on each asset based upon the consideration allocated to such assets minus the target's tax basis in the asset sold. (Note that gain may be taxed again to the target's shareholders when cash or property is distributed to them as dividends or in liquidation.)

The character of the gain or loss on sale (e.g., ordinary or capital) will depend on the nature of the asset being sold. The target must include gain in the year of sale unless the installment method is used. The target may be able to offset gain with loss carryforwards from previous years. Target's gain on the sale may also be subject to state and local taxes. Finally, unless the target liquidates, it continues as a legal entity and preserves its tax attributes. (See Examples 14.9 and 14.10.)

EXAMPLE 14.9

Suppose Shell Company purchased Modal Oil Corporation for $2.5 billion. Assuming that the purchase was for cash, and that the total stock basis of Modal's shareholders was $1 billion, the tax effects are as follows. The shareholders of Modal have a capital gain of $1.5 billion. There is no gain or loss to Modal, and its tax attributes (such as any unused tax credits or NOLs) carry over into the future. The basis of Modal's assets is not stepped up to their fair market values, unless an IRC Section 338(h)(10) election is made (see Chapter 15).

EXAMPLE 14.10

Assume the same fact as Example 14.9, except that Shell purchases Modal's assets. Assuming the assets have a tax basis of $2 billion, the tax effects are as follows. Modal has total gains of $.5 billion, which are allocated to its assets based on their relative fair market values. The basis of Modal's assets, in Shell's hands, are stepped up to their fair market values.

Financial accounting considerations in a taxable acquisition are important as well, as shown in Example 14.11.

EXAMPLE 14.11

Assume the same facts as in Examples 14.9 and 14.10. The excess purchase price of $.5 billion over the value of the assets must be booked as goodwill by Shell. The goodwill sits as an asset and is not amortized as an expense, which reduces financial statement net income, although, it is amortized for tax purposes straight-line over 15 years. Accounting income is only reduced to the extent that the goodwill is found to have been impaired by future events.

TAX PLANNING AND ACQUISITION COSTS

All M&A activity involves significant transactions costs. M&A activity also involves a variety of different acquisition costs. For example, legal and accounting fees can be substantial. This is especially true for tax-free reorganizations, where deals must be structured very specifically to meet IRS requirements. To that end, firms often apply to the IRS for a letter ruling in order to obtain an agreement on the tax-free status of a proposed transaction. The legal and accounting fees here are typically hundreds of thousands of dollars. Such costs are deductible.

However, there may be significant legal and accounting fees related to financing the acquisition. There also may be significant underwriter, broker, or loan fees, depending on the form of financing. Such costs must be capitalized into the debt or equity. If debt, the costs can be amortized over the life of the debt. If equity, the costs are nonamortizable.

ALLOCATING PURCHASE PRICE

To induce shareholders of the target corporations to sell their stock, the acquiring corporation usually must offer in excess of the stock's FMV. This usually exceeds both the book and tax carrying values of the underlying assets. If the acquisition is a tax-free reorganization, the excess cannot be used to step up the tax basis of the assets. Instead, it must be capitalized into an appropriate intangible (typically goodwill), which is amortizable over 15 years. If the acquisition is taxable, the purchase price is allocated to the target's assets based on their relative FMVs. The excess is capitalized as an intangible (that is, goodwill).

FINANCIAL ACCOUNTING TRADE-OFFS

Beyond the economic value-added by an acquisition, there are financial reporting implications which impact investors' perceptions of value. This issue is, fundamentally, how will conglomerate earnings per share (EPS) be affected by the merger? EPS is affected by the change in earnings and the change in number of shares. The M&A-related change in earnings results from both the earnings of the acquired firm, any conglomerate-related synergies (such as eliminating redundant costs), and transaction-related costs (such as financing and professional fees).

Like amortization of goodwill, another previous financial accounting concern was the method of accounting for the transaction. There used to be two basic choices: a purchase or a pooling of interests. The latter was uncommon and not allowed by many countries' GAAP. As of July 1, 2001, pooling was eliminated in the United States for almost all types of organizations. Previously, pooling in the United States typically involved a B tax-free reorganization (i.e., a stock for stock swap) and avoided book expense for amortization of goodwill.

Insight into tax-financial accounting trade-offs is further provided in the executive interview in Exhibit 14.5.

EXHIBIT 14.5   Interview with former chair of the U.S. accounting standards body, the FASB

EXECUTIVE INTERVIEW

Dennis Beresford
Retired Chairman
Financial Accounting Standards Board (FASB)

What tensions did you observe in financial reporting goals versus tax reporting?
Most companies are described as having two sets of books in that financial statements to shareholders and other external users of those statements often are quite

different from what is reported in tax returns. This is due principally to the fact that reports to shareholders and tax returns serve quite different purposes. Reports to shareholders are supposed to neutrally report operating results and financial position for the purpose of helping users of those statements make predictions about future cash flows of the company, while tax law is designed to accomplish governmental economic and social goals. Yet there often are more similarities than differences between financial reporting and tax, and there is an interaction between the two. Simply put, financial reporting conventions can affect what is reported for tax purposes and tax consequences often influence reporting as well.

What specific accounting issues come to mind?
The LIFO inventory method is an excellent example of taxes affecting financial reports. By law, companies desiring to take advantage of the favorable tax effects of LIFO must use that method in shareholder reports as well. (Of course, many companies believe that LIFO best reports periodic income anyway, but others clearly would use another method in their financial reports were it not for the tax benefit.) Business combinations and leases are other areas where the book treatment may significantly influence the tax treatment and vice versa.

Did such issues influence firm's discussions with the FASB?
In my time at the Financial Accounting Standards Board, it was unusual for the Board to discuss its new accounting proposals with the IRS or congressional tax writers. And it was unusual for the Service or Congress to seek the FASB's input on their initiatives. Yet constituents often challenged FASB proposals on the grounds that the resulting accounting could cause less favorable tax positions for companies. The FASB certainly does not set out to cause tax problems, but it has to keep its principal focus on trying to achieve the most informative reporting to shareholders and other current and potential investors or creditors.

Did it seem that, in at least some cases, firms structured their transactions with financial reporting and tax considerations in mind?
In the business world, of course, when potential transactions are considered, companies endeavor to structure the transactions in order to obtain both the most favorable financial reporting position and the most favorable tax treatment. When ideal treatments aren't initially possible, transaction structures often are modified to get closer to the ideal. Both financial reporting and tax considerations are important. In the final analysis, however, the economics and business purposes of transactions must be kept paramount and the book, or tax accounting treatments must result from the transactions and not be their objectives.

MAXIMIZING TAX BENEFITS

Net Operating Losses

As mentioned before, of the four types of acquisitions—taxable stock purchase, tax-free stock purchase, tax-free asset purchase, and taxable asset purchase—only the last results in the permanent loss of the target firm's

NOL carryovers. To discourage firms acquiring other firms solely for their tax attributes, a number of U.S. tax provisions limit the use of such tax attributes after an ownership change. The limits apply whether the acquisition occurs in taxable or in a tax-free exchange.

NOL Limits: Year of Acquisition   The first are the separate return limitation year (SRLY) limitation rules. These restrict the benefit of a target's losses in a consolidated tax return. Usually, losses incurred by one member of a consolidated group can be used to offset income of other members of the group. This is not the case if a new member has losses which arose before joining the group. These losses are restricted by the SRLY rules to offsetting income generated by that corporation. Accordingly, losses of the target can only be partly used by the acquiring corporation. This includes losses in the year of acquisition. (See Example 14.12.)

EXAMPLE 14.12

Little Co. has an NOL of $3 million. It advertises its NOL as an asset it would sell to another corporation having substantial taxable income. Big Corp. has taxable income of $5 million in 2000. It expects the same amount of income in 2001. Big's tax liability for 2000 is $1.7 million (i.e., $5 million × 34%). Big will probably incur approximately the same liability in 2001 unless it can use target's NOL. If Little is merged into Big and Little's NOL carries over to offset Big's taxable income for 2001, Big's taxable income would only be $2 million (that is, $5 million minus the $3 million NOL carryover). Big would save $1,020,00 in taxes (i.e., $3 million reduction in income times the 34% tax rate). Little's NOL would be an asset worth approximately $1,020,000 to Big.

Assume that Little merges with Big on December 16, 2000. Under the SRLY limitation rules, only $205,500 [i.e., $5,000,000 × (15 days/366 days)] of the $3 million NOL can be used to offset Big's taxable income in 2000. The remainder of the NOL can be carried forward to offset Big's income in future years.

NOL Limits: Subsequent Years   The second limitation comes from the rules under IRC Sections 382 and 383. Under these rules, the acquired company's use of its tax attributes is subject to an annual limitation if it undergoes an ownership change. An ownership change can occur by the purchase or sale of stock, a redemption, a reorganization, or the issuance of stock. Usually, an ownership change will occur if the value of stock ownership held by 5% shareholders increases by more than three percentage points within any three year testing period. Thus, a buyer's use of the seller's tax attributes is limited. The limitation is calculated by multiplying the value of the stock of the corporation immediately before the ownership change by the long-term tax-exempt bond rate. The IRS reports this rate monthly. (See Example 14.13.)

EXAMPLE 14.13

Chuck Corp. merges with Lynn Co. on January 1, 2002. Chuck's shareholders experience a more-than-50% ownership change. At this point, Chuck has an NOL carryover of $500,000. The value of Chuck's stock is $1 million, and the long-term tax exempt rate is 10%. The amount of the NOL carryover that can be used in 2003 is $100,000 (that is, $1,000,000 × 10%). If in 2003 Lynn has taxable income of $700,000 (before any NOL carryover), $70,000 of the loss can be used. The $30,000 remaining portion ($100,000 − $70,000) is carried over and increases the NOL limit for 2002 to $130,000 ($30,000 + $100,000).

Depreciation

For most corporations, the most significant tax shield is depreciation. If there is a taxable acquisition, the target company's assets are revalued to their FMVs. This normally means a step-up in basis, with a resulting increase in the depreciation tax shield. However, this simultaneously triggers a taxable gain to the acquired corporation equal to the entire step-up, making the present value of the tax savings negative. The issue is whether this extra tax cost can be negotiated into a lower purchase price, or the benefits of having an NOL carryforward are offsetting (or the nontax considerations more than outweigh these tax costs).

State and Local Taxes

Most state income tax laws are similar to the U.S. federal tax laws. Thus, transactions taxable (tax free) for U.S. purposes are also taxable (tax free) for state income tax purposes. If there is an asset purchase, state and local transactions taxes will apply, too. Many states impose a realty transfer tax on any realty owned by the target. Additionally, many states impose sales and use taxes on nonrealty assets owned by the target (not including inventory). To avoid such taxes, the stock of the target should instead be purchased. If shareholders of the target corporation prefer an asset purchase, the acquirer might be able to negotiate (that is, pay a part of the tax benefits).

EXHIBIT 14.6   Example of an LBO

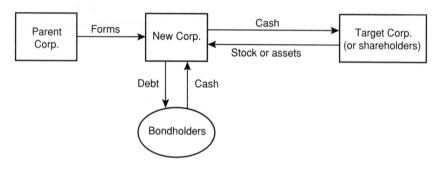

LEVERAGED BUYOUTS

In a leveraged buyout (LBO), the acquiring firm borrows to acquire cash to effect either a taxable or tax-free acquisition. If the interest rate is not too high, the economics of an LBO may surpass other forms of financing due to the advantage of leverage and the tax deductibility of the related interest expense. Often, the LBO follows the sequence shown in Exhibit 14.6.

A distinguishing feature of this scheme is the forming of a new entity which issues debt. Thus, if the acquired company turns out to be a bad investment, and New Corp. cannot pay bondholders, liability does not extend to the parent corp.

Some possible tax pitfalls are as follows. If the debt is discounted (or as an extreme, a balloon note is used), paper (noncash) interest expense can be created by tax authorities such as the IRS, which translates into taxable interest income to bondholders. Second, the debt/equity ratio of New Corp. might be so large that the tax authorities reclassify the debt as equity, converting deductible interest expense into nondeductible dividends.

To mitigate against this, the debt should be straight debt with no convertibility, fixed periodic interest payments, and enforceable (and certain) due dates. A third limitation is the overall acquisition indebtedness interest deduction limitation. (See Example 14.14.)

EXAMPLE 14.14

Big Corp. forms Newco, a wholly owned subsidiary. Newco issues $100,000,000 of 15% bonds. The rate is high because the bonds are not secured by any assets. Next, Newco purchases Little Co. stock for $100 million in cash, so Little Co. becomes a subsidiary of Newco. If Little Co. can earn an after-tax return in excess of $(1 - .35)(.15) = .0975$ which is the after-tax cost of Newco debt, and the IRS does not disallow some or all of Newco's interest deductions, the acquisition makes sense.

SOURCES OF MERGER AND ACQUISITION FINANCE

There are a number of financing sources for M&A activity. Typical pretax costs of capital for these sources are shown in Tax Management in Action 14.2.

Other Types of Merger and Acquisition Finance

In addition to the traditional sources of finance already noted, such as senior and subordinated debt along with common and preferred stock, some less conventional methods include

- Debt securities with investor put option
- Alphabet stock, where investors hold a company's stock but shares participate only in earnings of specified subsidiary (or assets)

TAX MANAGEMENT IN ACTION 14.2

M&A Financing Sources

Lender/Investor	Type	Cost
Management buyout	Common stock	Dividends + appreciation*
ESOPs	Convertible preferred or common stock	Dividends + appreciation*
Sellers	Subordinated debt or preferred stock	Negotiable
LBO funds	Common stock	High (>10% annually)
Venture capital funds	Common or preferred Subordinated convertible debt or bonds	Very high (>20%)
Pension funds	Subordinated debt Common or preferred	Treasury rate*(bonds) low (>6% annually)
Insurance companies	Any debt or stock	See pension funds
Investment banks	Common or preferred	Dividend + appreciation*
Commercial banks	Senior debt	Prime plus 1–4%*

*Adjusted for risk

- ARPS (adjustable rate preferred mortgages) where interest rates are reset periodically
- Sale/leaseback financing
- Junk bonds (high-yield, high-risk subordinated securities)
- Debt securities with detachable warrants
- Paid-in kind (PIK) securities, where interest or principal is payable in cash or securities

Other Issues Arising with Merger and Acquisition Transactions

In an LBO, as well as other M&A transactions, methods of compensating the target's management may have different tax and accounting ramifications. If managers are compensated through stock or stock options, the firm deducts these costs when paid.

Some other aspects of M&A are shown in Tax Management in Action 14.3.

TAX MANAGEMENT IN ACTION 14.3

TAKEOVER TERMS AND THEIR TAX IMPLICATIONS

Greenmail. A targeted stock repurchase where payments are made to potential bidders to eliminate unfriendly takeover attempts. No tax deduction to the repurchasing firm; capital gain to the selling firm, or potential acquirer (IRC Section 162(k)).

Poison Pill. A financial device designed to make unfriendly takeover attempts unappealing, if not impossible. The most prevalent form of this is a stock right plan (SRP), which gives existing shareholders the right, in the event of a merger, to buy stock at half price; with more shares to buy, this increases the price of an acquisition. The options are not deductible to the firm or taxable to the shareholder. If exercised, the purchased stock simply has a lower basis to the shareholder.

Golden Parachutes. Some target firms provide compensation to top-level management if a takeover occurs. For example, when the Scoville board endorsed a $523 million tender offer by First City Properties, it arranged for 13 top executives to get termination payments of about $5 million. For the firm, deduction is allowed only to the extent that the payment does not exceed three times the average pay (over the

TAX MANAGEMENT IN ACTION 14.3 (CONTINUED)

last five years) of the officers, shareholders, or highly compensated individuals receiving the pay (IRC Section 280G).

Poison Puts. A poison put is a variation on the poison pill. A poison put forces the firm to buy securities back at some set price. There is no deduction for the firm.

Crown Jewels. Firms often sell or threaten to sell major assets—crown jewels—when faced with a takeover threat. This is sometimes referred to as the *scorched earth* strategy. This tactic often involves a lockup, which we discuss later. Sales of such assets result in ordinary or capital gains or losses to the corporation, depending on the asset type.

White Knights. A firm facing an unfriendly merger offer might arrange to be acquired by a different, friendly firm. The firm is thereby rescued by a so-called white knight. Alternatively, the firm may arrange for a friendly entity to acquire a large block of stock. White squires or big brothers are individuals, firms, or even mutual funds involved in friendly transactions of these types. Sometimes white knights or others are granted exceptional terms or otherwise compensated. This has also been called *whitemail.* The stock purchase results in capital gain or loss to the selling shareholder. If white knights become officers of the corporation, compensation payments are taxed as ordinary income and are deductible by the corporation.

Lockups. A lockup is an option granted to a friendly suitor (a white knight, perhaps) giving it the right to purchase stock or some of the assets (the crown jewels, possibly) of a target firm at a fixed price in the event of an unfriendly takeover.

Shark Repellent. A shark repellent is any tactic (a poison pill, for example) designed to discourage unwanted merger offers.

DEFENSIVE STRATEGIES

In many cases a firm, in particular, its management, may wish to employ strategies to avoid a hostile takeover. A number of these strategies were mentioned in the Tax Management Action 14.3. Another strategy is for the firm (or its employees) to purchase enough stock on the open market such that the potential acquirer cannot acquire a controlling (such as a 50% or more) interest. Alternatively, the firm itself can buy back, or redeem, shares. If the acquisition is financed by debt, the LBO rules already discussed apply.

EXHIBIT 14.7   Corporate Buyout via an ESOP

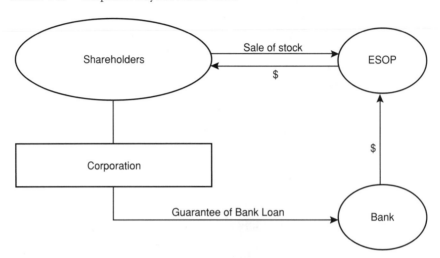

The firm's employees also can buy back their firm's stock through their pension funds, or through an employee stock option plan (ESOP). An ESOP purchase may work something like that in Exhibit 14.7. The following tax advantages apply. First, the corporation can tax deduct any payments made to pay principal on the loan (limited to 25% of aggregate compensation paid or accrued to ESOPs participants during the year), or to pay interest on the loan. Also, lenders to the ESOP (banks, insurance companies, and corporations actively engaged in lending) can exclude from taxation 50% of interest income from the ESOP if the loan was used to buy the firm's own securities. (This is discussed further in the next chapter.)

Beyond ESOPs, another defensive strategy is for the firm to borrow significant amounts, such that the debt service (combined with the acquirer's additional costs of capital for the acquisition) is too high for an acquirer. (See Example 14.15.)

EXAMPLE 14.15

Target's stock has been underperforming and management is fearful of a hostile takeover by Big Corp. Target's current capital structure consists of $10 million in 8% debt and $50 million par value of common stock. It issues another $50 million of 15% debt, which is used to buy back half of the outstanding common stock. The resultant capital structure makes Target a less appealing acquisition for Big.

MERGER AND ACQUISITION ACTIVITY
AND SCRUTINY BY TAX AUTHORITIES

Because of the substantial amounts of wealth at stake, many creative financing arrangements are invented by investment bankers, CPAs, and lawyers. In the United States, such arrangements are frequently challenged by the IRS under the *substance over form* doctrine. (Outside the United States, this doctrine is rarely applied, although it has been established by judicial decisions in the United Kingdom, Canada, and Australia. As noted previously, one good reason to study U.S. tax law is that the various restrictions that have been enacted to limit taxpayers provide a roadmap for tax planning in other countries.)

PUTTING IT ALL TOGETHER: MERGER AND ACQUISITION
FROM A SAVANT PERSPECTIVE

Big Corp. wants to acquire the assets of Little Co. These assets have a tax basis (and net book value) to Little of $300 million (assume 10-year MACRS depreciation) and a fair market value of $200 million. The Little Co. shareholders have a tax basis in their stock of $100 million. Little has incurred losses in its operations during the last several years and has NOL carryovers of $250 million. Big plans to continue the business conducted by Little, hopefully on a profitable basis. Big considers the following alternatives:

- *Using cash and/or other property, Big purchases the asset directly from Little. Afterward, Little liquidates and distributes the cash/property to its shareholders.*
- *Big purchases for cash and/or other property all of the stock in Little from its shareholders. Immediately after, Big liquidates Little.*
- *Using an A reorganization, Little merges into Big. In exchange for their stock, shareholders of Little receive stock in Big.*
- *Under a C reorganization, Little transfers all of its assets to Big in return for Big's voting stock. Little then distributes the Big stock to its shareholders.*

Tax management should focus on the preservation of Little's favorable tax attributes, the NOL carryovers, and the high tax basis in assets. The first alternative is poor. This is because the purchase price becomes the basis in the assets for Big Corp. Because Little's basis in the assets is $300 million and their value is only $200 million, the first alternative would result in lower depreciation deductions. Additionally, any unused NOLs disappear upon the liquidation of Little. Little has a realized loss of $100 million ($300 million basis in assets minus $200 million sales price) from the sale of the assets. Because of Little's history, it seems unlikely it will generate much income in the year of sale and thus this loss may generate no tax benefit to Little.

The second alternative has some drawbacks as well. As discussed in Chapter 15, when a subsidiary is liquidated, absent a special election the subsidiary's bases in its assets carry over to the acquiring corporation. Accordingly, what Big paid for the Little stock is irrelevant. Little's NOLs carry over to Big, however, IRC Section 269 (or the business and tax avoidance concepts discussed previously) could present problems. IRC Section 269 provides that if a subsidiary is liquidated within two years of acquisition, and the principal purpose is tax avoidance, any tax benefits may be disallowed.

The third and fourth alternatives should accomplish the results intended from the second alternative, but with less tax risk. Assuming Big can establish a business purpose to the acquisition, it should be able to acquire Little's favorable tax attributes using an A or C reorganization.

Next, consider the setting in the SAVANT framework.

Strategy

Can similar assets be purchased piecemeal on the open market instead of having to purchase the entire company? Also, are Big's shareholders willing to dilute ownership by giving its stock to Little shareholders?

Anticipation

The likelihood of IRS audit, and the subsequent disallowance of the NOL carryovers, is highest for the taxable acquisition. Accordingly, Big would offer a lower purchase price under this alternative, in order to adjust for this risk.

Value-Adding

What will be the impact of each alternative on Big's financial statements? If Big pays more than the fair market value of the tangible and identifiable intangible assets, the excess is goodwill. This amount is not amortized routinely, but to the extent it becomes impaired in the future, this would reduce earnings per share (EPS). Also, will Little continue to generate financial statement losses each year, which will reduce EPS?

Transaction Costs   These are probably high under the asset purchase alternative, since title to each asset must be transferred. They also are probably high for the A reorganization, because state law requirements must be met.

Timing   If the acquisition is made at the beginning of the year, Big can use more of the current year's NOL.

Negotiating, Transforming

Because the NOLs are worth something, how much extra must be paid? Assuming the U.S. interest rate is 10%, then the value of the NOLs is $250 million(.10)(.4), where the last term is the (rounded) 10-year annuity multiple, assuming the firm has a 10% discount rate as well. So, the maximum the firm would pay for the NOLs is $10 million. However, the Little shareholders may not demand that much for the NOLs. At a minimum, they would demand at least the FMV of their stock, which is $250 million. If Little is expected to run additional losses, and has low dividend history, Big may not have to pay much more than that.

Under a taxable acquisition, Little shareholders have an immediate tax cost, which they would not have under a tax-free reorganization. The difference is: (($200 million + NOL premium) − $100 million stock basis) × 20%. So, the tax difference may approximate the price difference between a taxable and a tax-free acquisition. In sum, Big will use transforming by acquiring tax deductions at its 34% tax rate, which only costs the sellers at their 20% tax rates.

CHAPTER 15

Other Topics in Changing Original Form

That didn't take long. On January 1, Germany abolished capital gains tax on the sale of shares held by one company in another. Six days later E.ON, a big utility, said it was selling a subsidiary.... The timing of the sale has saved E.ON perhaps ε (Euro) 500M in tax.

The Economist, January 12, 2002

This chapter covers other entity conversion topics. These are (1) the use of flow-through entities for divestitures, (2) the use of flow-through entities for acquisitions, (3) liquidations of a subsidiary, (4) the sale of a subsidiary, and (5) bankruptcies. Although knowledge of these topics can be of great use to managers, particularly in times of change, they have been reserved for last because they can be stunningly complex. Indeed, as the great twentieth-century American jurist, Learned Hand put it, they form a "fantastic labyrinth" whose words "merely dance before my eyes in a meaningless procession: cross-reference to cross-reference, exception upon exception...."

USE OF FLOW-THROUGH ENTITIES FOR DIVESTITURES

There were 2,503 major U.S. corporate divestitures in 1996 alone. With a value of $181.78 billion, these accounted for 33% of all M&A activity. Flow-through entities (such as partnerships and limited liability companies) are increasingly being used in divestitures and business split-ups. (Although other flow-through entities such as subchapter S corporations and trusts have advantages, they generally are less flexible than partnerships and LLCs.)

In some cases, a divestiture may result because a firm wants to distance itself from a part of its business. One reason to do so may be to get this part off the business's consolidated financial statements. Another reason might be to realize the part's current value by selling it to its current management team.

EXHIBIT 15.1   Shifting R&D off Financial Statements

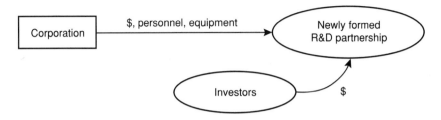

One advantage of using a flow-through entity in circumstances like these is that if a firm spins off one of its part into a flow-through (or starts a new business segment in one), under U.S. GAAP the flow-through entity is not reflected throughout the firm's consolidated financials. Instead, it is shown in the assets section on a single line as an investment. This keeps details away from shareholders, competitors, and other users of the firm's publicly available financial statements. The furor over excessive use of such special purpose entities (SPEs), sparked by the collapse of Enron, suggests caution in the use of SPEs.

In the 1980s, it was common to do this with research and development (R&D) efforts. Isolating R&D ventures was typically accomplished by forming R&D limited partnerships like those in Exhibit 15.1.

There were several advantages to using this technique. First, outsiders, particularly competitors, would not know the extent of the firm's R&D spending. Second, risk was diversified by spreading it to outside investors. Finally, because flow-through entities allow more flexibility than corporations in allocating cash flow, income, or expenses among owners, R&D credits and deductions could be effectively transferred to the outside investors partners as a kind of risk premium. (See Example 15.1.)

EXAMPLE 15.1

An electronics manufacturer decides to develop a new cellular telephone. The product is risky: It is a major innovation—a solar powered operating system—and may not be successful. Because the required R&D to develop this product is substantial, the manufacturer wants to keep the new product's R&D operations *off balance sheet* to avoid scrutiny by financial analysts and competitors. Accordingly, it forms an R&D limited partnership with itself as the general partner.

The partnership is capitalized by $1 million of its own and $10 million from outside wealthy investors, in a private placement. By agreement, the deductions as well as the R&D tax credits flow through to the investors. The tax savings is part of the return on their investment.

This type of investment scheme can be used with other new, risky ventures where outside investors can be found. Note that the firm cannot form such an entity alone, because most jurisdictions require that partnership have at least two owners of partnerships. The same applies to limited liability companies (LLCs). LLCs have some marked advantages. For example, unlike general partnerships, LLCs offer complete liability protection to passive investors.

Indeed, there even are problems providing limited liability with limited partnerships. This is because favorable tax treatment cannot be accomplished unless there is at least one owner that is a solvent general partner. This necessarily puts its other assets at risk.

However, partnerships have some advantages over LLCs. For example, LLCs often are subject to state franchise or gross receipts taxes that do not apply to partnerships. Valuation discounts for estate tax purposes have been higher for partnership interests, too. Furthermore, LLCs are fairly new in the United States, and thus there has not been time for clear governance rules to develop.

Another similar divestiture can occur when management wants to buy out part of the firm. This can happen when some executives want to privately own the part of the firm that they manage. To do this, the assets of the part can be transferred to a newly formed LLC owned jointly by the firm and the executives.

The tax consequences of such flow-through divestitures are as follows. The formation is generally tax free to all parties involved. The usual flow-through rules apply as the new entity is operated. For example, there is no tax at the entity level, and each year's taxable income (or loss) flows through to the owners. The owners can specially allocate income or loss between themselves to suit their tax status, subject to meeting substantial economic effect tests. (See Example 15.2.)

EXAMPLE 15.2

A software company has one product line that, due to its novelty, is expected to incur financial (and tax) losses. These are expected to drive the firm's earnings down by 20% for five years, until the new line begins to turn a profit. Management forms an LLC into which it transfers all personnel and assets related to this operation. The transfer is tax-free, and the LLC is reported only on the firm's balance sheet. If this is done, under U.S. GAAP the losses simply reduce the book value of the investment and do not reduce the firm's financial accounting earnings.

The asset transfer usually is free of sales-type taxes, but in some jurisdictions there could be a revaluation for property tax purposes (which can result in lower property taxes). If employees are transferred during the payroll tax year (e.g., in the United States at anytime other than January 1), there can be additional payroll taxes (such as the 6.2% employer's portion of the U.S. Social Security tax).

USE OF FLOW-THROUGH ENTITIES FOR ACQUISITIONS

For reasons similar to the above use of a flow through for a partial divestiture, a firm may use a flow-through for acquiring a new business venture. The other owners might be management, outside investors, or venture capitalists. In addition, to get such a venture off balance sheet, the firm might need outside investors to infuse capital for business expansion.

One variation on this is an acquisition via direct stock purchase, followed by the *drop down* of assets into a newly formed flow-through entity. Exhibit 15.2 shows how this can be accomplished.

EXHIBIT 15.2 Drop-Down of Newly Acquired Venture into Flow-through Entity

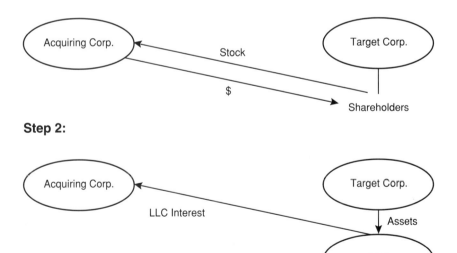

In Exhibit 15.2, step 1 may be structured as either a taxable or a tax-free acquisition. Chapter 14 discussed the tax consequences of these alternatives. Step 2 is generally a tax-free process to all parties involved.

LIQUIDATIONS

When a corporation liquidates, a taxable gain or loss can result at both the corporate level and the shareholder level. The liquidation process can take two forms, as illustrated in Exhibit 15.3.

In both types, the corporation recognizes gain or loss on the difference between the fair market value (FMV) of the assets and their adjusted bases. (For type 1 liquidations, sales price is used instead of FMV.) The corporation pays a tax on the gain or deducts the loss on this step. (To the extent the loss creates a net operating loss (NOL) which cannot be fully used as a carryback, the tax benefit of the NOL is lost).

In the second step, the shareholders recognize capital gain or loss on the difference between the adjusted bases of their shares and the cash (for type 1)

EXHIBIT 15.3 Basic Forms of Corporate Liquidations

Type 1:

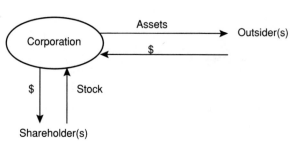

Type 2:

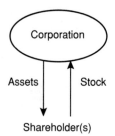

or FMV of assets (for type 2) received. Although this can trigger current taxes, it may reduce future tax effects if the shareholder(s) subsequently sell(s) the assets. This is because in a type 2 liquidation the assets' bases are adjusted to their FMVs upon receipt by the shareholder(s). (See Examples 15.3 and 15.4.)

EXAMPLE 15.3

Assume a corporation liquidates by first selling its assets and then distributing the cash to shareholders. Let the shareholders' basis in the stock be $200,000 and the corporation's tax basis in the assets be $150,000. The assets consist of $200,000 in cash, and equipment with a fair market value of $300,000. If the corporation is in the 35% tax bracket, then

If corporation sells assets first:		
Sales price of assets	$300,000	(1)
Less basis in assets	<150,000>	
Gain	$150,000	
Tax at 35%	52,500	(2)
Distribution to shareholder:		
$((1) - (2)) + \$200,000$ cash =	447,500	
Tax on distribution:		
$.2(447,500 - 200,000) =$	<49,500>	
Net cash to shareholder	$398,000	

EXAMPLE 15.4

Assume the facts as in Example 15.3, except that first the corporation distributes the assets to the shareholders, and then the shareholders sell the assets. This results in:

Distribution of assets	$300,000	
Less corporation's basis	<150,000>	
Gain to corporation	$150,000	
Tax on distribution to corporation:		
$.35(150,000) =$	52,500	
Distribution to shareholder:		
$(300,000 + 200,000) - 52,500 =$	447,500	
Tax to shareholder:		
$.2(447,500 - 200,000) =$	<49,500>	
Net cash flow to shareholder:	$398,000	

EXHIBIT 15.4   Basic Dissolving a Subsidiary

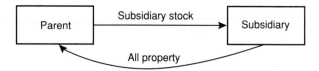

A special set of rules may apply if the shareholder is a corporate parent. They are triggered if the parent made an election under IRC Section 338 at the time it acquired the subsidiary. If this IRC Section 338 election was made, then gain was recognized by the subsidiary as if the parent bought the assets outright. This has the effect of stepping up the basis of the assets to their FMV, which in turn reduces the gain to the parent upon liquidation of the subsidiary. The following sections discuss IRC Section 338 elections.

Liquidation of a Subsidiary

Sometimes a parent wants to dissolve a subsidiary as a separate entity. In some cases it wants to keep at least part of the ongoing business. In other cases, it simply wants to sell the assets. This is depicted in Exhibit 15.4.

Subsequent to the liquidation, title to assets is transferred to the parent, the stock certificates are destroyed, and the subsidiary ceases to exit as a legal entity. What is the tax treatment to both parent and subsidiary? Unless the conditions for IRC Section 332 are met,

- The subsidiary recognizes gain or loss on each asset, measured as the difference between its FMV and adjusted basis.
- The parent recognizes gain on loss on sale of the stock, measured as the difference between the FMV of all assets received less the basis in the stock.

To qualify for IRC Section 332 treatment, the following conditions must be met:

- The parent owns at least 80% of the subsidiary's stock
- The subsidiary must distribute all of its assets within either
  - One taxable year
  - Three years from the close of the taxable year in which the first distribution occurs

Example 15.5 illustrates the results in a *taxable* liquidation of a subsidiary:

EXAMPLE 15.5

Suppose a parent corporation's basis in its 100% owned subsidiary is $10 million. The subsidiary has assets worth $5 million, with adjusted bases of $3 million. The subsidiary transfers title of the assets to the parent, and then is liquidated.

The result is that the subsidiary has a gain of $5 million – $3 million = $2 million. If it is in the 35% tax bracket, it pays taxes of $700,000 on its final corporate tax return. The parent then recognizes a loss of $5 million – $10 million = $5 million on its tax return. Because it is a capital loss, the parent cannot deduct it currently unless there are other capital gains against which to offset it.

What is the basis of the acquired assets in the parent's hands? The basis is their fair market value: $5 million. Accordingly, if the parent sells the assets immediately after acquisition, there is no gain.

There is a way for a parent and subsidiary to affect the timing of such gains and losses in the United States. This is through a IRC Section 332 liquidation. In one, the increase or decrease in the value of the subsidiary is not taxed. That is, if the requirements of this section are met, no gain or loss is triggered by the liquidation to either the parent or the subsidiary. The result is that any built-in gain or loss on the parent's investment in the subsidiary—that is, the difference between the subsidiary's FMV and the parent's basis in the subsidiary's shares—has no tax effect. Instead, the parent's basis in the subsidiary—the price the parent paid when it bought the subsidiary, or the amount the parent invested in the subsidiary that has not yet been repaid—merely disappears.

Nor is there a current tax (deduction) on the subsidiary's built-in gain (loss) on the liquidated assets. Instead, the subsidiary's basis in these assets becomes the parent's basis in the assets. Note that the tax effects avoided in the liquidation thus can be triggered if the parent later sells the assets. Thus, although this is labeled a tax-free transaction, as with many others mentioned throughout this book, it is really tax deferred. True, the transaction does not trigger current taxes. But they can be generated in the future, as shown in Example 15.6.

EXAMPLE 15.6

To see how a tax-free liquidation would work, assume the same facts as in Example 15.5. Under IRC Section 332, the subsidiary would recognize no gain on the assets and the parent no loss on the stock. The parent's tax basis in the assets acquired would be $3 million (because this is the subsidiary's basis in these assets).

If the parent then sells the assets for their $5 million FMV, it will be taxed on a gain of $5 million – $3 million = $2 million. To best manage taxes, the parent can select the timing of the sale. For example, if it never sells the assets (perhaps because it uses them up), there would be no taxable gain.

If management has decided on a subsidiary-liquidating transaction, should it meet the IRC Section 332 criteria? An analysis from a SAVANT perspective can help in this decision.

Strategy

If the parent plans on keeping much of the subsidiary's assets as an ongoing business, IRC Section 332 usually is preferable. This is because taxation is deferred until the parent disposes the assets. If instead the assets are to be stripped and sold, a tax-free liquidation helps only if the parent plans to delay the sale.

Value-Adding

Here, management's assessment of the NPV of cash flows hinges critically on tax effects to both the parent and subsidiary. Looking at the tax attributes of the parent and subsidiary individually:

Adjusting Value-Adding for Risk   A primary advantage for many liquidations is to get assets out of a subsidiary that may have some potential liability at the entity level. Here, tax treatment (IRC Section 332 or not) has little differential impact.

Transaction Cost and Value-Adding   The legal cost (primarily for title transfer) will be about the same, although advice on compliance with IRC Section 332 may make that option slightly more costly. Note that a liquidation of a controlled subsidiary usually does not trigger a sales-type tax or increased property taxes, but may result in fairly modest document transfer taxes. Exhibit 15.5 summarizes these trade-offs.

Anticipation

The analysis presented above may need to be adjusted if IRC Section 332 treatment is desired but the parent's tax rate might change during the liquidation period. In terms of timing, both the tax rates of the parent now, and its tax rates in future years affected by the liquidation, need to be considered. Regarding time value, if the subsidiary's assets are not to be resold, or there is a built-in gain on the assets, there is a definite time value advantage to tax free treatment.

EXHIBIT 15.5   Situations Shaping Trade-Offs for IRC Section 332 Elections

Subsidiary assets appreciated*	Subsidiary assets not appreciated or or depreciated*
Subsidiary & parent in taxpaying status: **Elect Section 332**	Subsidiary & parent in taxpaying status: **Do not elect Section 332**
Subsidiary & parent in nontaxpaying status: **Do not elect Section 332**	Subsidiary & parent in nontaxpaying status: **Depends**
One of entities in NOL status & other in tax-paying status: **Depends on overall tax conditions**	One of entities in NOL status & other in tax-paying status: **Depends**

*If subsidiary's assets are appreciated, their FMVs probably exceed the parent's basis in the subsidiary's stock, too.

Negotiating

If the managers of the subsidiary are to be retained, and their compensation is based on profits, the managers might prefer not to use IRC Section 332 if there is a potential gain on the corporate assets.

Transforming

If there are built-in losses on the subsidiary's assets, these non-deductible losses can be transformed into deductible ones. Under IRC Section 332, when the parent subsequently sells the assets, it can recognize the losses.

BUYING A SUBSIDIARY FOR ITS ASSETS

In many cases, a company wants some but not all of the assets of a target company. Moreover, it may intend to downsize the existing business, for example by laying off employees or ridding itself of unwanted assets. This often is referred to as cherry-picking. One way to accomplish this is merely to buy the desired assets, and hiring the desired employees, of the target. However, the target's shareholders may not want to be left with a corporate shell. This usually is because what is left is not viable as a business, and thus accumulated earnings or personal holding company taxes (as discussed in Chapter 3) may be triggered.

A way to satisfy both the new parent corporation and the target's shareholders is to acquire the company's stock, followed by an immediate liquidation and subsequent sale of unwanted assets. Exhibit 15.6 shows how this can be done.

EXHIBIT 15.6   Illustration of a Cherry-picking Acquisition

Step 1—Purchase

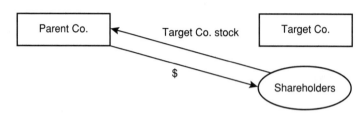

Step 2—Liquidate

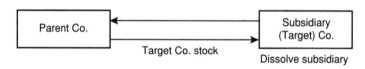

Step 3—Sell unwanted assets

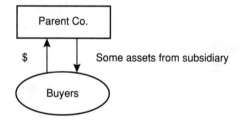

The potential U.S. tax issues are in steps 2 and 3, where the parent could be taxed on gains. How does the firm manage taxes in this case? An excellent way is by making an IRC Section 338 election. If a valid IRC Section 338 election is made, there is only gain at the subsidiary level, and no gain when the parent sells the assets. Further, upon purchase of the subsidiary, the tax bases of the acquired assets are stepped up to their fair market values. (See Examples 15.7 and 15.8.)

EXAMPLE 15.7

Suppose an acquiring company is willing to pay $10,000,000 for a company that holds a patent on an asset that the acquirer would like. The acquirer has no interest in the other assets, and plans to sell them immedi-

Asset	Adjusted basis to target	FMV
Plant, equipment	$3	$3
Patent	1	7
	$4	$10

ately after the acquisition. The subsidiary's assets (in millions of dollars) are as follows (assume there are no liabilities):

Assume both the acquirer and the target are in the 35% bracket.

If IRC Section 338 is elected, the following tax consequences occur: (1) there is $6,000,000 ($10,000,000 – $4,000,000) gain to the subsidiary, resulting in a tax of $2,100,000; (2) the acquirer has a $10 million tax basis in the target corporation's assets; (3) as a result of (2), the acquirer will have no gain if it sells the plant and equipment for $3 million; and (4) its annual tax amortization for the patent is $7 million / 15 years = $467,000, which at the firm's bracket yields $163,000 of tax benefits. Under this option, the NPV of taxes is: $2,100,000 – ($163,000 × 7.606) = $860,000. (This calculation assumes a 10% cost of capital and a 15-year planning horizon.)

EXAMPLE 15.8

Assume the same facts as in Example 15.7, except that 338 is not elected. The following tax consequences occur: (1) There is no gain or loss to the target; (2) the acquirer has the same tax basis in the assets as did the target; (3) as a consequence of (2), the acquirer pays no tax on the sale of the plant and equipment because their FMV already equals their basis; and (4) the annual tax benefit from amortizing the patent is (.35) (1,000,000/15) = $23,000. Under this scenario, the NPV of taxes is: –(23,000)(7.606) = <$174,938> (This calculation also assumes a 10% cost of capital and a 15-year planning horizon.)

Under these facts, the IRC Section 338 election does not provide the best time value of tax benefits.

Generally, IRC Section 338 provides better tax benefits if either

- The subsidiary is in a lower tax bracket than the acquirer (because gain is shifted to the target).
- The parent plans on disposing of, or using rapid write-offs for, the acquired assets.

Acquiring a Company with NOLs: The IRC Section 338(h)(10) Election

One of the hottest methods in M&A activity in the United States over the past decade has been the IRC Section 338 (h)(10) election. The main reason is that a IRC Section 338(h)(10) election allows the maximum use of NOLs in an acquired corporation.

As discussed in Chapter 14, there is an annual limit to the amount of a target's accumulated NOLs that an acquiring company can use. The limitation provides that the taxable income of the acquirer can be reduced each year only by a portion of the NOL carryover. The portion is the value of the loss corporation's stock on the date of the ownership change, multiplied by the long-term federal interest rate. An exception to this limit can result from an IRC Section 338(h)(10) election.

Here, similar to an IRC Section 338 election, the acquirer is taxed as if it immediately liquidates the target after acquisition. Gain or loss is recognized to the target, and the acquirer gets a step-up in the tax basis of the acquired assets. The major difference is that if the target has NOLs they reduce the target's gain. NOLs in excess of this gain then carry over to the acquirer. (See Example 15.9.)

EXAMPLE 15.9

Refer to Example 15.7, when an acquirer is after a target's patented assets. Add to this the assumption that the subsidiary has a $5 million NOL carryover. If IRC Section 338(h)(10) is elected, then: (1) gain to target = ($10 million − 4 million) − $5 million NOL = $1 million, (2) basis of target assets acquired = $10 million, and (3) annual tax amortization of patent = $7 million / 15 = $467,000.

What are the requirements to elect IRC Section 338 or 338(h)(10)?

- An IRC Section 338 election must be made by the fifteenth day of the ninth month after a qualified stock purchase occurs. Once made, the election is irrevocable.
- The target must be acquired by a stock purchase of at least 80% of the target's stock. The percentage is measured both in terms of voting power and in terms of value. This dual measurement is common where, as here, tax treatment depends on virtually complete control of a corporation.
- From the time the first stock purchase occurs until the purchase is consummated, less than 12 months must have transpired.

- The target must be acquired in a taxable transaction. Thus, one of the tax-free reorganization provisions cannot also be used in conjunction with the acquisition/liquidation.

The use of IRC Section 338 or 338(h)(10) acquisitions and liquidations creates some potential tension between buyer and seller. An important tension is with respect to the taxable nature of the transaction. The seller (more specifically, its shareholders) must recognize gain on the sale of their stock; they cannot use a tax-free reorganization provision to postpone gain. Accordingly, they may demand a higher purchase price. However, the purchaser may be willing to accept this higher price to obtain the benefits of IRC Section 338 or 338(h)(10). Thus, the tax benefits on the table may be an item both sides are willing to negotiate. (See Example 15.10.)

EXAMPLE 15.10

Referring to Example 15.9, how much more would the acquirer be willing to pay to get IRC Section 338(h)(10) treatment?

PV of using NOL now: (e.g., through a Section 338(h)(10) election)	$5,000,000(.35) =	$1,750,000
PV of using NOL over a number of years:		
6%(10,000,000) = 600,000/year		
10,000,000/600,000 = 16.66 years		
PV: (600,000)(7.824) = $4,694,440(.35%) =		1,643,040
Difference		$ 160,960

(This example assumes a 6% tax discount rate and a 10% firm discount rate.)

Generally, the lower the purchase price relative to the NOL carryforward, the more the value of accelerating the NOL deduction via electing IRC Section 338(h)(10).

FIGHTING OFF TAKEOVER ATTEMPTS WITH ESOPs

In many situations, one firm attempts to take over another in a hostile manner. That is, the target's management does not approve the takeover attempt. If many other employees are also against the takeover, one way to fight it off is to have the employees buy as many shares as they can. In the United States, this can be done through an employee stock ownership plan (ESOP). (See Example 15.11.)

EXAMPLE 15.11

Suppose a hostile company seeks to buy 51% of a target firm's outstanding shares on the open market because 51% would give the acquirer voting control. The firm wants to acquire the same 51% of the stock. Assume the firm's one million shares are trading for $100 each. Also, assume that if the ESOP borrows from a bank to finance the purchase, it can do so at 10% interest.

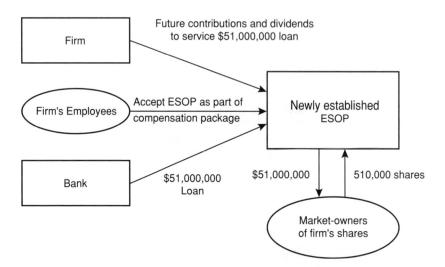

Because the firm's employees end up owning controlling interest in the firm, the hostile suitor cannot acquire the firm in the open market. Although 10% interest must be paid on the bank loan, part of this cost can be defrayed by tax-deductible dividends paid to the ESOP. (Recall that in the United States, dividends are not normally tax deductible).

What are the SAVANT attributes of this transaction?

Strategy

Management may not want ownership control in employee's hands. This is because future negotiations with unions might be weakened, and other labor-management disputes could see a costly shift of power to workers. For that reason, the firm may want less that 51% of the firm's stock owned by the ESOP, with the remaining stock instead purchased by an investor favored by management (a white knight). Other options include a management buyout (MBO), or a recapitalization (e.g., bonds issued for stock).

Value-Adding

The NPV of cash flows depends on (1) the amount and interest rate of bank borrowings, (2) dividends paid to ESOP (less the firm's tax deduction for doing so), (3) the firm's tax rate, and (4) the market price of the stock, among other things.

Adjusting Value-Adding for Risk   There is always some risk the suitor will outbid the ESOP, and shareholders will still tender their stock to the suitor and not the ESOP. Fortunately, the legal and accounting costs of setting up the ESOP are deductible, regardless of the outcome.

Adjusting Value-Adding for Transaction Costs   While tax-deductible, the setup and annual costs for an ESOP trust are high.

Anticipation

There very likely will be market price reactions as the hostile suitor competes with the ESOP. If capital gains rates are scheduled to fall (increase), the firm (through the ESOP) may want to adjust the timing of the share acquisitions accordingly. In terms of time value, the NPV analysis (discussed previously in value-adding) is important.

Negotiating

The employees must be persuaded to provide some capital to finance the ESOP, and to accept the ESOP as part of their overall compensation packages. This probably means they have to give up some other part of the compensation, such as reduced salary or pension benefits.

Transforming

This is not readily applicable here.

Instead of selling off an entire subsidiary, many firms sell off up to 19.9% of the stock of a subsidiary. This generates cash to the firm, and does not lose voting control. More importantly, retaining 80% control is important because it allows the consolidated group to use the subsidiary's tax benefits (such as NOLs).

These partial sales can involve significant transactions costs. This is because they often involve listing the subsidiary on a public stock exchange. Listing involves costly Securities and Exchange Commission (SEC) procedures, such as filing and public audits.

BANKRUPTCIES

In the United States, if a corporation goes through a regular bankruptcy proceeding, subsequently liquidates, and the company's business continues post-bankruptcy, then it is eligible for tax-free treatment as a G Reorganization. Here, shareholders in the bankrupt corporation recognize gain as the lesser of realized (total) gain or boot received.

The requirements are as follows. First, part or all of the assets of the corporation are transferred to another corporation (either the old corporation, a newly reorganized one, or another acquiring corporation). Second, only stock, securities, and other property of the acquiring corporation can be used as consideration. Third, stock and securities of the new or acquiring corporation received by the bankrupt corporation must be distributed to its shareholders, security holders, or creditors.

Basic Tax Research Skills

This appendix outlines some fundamental research skills for managers, and for consultants who are not tax specialists. After doing basic research, one should consult a tax specialist for corroboration of the findings.

STEPS IN THE RESEARCH PROCESS

When a tax issue arises, the simplified program in Exhibit A.1 may be followed.

EXHIBIT A.1   How Tax Issues Are Solved

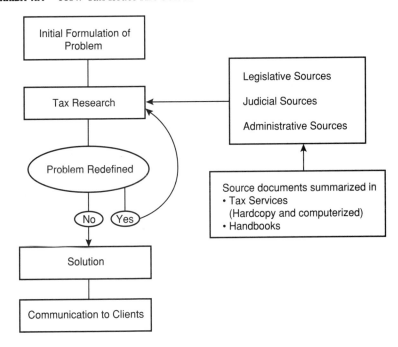

SOURCES OF THE LAW

Tax rules stem from three sources: (1) Laws passed by legislatures like the U.S. Congress (including tax treaties), (2) administrative rules issued by tax agencies, such as the IRS, which are more detailed (and thus provide more guidance that statutes), and (3) court interpretations of these laws and rules for specific taxpayer situations. These sources are not usually in conflict, although courts of different jurisdictions may sometimes disagree. It is generally best to find a source that conforms most closely to the client's set of facts, such as a court case or an administrative pronouncement (like an IRS Revenue Ruling for a federal tax issue).

Sometimes general rules must be assumed to apply to the client's situation. This is easy to do in some situations. For example, IRC Section 103 states categorically that interest from state and local bonds is tax free for federal purposes. Thus, if a company owns a State of Connecticut bond, it is safe to assume that its interest income is tax free. In many cases, though, general rules are vague enough so as to leave room for interpretation. These gray areas allow some risk-taking on interpretation that may save tax dollars. (Interestingly, the company effectively wins on the interpretation if its tax return is not audited. Even if audited, the tax authorities often negotiate a settlement.)

GETTING ANSWERS TO SIMPLE QUESTIONS

As discussed in Chapter 1, a great deal of tax information is available on the Web. It is accessed easily through gateway sites like *www.taxsites.com*. Most of the material is primary sources: These are documents issued by official, government sources such as actual statutes, administrative pronouncements, and judicial opinions. However, a growing body of secondary sources— mostly short articles and calculation sites—is becoming available.

For most circumstances, the primary sources are too difficult to use, and the secondary sources are too incomplete to be more than more general guidelines. In response, tax specialists typically use a number of highly organized, up-to-date, and thorough tax reporter services that reference all sources of tax law. They are available as hard copy or can be accessed by computer (including both Web based and CD ROM) from publishers like Commerce Clearing House (CCH), Research Institute of America (RIA), and West Publishing.

Because the complete services are complex, the nontax specialist is better off using a tax handbook. These are designed to give easily accessed, easily digested answers to more common tax questions. For U.S. federal rules, along with those of some states and other countries, these handbooks are published by CCH and RIA; Butterfields publishes similar guides throughout the former British Commonwealth. Even if an answer can be found in one of the handbooks, managers should confer with a tax specialist just to make sure.

Here is an example of research using a handbook. Suppose a company is considering acquiring a firm for cash. The market value is $10 million and the book value of assets is $8 million. Thus, under U.S. GAAP, the $2 million excess is goodwill. Can the goodwill be amortized for tax purposes? To find out, one should start by brainstorming to find as many related words as possible. This is done in case some of them are not listed in the handbooks' topical index. Here, the following words might come to mind: goodwill, amortization, acquisition, and intangible.

Turning to goodwill in the index of a handbook (see Exhibit A.2), for example, one might find the following:

EXHIBIT A.2   Example of Tax Rule Handbook Index

GOODWILL

- Amortization . . . . 1994 et seq.
- Capital assets,as 2620
- Capital expenditures. 1650
- Cost of 2466
- Entertainment expenses for promotion of. 1564
- Partnerships. 3767 et seq.

Turning to paragraphs 1994 and 1995, one would find:

1994 Amortization of Intangibles
      The cost of most acquired intangible assets, including goodwill and going concern value, is amortized ratably over a 15-year period.

1995 Fifteen-year amortization of intangibles
      Taxpayers can claim a deduction on Form 4562 for "amortizable section 197 intangibles" by amortizing the adjusted basis (for purposes of determining gain) of that intangible ratably over a 15-year period beginning with the month in which the intangible is acquired. (Code Sec. 197 (a)) No other depreciation or amortization deduction is permitted with respect to any amortizable section 197 intangible. (Code Sec. 197 (b)) [L-7951; 1974; TD 26,902]

Thus, goodwill is amortized over 15 years. The statutory source of the law is Internal Revenue Code Section 197.

Present Value Analysis: Lump Sums

The present value of a sum due n years in the future is the amount which, if it were on hand today, would grow to equal the future sum. Since $100 would grow to $141.85 in six years at a 6% interest rate, $100 is defined to be the present value of $141.85 due six years in the future when the appropriate interest rate is 6%.

Finding present value (or *discounting*, as it is typically called) is simply the reverse of compounding, and equation B-1 can readily be transformed into a present value formula (where r is the interest rate):

$$FV_n = PV(1 + r)^n \qquad \text{(B-1)}$$

which, when solved for PV, gives

$$PV = \frac{FV_n}{(1 + r)^n} = FV_n \left[\frac{1}{(1 + r)} \right]^n \qquad \text{(B-2)}$$

This last equation shows the term in brackets for various values of r and n.

Exhibit B.1 shows values for various combinations of interest rates and periods. For the example given in the first paragraph of this Appendix, Exhibit B.1 would be used as follows. Look down the 6% column in Exhibit B.1 to the sixth row. The figure shown there, 0.7050, is the *present value interest factor* $(PVIF_{r,n})$ used to determine the present value of $141.85 payable in six years, discounted at 6%:

$$PV = FV_6(PVIF_{r,n})$$
$$= \$141.85(0.7050)$$
$$= \$100$$

EXHIBIT B.1 Present Values of $1 Due at the End of n periods

$$PVIF_{r,n} = \frac{1}{(1+r)^n} = \left[\frac{1}{(1+r)}\right]^n$$

Period = n	1%	2%	3%	4%	5%	6%	7%	8%	9%	10%	12%	14%	15%
1	.9901	.9804	.9709	.9615	.9524	.9434	.9346	.9259	.9174	.9091	.8929	.8772	.8696
2	.9803	.9612	.9426	.9246	.9070	.8900	.8734	.8573	.8417	.8264	.7972	.7695	.751
3	.9706	.9423	.9151	.8890	.8638	.8396	.8163	.7938	.7722	.7513	.7118	.6750	.6575
4	.9610	.9238	.8885	.8548	.8227	.7921	.7629	.7350	.7084	.6830	.6355	.5921	.5718
5	.9515	.9057	.8626	.8219	.7835	.7473	.7130	.6806	.6499	.6209	.5674	.5194	.4972
6	.9420	.8880	.8375	.7903	.7462	.7050	.6663	.6302	.5963	.5645	.5066	.4556	.4323
7	.9327	.8706	.8131	.7599	.7107	.6651	.6227	.5835	.5470	.5132	.4523	.3996	.3759
8	.9235	.8535	.7894	.7307	.6768	.6274	.5820	.5403	.5019	.4665	.4039	.3506	.3269
9	.9143	.8368	.7664	.7026	.6446	.5919	.5439	.5002	.4604	.4241	.3606	.3075	.2843
10	.9053	.8203	.7441	.6756	.6139	.5584	.5083	.4632	.4224	.3855	.3220	.2697	.2472

ANNUITIES

Assume you were offered the following options: (1) a two-year annuity of $1,000 a year, or (2) a lump-sum payment today. If you have no need for the money during the next two years, then if you accept the annuity you could simply deposit the receipts in a savings account. Let this account pay 6% interest.

If this is the case, how large must the lump-sum payment be to make it equivalent to the annuity?

The following time line will help explain the problem.

The present value of the first cash flow (cf)—the payment at the end of the first year—is $cf[1/(1 + r)]$. That for the second is $cf[1/(1 + r)]^2$. Let the present value of an annuity of n years be called PVA_n and let $PVIKA_{k,n}$ be the designation for the present value interest factor for an annuity. This allows the problem to be expresseed with the following equations:

$$PVA_n = cf\left(\frac{1}{1+r}\right)^1 + cf\left(\frac{1}{1+r}\right)^2 + \dots + cf\left(\frac{1}{1+r}\right)^n$$

$$= cf\left(\frac{1}{(1+r)} + \frac{1}{(1+r)^2} + \dots + \frac{1}{(1+r)^n}\right)$$

$$= cf\sum_{t=1}^{n}\left(\frac{1}{(1+r)}\right)^t$$

$$= cf\left(PVIFA_{r,n}\right) \tag{B-3}$$

The last line of these shows $PVIFA_{r,n}$ as the term in parentheses.

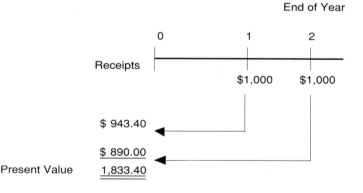

Time Line for an Annuity:
Present Value with $r = 6\%$

End of Year

	0	1	2
Receipts		$1,000	$1,000

$ 943.40

$ 890.00

Present Value   1,833.40

Just as Exhibit B.1 showed values for various combinations of interest rates and periods for the present value of a lump sum, Exhibit B.2 shows this for the present value of an annuity. For the example being discussed in this section of this Appendix, Exhibit B.2 would be used as follows.

From Exhibit B.2, the $PVIF_{r,n}$ for a two year, 6 percent annuity is found to be 1.8334. Multiplying this factor by the $1,000 annual receipt gives $1,833.40, the present value of the annuity. This amount is identical to the long-method answer using formulas.

$$PVA_n = cf\left(PVIFA_{r,n}\right)$$
$$PVA_3 = \$1,000(1.8334) \qquad \text{(B-4)}$$
$$= \$1,833.40$$

Notice that the entry for each period n in this exhibit is equal to the sum of the entries up to and including period n. For example, in the $PVIFA$ for 6%, two periods as shown in Exhibit B.2 could have been calculated by summing values from Exhibit B.1:

$$.9434 + .8900 = 1.8334$$

EXHIBIT B.2   Present Value of an Annuity of $1 per Period for n Periods

$$PVIFA_{r,n} = \sum_{t=1}^{n}\frac{1}{(1+r)^t} = \frac{1 - \dfrac{1}{(1+r)^n}}{r}$$

# of Payments (n)	1%	2%	3%	4%	5%	6%	7%	8%	9%	10%
1	0.9901	0.9804	0.9709	0.9615	0.9524	0.9434	0.9346	0.9259	0.9174	0.9091
2	1.9704	1.9416	1.9135	1.8861	1.8594	1.8334	1.8080	1.7833	1.7591	1.7355
3	2.9410	2.8839	2.8286	2.7751	2.7232	2.6730	2.6243	2.5771	2.5313	2.4869
4	3.9020	3.8077	3.7171	3.6299	3.5460	3.4651	3.3872	3.3121	3.2397	3.1699
5	4.8534	4.7135	4.5797	4.4518	4.3295	4.2124	4.1002	3.9927	3.8897	3.7908
6	5.7955	5.6014	5.4172	5.2421	5.0757	4.9173	4.7665	4.6229	4.4859	4.3553
7	6.7282	6.4720	6.2303	6.0021	5.7864	5.5824	5.3893	5.2064	5.0330	4.8684
8	7.6517	7.3255	7.0197	6.7327	6.4632	6.2098	5.9713	5.7466	5.5348	5.3349
9	8.5660	8.1622	7.7861	7.4353	7.1078	6.8017	6.5152	6.2469	5.9952	5.7590
10	9.4713	8.9826	8.5302	8.1109	7.7217	7.3601	7.0236	6.7101	6.4177	6.1446

UNEVEN CASH FLOWS

The definition of an annuity includes the words *fixed amount.* In other words, annuities involve situations where cash flows are *identical* in every year. Although many financial decisions do involve constant cash flows, some important decisions are concerned with uneven flows of cash.

The *PV* of an uneven stream of future income is found as the sum of the *PV*s of the individual components of the stream. For example, suppose we are trying to find the *PV* of the stream of receipts shown in Exhibit B.3, discounted at 7%. As shown in the table, we multiply each receipt by the appropriate $PVIF_{r,n}$, then sum these products to obtain the *PV* of the stream, $9,347.70.

EXHIBIT B.3 Present Value of Uneven Stream of Receipts

	Streams of Cash Flows	×	$PVIF_{r,n}$ (7%)	=	PV of Individual Cash Flows
Year 1	$1000		0.9346		$ 934.60
Year 2	2000		0.8734		1746.80
Year 3	1000		0.8163		816.30
			PV = sum		$3,497.70

Bibliography

Buffett, Warren. Chairman letter to Berkshire, Hathaway shareholders, 1994. *http://www.berkshirehathaway.com/letters/1994.html*

Dell, Michael. "Michael Dell turns the PC world inside out." Article by Andrew E. Serwer. *Fortune* 136, no. 5 (Sept 8, 1997): 76–77.

Drucker, Peter F. *Management: Tasks, Responsibilities, Practices.* New York: Harper & Row, 1974.

Fisher, George. "Missed moments: Critics say Kodak's Fisher made three big mistakes." Article by Linda Grant. *Fortune* 136, no. 8 (Oct 27, 1997): 188–191.

Ford, Henry J. (in collaboration with Samuel Crowther.) *My Life and Work.* Manchester, New Hampshire: Ayer Company Publishers, 1996. Originally published by Garden City, N.Y: Doubleday, Page & Co., 1926.

Freeland, James J., Stephen A. Lind, and Richard B. Stephens. *Cases and Materials on Fundamentals of Federal Income Taxation.* 8th ed. New York: The Foundation Press, 1994.

Frieden, Karl. *Cybertaxation: The Taxation of E-Commerce.* Chicago: Commerce Clearing House, 2000.

Gates, Bill, Nathan Myhrvold, and Peter Rinearson. *The Road Ahead.* New York: Viking Press, 1995.

"Germany's tax reform makes an impact." *The Economist.* January 10, 2002. *http://www.economist.com/library/articlesBySubject/moreArticles.cfm?subject=Germany*

Kotler, Phillip. *Marketing Management: Analysis, Planning, Implementation, and Control.* 9th ed. Englewood Cliffs, New Jersey: Prentice Hall, 1999.

McNealy, Scott. "The Adventures of Scott McNealy: Javaman." Article by Brent Schlender. *Fortune* 136, no. 7 (Oct 13, 1997): 70–77.

Penman, Stephen. *Financial Statement Analysis and Security Valuation.* Boston: McGraw–Hill, 2001.

Schultz, Howard. "Starbucks: Making values pay." Book excerpt from *Pour Your Heart into It* by Howard Schultz and Dori Jones Yang. *Fortune* 136, no. 6 (Sept. 29, 1997): 261.

Slater, Robert. *Soros: The Unauthorized Biography: The Life, Times, and Trading Secrets of the World's Greatest Investor.* New York: McGraw–Hill, 1997.

Smith, Richard L., and Janet Kiholm Smith. *Entrepreneurial Finance.* New York: John Wiley and Sons, Inc., 2000.

index

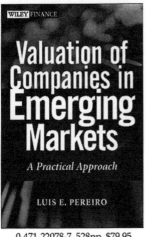
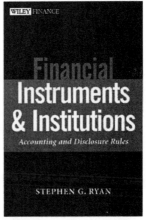

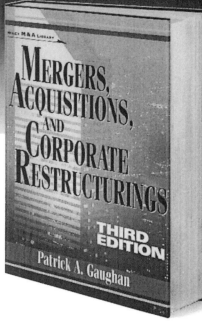